Also by Elizabeth Pepper and John Wilcock

The Witches' Almanac

Magical and Mystical Sites

ELIZABETH PEPPER

and

JOHN WILCOCK

Magical and Mystical Sites

EUROPE AND THE BRITISH ISLES

Harper & Row, Publishers
New York, Hagerstown, San Francisco, London

Illustration on title page: A medieval talisman used to insure safety on a journey.

Designed by Gloria Adelson

Chapter openings: styling and artwork by Elizabeth Pepper

Library of Congress Cataloging in Publication Data

Pepper, Elizabeth.
  Magical and mystical sites.
  Includes index.
1. Occult sciences—Europe. I. Wilcock, John,
joint author. II. Title.
BF1434.E85P46   1977   914'.04'55   76-5533
ISBN 0-06-014614-1

77 78 79 80 10 9 8 7 6 5 4 3 2 1

For Martha and Martin

Contents

Introduction

THIS QUEST FOR MAGIC has been the most fascinating study we have ever undertaken and the very elusiveness of our subject has acted as a continual goad to our imagination. Through a score of countries we have followed the tenuous trail, visiting places whose reputation for enchantment we have joyously confirmed. We have tried to be "objective" reporters, and if at times we have, unhappily, succeeded too well the fault lies not in our stars but in ourselves. We were aware, of course, before we began that a belief in magic or supernatural forces was as old as mankind and that all through history, and still today, there are those who seem to possess extraordinary powers. And it took very little to convince us that latent, and usually untested, powers lay dormant in every human being, including ourselves—a remnant, perhaps, of ancient skills that were indispensable in less technological times.

The ability to read the future or to project one's astral spirit has become a relatively commonplace goal among the millions who practice occult disciplines. Not everyone can master such accomplishments, but almost everyone knows somebody who has tried. And what is telekinesis or psychometry, ESP or dowsing if not a calculated development of powers beyond the norm—powers we might readily define as "magical"?

To dismiss all personal and historical manifestations of magical phenomena as merely coincidence, superstition, or trickery is to defy logic. Few people that we have met, however skeptical they might have been, had minds so closed that they could not be intrigued by or involved with some aspect of this far-reaching subject. It is the scientific mind that remains the most immovable; scientists tend to dismiss anything they cannot explain. Yet most theories are merely tentative, all rules have exceptions, and one generation's heresy becomes the following era's history.

To study magic then, is to push off with one's flimsy raft onto a stream whose deceptively slow-moving waters carry one with surprising swiftness into more and more unfamiliar territory. There are few recognizable landmarks and a bewildering array of tributaries from which to choose. The mainstream is never far away, but a million different channels feed into and out of it, all equally fascinating, all full of surprises, all hinting at further vistas, still unseen.

The very word *magic* seems capable of evoking a spell, as anybody who tries dropping it into casual conversation can testify. It seems to be a subject in which everybody would like to believe, if only they could produce some evidence to silence the scorn of hard-headed friends. Magic is a word with endless interpretations, of which possibly the most accurate might be the least binding. Perhaps magic merely means forces as yet undefined, or uncategorized. And finding magic may require an ability to look within rather than outward.

Believing in magic is ultimately to pay tribute to the ancient idols, the gods of pagan times, when men worshiped nature or the symbols which represented its different manifestations. The most powerful of these has always been the sun, the major source of heat, light, and life, whose boundless energy—we are now being told—is once again to be harnessed on a global scale. All eras and cultures have deified the sun, which has been worshiped under many different names and with many different rites, most of them having something to do with fire or the perpetual battles that rage between the forces of light and darkness.

But what did "worship" mean? Was it merely the innocent tribute paid to this supreme power by ignorant savages who recognized its life-giving qualities? Or were these invocations rewarded—with a knowledge that we have yet to relearn? Are we "worshiping" the sun with our plans to harness solar energy? In short, did the ancients know something that we do not?

The moon, too, has always been worshiped (usually as a goddess, the female counterpart of the sun), and the fact that space travelers of our era have visited it (are we *sure* we were first?) has done little to lessen its mysteries. That the moon affects tides and even the flow of blood through the body has always been a common knowledge. Ancient almanacs emphasize the importance of selecting the correct phase for planting crops or casting spells: we can prove the efficacy of the former, so why we do question the latter?

Our original plan was to combine thorough research into occult history with an actual trip to all the ancient sites of myth and mystery, all the fabled places of power renowned in the annals of magic. Time, money, and distance soon limited us. After all, we concluded, the Greeks borrowed Eastern themes but quickly made them their own, and who could deny that Greece was the fountainhead of Western culture? With a bow to Ephesus in Turkey we began our quest in the Aegean Islands, searching for truths among the legends about Pythagoras, Hippocrates, and Plato's Atlantis.

We visited tiny Delos, which as the reputed birthplace of Apollo and Diana (god and goddess of the sun and moon) retains a significance far out of proportion to its size, then headed northward to Eleusis, whose cult, the Eleusinian mysteries, inspired a moral and intellectual touchstone for the ancient world, and then traveled to Delphi, where the Apollonian and Dionysian oracles for centuries determined the course of history.

The witches of Thessaly and the Orphic myths of Thrace, both originating in what is now northern Greece, together produced a heady mix of arcane lore which spread rapidly westward. By Christian times the witches of Thessaly were a constant theme of the Roman historians, and of course, Rome itself, that eminently pagan city, disseminated the wisdom of its day through a vastly expanding empire. But others, too —Phoenicians, Jews, Celts, Goths, Saxons, Greeks, Normans, Crusaders, Moors, and Gypsies—carried the mystic wisdom along myriad routes through the centuries. And all along the way are scattered the landmarks of its passage: caves, temples, shrines, sacred groves, magic mountains. They mark the sites where natural met supernatural, all of them once "places of power" whose secrets, perhaps, have been merely forgotten or mislaid.

As we proceeded west, assuming as many before us that that was indeed the direction of all cultural flow, we began to sense the presence of another kind of magic, one even more mysterious and compelling than hitherto encountered. The first hint was on Malta, a curious anachronism with its temples older than the Great Pyramid. But again in Spain, on the coast of Brittany, and then in the British Isles, the rhythm became more insistent. And in Ireland, the last stop on our journey, it seemed as though we had reached the very heart of this other magic.

Here was evidence of a people who might well have held the keys to an awe-inspiring wisdom. They were contemporary with the world's oldest cultures—the Egyptian, the Chinese—and, if anything, were more sophisticated.

We proved to our own satisfaction that Western magical thought is composed of two major themes. The first was shaped and vitalized by the Greeks at the height of their culture during the millennium before the Christian era. The second, far older, still mysterious, sprang up in the West. Today, five thousand years later, the fruits of this magic wait to be harvested.

There are, of course, many byroads along our quest, and often we have let fancy and/or history lead us. With the death of the Emperor Julian in the fourth century and Rome's adoption of Christianity as virtually the state religion, pagan beliefs and occult wisdom went into hiding for centuries. But it re-emerged, strengthened and expanded, with the arrival in Spain of the Moors. From their strongholds, at Toledo and Granada, the Moors spread the treasures of Greek and Hebrew mysticism once more across Europe, along with Arabic numerals, medicine, and the neo-Platonic philosophies which so influenced the occult scholars of the Renaissance.

Christianity fought back relentlessly to eventually expel the dark-skinned invaders, but their legacy of neo-Pythagorean doctrines and the alchemical search for the philosopher's stone (or one's own soul?) have endured to this day. We follow these themes from the Faust country of southern Germany, into the folkloric regions of the Auvergne, the Basque country and Brittany, to Chinon, once a prison for those mystical heretics the Knights Templars, as well as the starting point for the ambiguous career of Joan of Arc.

At Chartres we pick up on the legends of the pre-Christian Druids whose beliefs and customs made an imprint on society which survives in the twentieth century and in quest of which we explored both sides of the English Channel and both shores of the Irish Sea.

A search for magic, then, inspires our journey from beginning to end and we undertake it as the ancients advised, with a happy heart, an open mind, and eyes that see beyond the darkness. It is a light-hearted quest and from it we seek nothing more than to recover lost knowledge, revitalize psychic energy and perhaps to awaken a slumbering memory or two along the way.

We extend our gratitude to the many people who proffered help, advice, and documentation. We wish to thank particularly Tony and Jan Roberts, Barbara Stacy, and Martha Zenfell, whose endless patience and superb navigation played an invaluable part in the quest.

1

Ephesus

CITY OF MAGICIANS

LONG BEFORE THE ADVENT OF CHRISTIANITY, the ancient city of Ephesus on the coastal plain of Asia Minor (now part of Turkey) was renowned as a center for the study of magic and all the secret and hidden arts. The nineteenth-century historian Edward Falkener, who asserted that Ephesus was noted for its magic "above all other places in the world," explained that it was here that Eastern and Western magic met. "Building on the confines of Greece and Asia," he wrote in his *Ephesus and the Temple of Diana*, "it engrafted the philosophy and mythology of the one country on the mystical ceremonies and belief in magic of the other."

The city's very origin, in fact, was based on a prediction by the Delphic oracle. Up to that time, the Ionians who had migrated from Greece, were settled on an island off the coast, but by the eleventh century B.C. overcrowding had made the founding of a new colony inevitable. Under the leadership of Androclus, son of the Athenian king Codrus, the immigrants sent messengers to Delphi to ask what site for a new city would be favorable. They were told that a fish and a boar would indicate where that was to be.

Illustration: The Hectate Wheel. The symbol of the city of Ephesus, associated with the "dark" side of the Goddess of the Moon. From a stone disc, Ionia, sixth century B.C.

3

Shortly afterwards a group of fishermen who had gone ashore for a picnic were frying their lunch when one of the fish jumped from the pan, causing a spark to set fire to nearby bushes. A frightened boar, seen to run from the bushes, was chased and killed; the Delphic prophecy appeared to be fulfilled. Thus was Ephesus first built, ten centuries before Christ.

For generations the effigy of a wild boar stood in the main square, although the city itself changed locations after numerous attempts had been made to stop the adjoining River Kaystross from silting up the harbor. Today the ancient city, in what is now western Turkey, is three miles from the water—successive earthquakes had caused its destruction and rebuilding.

A century and a half before the birth of Christ, the Greek mathematician Philon wrote a short treatise called *De Septem Orbis Spectaculis (The Seven Wonders of the World)*. "I have seen the walls and hanging gardens of ancient Babylon, the statue of Olympian Zeus, the Colossus of Rhodes, the lighthouse at Pharos, the mighty work of the high pyramids, and the tomb of Mausolus. But when I saw the temple at Ephesus rising to the clouds, all these wonders were put in the shade."

What Philon saw was the fifth shrine to be built on the coastal plain near Ephesus. From the eighth century B.C. to the fourth century A.D., pilgrims from every quarter of the Mediterranean journeyed there to pay homage to the graceful deity called Artemis by the Greeks, Diana by the Romans.

The history of her worship extends even further back in time. Ephesus was the traditional home of the Amazons, a nation of female warriors. To prevent their race from dying out, it is said, the Amazons paid annual visits to the neighboring tribes. Male offspring resulting from these visits were returned to their fathers; female children were kept and trained in the arts of hunting and warfare. Although the Amazons are largely dismissed by scholars as mythical, the persistence of their appearance in Greek legends indicates a possible basis in fact. When the Ionian Greeks conquered and colonized Ephesus, the deity of the city was Amazonian in character. A chaste huntress, protecting wild animals and youth, she was so akin to their own Artemis that the worship of the two deities was combined.

So Ephesus became a city belonging to the goddess of the moon, Diana, who personified hidden knowledge. It is no wonder that such a city soon became renowned in the ancient world as an appropriate dwelling place for magicians and necromancers.

Today nothing but a turf-covered mound remains of the famous temple. Its site is three-quarters of a mile outside the walls of Ephesus. The great shrine stood where the fig gardens are now, to the right of the road to Kuşadasi, some 400 yards from the mosque of Isabey. The area, recalling the British excavations there during the nineteenth century, is called Ingiliz Cukuru, "the English Pit."

It was characteristic that the site of Diana's temple should hold for a while a church dedicated to the Virgin Mary. Centuries passed and it, too, disappeared. The plain of glory became a deserted marsh, malaria-ridden, its remnants of majesty hidden from sight by swamp grass, and so it remains.

Twentieth-century tourists seem to be most interested in the Christian legends, superimposed as elsewhere on more ancient lore. The massive *agora* ("marketplace"), for example, is associated with St. Paul. The enormous theater (it could seat 24,000) was where the silversmith Demetrius gathered with an angry crowd to protest Paul's preaching.

Ephesus during the first century A.D. was a wealthy city and devoted to the service of the mystic goddess of the moon. St. Paul's visit and the subsequent burning of "books of sorcery of great value" suggests the menace Ephesus represented to the early Christians.

A curious local legend concerns the Caves of the Seven Sleepers, said to be Christian refugees who hid themselves during the pagan festival ordered by the emperor Decius when he entered the city about A.D. 250. Supposedly the seven slept well into the reign of Theodosius (A.D. 408–450) when they were able to emerge with their beliefs safe from attack.

Although the temple site offers little to view, the magnificent ancient city of Ephesus itself is today a tourist attraction. The uncovered and reconstructed ruins, mostly Roman, sprawl over a site of twenty-six square miles, of which but a quarter has been excavated. What can be seen, however, is awe-inspiring: marble-paved streets bearing grooves from centuries-old chariot wheels are lined with impressive headless statues (it was the custom of conquerors to top off statues of previous heroes with the heads of their own); arcades where once shops used to be; temples and fountains dedicated to successive emperors; six-foot-high tablets bearing the city laws; public baths and toilets, the water from the former washing away the refuse of the latter; and a carved sidewalk inscription clearly indicating the location of the city's brothel with its inscription of a heart, a woman, and a left foot (indicating the next building on the left). Unmistakably erotic statues of Priapus (the male generative power personified as a god) have been discovered on the site of the brothel itself.

The worship of Priapus was the acknowledgment of the phallus as the cause of fertility and was practiced by Greeks and Romans especially around the beginning of the Christian era.

Reconstructing the city whose population must have exceeded 100,-000 has been made easier because of the discovery of a sarcophagus containing a plan from the fifth century, on which most streets and buildings were clearly marked. The excavation of Ephesus, which has been hindered many times by earthquakes that still rock the region today, is continuing. Recent discoveries have included an elegant villa with mosaics and painted walls in color so true that the pictures of the peacocks and trees are still clear.

Most of what we know about the wondrous temple of Artemis at Ephesus is through the work of J. T. Wood, an English engineer, who got permission to start probing the site in 1863 and who kept up his work for more than a decade through constant hardship and frustration. That the ancients chose the placement of their sacred shrines with an eye for grandeur is apparent in his description of the physical landscape:

> The great beauty of Ephesus can scarcely be exaggerated, surrounded as it is by mountains which, in their broken forms exhibit in every direction a varied picturesque skyline. In the Spring of the year the angelica, with its bright yellow blossoms, covers Mount Coressus, making it most prominent in the landscape from every point of view. Although my sojourn there was extended over the greater part of 11 years, I never became weary of the scenery by which I was surrounded, for the mountains on which my eyes daily rested changed from hour to hour as the sun travelled on its course, and the desolation of the place was fully compensated by its constant and never-ceasing loveliness.

Desolation was only part of the story. In his immense book, *Discoveries at Ephesus,* Wood tells of loneliness, scorpions, and thefts from the site by ruffians who, in the nearby village, would offer him bits of sculpture for sale that he himself had excavated. He had constant problems with the Turkish authorities about getting his permit renewed.

In his first year at Ephesus there was a serious drought, and Wood was amazed one day to see 2,000 Turks, all dressed in white, ascend nearby Mount Pagus and with arms outstretched pray for rain (soon afterward it rained). In later years there were incessant thunderstorms and rains.

He also had constant trouble with workmen, one of whom was suffocated when a trench fell in; others were jailed for stealing a lamb. About evenly divided among Arabs, Turks, and Greeks, the workmen would fight constantly. The Greeks especially took numerous religious holidays, when they would don their best suits and sit around drinking. At one time he had as many as 100 men working simultaneously and their frequent demands for 15 piastres a day, instead of the usual rate of 10 piastres (about 21 cents at that time), made big inroads into his £16,000 budget which had been provided by the British Museum.

One day a Turkish merchant from nearby Smyrna (only fifty miles, but three hours away by train) turned up to report having dreamed there was a treasure on the site and persuaded Wood to let him hire his own diggers and join in the search. Finding nothing, he tried to stick Wood with his bills, but the Briton, understandably, resisted this. A year or two later the Turk's premonition was proved correct when Wood's men dug up an earthenware vessel containing 2,000 coins from the years

1285 to 1315. Turkish authorities scoffed at what they considered the negligible value of this find.

Finally, Wood was able to report success. From fragmentary inscriptions discovered nearby, he was able to establish that whenever a performance was held in the ancient theater, the sacred images were carried from the temple and returned afterward. The route proscribed was by way of the Magnesian Gate. This was uncovered fifteen feet below the ground, and a marble street, twelve yards wide, was discovered leading right to the site of the temple—the fifth and last one to be built on the site.

The temple had been enormous: 342 feet long by 163 feet wide, brightly painted and glowing with metal adornments. Wood also found sections from the temple built by Croesus and then ran into difficulty excavating further in the marshy ground. But he succeeded in taking twenty-three vases and sixty-three loose blocks of marble back to England (now in the British Museum), and among them was a piece of marble column on which was an inscription in Greek relating to divination by the flight of birds:

> In flying from right to left if the bird [conjecture] shall get out of sight
> it is lucky, but if it shall raise its left wing and whether it raises it or hides,
> it is unlucky: and if, in flying from left to right, it should get out of sight
> in a straight line it is unlucky: but if raising the right wing . . .

At the turn of the century, D. G. Hogarth continued the work begun by Wood, again sponsored by the British Museum, and uncovered the remains of earlier temples. In their ruins he found a collection of statuettes, in gold and ivory, of the goddess Diana and her wild animals.

The attribute of the goddess most noteworthy, and perhaps the reason for her deification, was her ability to tame wild creatures. Throughout history and down to the present day, we read of those humans who seem to possess a peculiar ability to communicate with birds and animals. One can easily imagine how revered this quality might have been in ancient times when human/animal relationships were closer, when a nomadic existence depended on a successful hunt. Even today when hunting is called sport, those who can mysteriously put themselves in the animal's position, sense its movements, command the respect of their fellow nimrods. The curious relationship between hunter and hunted has often been explored in fact and fiction. Diana, the huntress who was also the protectress of wild things, is possibly the earliest example of this ambivalence.

The first temple, or tree shrine, raised to honor her was destroyed by the Cimmerians in 650 B.C. It was rebuilt twice and successively sacked. The fourth temple was sponsored by Croesus of the Lydians and its splendor lived up to his name. It took over 120 years to complete and was of white marble, surrounded by Ionic columns, and adorned with a variety of ornament unusual to the period. Its magnificence excited Herodotus to admiration upon his visit there around 450 B.C. But a century later, the temple was destroyed once more. On an October night in 356 B.C. (said to be the very night Alexander the Great was born) a man called Herostratus, who had the strange ambition to immortalize his name by committing a great crime, set its wooden precincts afire.

His name, ironically, was immortalized because of the universal denunciation of his crime: the public council of Asia decreed that he be declared the worst and basest of men and the perfection of all wickedness and worthy of neither remembrance "nor even to be named."

This time an indignant population joined together to rebuild the profaned shrine. We read of donations from individuals, rich and poor: kings from neighboring communities vying with each other for the honor of contributing treasures to the temple. Alexander the Great, passing through on his way to the East, proffered a large donation, on the condition the temple be dedicated in his name. The Ephesians handled the matter with admirable tact: "But how can one God dedicate a temple to another?" In 323 B.C. the edifice was finished; this was the fifth temple and the one Philon called the greatest of the Seven Wonders of the World. Its 127 columns soared 60 feet above the plain and Pliny the Elder tells us it was full of the genius of Greece: statuary by Praxiteles and wondrous paintings. Pliny (whose thirtieth book, incidentally, is about magic and includes a list of necromancers starting with Moses) explains that the massive columns were raised on baskets of sand which were gradually emptied, allowing the columns to settle into their bed. The great lintel, however, was so huge that the architect Dinocrates despaired of ever adjusting it correctly and was on the verge of suicide when Diana herself appeared to him in his sleep and assured him that the lintel was now in place. Which, on waking, the architect found to be the case.

And what of the image of the goddess herself, she who had inspired this awesome monument?

The goddess of the Amazons was originally symbolized in the form of a date-palm tree, upon which had fallen a *diopet* (a small stone, perhaps a meteorite) and around which the first shrine was built. For centuries thereafter the *diopet*, said to have come from Zeus, would be encased in the mural or towerlike crown of the statue of the goddess, which was created by the Greeks to replace the palm tree. The *diopet* was acknowledged to be the most sacred object in the temple and may have survived the ultimate destruction of the shrine.

One report has it that the original *diopet* now rests in the City of Liverpool Museum. The museum acquired the stone from the antiquarian Charles Seltman, who bought it at Ephesus in the 1940s.

Liverpool's Keeper of Archaeology, Dr. Dorothy Downes, says that just because it was purchased at Ephesus doesn't prove its origin but that "it may well have come from one of the Ephesian temples." The stone was originally a neolithic pestle of volcanic greenstone, she adds, "and was converted into an object of worship sometime after c. 700 B.C. by reshaping and the addition of iron bands. Many people believed that such stray finds were meteorites and therefore sacred."

The figure called "the Diana of Ephesus" is known to us through the small facsimiles produced for sale to the thousands of pilgrims who annually visited the shrine. These tokens are mentioned in the Bible (Acts 19) and were made by, among others, the silversmith Demetrius, who after hearing Paul speak gathered his colleagues together and said: "Not only this our craft is in danger to be set at naught, but also the temple of great Diana shall be reputed for nothing! Yea, and her majesty shall begin to be destroyed, whom all Asia and the world worshippeth." Roused to anger the silversmiths cried: "Great is Diana of the Ephesians!" So began the tumult which spread through the city and forced St. Paul to leave.

The figurines vary in detail and the standard interpretation of their symbolism is open to question. Most often one reads how the fertility goddess of Eastern origin cloaked in bizarre Oriental splendor was combined with the pure Artemis/Diana deity of nature. Nearly every scholarly source describes the image as monstrous and having multiple breasts.

Yet when we read of the custom of dressing the statue in vestments and bedecking it with ornaments, the significance of the girdle of "breasts" becomes clear. The sacred tree, the date-palm, would have been heavy with fruit at the time of Artemis' festival. It seems more than likely that a festoon of ripe dates adorned the figure of the deity at the celebration. The token replicas conceivably portrayed this traditional decoration. Probably this interpretation better suits the Amazon heritage and is more in keeping with the character of classical myth: "Queen and huntress, chaste and fair." The figure itself is slender, high-breasted, similar in form to other representations of the same period. Both arms are extended outward, palms open, and tiny lions climb to the shoulders. The lower body is as if swathed in three bands, or friezes, of stag, bull, and lion heads.

Many of the statuettes bear a pendant: scorpionlike, with a half-moon, horns pointing downward, suspended around the neck. All wear the curious towerlike crown in which the sacred *diopet* was stored. The faces are Hellenistic in style with pure, regular features, and on each side of the head are five tiny busts of female figures, arms upraised. No trace of the original statue has ever been found. It must have been formidable, for it rested on an altar which was seventy feet wide and encircled by a double row of columns. Its destruction was accomplished in A.D. 400 by a Christian zealot who boasted that he had torn down the image of the "demon Artemis."

The Diana cult survived the destruction of the temple by the Goths but was forced underground when by proclamation of the Emperor Constantine, Julian's predecessor, Christianity became the official religion of the Roman Empire. The mystic themes of the old faith which Julian tried vainly to revive continue to reappear even to the present day.

Perhaps the best-known native of Ephesus in Roman times was the philosopher-magician Maximus, who after initiating the emperor Julian into the Eleusinian mysteries introduced him to many mystical practices, including, it is said, midnight rites to the goddess Hecate.

Hecate was a phase of Artemis (Diana). At dark-of-the-moon the temple belonged to her and it was then that magic took place.

It should be noted that all ancient goddesses are actually one. The Earth Mother as personified by Cybele, Demeter, and Isis and the Virgin known as Artemis, Persephone, and Hecate are all aspects of the female —mistress of mystery and intuition. Robert Graves speculates that when the Western world adopted the all-male deity (godhead) of Jesus, a decline in psychic meaning in life began. An eventual attempt by Roman Catholics to return to the veneration of Mary, Virgin and Mother, was thwarted by the force of the Reformation.

Maximus convinced Julian, a believer in the principle of metempsychosis (reincarnation) so beloved of the Pythagoreans, that he was animated by the soul of the emperor Alexander and as such was destined to conquer the world.

Giuseppe Ricciotti, in his *Julian the Apostate,* recounts an interesting story of how Maximus and Julian first met. At the time, Julian, still nominally a Christian to avert the wrath of his uncle the emperor Constantine, was studying with Eusebius at Pergamum. His teacher did not entirely approve of Maximus, already notorious as the high priest of Hellenic paganism, and told Julian of the time the latter had invited Eusebius and some friends to the temple of Hecate where Maximus burned incense and recited a hymn. Then they were amazed to see the statue of the goddess smile and laugh out loud. Maximus calmed them by asking them to watch closely, as the torches she held were about to burst into flame—which they did.

Eusebius was sure that this incident would quench Julian's curiosity about Maximus, yet it had quite the opposite effect. Julian replied: "Farewell, keep your books; you have shown me my man." And he set off forthwith for Ephesus, where he completed a regular course of studies in the occult arts. He was officially initiated into the mysteries with all attendant trappings—the underground ceremonies with strange sounds, revolting exhalations, and fiery apparitions. From that moment on, avers his unsympathetic biographer, the Christian priest Gregory, Julian was possessed.

All through his childhood he had kept his thoughts to himself, knowing full well that to reveal his beliefs would have signed his death warrant. His uncle Constantine, having murdered his own three sons, embraced Christianity as the state's semiofficial religion, perceiving that it might become a powerful instrument of imperial authority.

Julian, born Flavius Claudius Julianus at Constantinople on November 6, 331, was a sun worshiper, although during his youth he had been deferential toward his uncle and paid lip service to Christianity, a religion about which he was scornful. Like most of his contemporaries he used the term "magic" as one of opprobrium and once commented that Paul "surpassed all the magicians and imposters that ever lived."

Julian was sarcastic about Christian spells, making the point that fornicators, idolators, adulterers, thieves, covetors, and extortioners could apparently all be washed clean by baptismal water that was nevertheless incapable of curing any bodily ailments. He, on the other hand, believed in every form of pagan divination, including the examination of entrails and the interpretation of dreams and omens.

Julian was twenty when he first went to Ephesus, at the beginning of a short and crowded career which eventually found him studying magic in Athens, being admitted to the Eleusinian mysteries, being appointed western military commander in 355, and becoming Roman emperor on Constantine's death in 362. The new emperor's first act was to reopen all the pagan temples and attempt to roll back the Christian tide. But this force was too powerful for him; barely a year later, while conducting a successful campaign against the Persians, he was murdered. He was thirty-two and with his death virtually the last opposition to Christianity disappeared.

His Christian enemies, incidentally, made great sport of the fact that the javelin's death blow went through Julian's liver. They were not above believing, as did the pagans, that this particular organ was of great significance in divination.

Historians have speculated endlessly about the extent to which Maximus ("the high priest of Hellenistic paganism, a user of curious arts who habitually consorted with the gods") influenced the young emperor-to-be. The magic that Maximus taught Julian was of a theurgical nature, which the dictionary defines as a kind of occult art in which the operator "by means of self-purification, discipline, sacred rites and the knowledge of divine marks or signatures on nature" was felt to be capable of evoking "beneficient spirits." Medieval ecclesiastics, following the condemnations of St. Augustine, refused to make any distinction between theurgy and magic, outlawing both equally.

In *Julian the Apostate,* Ricciotti comments that it would be a mistake to dismiss the kind of magical effects that Maximus produced as being a total fraud. "If for a theurgist the divine was invisibly diffused throughout the whole cosmos . . . whatever induced the divine to reveal itself was a legitimate theurgic activity. And to obtain such a revelation one had recourse to all the then-known physical, chemical and optical laws. But one could also enrich and complement the picture with additional props which would enhance the desired theurgic effect." Saltpeter mixed with charcoal, for example, could stimulate the effects of thunder.

Julian's philosopher-friend Libanius described Maximus as the "good physician" of Julian's changed opinions and reported that Maximus confirmed for the soon-to-be emperor, what his dreams had hinted—that he would be the restorer of the old gods and the overturner of Christianity.

But other commentators about Maximus are not so sympathetic. The soldier-historian Ammianus, who once wrote that even a confessed atheist of that time did not make a journey without casting a horoscope, thought that the boisterous way in which Julian greeted his old sorcerer-friend after becoming emperor was "unbecoming." And it certainly seems that Maximus exerted an extraordinary influence on a man whose actions governed the fate of millions.

"Probably a quack, certainly a schemer . . . reputed as a user of curious arts who habitually consorted with gods." This is the verdict of W. Douglas Simpson, author of another book also with the title *Julian the Apostate.* It is probably a typical appraisal. After Julian's assassination, Maximus himself came to a bad end. Christian authorities returned the magician to Ephesus where he was beheaded in A.D. 376.

Maximus was the last of a long line of Ephesians whose lives were devoted to occult pursuits under the aegis of the Moon Goddess.

Heraclitus (c. 540–475 B.C.), "the Dark Philosopher," was born and lived his life in Ephesus. In a sense he is the founder of metaphysics. "All things are one, and this one is made up of many opposing tensions, such as hot and cold, good and evil, day and night . . . inseparable halves of one and the same thing. The basic actuality of life is change and the basic element is fire." Fundamental occult precepts.

Falkener tells us that the Jews in Ephesus at this time were "sunk in great superstition" and believed that Solomon had discovered the power of exorcising evil spirits "by the aid of some wonderful herb he was acquainted with." Solomon was Israel's king in the tenth century B.C., and the son of David and Bathsheba. Famed for his wisdom and wealth, he was legendary as a master magician. The famous medieval *grimoire,* or textbook of magic, *The Key of Solomon,* is attributed to him. Called "the Archmagician," "the Lord of Occult Realms," his fame came to be celebrated in the magic folklore of many lands.

Another Ephesus phenomenon were tokens known as the Ephesian letters. These, according to Eustathius, may have been the spells that were engraved on the feet, girdle, and crown of the statue of Diana. They achieved some local fame in ancient times for being charms that could make one invincible. There were many references to them being secretly employed by athletes or those in competition. One wrestler was said to have defeated 300 opponents before the charms in his possession were discovered and taken away from him, and Anaxilaus once wrote: "The athlete and other candidates at the Olympic games fly to the magic art from desire of victory."

In these modern days racetrack officials check for the unfair advantage that drugs might give. But in Roman times, according to Marcellinus, a certain horse racer named Hillarius was actually put to death for sending his son to a magician to be taught secret spells and charms, "by which, without any man's knowledge, he might be able to effect all he desired in the way of his profession."

Falkener suggests that perhaps this "superstition," lingering on into the Middle Ages, was the reason for the oath of asseveration (i.e. denial of magical aid) required from combatants prior to trial by battle.

The celebrated King Croesus is said to have escaped being burned alive by having Ephesian letters pronounced on his pyre, and many a magician, like Solomon, was supposed to have exorcised evil spirits by causing them to recite to themselves these famous letters.

What *were* the letters actually? So far as can be ascertained, they consisted of certain basic words written in Greek—the words for darkness, light, earth, the year, the sun, the truth. Probably they were written, on parchment, and certainly they were carried in sewn leather bags, as a passage from *The Metrical Proverbs of Athenaeus* makes clear:

> The skin anointed with golden ointment
> Effeminately dressed in soft robes
> And delicate slippers—
> Chewing onions; munching cheese;
> Eating raw eggs; sucking shellfish;
> Quaffing goblets of rich Chian*
> And carrying in sewn leather bags the
>   Ephesian letters of good omen.

So we find only fragments remain to illuminate the magic that once lived in Ephesus, symbolic home of Diana, goddess of night and wild nature.

The herb associated with Diana of Ephesus is the amaranth, named for the Greek word meaning "unwithering." Its choice was prophetic, for Diana remains ever a fascinating concept, curiously relevant in today's world as women seek to redefine their roles in a society so long in disharmony with the world of nature.

Although the site of Ephesus is on the west coast of Turkey, it is easily reached by boat from various nearby Greek islands, the most

---

*A mixture of garlic, leeks, cheese, oil, vinegar, and dried herbs.

charming of which is Kos. There the Viking Travel Agency (and others) operates at periods when the tensions between the two countries are not too high.

The site at Ephesus is huge and well excavated, and both the ruins and the small museum in the nearby town can be covered amply in half a day, particularly if time is not spent on the various Christian relics which seem an unavoidable part of guided tours.

2

Samos

THE FATHER OF NUMBERS

ONE OF THE GREENEST of Greek islands, which also happens to be the one closest to Turkey, held an unusual celebration in 1955, marking the twenty-five hundredth anniversary of the founding of the world's first school of philosophy by Pythagoras who was born on the island. He was, in fact, the first person to use the word *philosopher,* meaning "lover of wisdom," and what he discovered influences our thinking to this day. If it were only for his contributions to mathematics and music alone—both basic forms of magic—he would be revered. But there was much more to him than that.

Some ancient writers believed that this man, whose wisdom had been predicted by the Delphic oracle, was himself a god, sent to earth to impart knowledge. In his *Anacalypsus,* Godfrey Higgins speculates that this might have been the origin of the Jesus legend. At any rate, the prescience ascribed to Pythagoras has no other parallel.

Manly P. Hall in *The Secret Teachings of All Ages* records that Pythagoras was able to speak to the spirits in the water, through whom he predicted things. "By the exercise of mental influence he caused a bird to change

Illustration: Pythagorean Pentalpha. Sign of recognition used by Pythagoras, a native of Samos, and his disciples. Also a symbol of health. Drawing from medieval text.

15

the course of its flight, a bear to cease its ravages on the community and a bull to change its diet. He was also gifted with second sight, being able to see things at a distance and accurately describe incidents that had not yet come to pass."

Pythagoras was said to have possessed a remarkable wheel by means of which he could predict future events. He believed that everything in nature could be divided into three parts and said that no one could become wise until he viewed every problem as being diagrammatically triangular. "Establish the triangle and the problem is two-thirds solved," he declared.

Needless to say, the world, too, could be divided into three parts. Most creatures, including humans, who subsisted on material things were in the lowest, inferior, portion. Above men was the Superior World, and above that, topping the other two, was the Supreme World. This man could aspire to only by rising above his material nature, said Pythagoras, until he was acceptable to the gods and able to partake of their immortality.

Pythagoras was born the son of a wealthy jeweler named Mnesarchus on Samos in 582 B.C. Even before his birth he was consecrated to Apollo, god of light, and when he was only one year old his mother took him to a temple in Lebanon where an Israelite high priest gave him a special blessing. Influenced at an early age by Thales, who was considered chief of the seven "wise men" of Greece, Pythagoras is believed to have spent some of his youth in Egypt where geometry is said to have been invented as a necessary means of calculating the River Nile's annual overflow onto surrounding lands.

Mathematics quickly became the young Pythagoras' passion, with the number 10—the addition of 1, 2, 3, and 4—assuming mystical significance, partly because it fulfilled his requirements that the perfect number must contain an equal number of odd and even numbers, and partly because he believed it to be "the principle of health." To demonstrate his theory, Pythagoras would lay pebbles out in four pyramidal rows to form the perfect triangle. The heavens contained ten moving bodies, the philosopher averred: earth, counter earth, sun, moon, five planets, and a sphere of fixed stars.

Mathematics led him inevitably into music and to experiment with strings of different lengths and thicknesses whose tension (and resulting tone) could be changed by turning a screw. The shortest string produced the highest note, the longest the lowest.

Proportions and ratios being the next obvious step, he noted three consonances: the octave (1:2), the fifth (2:3), and the fourth (3:4); their harmonies (he concluded) depending on matching proportions. One story about this is told by the sixth-century Roman statesman, Boethius, who recounted that as Pythagoras was passing a blacksmith's shop one day, he stopped to listen to the musical sounds of the hammers upon the anvil. His keen ear was aware of an unharmonious note. He walked in and weighed the hammers, finding four of them in proportion: 12 – 9 – 8 – 6, and the fifth's weight bearing no relation to the others. Eliminating this one, he played the others again, finding that the heaviest hammer—double the weight of the lightest—was a full octave lower.

It's a charming story, but unfortunately, says Benjamin Farrington in *Greek Science,* "there is some confusion in tradition, for the experiment with the hammers could not give the results said to have been given."

Nevertheless, as Plutarch wrote, "the function of geometry is to draw us away from the sensible and perishable to the intelligible and eternal. For the contemplation of the eternal is the end of philosophy as the contemplation of the mysteries is the end of religion."

Turning his attention to the eternal, Pythagoras next devised his theory about "the music of the spheres," speculating that as the distance of the sun from the earth was twice that of the moon, and that of Venus three times as great, and that of Mercury four times, with the other planets in proportion, then it followed that this universal harmony produced "a fuller and more intense melody than anything affected by mortal sounds."

Aristotle, who had been skeptical about the magical 10, suggesting that the Pythagoreans had invented the "counter earth" to make the facts fit their opinions, was rather more enchanted with the concept of heavenly music and tried to explain why, if it was literally true, people were not able to hear the music of the spheres. These sounds, he said, had been with us since birth and so we had never had pure silence to contrast them against—just as a coppersmith "becomes by long habit indifferent to the din around him."

Pythagoras was a natural-born teacher, acquiring disciples first at the school on Samos and in 529 B.C. at Crotona in Italy. Pythagorean brethren were required to meditate daily and examine their consciences. The philosopher once advised his pupils that "the subjugation of the tongue" was the most difficult of achievements, a thought echoed centuries later by his follower Apollonius of Tyana, who once went five years without speaking, expressing the opinion that "loquacity has many pitfalls but silence none."

Although Pythagoras had been dead four centuries by the time Apollonius was born in Asia Minor (about 4 B.C.) his teachings were still current and Apollonius took the Pythagorean vow in his teens, submitting himself to strict disciplines and traveling widely as had his long-dead mentor. His life, written by Philostratus, is about the only source of information about Apollonius of Tyana. It has many references to the miracles he performed and the mysterious way he disappeared rather than merely dying.

At his school, Pythagoras opened and closed each day with songs, reportedly curing many ailments by playing to the sufferer specially prepared musical compositions. New initiates to his school, once they had proved themselves worthy, were first allowed to wander freely in a sort of vestibule to the inner temple. "In this gymnasium people were encouraged to express their opinions and beliefs," wrote W. J. Colville in *Ancient Mysteries and Revelations,* "and Pythagoras himself would unexpectedly appear to the stranger, studying his words and gestures in estimating which he was never at fault. He paid particular attention to gait and laughter which are always faithful indexes of character. He also made so profound a study of the human face that he read dispositions at a glance."

After a few months of preliminary training, the Pythagorean candidate was subjected to various ordeals, one of which was spending the night in a cave haunted by mysterious elementals who assumed gruesome shapes. If his courage withstood this ordeal, he passed from the initial stages (which might last anywhere from two to five years and during whose lessons he must maintain complete silence) and was welcomed into the philosopher's home along with the other disciples.

"Real initiation now began. A rational exposition of occult doctrine was now given which consisted especially of the science of numbers, the esoteric meaning of which was kept from the people at large and communicated only to students who had proven their worth. A great distinction was made between secular and sacred mathematics."

The early lessons took place in daylight, usually in the full blaze of the outdoor sun. The noted mathematician, like the emperor Julian who followed his precepts almost 700 years later, believed in the sun as "the central fire" and felt that energy emanated from all living things and from all patterns, forms, and organizations existing in nature.

From time to time Pythagoras would go into the temple for extended periods to meditate. On these occasions the food he took with him consisted of poppy seeds and sesame seeds, the juiceless skin of the sea onion (which he thought had great healing properties), flower of daffodil, leaves of mallows, and a paste of barley, peas, and wild honey. He also favored a mixture of cucumber seeds, dried raisins, flowers of coriander, seeds of mallows and purslane, scraped cheese, meal, cream, and wild honey. Although it doesn't sound very appetizing, it kept him alive until he was almost a hundred years old.

Much of the knowledge that he handed down to his pupils he apparently acquired during his extensive travels. The Roman historian Porphyry (A.D. 233–c. 304) and the Syrian philosopher Iamblichus (c. A.D. 250–c. 330) both note that Pythagoras learned geometry and astronomy in Egypt; astrology and the science of numbers in Babylon and Phoenicia. His prohibition against the eating of beans had a parallel in ancient Indian texts, but the Egyptians, too, were not allowed to eat beans, according to Herodotus, because their priests considered beans to be unholy food.

Some say Pythagoras acquired his doctrine of metempsychosis, or reincarnation, from his early teacher Pherecydes. Others credit India as the source but this is unlikely. Ralph Linton in *The Tree of Culture* remarks that belief in reincarnation did not originate in India for no mention of it occurs in the older Vedas nor did the belief form part of the general Indo-European cultural heritage, although, he remarks, there are references to it in Celtic mythology. In this regard it is interesting to note that Diogenes Laërtius, biographer of the Greek philosophers, writing in the third century A.D. says Pythagoras studied under the Druidic priests of the Celts.

"He traveled everywhere, underwent immense labors and dangers, choosing to leave his country and dwell among strangers," wrote Pythagoras' biographer Iamblichus. "Likewise he dissolved tyrannies, gave orderly arrangements to confused politics and emancipated cities. He also caused illegality to cease and impeded the operations of insolent and tyrannical men."

Although he visited much of the known world—Syria, Arabia, Chaldea, Phoenicia, Egypt, and conceivably even India and Gaul—always advising tourists to leave their prejudices at home, Pythagoras was fond of his native Samos which was and still is one of the most verdant of Greek islands. Unique in that it is heavily wooded, it was referred to by the ancients as phyllas ("leafy") and dyoussa ("oak-tree clad"). Another characteristic is its mountains and, indeed, the island gained its name from the early Phoenician settlers who called it *samos,* meaning "high" or "lofty." The mountains are believed to be extinct volcanoes, a theory bolstered by their numerous cavities, one of which is called "the Candle" because of a mysterious light that seems to issue from it and has been observed by seafarers on misty nights. Samos was also the birthplace of Hera, wife of Zeus, and there a famous temple was built for her in ancient times, of which one column remains.

The famous philosopher's own birthplace, a tiny port now called Pythagorion, is on the southern side of the island and was once the capital. Nearby is a 1,300-yard tunnel carved through the mountains to bring in water, and for which Pythagoras is said to have provided the necessary calculations. It was built by the notorious Polycrates who ruled from 535 to 515 B.C. and who tried tirelessly to win popularity by donating money to the poor and adorning the city with public works on a grand scale.

Polycrates first came to power with the help of his two brothers, taking advantage of a festival to Hera when most citizens were celebrating outside the town. Shucking off his siblings, he next acquired a fleet of 100 pirate ships with which he terrorized the Aegean, allying his forces with those of Amasis of Egypt against the Persians. He had the reputation of being very lucky and once, to test his fortune, cast his emerald ring into the sea: it reappeared in the belly of a fish served to him three days later.

"Polycrates the Tyrant" was how historians described him and for a while there were few who could withstand him. His opponents on Samos combined with Spartans, Corinthians, and Persians to assault his power, but he fought off the siege and it was only after being lured to the mainland with promises of gold by Oroetes, Persian governor of Lydia, that he was captured and killed. Herodotus noted that the manner of his torture and death was too horrible to describe.

It was because of Polycrates that Pythagoras left his beloved Samos and took up residence at Crotona. But he was already famous when he left, one of his well-known maxims being: "Numbers take man by the hand and conduct him unerringly along the path of reason."

Pythagorion today must be one of the sleepiest towns in Greece. It is accessible by bus only three times daily from Samos' main port of Vathy and has almost nothing to interest the visitor except a few harborside tavernas. There are no traces of the great philosopher. The only statue in town is one commemorating Lycurgus Logothetis, leader of the 1821 revolt against the Turks.

Samos was the birthplace of other remarkable Greeks: Aesop, author of the fables; the philosopher Epicurus; the astronomer-scientist Aristarchus; and Callistratus, who first devised the twenty-four-letter Greek alphabet.

Today the island is best known for its wine, which was a favorite of Lord Byron, and few tourists miss visiting the winery for some free samples. The inhabitants are extremely healthy and longevity on Samos is common. They have a reputation for being highly intelligent and can often "forecast distant events with uncanny certitude."

Pythagoras founded his academy in Crotona, possibly choosing this small Italian town, the only natural harbor between Tarsus and Sicily, because of the meaning of its name: "mouthpiece of the Pythian," a reference to the Delphic oracle after which Pythagoras himself had been named. Some of the Pythagoreans considered their master to be a reincarnation of the great god Apollo.

He was over fifty years old when he opened the Crotona academy, a school to which his disciples gave everything they owned, reserving the right to reclaim their share if they chose to leave afterward. (When this did happen the other pupils erected a tomb in the departed one's name and thereafter never spoke of him.)

Following Plato's doctrine of equality for the sexes, he allowed women to join the school, but enjoined men and women alike to dress simply and behave modestly, "never yielding to laughter and yet not looking stern" as Will Durant expressed it in his *Life of Greece*. Students were forbidden to practice sacrifices, kill any animal harmless to man, or chop down trees. They were not to eat flesh, eggs, or beans, the latter prohibition having been interpreted in many ways. Cicero thinks it was because of the way they disturbed the mind during sleep; Aristotle says beans signify lasciviousness, so that the ban might imply chastity. The bean being an archaic symbol of the female, it might have been veiled advice to practice celibacy. In those times votes were recorded by casting beans, so some have theorized that the admonition was an allegorical prohibition against taking political office. The philosopher himself merely said beans were the souls of the dead.

About eating meat, Pythagoras was much less ambiguous, declaring that it clouded the reasoning faculties. He suggested that judges should abstain from meat before a trial if they hoped to give honest and astute decisions.

By the time his students were ready for the higher degrees, they were sufficiently conditioned that such inner faculties as ESP and clairvoyance would rapidly assert themselves, particularly as these deeper teachings invariably took place at night beside the sea or in the crypts of temples lit by gentle naphtha flames.

His conditions for initiation were harsh, and many of them appear quite arbitrary at this date when we don't know the reasoning behind them. Why, for example, did he caution against looking into a mirror near a light source or picking up what had fallen down? What superstition warned against touching a white cock or sharing one's roof with swallows? Possibly some of these beliefs were the surviving fragments of ancient religious rites.

At any rate, Pythagoras was strict in enforcing them and in the end it was that that led to his death (although at the ripe old age of almost one hundred, after marrying one of his students when he was sixty and having seven children). A certain Cylon, a wealthy and prominent local citizen of Crotona, was so infuriated at being refused admission to Pythagoras' academy that he gathered together a band of assassins who set fire to the school and killed its leader. Other Pythagorean communities were sacked and burned, their influence having been perhaps mistakenly regarded as a threat to existing political powers.

Most of his mathematical secrets, which had never been committed to paper, died with him, although for centuries afterward his teachings were the basis of a somewhat mystical secret society in the cities of Magna Graecia, or what is now southern Italy.

Pythagoreans believed that everything that existed had a voice and that all creatures were, in Emil Naumann's words, "eternally singing the praise of the creator."

Plato, who was an active neo-Pythagorean about 150 years later, was a great believer in the efficacy of music, maintaining that it should not merely create cheerful emotions but "inculcate a love of all that is noble and a hatred of all that is mean." In his *History of Music*, Emil Naumann says that both Plato and Damon of Athens (Socrates' music teacher) were in agreement that the introduction of a new and presumably enervating scale would endanger the future of the whole nation and that it was not possible to alter a key without shaking the foundations of the state.

The seven sacred vowels—*alpha, epsilon, eta, iota, omicron, upsilon,* and *omega*—were recognized as having some fundamental relationship to the seven planets, and the names of God were believed to be formed from combinations of these seven planetary harmonies. Early instruments had seven strings and the ancient Egyptians confined their sacred songs to the seven primary sounds, forbidding any others to be uttered in the temples.

Plato wrote that the Greeks gained their knowledge of the therapeutic and philosophical aspects of music from the Egyptians, who in turn considered Thoth (Hermes) the founder of the art. Some poems and songs had existed in Egypt for at least 10,000 years, he declared, and these were of such an exalted and inspiring nature that only the gods could have composed them.

There did exist at one time in Greece a prohibition against dissonance, and any musician composing music that was regarded as harmful in this manner could be banished for what was regarded as a crime against the common good. The same held true for an architect who built an asymmetrical building.

Pythagoras believed that in ancient days when an architect designed a great building, temple, or shrine, he conceived of it as a magnificent symphonic chord unfolding the structure in harmony with this specific vibration. He explained to his disciples that they could walk through the streets with a lute and strike the keynote of any building—a destructive keynote that if carefully studied would demolish the structure. "We also realize that every tone of sound, every color, will have some kind of effect either upon the mind or the imagination or upon the building."

What might be termed "musical medicine" was a Pythagorean concept. He used music to calm his disciples before going to sleep and to render their dreams prophetic. He is said to have calmed the frenzy of a youth who was gathering wood to burn down his girl's home by persuading a man playing a flute nearby to change his tune.

"There are certain melodies devised as remedies against the passions of the soul and also against despondency and lamentation," wrote Iamblichus, "which Pythagoras invented as things that afforded the greatest assistance in these maladies. And again he employed other melodies against rage and anger and against every aberration of the soul. There is also a kind of modulation invented as a remedy against desires."

It was Iamblichus in his *Life of Pythagoras* (translated by Thomas Taylor in 1818) who recorded some of the famous Pythagoric aphorisms, whose brevity encompasses more wisdom than would at first appear. Here are some of them:

Govern your tongue before all things, following the gods.

The wind blowing, adore the sound.

Offer not your right hand easily to anyone.

Sacrifice and adore unshod.

Declining from public ways, walk in unfrequented paths.

Cut not fire with a sword.

Remove from yourself every vinegar bottle.

Step not beyond the beam of balance.

Having departed from your house turn not back, for the furies will be your attendants.

Eat not the heart.

The pentagram, or pentacle, a major symbol of magic, was the sign of recognition used by Pythagoreans who called it "Health." One of the lesser-known Pythagorean symbols was the T, whose cross-stroke was supposed to indicate the forking of the ways, the left pointing to the earthly, the right to divine wisdom. In many nations this forked stick symbolizes life, and in the desert is an indication of the presence of water.

It is worthy of note that recent discoveries in such esoteric mathematical areas as quantum physics, wave mechanics, and the theory of relativity have led some contemporary academics to describe themselves as neo-Pythagorean.

Pythagoras and Confucius (550–478 b.c.) were contemporaries, and much of the *I Ching,* of which the latter thought so highly, shares the "elements of numbers as the elements of realities," according to the *Encyclopaedia Britannica.*

Pythagoras left no writings, religious or mystical, but during his long life he had instructed many pupils and his teachings survived for centuries after his death. Because of the strict rules of secrecy imposed upon his pupils, however, later writers have a tendency to attribute too much to the master. He "rapidly became an almost superhuman figure," as D. R. Dicks tartly puts it in *Early Greek Astronomy.*

And, observing that Pythagoras believed in divination by stars, dreams, delirium, the flight of birds, the entrails of sacrificed animals (and sometimes, because of his vegan beliefs, *vegetables*), Benjamin Farrington in *Science and Politics in the Ancient World* contrasts Pythagoras with the philosopher Epicurus, who "alone rejected these lying sciences and exposed the imposters." Epicurus, he writes, had a school in Athens about 200 years after the death of Pythagoras and was "the first man known in history to have organized a movement for the liberation of mankind from superstition."

But Pythagoras' critics are few and far between, and he appears to have been truly one of the illuminati. The first philosophic master to establish a mutual assistance school, Pythagoras insisted that his pupils be familiar with mathematics, music, and astronomy. The first rule he taught his disciples was silence, the rudiment of concentration.

He was, says Manly P. Hall, "the personification of majesty and power and in his presence all felt humble and afraid. . . . The influence of this great soul over those about him was such that a word of praise from Pythagoras filled his disciples with ecstasy while one committed suicide because the Master became momentarily irritated over something he had done. Pythagoras was so impressed by this tragedy that he never again spoke unkindly to or about anyone."

A sojourn on Samos, however brief, allows a visitor to experience a strange sense of kinship with Pythagoras, a man of grace and wisdom, whose name remains paramount in the annals of mystery and magic.

3

Kos

MAGIC AND MEDICINE

"Nature is the cure of all illness" was the maxim of Hippocrates, the father of modern medicine, who one century after Pythagoras was practicing his craft and laying the foundations of a philosophy just as durable, on the island of Kos only a few miles away from Samos.

The first man to make a thorough study of the human system, Hippocrates defined most of the basic scientific truths which still govern medicine today and formulated the oath, now called the Hippocratic oath, ("I swear by Apollo physician, by Asclepius [Greek god of healing], by Health, by Panacea and by all the gods and goddesses, making them my witnesses, that I will carry out, according to my ability and judgment . . .") universally accepted by its practitioners.

He is understandably revered on Kos, one of Greece's more beautiful islands and which, like Samos, possesses a local winery. The Asclepieon, or "hospital," at which he practiced can still be inspected atop a hill about two miles east of town. Only ruins remain, of course, but as it was Hippocrates' philosophy that the surroundings were almost as important as the cure, just climbing the hill to look at the view undoubt-

Illustration: The caduceus, symbol of medicine, associated with Hippocrates who lived in Kos and founded a hospital there. From a Greek amphora, fourth century B.C.

25

edly will do you good. According to Pausanias, it was prohibited to die or give birth here and the sacredness of the spot is enhanced by the remains of a temple to Apollo dating from Roman times. Kos has quite a number of Roman ruins, most of them in a tree-shaded glen at the fringe of the little harbor town. Kos is a lovely island and well worth a few days' stay, quite apart from its proximity to Turkey to which many daily cruises operate. The island also has an airport.

Until Hippocrates, born on Kos in 460 B.C. the year of the eightieth Olympiad, medical practice was a jumble of guesswork, gamble, and superstition. Magic it might certainly have been—when it worked—but after him it was magic that was *proven* to work when conducted under codified formulas.

Hippocrates' importance, and certainly his long-lasting fame, is as much due to his meticulous recording of his research and experiments as to his actual practice. All the great Greek writers—Sophocles, Socrates, Euripides, Plato, Aristotle—paid tribute to his work and he was the equal of them all. For twelve years he traveled the world of his time, Europe, Asia, and Africa, and met anybody who had anything to contribute to his already-encyclopedic knowledge.

In Militos he discussed "substance and infinity" with the great philosopher Anaxagoras (500–428 B.C.), and this helped him to correlate man's cycle of health with his natural environment. Studying the papyri left by Heraclitus in the sixth century B.C., he learned that "nothing in this world remains unchanged but for one moment only. Everything changes aspect, it dissolves, merges with other elements and displays a new aspect, different from the previous one."

But perhaps in Samos, birthplace of Pythagoras, he received confirmation of his most heartfelt theory: that it was not possible to ignore the patient's psychical condition when his body was undergoing treatment, that body and soul were to be examined as a whole.

Before the advent of Hippocrates the practice of "medicine" was almost a primitive form of magic, a combination of spells and incantations to exorcise the evil spirits who it was believed were the cause of the disease. Some ailments were regarded as "sacred" and Hippocrates once commented: "I do not believe the Sacred Disease is any more divine or sacred than any other disease, but on the contrary has specific characteristics and a definite cause."

And, just as today, there were practitioners of medicine whose main motivation seemed to be acquiring money, and in *Ancient Culture and Society: Early Greek Science,* G. E. R. Lloyd refers to "a post-Aristotle treatise" which warned doctors not to discuss fees with sick patients, as it tended to cause anxiety.

In the year 430 B.C. Hippocrates arrived in Athens during a major famine and epidemic, occasioned by the Peloponnesian War (against Sparta) which had begun the year before. He studied the crowded conditions under which the Athenians lived, the humidity that spread germs, the infected bodies that were left untreated, the impure water that was drunk by the ill and healthy alike. And by such strict measures as segregation of the sick, incineration of the dead, and boiling of all drinking water he brought the epidemic to a close. But too late to save the life of the famous Athenian statesman, Pericles, who had first sought his aid.

Then he returned to Kos to take charge of its medical center, Asclepieon, which, understandably, became one of the most famous in the world, adding to its earlier reputation for mystic healing by application of practical measures.

Hippocrates, who himself reputedly lived to 109 years, prefaced his major work on the medical art with the admonition: "Nobody ever can attain to the height of perfection in this art since our life is so very short and the art itself so long and full of perplexities."

His advice tended to take the form of short aphorisms, which displayed not only a great deal of common sense but also a shrewd knowledge of psychology long before the concept was formulated. The aphorisms of Hippocrates with amplifications and annotations by later Greek and Roman physicians (such as Dioscorides, a Greek army doctor of the first century B.C., and Galen, who lived in the second century A.D.) were translated and published in London in 1708 by C. J. Sprengell, an English doctor who observed in his introduction: "This work has cost me not only a great deal of Labour and Pains but Expences too; these are inconsiderable in respect of the Satisfaction I shall have if the reader received any Advantage from it."

The book, a handsomely printed volume with *f* for *s* throughout, quotes Hippocrates on a variety of subjects, from milk ("It is not good to allow milk to those that are troubled with the headache or those that are in fever.") to sadness and the effects thereof: "Some may be sad and fearful but for some small time having manifest reasons for it. But those that are so without any outward cause have their blood thick and heavy, their perspiration suppressed and a disorder in their animal functions. For which a timely lobotomy is the only remedy, or else a well-prepared vomit."

Hippocrates was a great believer in balance. The person who got sick from eating too much should take steps to move his bowels. "Whatever disease is caused by repletion must be cured by evacuation." Like most medical practitioners of his day he was a strong believer in purges and emetics to rid the body of tainted or excess food. But he cautioned: "Bodies that are not easily purged upwards must, before the taking of Hellebor, be well prepared with a moistening and plentiful diet and rest. For if Hellebor or any other strong emetics or cathartics are given upon an empty stomach, or presently after the body has been heated by exercise or otherwise they may by their violent irritation cause convulsions and death of which we have had not a few instances."

Very few of his writings, unfortunately, refer to specific herbal remedies (hellebore, a white poisonous flower, is used as both a sedative and a depressant), but we can make a fairly good guess at what some of them were from the writings of his later colleagues.

The Greek Herbal of Dioscorides, translated by John Goodyear and published in England in the seventeenth century, is a comprehensive guide to many of the healing herbs that still flourish today. And a current book, *Herbs of Greece* by Alto Dodds Niebuhr, quotes lavishly from Dioscorides as, for example, in the case of the Roman nettle *(Urtica pilulifera)*, a weed with long-stalked leaves that grows up to three feet in height. Its Greek name is *tsuknes,* and about it Dioscorides writes: "Ye leaves being sodden together with small shell fish do mollify ye bellies, dissolve windiness, move ye urine."

Also much in use in ancient times—and almost certainly in Hippocrates' day—was the yellowish-green plant *Ruta graveolens,* or rue, later referred to by Shakespeare as "the herb of grace." It grows two or three feet high, is prevalent in May to July and, despite its fetid odor, was used in salads. But its major value to the ancients was that its smell gave it insect- and germ-repellent properties and it was strewn in courts and homes for that purpose.

Its Greek name is *apigheros* and Dioscorides commented that "being chewed it ceaseth ye rank smells which come from garlic and onions." He also recommends it "to cause the menses to flow."

Of course the most widely-known herb was undoubtedly what the Romans called *Conium maculatum* (Greek name: *amaranghas*)—a biennial with white roots, white flowers, and purple spots on the hollow stem, and which is still famous today as hemlock, the poison that killed Socrates.

During his life, Hippocrates made many foreign excursions to spread his knowledge but usually returned to Kos where jealous rivals once tried to burn the Asclepieon and put the blame on him. But he was much revered on the island.

During the past century, archeologists have uncovered the remains of an earlier Asclepieon on Kos, dating back to the year 336 B.C., but the last building to stand on the site was destroyed by an earthquake many centuries later, in A.D. 554. The site today is surrounded by beautiful cypress trees and what was a sacred park, whose springs still bear traces of sulphur and calcium used in many ancient cures.

Perhaps the most charming monument to the father of medicine is the immense Hippocrates' plane tree which spreads its branches over a tiny town square, Plateia Platanos. The tree, which in winter appears lifeless, sits over an ancient spring whose refreshing waters renew its vigor yearly, causing its cool, green leaves to cast a shade over the area around it. It is said to have been the very same tree under which the immortal Hippocrates sat and expounded his theories to all who cared to listen.

4

Atlantis

THE PERFECT CIVILIZATION?

THE ROMANTIC NOTION of an ancient island civilization that flourished until its overnight disappearance into the ocean is common to many societies and has persisted for thousands of years. Magic thrived in that ancient land, so tradition tells us, and many mystical secrets were known which have never been rediscovered; its fortunate citizens were rich, powerful, wise, and supremely happy, living in perfect harmony with nature and desiring nothing more than the eternal bliss they already possessed.

Over the centuries this Utopia has become the repository of all our far-fetched dreams and fantasies, a perfect land where polluting technology was unknown (and unneeded) and peace prevailed. The legend constantly renews itself: Shangri-La, Bali-hai, Brigadoon have each been literary manifestations of the age-old dream. It is a convenient and all-embracing myth which enables us to measure our contemporary inadequacies, our lack of perceptions, against an idealistic but probably impossible standard.

But so persistent is the myth, so various the locations of this supposed

Illustration: Sunwise Spiral. A magical symbol suggesting scientific sophistication; mystery and science are both integral to the Atlantis legend.

magical island—the Atlantic, the Pacific, the Aegean, the Sargasso Sea —it seems not unreasonable to conclude that it has some basis; that there was, in fact, more than one such place where a flourishing civilization suddenly disappeared and which, in retrospect, appears to have been an enchanted land.

An Egyptian version of the legend, preserved on papyrus in the Leningrad Museum, tells of a traveler who was shipwrecked while sailing to Pharaoh's mines and who was cast upon a strange shore. Here he met a wonderful golden dragon which told him: "This is an island of blissful beings where all the heart may desire can be found." The traveler would be rescued by his own people, the dragon predicted, but "never more shall you see this island because it will be swallowed up by the waves."

Centuries later it was Egypt, wrote Plato, where the story of Atlantis first originated. About the year 355 B.C. Plato set down for the first time what purported to be a dialogue between his old teacher Socrates and two friends, Timaios and Kritias, in which they discussed this long-lost kingdom of Atlantis. Even then the story was second-hand, the main protagonist being Kritias' ancestor Solon, the legendary Athenian lawmaker who had visited Egypt more than a century before.

During this visit, according to Plato's narrative, Solon met with the priests of Saïs, an ancient town in the Nile Delta, and over a discussion of ancient history these priests scoffed at Solon's knowledge, which they said was incomplete even when it concerned his own country. Saïs' own historical records went back for at least 8,000 years, they claimed, because Egypt was a divinely preserved, sacred land. These manuscripts (said the priests) contained the description of a war between the Athenians and an ancient nation which inhabited a great island in the Atlantic Ocean.

"In the neighborhood of that island," Plato quoted the priests as having explained, "there were others, and beyond them at the limit of the ocean a great continent. This island, called Poseidonis or Atlantis, was ruled by kings to whom belonged the neighboring islands. Moreover they were masters of Libya and of the islands around the Tyrrhenian Sea. When Europe was invaded by the Atlantean army, the valor of the head of a Greek coalition, the City of Athenae, saved Greece from the Atlantean yoke. These events were soon followed by a dreadful catastrophe: a violent earthquake tore the earth asunder and heavy and lasting rains flooded it. The Greek troops perished and Atlantis sank beneath the ocean."

This extract is from Plato's *Timaios,* but the Atlantis story is picked up and amplified in his *Kritias,* in which the date of Atlantis' foundering is given as 9,600 years before Plato's time. It gives details of the government of the country and describes it as a rich and fertile place with a very advanced civilization. According to Plato, there existed great cultivated plains and forests of unusual trees, and there were many mines producing metals and precious stones. Plato mentioned with awe the wonder metal *oreichalkos,* which shone like gold and possessed magical qualities.

In his manuscript essay *Giants in the Earth,* the British occultist Anthony Roberts quotes other classical texts to suggest that the Atlanteans fell prey to, and finally practiced black magic "and so were destroyed through their subservience to the dark powers of the spirit of evil." Roberts believes that there is more to the story of Atlantis than a fable and that some society existed in the Atlantic Ocean thousands of years before the Christian era. "What it really was will be seen to be very different from anything the classical scholars could interpret or understand. All they could convey were faint hints and memories of the grandeur and civilization that had actually existed," he comments.

Almost all of the writers who have discussed the Atlantis legend, and since the time of Plato there have been more than two thousand books on the subject, have been confronted with one basic problem: was Plato's account fact or fiction? Many of the earlier commentators, such as Iamblichus, Porphyry, and Origen, seemed to feel there was substance to the tale, although their interpretations of it differed. At least they were more or less contemporaries of Plato, whereas latter-day speculators have built their cases mainly on the store of wishful thinking and fantasy that have accumulated over the centuries.

Plato's reputation alone is not enough to go on. In his long life he had written both fact and fiction, and most people would agree that he was quite capable of producing an allegorical tale, his idealistic outline for a "perfect" society. The Atlantis tale might also have been his personal version of a story whose central facts were true but distorted enough to make a better story.

In *Lost Continents: The Atlantis Theme in History, Science and Literature,* L. Sprague de Camp concludes that "Plato wrote a fascinating fiction that has had a large and continuing influence on Western literature and thought, but has nothing to do with geology, anthropology, or history, about which Plato knew very little."

For almost one thousand years, from the sixth century until the discovery of the Americas, the subject of Atlantis lay dormant. But then interest revived with a vengeance. Queen Elizabeth's astrologer John Dee, defying both reason and Plato himself, actually listed America as Atlantis on one of his maps and the speculation was picked up by, among others, Francis Bacon.

Among the more renowned Atlantis buffs of modern times have been the Minnesota congressman Ignatius Donnelly (1831–1901), whose *Atlantis: The Antedeluvian World* went through fifty printings, the last only a few years ago; Paul Schliemann, grandson of the renowned archeologist, who claimed to possess some Atlantis relics but never produced them; James Churchward who produced some doubtful documentation not only of Atlantis but of two other vanished civilizations, Lemuria and Mu; Madame Helena Blavatsky, who said she had examined a manuscript (written on palm leaf pages) from Atlantis while in a trance; and Rudolf Steiner, who explained that Atlanteans had mastered both the magic power of words and the "life force" and with one or the other could accomplish just about anything.

The most thorough documentation, not of Atlantis itself but of the different theories that people have had about it, is de Camp's *Lost Continents.* In one of the appendices the author lists 215 different "Atlantis interpreters" together with the date of their comments and their suggested location for the sunken paradise.

"Perhaps the very impracticality of Atlantism constitutes part of its charm," suggests de Camp. "It is a form of escapism that lets people play with eras and continents as a child plays with blocks."

Current speculation about Atlantis has taken some rather wide liberties with Plato's original text. His assertion that the cataclysm which swept Atlantis away had taken place 10,000 years before his time is now being explained as either a misapprehension or misprint. What he really meant, say some contemporary Atlantists, was a date much nearer—say 1,200 years before. And there *is* a slight case for assuming that Plato's date was an anachronism: the oldest nations in Europe, including Greece, cannot trace any historical continuity back much further than 3,500 years. Even the Egyptians and Sumerians (the "records" of the priests of Saïs, notwithstanding) go back little further than 5,000 years.

But it may be necessary to tamper not only with time but with place. Plato's Atlantis was an island "west of the Pillars of Herakles" (the Straits of Gibraltar), which would place it somewhere out in the Atlantic. The Sargasso Sea has been suggested as a possible location because of Plato's statement that the sea became unnavigable after Atlantis sank. And the historian Diodorus Siculus refers to a report brought back by Phoenician sailors about an island to the west "several days sail from the coast of Africa." It abounded in all manner of riches, they said. "Fish and game were found in great abundance; the climate was delicious, and the trees bore fruit at all seasons of the year."

Yet the search for Atlantis has continued for centuries in the Atlantic Ocean and nothing has been found to fit Plato's story. Heinrich Schliemann, the noted archeologist who uncovered Troy and Mycenae, wrote about the ancient papyrus in Russia's St. Petersburg (Leningrad) Museum, referring to an expedition sent by a Pharaoh of the Second Dynasty (2890–2686 B.C.) "in search of traces of the land of Atlantis from whence 3,500 years before the ancestors of the Egyptians arrived carrying with themselves all of the wisdom of their native land." After five years the expedition returned reporting "that they had found neither people nor objects which could give them a clue to the vanished land."

Of course, just because no traces of Atlantis have been found west of Gibraltar doesn't mean it was never there. But some contemporary historians have begun to turn their attention in the other direction: eastward to the Greek island of Santorini, which has had a long record of volcanic eruptions, the most recent being about twenty years ago.

It is the massive eruption that took place almost 3,500 years ago, however, that appears to fit most closely the Atlantis legend. On that terrible day in or around the year 1520 B.C. the entire center of the island, an area of thirty-five square miles, sank into the ocean causing a fallout that covered the island (then called Thera) with volcanic ash more than 100 feet deep and, more significantly, causing a tidal wave that flooded parts of Crete sixty miles to the south. Crete, or more specifically the flourishing civilization centered around the Minoan capital of Knossos, may have been Atlantis, and Santorini's submergence may have been the *cause* of its demise.

Some idea of the scale of the disaster can be gained from a comparison with the effects of a similar eruption in modern times, that of Krakatoa, between Java and Sumatra, in 1883. On this occasion the volcanic ash reached the stratosphere and was carried on the winds as far as Europe, turning day into night for a radius of 100 miles and making a noise (the loudest ever recorded in our history) that was heard in Australia, 2,000 miles away.

And yet the eruption at Krakatoa, historians agree, must have been less than half the magnitude of the one at Thera 3,000 years earlier. This assumption is made from the enormous size of the crater, now an immense bay which separates Santorini from the other islets to which it was once joined.

Today's Santorini is certainly unique and more than a little eerie. The daily boat from Piraeus (it lies on the direct route to Crete) ties up below the steep, red cliffs which are then climbed via a zigzag path up a hillside sheer enough to appear almost vertical. Donkeys carry the luggage, and also the less energetic passengers. At the top the charming Hotel Atlantis is a delightful spot from which to gaze out over the deep bay, which is really the "mouth" of the still-not-quite-extinct volcano.

The path to the harbor is named after the late Spyros Marinatos, a professor of archeology at Athens University, whose excavations on the island, notably at the abandoned village of Akrotiri, convinced him that this former Minoan colony was the very one that gave birth to the Atlantis legend.

"The Egyptians must undoubtedly have heard of an island becoming submerged," Professor Marinatos suggested, "and this was Thera (Santorini), but being small and insignificant they did not know of it. They transferred this event to Crete, the island so grievously struck and with which all contact they had suddenly lost. The myth of an army being engulfed stemmed from the news of the loss of thousands of souls. With the lack of cohesion and logic that characterizes myths, not even Plato sensed the inconsistency of Atlantis in the Atlantic Ocean and the entire armed forces of the Athenians, in Athens of course, being submerged at one and the same time."

Among the discoveries made in the buried city of Akrotiri is the remains of a magnificent wall painting, 10 feet by 14 feet, in which six nymphs are seen presenting flowers to a bare-breasted goddess near to whom stands a peacock. The peacock was sacred to the Olympian goddess Hera, wife and sister of Zeus, to whom a magnificent temple once stood on the island of Samos. The fresco is now being pieced together at the Byzantine Museum in Athens.

Professor Marinatos was slightly puzzled that his investigations had yielded so little proof of life. "We have not found a single skeleton," he said, "although we know that thousands must have died as a result of the earthquake and volcanic eruptions."

It is certainly true that a disaster struck Crete about 1,500 B.C. and the flourishing Minoan civilization which until then had kept up steady contact with the Egyptians came to an inexplicable halt. From then on, Egypt's king, Amenhotep III, maintained close ties with Mycenae, in the Peloponnese, and Crete disappeared from the records.

How close that original contact used to be between Crete and Egypt can be seen from the Egyptian flavor of the ruins at Knossos, the re-created palace of the ancient Minoans just outside Crete's present-day capital of Heraklion. The tranquil setting, between two hills, is beautiful, and the reconstructed palace—the work of Sir Arthur Evans, a British archeologist who spent his own fortune upon it at the turn of the century—impressive.

King Minos ruled Crete in the days of its greatest glory and of all the legends connected with his name none has lingered more persistently than that of the half bull/half man who took his name, the Minotaur. This fearsome beast was imprisoned in a labyrinth and every year seven youths and seven maidens were offered to it in sacrifice.

It is this, one of the earliest examples of a maze on record, that may have inspired medieval church labyrinths: the tiled mazes through which early Christians felt obliged to crawl on hands and knees. "The labyrinth, so easy of access but from which no one can escape is symbolical of human life," as one turn-of-the-century writer put it.

While Sir Arthur's excavations were still continuing at Knossos a minor earthquake took place. It did no damage but reminded one and all of the Minoans's belief that such tremors were due to this earth deity they so respected—a giant bull tossing the earth on his horns. The sea god Poseidon, too, was referred to in Homer as "the earth shaker."

Crete, the largest of the Greek islands, is one of the most interesting and has been an archeologist's paradise for the past century. Cretans are ruggedly independent people, many of them mountain men who can still be seen wearing their traditional black costume with its high boots. Something of their vigor and individuality can be gleaned from the works of Greece's most famous novelist, Nikos Kazantzakis, whose most famous book, *Zorba,* was set on this island where he lived and died.

The nearest town to Knossos is Heraklion, which has always served as a port for that splendid city and achieved some stature in the ninth century when the Arabs built a fort there. It was later occupied by the Venetians, then the Turks. Some traces remain of all these conquerors. Today, with a population of 70,000, it is a cosmopolitan city with a tranquil beauty that charms visitors who sit at its outdoor cafés, within sight and sound of the sixteenth-century fountain in the central square. The painter El Greco (1542–1614) was born near here and novelist Nikos Kazantzakis (1883–1953) is buried near the city wall. Boats from Piraeus dock at Heraklion every day.

But, in conclusion, we must accept that even if there was a real Atlantis, and even if it existed in Greece, it may have been but one of many similar vanished societies.

Atlantis, then, has become for some people a metaphor of a lost land that disappeared long ago and may yet appear again. It has many counterparts in various parts of the world, not the least of which is the enduring myth of the "lost land of Lyonesse," somewhere off the Cornish coast of England, where the remainder of King Arthur's band disappeared after the king's final, fatal battle.

As late as the sixteenth century the British historian William Camden was recording that fishermen off Land's End continuously dragged up broken pieces of masonry in their nets and in the area around the Scilly Isles lines of ancient stone walling have been uncovered at low tide.

The main drawback to this particular theory is that geologists believe most of the land subsidence that took place in the volcanically volatile Atlantic fringes was well before the Bronze Age (2,000 B.C.) and King Arthur's era is usually assumed to be around A.D. 500. Of course it is true that erosion and land subsidence continue even today and there are innumerable examples of volcanic islands that disappear and reappear from below the oceans with almost clockwork regularity. Exact dating, of course, must remain conjectural, but geologists believe that the British Isles were actually a part of continental Europe until somewhere around eight or nine thousand years before the Christian era.

5
Delos

SACRED TO THE SUN
AND MOON

THE 10 A.M. BOAT which leaves Myconos harbor each morning for the barren island of Delos is of only passing interest to most of the holiday makers having their breakfast of bread and honey at the sidewalk cafés. Most have already made their plans for the day—nude sunbathing at Paradise Beach or shopping for souvenirs in the labyrinthian back streets of the port—and such plans do not include four hours' traipsing through ruins in the scorching midsummer sun. Besides, they have heard about Delos with its inch-thick cheese sandwiches, warm beer, no shops, no beaches, and reputedly poisonous snakes awaiting anybody unwary enough to stray from the beaten paths.

But Delos needs none of the normal tourist pleasures, nor indeed, any of the normal tourists. None of its disadvantages will ever be enough to discourage those who are fascinated by its history, those who are aware that this tiny, barren islet was once the religious, artistic, and commercial center of the Greek and Roman worlds.

For apart from its excellent harbor and its situation at the center of the Cyclades (which, according to legend, arranged themselves around it), Delos has a supernatural reason for its importance. It was the birth-

Illustration: Artemis and Apollo. From a hand mirror. Greece, fifth century B.C.

place of the sacred twins Apollo and Artemis, god of the sun and goddess of the moon.

Homer's *Hymn to Apollo* (about 800 B.C.) tells the story of how a beautiful mortal named Leto was made pregnant by the god Zeus but how none would give her sanctuary because they feared the wrath of Zeus' wife Hera, should she learn of the infidelity.

In the nick of time, a tiny island floating on the sea consented to receive Leto, and Zeus in gratitude moored it by causing four pillars to rise from the bottom of the sea and secure the island. Delos' 370-foot Mount Cynthos (Cynthia is a name for Artemis/Diana in her aspect as goddess of the full moon) was thought to be the place the twins were delivered.

The view from Mount Cynthos is magnificent, one commanding the whole of the island and its surrounding isles of the Cyclades including Myconos, about two miles away. Today it is tranquil Delos that fills us with awe, imparting to the visitors a strange suspicion that their every move is being watched by unseen presences. People who have slept overnight on the island (the Tourist Pavilion has a few spartan rooms) speak of having curious dreams.

In ancient times the roles of the two islands were reversed, Delos being the center of activity and Myconos the place that provided subsidiary services. A primitive cave temple just beneath the summit of Mount Cynthos was once believed to be the actual birthplace of the twin deities, but later research disclosed the shrine to be of Hellenistic time and dedicated to the hero-god Hercules. A host of ruined temples and shrines dot the peak: antiquities honoring Syrian deities, the Egyptian gods Serapis and Thoth (Hermes), the aforementioned Hercules, the jealous Hera (Juno). A theater built for religious drama and remains of many other shrines and sanctuaries may also be found here. The visitor climbs by a pathway 3,000 years old.

The Ionian Greeks from colonies on the coast of Asia Minor considered Delos a religious cult center (tenth to eighth centuries B.C.) where Artemis (Diana) was honored. Homer's *Iliad* relates not only the Leto legend but also her oath upon being welcomed there to make Delos the center of her son Apollo's worship—that all the world should bring offerings to his altar. So the island bloomed with flowers and gold. It was to become, as the sacred island of Apollo, the greatest cult center in ancient Greece, and even today exerts a potent magnetism.

The excavations begun by French archeologists in 1873 continue to the present day. They have uncovered a wealth of shrines, sanctuaries, and the ruins of a brilliant cosmopolitan city, the most complete, save for Pompeii, of all antiquity.

Because the island is never more than just over one mile wide, the visitor is confronted by ancient relics at almost every step. (It is true that poisonous snakes have been reported, but they are few and far between.) Brightly colored flowers flourish between the ruined buildings, echoing the tinted mosaics astonishingly well preserved in the floors of some of the private homes. Artisans and craftsmen from all over the known world came here to pay tribute to Apollo, the most Greek of all the gods, who was worshiped as patron of poetry, music, and art. He was lord of truth and light, a healer who fathered Asclepius, and the god of reason whose motto "Nothing in Excess" adorned the oracle at Delphi. His festivals were an occasion for rejoicing at which the poets who were presumed to be pleasing to him were rewarded with a garland of laurel, a tree sacred to Apollo.

In *The White Goddess,* Robert Graves explains that poetry's connection with laurel is not merely that the tree is an evergreen and thus an emblem of immortality, but that it is also an intoxicant: the female celebrants of the Triple Moon Goddess at Tempe chewed laurel leaves to induce a poetic and erotic frenzy. "And when Apollo took over the Delphic oracle the Pythian priestess who continued in charge learned to chew laurel for oracular inspiration."

In spite—or maybe because—of Delos' religious importance it also achieved renown in pre-Christian times as headquarters first of an Ionian Council, then of a league of city-states and islands united against the Persians and other possible enemies. Each member contributed ships and a lump sum of money which, at first, was entrusted for safekeeping to the island's temple of Apollo.

By the middle of the sixth century B.C. Athens was beginning to take major interest in the tiny island and in the year 540 Peisistratos ordered Delos purified and all corpses removed from ground visible from the sanctuary.

Over the years more and more religious prohibitions were added so that eventually all ancient tombs were removed and births and deaths were completely forbidden on the island. Neighboring Rhenea became the burial ground.

Plutarch writes that the ruler Nicias organized ceremonies on Delos "both as acts of devotion to the god and demonstrations of lavish public generosity." On at least one occasion he filled the narrow channel between the two islands with a bridge of boats, which were "magnificently gilded and painted and hung with garlands and tapestries," leading a procession across the bridge at dawn.

The dictator Polycrates of Samos held sway over the Cyclades islands at one time and to show his devotion to Apollo also dedicated Rhenea to the god by fastening the two islands together with a big chain.

The regular pilgrimages to Delos, known as *theoria,* came to be important state occasions when the pilgrims were accompanied by choirs and special treasurers bearing offerings and a gold crown for the god. The island's own choir, the Delos Maidens, became famous for its skill at mimicking dialects and its intricate dance rhythms.

Whenever a pilgrimage was taking place, said Plato, Athens itself had to be kept pure, and tradition decreed that no executions could take place until the ship had reached Delos and returned again, "which sometimes takes a long time if the winds hold it back." Even today the voyage takes five or six hours by boat and the ancients, relying on oars and sails, must have found the journey very unpredictable. Socrates' execution was said to have been delayed in 399 B.C. because a pilgrimage to Delos was taking place.

As always, of course, there were skeptics, unbelievers, and malcontents. The poet Crito described Delians as "Apollo's parasites," and Pliny wrote that the island became known as a "fattener of hens and deviser of sauces." By the third century B.C. the island's major fame was as a grain market, and a century later it was serving as a center for the local slave trade, well known to Mediterranean pirates whose customers were the wealthy Roman estate holders.

From the time the daily boat docks on Delos to when it leaves again for Myconos, visitors have four hours to visit the ruins, inspect the museum, and pause for a coffee and a sandwich at the Tourist Pavilion. There are a handful of inexpensive, simple rooms available for those wishing to stay the night, but no distractions of any kind occur in the evening. Better bring a book if you plan to stay over.

Our tour begins at a flagstone-paved square near the landing stage. This was the ancient *agora* from which a paved road leads to Apollo's sanctuary. At one time this was lined with porticos and statues on pedestals; on the left can still be seen the remains of an immense building, fronted with sixteen Doric columns, that Philip of Macedonia (father of Alexander the Great) dedicated to the god Apollo in the fourth century B.C. It was commonplace for powerful rulers, and wealthy states, to dedicate statues and buildings to Apollo, and in the sanctuary itself is still the pedestal to a colossal statue of Apollo set up in the seventh century B.C. by worshipers from the wealthy island of Naxos. The statue itself, now in fragments, is in the Artemission sanctuary to the west.

We find the ruins of only two temples to Artemis on Delos. The power of Diana's cult was waning as Apollo's sun rose to light and personify the Greek's Golden Age of intellectual achievement. But the Greeks were wise enough to continue to pay heed to their *chthonian,* or underworld deities. In the museum is an excellent statue of Artemis, her knee resting lightly on the back of a now-headless stag.

Three temples to Apollo have been excavated. The area containing them is called the Sanctuary of Apollo and is entered by climbing four white marble steps (dating from the second century B.C.) into the Propylaea ("gateway"). The first and largest temple was dedicated to the god by the Delians themselves and was never completed. Work commenced in 476 B.C., but a takeover by the Athenians of the Delian treasury suspended operations. When in 314 B.C. Delos was once again independent, work resumed briefly. The Macedonians swept down in 322 B.C. and in 166 B.C. the Romans restored management of Delos to Athens. In 88 B.C. Menophanes, a general of Mithradates VI of Pontus, sacked the island.

The second temple of Apollo was dedicated by the Athenians, and is of Doric style built of white marble carried over from Athens in the early fourth century B.C. The third and oldest temple (late sixth century) is built of porous stones and contained a cult statue. On the west of the second temple is a small temple to Artemis.

On its east is the most curious monument of the island. Called the Sanctuary of the Bulls, it was considered to be the eighth wonder of the world. Here, it is said, the famous *geranos,* or "crane dance," took place, having been first performed by Theseus on his way back home after he killed the Minotaur. A maze-like dance, then perpetuated, took place around an altar built by Apollo from the left horns of goats killed by his twin, Artemis, on Mount Cynthos and is mentioned more than once in ancient writings. Writer Callimachus refers to young men with hands tied behind their backs buffeting the Horned Altar and circling the sacred olive tree from which they bit the bark. Such things, he notes, "did the nymphs of Delos devise for sport and laughter to young Apollo."

The crane, or stork, like the Egyptian ibis, was a symbol of Thoth, or Hermes, and sacred to many ancient peoples. The Thessalians considered the killing of one as heinous as murder. It was associated from the earliest times with child-bearing and therefore the stork dance could have had some connection with the birth of Apollo and Artemis.

The horned altar, around which the dance took place, stood at the north end of a narrow gangway surrounding the paved hall—the structure gets its name from two statues of foreparts of bulls—and it is surmised that this was also the site of the Oracle of Apollo (Pythian), which is known to have existed on Delos. Plato tells a curious story about how the Delians were once told by their oracle that to get rid of the plague they should double the size of their altar but retain the shape. The gods, Plato explained, wished to shame them for their neglect of geometry.

Probably the best-known statues on Delos are those of the magnificent lions—a gift to the temple from the wealthy island of Naxos— which sit on oblong pedestals guarding the now-dried-up Sacred Lake. From a spring atop Mount Cynthos a river called Inopos rose and used to feed this lake, which is mentioned in writings as early as the sixth century B.C. Both river and lake dried up in 1925. The lake is said by some sources to have been the true birthplace of the twin gods, and a palm tree which stood in its center was what Leto clung to in her hour of travail. Plutarch mentions that a massive bronze palm tree dominated the gateway to Apollo's sanctuary in 417 B.C.

Outside the sanctuary's precincts, to the south, are a set of small structures known as the tombs of the Hyperborean maidens, a mysterious "people from beyond the north wind" who, according to Herodotus, came to Delos to help Leto deliver her godly children and stayed on as priestesses. At one time worshipers would climb the steps to the graves and offer locks of hair and other sacrifices. There are scattered references to the Hyperboreans in Greek literature—the "winged temple of the Hyperboreans," mentioned by Herodotus is thought to refer to Callanish in Scotland—but the name itself means "those who carry over" in Macedonian and other northern languages.

Delos abounds with shrines to diverse deities. Dionysus is honored in the House of the Dolphins (one of his symbols) and in the House of Masks. Private homes contain marvelous mosaics, one depicting Dionysus seated on a panther's back flourishing a tamborine in one hand and the *thyrsos* (staff with pine cone on its end decked with spirals of ivy leaves) in the other. Lovely dolphins are pictured rising out of the sea. These are in the area known as the Theater Quarter and are of the Hellenistic and Roman periods.

The Romans, in an attempt to diminish the importance of Rhodes, declared Delos to be a free port around the second century B.C. and this attracted merchants, traders, and travelers from all parts of the world, notably Phoenicia, Palestine, Egypt, Syria, and Italy. Many brought their own cults with them and traces of these remain on Delos to this day. Among the most significant are the remains of the temple of Isis, the Egyptian goddess who, said Herodotus, the Greeks identified with Demeter, Isis having first shown the Egyptians the uses of wheat and barley. The columns of her temple still stand on the western slope of Mount Cynthos, together with a headless statue of the goddess whom Plutarch quoted: "I am all that hath been, is, or shall be; and no mortal has lifted my veil."

Isis is the embodiment of all goddesses: Demeter, Artemis, Cybele, Persephone, and her Mysteries became a vital worship during Hellenistic and Roman times, challenging the rise of Christianity. Although the Greeks did not usually extend a welcome to foreign gods, the worship of Isis was already incorporated by the fourth century B.C., when a temple in her honor was erected at the foot of the Acropolis. As the goddess of the earth and its fruits, the sea, the underworld, love, healing, the moon and magic, she had something to offer almost everybody and through her Mysteries the worshiper could receive the priceless gift of immortality. As the mother of Horus, the sun god, she also seemed to the Greeks to parallel Apollo himself, and so her shrine on Delos would be particularly appropriate.

According to the *Encyclopedia of Religion and Ethics,* there were two regular services daily in the temple of Isis, the first at sunrise when the priest "waked the deity" and performed certain sacred ceremonials, and the second in the afternoon. At this later service the priest held up a vase of consecrated water which the worshipers venerated as the first principle of all things.

The history of Delos after Christian times parallels that of most of the Mediterranean world. As Roman influence declined, the invaders and the pirates moved in, looting and devastating until it seemed there was little left of value to protect. By the eighth century A.D. the island was silent and deserted and, apart from archeologists and visitors, it has remained so to this day. To the seeker after magic, though, the ancient gods are never far away, and to climb Mount Cynthos in the light of the full moon is to transcend time and be in their presence.

6

Eleusis

CREDENTIALS OF ANCIENT
WISDOM

ELEUSIS (Elefsis in modern Greek) is a small, shabby town on the main highway between Athens and Corinth. Buses from the Peloponnese and northern Greece roar through without stopping, their passengers diverted but briefly by the flaming pillars of natural gas marking the big oil refineries that line the highway.

Few sightseers visit the town, and a passenger in an Athens-bound plane would find it hard to distinguish anything below through the pall of smoke and cement dust that hangs constantly over the little community.

And yet, at the time when the world looked to Greece for its culture and its inspiration, this now-undistinguished hamlet was a symbol of the highest civilization. A secret society was the key to it, a repository of knowledge to which everybody sought access but to which neither wealth nor influence alone could gain one admittance. Only the wise could be initiated into the Eleusinian mysteries, and wisdom then as now transcended both class and country.

"Happy he of the mortals who has seen this;" wrote Homer, "in the dark kingdom of shadows, the fate of the initiate and the uninitiate is

Illustration: Hades and Persephone banqueting. From a plate. Greece, fourth century B.C.

44

not the same. Those mysteries of which no tongue can speak—only blessed is he whose eyes have seen them; his lot after death is not as the lot of other men!"

Whatever the secrets imparted at Eleusis (and disclosure of them was punishable by death), they were obviously potent. More than twenty-six centuries after Homer, Jung was to conclude: "The ordinary man was somehow liberated from his personal impotence and temporarily endowed with an almost superhuman quality. The conviction could be sustained for a long time and it gave a certain style to life—and set a tone for a whole society."

The Eleusinian mysteries flourished from the sixth century B.C. through the destruction of the sanctuary by invaders in A.D. 395, until finally suppressed early in the seventh century of the Christian era.

Like most great cults it began with a legend long since obscured in the mists of prehistory. Eleusis was honored, for it was there that Demeter, goddess of agriculture, fertility, and marriage (and symbol of the Earth Mother), was reunited with her lost daughter Persephone (called Kore, "the maiden," by the Greeks).

The tale is told in one of the earliest of the Homeric hymns. Persephone, born to Demeter and the god Zeus out of wedlock, attracted the attention of the dark lord of the underworld who carried her off to his realm beneath the earth. No one would tell Demeter of her only daughter's fate and in grief she withheld her gifts of fruitfulness from the land. Leaving Olympus disguised as an old woman she wandered, fasting, for nine days and nights in search of her child.

Near Eleusis enlightenment came. She was told by Helios ("the sun") about Persephone's fate and as she rested, tired and unhappy, by a wayside well, the daughters of a noble family of Eleusis tried to cheer her and invited her to join their household. She assented and her grief was assuaged by their hospitality and the light-hearted jests of the family's servants.

Declining wine, she broke her fast by drinking instead the humble beverage of the harvester—barley water flavored with the herb pennyroyal. She became nurse to the family's baby son, anointing him with ambrosia and placing him in the heart of the fire each night to give him immortality. Discovering this, the child's mother was understandably horrified and upbraided the old woman who responded angrily by revealing her true identity. Demeter then commanded the family to build a great temple to regain her favor.

Meanwhile, because of Demeter's neglect, crops had been failing and famine approached. Zeus who had formerly refused help to Demeter in finding their daughter was obliged to appease her. This he did by persuading Hades (Pluto) to return his captured bride.

But while down under, Persephone carelessly ate the seeds of a pomegranate (traditionally the food of the dead) and was therefore obligated to return to the shadowy domain for one-third of every year. Demeter and Persephone, in joyful reunion, became reconciled to the inevitable annual parting and taught their mysteries to the townspeople of Eleusis. The myth is an allegory of spring and rebirth.

Like most myths, Greek or otherwise, the fable of Demeter and Persephone has been interpreted in different ways. Patrick Anderson in *The Smile of Apollo* quotes Robert Graves' supposition that Demeter originated in a fertility rite. Anderson adds that the relationship between the Earth Mother and her Virgin daughter was one of great interest to the Swiss psychiatrist Carl Jung. In *Greece and the Islands,* Eric Whelpton suggests that the mysteries were the origin of the cult of Satanism because the gods worshiped were those of the underworld. And a little more profoundly Philip Sherrard, in *The Pursuit of Greece,* explains that Demeter represents the intellect, Persephone the soul, and Pluto the material nature with which the former must fuse.

But whatever the true meaning, Demeter (*de*—an ancient term for the earth; and *meter*—"mother") was a more sympathetic figure than the other Olympians and truly captured the hearts of the people.

Pausanias wrote in the second century A.D. that there were just two things in all of Greece "which are in a class by themselves: the games at Olympia and the Mysteries of Eleusis."

And Cicero (106–43 B.C.) commented: "Nothing is higher than these Mysteries. They have sweetened our characters and softened our customs; they have made us pass from the condition of savages to true humanity. They have not only shown us the way to live joyfully, but they have taught us to die with better hope."

The act of dying, of course, is a subject that has at some time or other preoccupied every person in every society at every stage of history. The ancient Greeks believed that it was necessary to come to terms with death by abolishing one's fear of it. It was a worthy state to achieve and such persons who did so comprised an intellectual elite; self-confident, unencumbered by trivial concerns, and truly free. It was this happy condition that the rites of Eleusis were designed to induce.

Aristotle said that one did not go to Eleusis to learn, but to experience certain emotions and to be put into a receptive frame of mind. And Aristophanes added: "To us alone initiated men, who act aright by stranger and by friend, the sun shines out to light us after death."

At the beginning, the mysteries was merely a local cult, but with the rise to power of Athens fourteen miles to the south, it was extended to include that city. A preliminary initiation known as the Lesser Mysteries took place at Agrae in the spring. Sacred objects were brought there and annually carried back in solemn procession to Eleusis. The positions of power—*hierophant* ("high priest"), *daduchus* ("torch bearer"), and *keryx* ("herald")—were always held by citizens of Eleusis.

In the second century B.C., during the first Illyrian war, Romans were admitted for the first time. They sent a fleet of twenty vessels to suppress the pirates of Queen Teuta and the grateful Hellenes offered to initiate those who wished it. In essence this was a recognition of Rome as a civilized power; a testament to the veneration in which the Mysteries of Eleusis were held.

In time, Dionysus, the god of wine and abandon, would be joined with Demeter and his orgiastic rites of initiation would be celebrated in her temple. Orphic and Pythagorean themes would blend, too, yet the mysteries retained much of their original character—symbolic ritual which was said to open the inner eye of man and exalt his powers of perception in order to perceive a higher degree of reality.

Scholars write that very little is known about the mysteries. The initiates were sworn to secrecy, their lips being "locked" with a golden key, and they kept their vows. Socrates is said to have declined initiation because it would seal his tongue. Yet some facts can be reconstructed from poetry, fragments of hymns, bas-reliefs, vases (most of the early pottery patterns were believed to be copies of scenes from the temple), and other art created during the centuries when Eleusis was called "the sanctuary of the whole world."

The Greater Mysteries were celebrated from mid-September to late October before the sowing—roughly the time of Virgo, for whom the grain-carrying virgin Persephone is clearly the zodiacal personification —and were preceded by guides *(spondophori)* who went around Greece offering safe conduct to the rites no matter what war might be going on at the time.

All candidates were required to have a sponsor, and barbarians, murderers, and immoral women were specifically barred, although, says François Lenormant in *Chaldean Magic,* "the compliance of a *mystagogos* who was not over-scrupulous sufficed to introduce them in spite of rules to the contrary." He doesn't cite his authority for this.

Personal slaves were allowed to follow their masters into the interior of the temple and had a right to regard themselves as initiated. "My master taught me letters and had me initiated," reads one epitaph found at the site.

"Magicians," according to Apollonius of Tyana, were also excluded and so were many noble aspirants who had achieved fame in other fields as, for example, the fearsome Roman emperor Nero. A reason for exclusion appears in Plato's statement: "He who not being inspired and having no touch of madness in his soul comes to the door and thinks he will get into the temple by the help of art—he, I say, and his poetry are not admitted."

Candidates for initiation had to abstain from fish (an emblem of fecundity) and also avoid chicken, beans, pomegranates, and apples. The priests, in addition, had to be chaste and avoid contact with the dead and with reputedly "unclean" animals, such as weasels.

The *hierophant* was chosen by lot from among those eligible and wore a purple cloak signifying royalty. Although he could be a married man, he had to remain chaste during the festival, a condition reputedly made easier by his partaking of a mild dose of hemlock, which inhibited desire. He assumed a new name on taking office, writing his old one on a lead tablet which was then flung into the nearby bay. (There are no reports of the bay being dredged in search of these antiquities.)

Emulating the wanderings of Demeter, the preliminary ceremonies lasted nine days and began with the assemblage outside the goddess' house, the Eleusinium, in Athens. The names of the two or three thousand would-be initiates were then read out.

The next day, meeting at an agreed time, every initiate took charge of a young pig. "To the sea, ye mystics," came the cry, and all set off on the four-mile walk to the water, where they ceremonially washed both pig and themselves.

"It was not an orderly procession," relates one authority solemnly "and of that fact we have no doubt at all," says W. A. Wigram in his *Hellenic Travel.* The writer theorizes that the occasion was a moment of light relief, a letting-off of steam before the serious encounters to come.

At any rate, the pigs were then ritually sacrificed, their keepers sprinkled with blood, and a day of rest observed. Then, assembling once more at sunrise, the pilgrims began their fourteen-mile parade to Eleusis. This parade was called the Iacchus procession (Iacchus—a name of Dionysus), the reference being to a particular cry made by the participants during the march.

Although a man on foot could cover the distance from the *agora* ("marketplace") in Athens to Eleusis in four hours, many stops were made at temples along the Sacred Way, where singing, dancing, and dedication of boxes containing sacred objects *(hiera)* would take place. There was much bawdy humor, echoing the servants' jokes that had once lightened the mood of Demeter. At Rhetoi a stop would be made at the home of a family named Krokonidai, who held the ancient privilege of attaching saffron-colored bands to the right wrist and right ankle of all pilgrims. This was to protect against the evil eye.

Strange mocking games with the central character a woman, or a man disguised as a woman, would provide light relief for a while as the procession made a stop on the bridge across the Kephissos River.

Darkness had already fallen when the pilgrims arrived at Eleusis and here began the night of torches with dancing around the well to the music of a crude oboe, the *aulos,* and crashing cymbals. Then, again emulating Demeter's search, participants wandered randomly along the shore, their flickering torches brightening the night like a swarm of fireflies.

Finally the symbolic fast period was ended with, according to the Roman historian Clement of Alexandria, the drinking of *kykeon* (Demeter's barley water) and a meal of cakes of sesame and wheaten flour, pies and cakes with numerous protuberances on the surface, lumps of salt, pomegranates, young shoots of the fig tree, giant fennel, cheesecake, and quinces.

After this night of revelry the crowd waited with mounting tension outside the telesterion, the immense hall whose forty-two massive columns supported a wooden roof big enough to shelter several thousand people. At this point there was a division into two groups: the *mystai,* who were told to wait another year before they were eligible for initiation, and the *epoptai,* who were given a password and allowed to enter. Authorities are vague on how the selection was made, but the password was essential. On at least one occasion men who tried to bluff their way in without it were put to death.

Of the ceremonies that came next, the Christian Clement of Alexandria was not so well informed. He was inclined to think of the mysteries as "schools for atheism," but he, like other commentators clearly felt that the experience must have been a subjective one and possibly unique to each individual.

"Here ends all instruction," he wrote, "nature and things are seen."

The historian Diodorus Siculus wrote that magicians officiated in the temples and by their incantations "struck the vulgar with awe." And an anonymous author writing in the *Classical Journal* of December 1827 added: "Not only the vulgar but even the most enlightened philosophers either were or pretended to be struck in a similar manner by the arts of men who have never been equalled for impudent imposture." The priests, he said, were professed magicians who boasted of their influence over the spirit world.

It was noted by several nineteenth-century occult writers that those who presided over the mysteries attributed their ability to evoke spirits of the dead to "magical songs" and the sacrifice of cocks and hens.

Despite all the secrecy, suggests Wigram, the rites almost certainly paralleled those of similar societies in every part of the world. He says:

> What any tribe needs for its strength is a good supply of food and a good supply of men, and youth is taught in initiation that he or she has to do his or her part in providing both.
>
> Thus the mysteries are usually corn [grain] ceremonies and birth ceremonies. The corn mystery culminates here, as in many another land, in an initiation drama in which Kore (Persephone), the corn maiden, the divine being who dies and goes beneath the earth to come back again bearing life for man, becomes the symbol of man's resurrection and every candidate for entry to her mystery is taught, "This is what you will have to do to serve the tribe and at last you will die, and remember this, that death is not the end."

The *Encyclopaedia Britannica* points out that "corn" can be a generic term meaning almost any cereal crop but that Demeter (whose Latin name is Ceres—"cereal") is usually pictured as carrying a sheaf of wheat.

It has been suggested that the Eleusinian ceremony was originally transplanted from Egypt; there is a parallel in the Egyptian Book of the Dead where man, at the moment of death, is a grain of corn which falls into the earth in order to draw from its bosom a new life.

Plutarch wrote: "When a man dies he is like those who are initiated into the Mysteries. Our whole life is a journey by tortuous ways without outlet. At the moment of quitting it come terrors, shuddering fear, amazement. Then a light moves to meet you, pure meadows receive you, songs and dances and holy apparitions."

The ancient writer Synesius quoted Aristotle who, he said, "is of the opinion that [inside the telesterion] the initiated learned nothing precisely but that they received impressions, that they were put into a certain frame of mind for which they had been prepared."

The inner rites took three forms: the things spoken—*legomena;* the things performed—*dromena;* and the things revealed—*deiknymena.* From the language of the ancient Greeks we know they thought of themselves as stationary—as if time moved toward them, overtook them, and moved on to become the past. This illuminates the description of a preliminary ritual when the initiate is seated on a stool, head veiled and one foot resting on a ram's fleece while the ceremonies take place before him.

Several Christian writers mention a "sacred marriage" and imply erotic excesses, but it is more likely a part of the *legomena* when rain, the "love union" between heaven and earth, is called the sacred marriage of the gods. Water is symbolically sprinkled as the words "Let it rain" are spoken to the heavens, and "Be fruitful" are spoken down to the earth.

Evidence indicates the *dromena* was a pantomime recalling the rape of Persephone, the wandering search of Demeter, and the final joyous reunion.

The possibility that the candidates were drugged in some manner cannot be totally discounted. Poppy capsules (source of opium) are represented on several Eleusinian monuments. Fasting, too, can promote visionary states.

At one point the blindfolded candidates were supposedly conducted on a kind of obstacle course around the telesterion accompanied by "sudden graspings by unseen hands," thunderpeals in the ear, noises, and lights. Female candidates occasionally fainted. When the blindfolds were removed they were told: "You have seen what I passed through and yet I rose again and so will you. Here is the initiate's secret: that death is a passage and no more."

Eventually the sacred boxes were opened and the contents revealed by the hierophant. It is speculated that the supreme revelation was the showing of a sheaf of grain. Hippolytus speaks of "a green ear of corn reaped in silence" and the analogy between the life of the plant and the life of mankind could have provided the vision: the *epopteia.*

This is speculation, however, because the vows of secrecy concerning the actual ceremonies were well kept, understandably, as the death penalty and confiscation of property was ordained for those who divulged or profaned the sacred rites. Pupils of a teacher named Sopatros were once informed that an initiate who was asked by somebody who had dreamed of the mysteries if the dream was true merely nodded his head—and was accused of impiety.

Aeschylus, accused of giving away the secrets in his writings, "escaped popular resentment" only by proving that he hadn't himself been initiated. Alcibiades and Andocides parodied the ceremony while drunk and were condemned to death for their irreverence.

One story about Eleusis concerns the famous courtesan named Phryne, who was so wealthy that she once offered to rebuild the walls of Thebes if they could be inscribed "Destroyed by Alexander, Restored by Phryne the Courtesan." This same Phryne was once accused of profaning the Eleusinian mysteries because, carried away with ecstasy at a festival, she removed her clothes, let down her hair, and stepped into the sea. When it seemed at the trial as though she was doomed, the orator Hypereides revealed her breasts to the judges who were so moved they acquitted her. The sculptor Praxiteles, too, was obviously impressed by Phryne, as he placed his bust of her beside his statue of Aphrodite in a temple at Thespiae, Phryne's birthplace.

Under the law of Solon, the Athenian *Bule* assembled every year on the day after the Eleusinian mysteries ended to try any cases of profanation, although it is recorded that particularly flagrant offenders were arrested, tried, and executed without appeal even while the ceremonies continued.

For most of the dozen centuries Eleusis held sway it remained immune to outside strife. The Persians burned down one temple, which was then replaced by an even grander one of white marble, built under the auspices of the renowned Pericles, whose architect Ictinus had already achieved fame with the Parthenon in Athens.

The new temple's "beauty and prodigious magnitude" were said to have excited a degree of astonishment only equaled by the awe that its sanctity created. It was 230 feet long by 180 feet wide.

But this, too, was eventually razed at the close of the fourth century by Alaric the Goth who, with 200,000 men laid waste not only to Eleusis but to the whole surrounding province of Attica.

After the seventh century A.D., by which time the cult of Eleusis had considerably declined, the ruins lay untended and forgotten for centuries.

In 1675 the English traveler Sir George Wheler paid a visit to the deserted place, noting: "One of the first things we came into was the stately temple of Ceres, now laid prostrate on the ground, not having one stone upon another, for it lyeth all in a confused heap together."

Half a century later (in 1716) Richard Chandler observed "the bust of a colossal statue of excellent workmanship maimed and the face disfigured. . . . A tradition prevails that if the broken statue be removed the fertility of the land will cease."

This tradition, which first surfaced in Cicero, was still being preserved at the end of the nineteenth century by local peasants who could be found dancing around the statue at the time of the harvest moon.

In 1801, however, the deplorable theft of the statue took place, over local objections, by two British academics who bribed the local governor (then a Turk), hired a ship, and hauled the immense statuary to the nearby dock for eventual removal to the Fitzwilliam Museum at Cambridge, where it still remains.

The audacity of this theft was compounded by the robbers' arrogance, expressed in a twenty-five-page book published in Cambridge at that time and in which they boasted about their coup "which required equal promptness and secrecy amidst the opposition to be expected from a herd of idle and mercenary Greeks."

It seems hard to believe that men of learning could so willfully deny such ancient traditions. It is undeniable that the area has suffered, the land's original fertility exorcised and made arid and dusty by the heat, smoke, and waste from surrounding oil refineries and industry. Doubtless the region is prosperous from the processing of oil, aluminum, and soap, and from the extensive shipyards, but the ecological cost has been high. For miles around, the trees, turning wistfully toward the sun, appear to be choking from a pollution unknown in previous centuries. During the past few years residents have been protesting plans for the nearby Petrola refinery to expand its site.

Being so close to industry, Eleusis, which is only a half-hour bus ride from Athens (bus #68 from Eleftherias Square), is not popular with tourists. This is a pity because it is a pleasant and easy excursion. Adjoining the site itself (admission free on Sundays and Thursdays) is a charming open-air café called the Cava Doro, where lunch is inexpensive and quite good.

The ruins possess much of their original mystical charm—all the more so, ironically, because of its relative lack of attention. It possesses an unspoiled atmosphere that the more visited sites totally lack. Immense broken pillars lie everywhere, many with their ancient lettering and ideograms still clearly visible. Patches of pale blue and white tile in intricate patterns define what was once a floor.

Great stone stairways lead up to the gentle, tree-covered hill which sits behind the remains of the vast telesterion, its back to the rock and its façade toward the east-southeast of the early morning sun. Strabo says it was capable of holding 2,000 initiates. Underground chambers and a still-unmarred circular well are almost overgrown with waist-high grass. The panorama from the ancient tower atop the hill is magnificent, notwithstanding the rusty hulks that anchor offshore.

A tiny museum (open 10 A.M. to 1 P.M. and 3 P.M. to 7 P.M.) displays a big, white plaster reproduction of the immense site in its most glorious days. Its buildings, in reconstruction, appear to be almost walled in, indifferent to the light—an uncharacteristic style for the sun-loving Greeks of today. The face of Demeter, in almost all of the museum's statues, is unclear or chipped away, but the busts of Hadrian, the marble pigs, and the vases from the seventh century B.C. help to depict an era when this now-deserted hill was the spiritual center of the universe.

Dr. Elisabeth Kübler-Ross, one of America's leading authorities on death and dying, is convinced of life after death. Her observation of over a thousand terminal patients has produced a pattern of experience at the moment of death that remarkably corresponds with the Greek philosopher Themistius' description of the secret of Eleusis.

> The soul at the point of death suffers the same feelings as those who are being initiated into the great Mysteries. First there are wanderings and weary devious hurryings to and fro, journeyings full of fears and uncompleted. Then before the end every sort of terror, shudderings and tremblings, sweat and horror. Then after that a marvellous sight meets you and pure regions and meadows receive you and there are voices and dancing and wonderful and holy sounds and sacred lights. And he that is completed and initiated wanders free and unrestrained and is crowned and joins in the worship and is among pure and holy men.

The well where it is said Demeter met the daughters of Keleos is believed to be in existence still, on the road to Megara, but if true, it is hard to locate and beyond the talents of the authors. The ancient Sacred Way to Athens still goes through Daphni but is now obliterated by the National Road, charged perhaps by its ancient energy. It is lined at its southern end by small factories, used-car lots, and shabby tavernas.

But it does, for the most part, follow the old route along which so many pilgrims once trod in ancient times and somewhere, as it crosses the River Kephissos, may be traces of the bridge built by Hadrian to mark the point where Persephone was reputedly carried off into the infernal regions.

In *The Pursuit of Greece,* Philip Sherrard speculates on how the pattern of such places as Eleusis is constantly repeated. First, he says, is the genuine inspiration, the revelation of a mystery, the great dynamic force, the spiritual teaching.

Then gradually the inner fire goes, the initiates become a caste holding behind closed doors the letter of the law, imposing superstition, stamping out any new revelation. . . . The creative life is formalized, given a hierarchy, a set of dogmas, an authority. Ossification.

New people, barbarians probably, but full of energy, come destroy the suffocating structure and set the blood flowing again.

What secrets still lie far beneath the ruins of Eleusis, as old as time, older even than the rocks themselves? One day, in some distant future when our own civilization will be but an archeologist's plaything, might a force not again emerge to still the death fears of a race not yet conceived?

7

Epidaurus

THE SERPENTINE SLEEP HEALERS

ATHENS itself offers all the predictably famous sites, but it's worth a trip across the gulf from Piraeus to ancient Epidaurus, which comes alive for a few weeks in midsummer when the centuries-old amphitheater becomes the site of an annual festival of Greek drama.

In pre-Christian times Epidaurus was one of the most celebrated places for followers of the god Asclepius, who it was believed visited invalids as they lay asleep on beds of animal skins and brought them dreams which would reveal a cure for their malady. In *Greek Oracles,* Robert Flaceliere says that the preliminary rites included drinking from a salt spring, various forms of abstinence and fasting, and religious ceremonies calculated to put people in a mood of expectation. Aristotle's observations in *On Divination Through Dreams* agree with the findings of modern psychologists, Flaceliere says, especially in regard to the significance of dreams, to which today's physicians attach great importance.

Asclepius was said to be one of Apollo's bastard sons, his mother being Coronis, a king's daughter, who abandoned him on Mount Thittion. (Edith Hamilton says Apollo put Coronis to death for her cruel act and saved the child.) Suckled by a goat and brought up by a goatherd,

Illustration: Seal of the Seven Serpents. From an amulet. Greece, first century A.D.

Asclepius was eventually tutored by the wise centaur Chiron, who lived on Mount Pelion and whose pupils included Achilles, Jason, and Odysseus. Chiron taught medicine to Asclepius, also the usefulness of the snake, which was used to find the healing herbs and later became the symbol of the god of medicine.

It was this snake that patients hoped would visit them when they slept in the precincts of Asclepius, and to aid their cures the priests of the temple would keep real (nonpoisonous) yellow snakes around. Many of the cures, especially for psychic ailments, were brought about by such self-suggestion at first; it was only later that baths, dieting, herbs, and stones were added to the therapeutic treatments.

Patients flocked to Epidaurus from all over to try the cures, and the 15,000-seat stadium was originally created to provide diversion for all these sick visitors and their friends and relatives.

Little remains of the temple today beyond the ruins of a two-storied temple in which the patients slept and to which they presented votive gifts representing the limb or organ that had been cured. Such tokens, made out of tin, are still presented by the faithful to Greek churches today, and similar examples have been found at other ancient Asclepieons, notably in England and Italy.

Although the Greek National Tourist Board runs a boat between Piraeus and Epidaurus in midsummer, the site is virtually deserted for the rest of the year, and access must usually be made via a couple of buses with a change at the Peloponnese town of Napflion. There is a good hotel, the Xenia, at Epidaurus.

The place where Asclepius was first worshiped was Trikkala in Thessaly—Homer in his *Iliad* refers to him as a wonderful doctor of Thessaly —and it was this part of northern Greece that was associated in ancient times with magical deeds of another kind. Thessalian witches had a reputation for the cures they could effect with herbs and there are innumerable references to their deeds in the writings of early Roman historians.

Today Thessaly is that portion of Greece least visited by tourists. This area of the mainland is very barren, and compared with the islands, least conducive to vacationing. In ancient times it was "notorious for witchcraft" and "universally known for magic incantations," as the second-century Roman author Apuleius puts it.

"What witch, what magician will be able to free you from Thessalian sorceries?" asked the Roman poet Horace in the first century B.C. Thessalian witches were believed to have powers over the moon, according to an old Greek papyrus dealing with magic: "If I command the moon, it will come down; and if I wish to withhold the day, night will linger over my head; and again, if I wish to embark on the sea, I need no ship; and if I wish to fly through the air, I am free from my weight."

Pythagoras is said to have learned from Thessalian sorcerers how to hold a polished silver disc up to the moon to divine its message, and a character in one of Aristophanes' comedies (c. 400 B.C.) comments: "Tell me, if I purchased a Thessalian witch, I could make the moon descend during the night and shut it, like a mirror, into a round box and keep it there carefully."

Sophocles, the Greek dramatist, and the comic writer Menander both refer to Thessalian magicians, while the Roman poets Virgil, Ovid, and Lucan describe Thessaly as the home of magic. The latter two, writing at the beginning of the Christian era, discuss the mephitic herbs gathered by witches for their philters in the fastnesses of Thessaly, the breeding ground of ancient Greek witchcraft. Here, too, were collected the mystic willow wands for divination.

Robert Graves points out that the willow, much worshiped by witches, was sacred in Greece to the goddesses Hecate, Circe, and Persephone—"all death aspects of the Triple Moon Goddess." As Culpeper succinctly says of the willow in his *Complete Herbal* (1653): "The Moon owns it." The legendary Orpheus has been depicted holding a willow branch on his sojourn through the underworld.

Thrace, that semimythical region in northern Greece we now associate with Thessaly, is said to have been the birthplace of Orpheus, an elusive, ambiguous figure who may or may not have been a god. To Orpheus is attributed the origin of the Grecian mythological system, permeated, like the Egyptian mysteries which instructed him, with sorcery, astrology, magic, and medicine.

It is in the Orphic poetry we encounter the principles of magnetism, that magical force embodying the powers to attract or repel. The eclipses of the sun and moon, the phenomenon of comets, the tempest of wind, thunder, earthquakes, the rainbow, all are its progeny. It is, says Joseph Ennemoser in *The History of Magic,* the Law of Nature, "the living power which drawing and repelling, creates and keeps together the parts of the world through which the stars are propelled and whirled around in their courses; while the opposite poles seek each other."

The magnet is the symbol of this power; as it creates and turns, it produces life. "Production is the highest assertion of the power of magnetism," Ennemoser asserts, "and this power is symbolized by Hercules."

Pliny derives the word *magnet* from the name of a shepherd, Magnes, who was tending his sheep on Mount Ida when he discovered a lodestone fastened to his iron-bound staff. Others have called it Heraclean because of its frequency near the ancient city of Hercules. Its attributes as a compass were discovered early because there is a first-century reference to its use in France.

Occultists have long associated the magnet with the magic (magnetic) wand of Hermes (Mercury): a magic staff with which the god Hermes, in Homer's words, "the eyelids of mortals closes at will, and the sleeper at will reawakens." Some say Asclepius was the son of Hermes and he, too, had a magic rod, the famous wand "through the possession of which a man becomes the master of healing."

Homer, Pythagoras, Epicurus, Aristotle—all were familiar with the magnet, and the Renaissance magus Agrippa also alluded to it when he commented: "In all things there is a secret power concealed and thence comes the miraculous powers of magic." The magnet had power to attract iron, he marveled, yet a diamond could deprive it of its strength. (Agrippa also had a word of counsel for the aspiring sorcerer. "The magician who will acquire supernatural powers," he warned, "must possess faith, love and hope.")

Claudian's *Riddles of the Magnet* refers to "the dark, invisible stone which in storm and lightning its power seems to rule" and talks about the magnetic image of Venus held suspended in the air at one of the temples, an iron one of Mars at another. "The war-like Mars loves the magnet," is, in the Orphic poetry, our first encounter with the word.

Plutarch speculates about something that sounds very like electricity. In his *History of Magic*, Joseph Ennemoser describes the two casks in a Samothracean sanctuary through which the priests mysteriously contrived to produce a spark from a brass ball on an altar.

Ennemoser says that the priests traditionally guarded their knowledge about magnetism from the uninitiated, but that less important secrets, such as amber's magnetic properties, were commonly known. There are frequent references in ancient Egyptian writings, he explains, to temple images suspended by what must clearly be magnetic force, and all kinds of magical tricks were demonstrated, such as carrying about an iron ball from which smaller ones were suspended. To the uninitiated this would surely seem like magic.

Magnetism is also a physical quality, a vibration that directs the senses of all living things, impelling them irresistibly this way or that. Its force constitutes an art of healing, not through a substance but by a power, a power borrowed "from the stars and nowhere else," says Paracelsus, the sixteenth-century alchemist.

Paracelsus attributed many of his healing powers to magnetism, offering precise instructions on laying the magnet in the center from which the sickness proceeds. "It is not a matter of indifference to which of these poles a man applies." People had something magnetic in them, he maintained, without which they could not exist and through which they were linked to the sun and the stars.

8

Delphi

THE AMBIGUOUS ORACLE

KINGS AND EMPERORS have always gone to war, and weak and powerful alike they have always sought to know in advance the outcome of their adventures. At one time, centuries before the emergence of Rand Institutes and batteries of computers that attempted to predict such things, they consulted oracles.

The Roman historian Pausanias tells us of the Messenian king Aristodemus who asked for ways in which he could conquer the Spartans. The oracle suggested to the king that he sacrifice to the gods a virgin of his own royal race. This Aristodemus did, delivering up his own daughter, that he might be compensated with victory. Unfortunately, he lost the war and we will never know whether or not his daughter was a virgin. But was the oracle to blame?

Centuries before the birth of Christ, pilgrims from all over the world were journeying to a sacred shrine on the slopes of Mount Parnassus to ask questions of the Delphic oracle. And for a price, all got an answer of sorts, although as we have seen, a person's interpretation of what the answer meant often left him with a worse dilemma than before.

Illustration:King Aegeus of Athens consulting the Pythia. From a vase painting. Greece, fourth century, A.D.

For six centuries or more, until the oracle's shrine was destroyed by the Christian emperor Arcadius in A.D. 398, Delphi shaped the history of the world.

The ruins of the temple lay untouched for more than twelve hundred years after its abandonment, but in 1671 Delphi was "rediscovered." In the last century, serious archeological excavations reached a peak, and today Delphi is once again, for different reasons, a shrine for pilgrims from many countries who, expecting less than their ancient counterparts, are nevertheless just as impressed and awestruck by the grandeur of the terrain and the age-old associations. Do some still ask—and receive answers to—their questions? We can only guess.

According to legend, Delphi's origins were associated with the god Apollo who came down from the north and killed the Python. (This could be another ancient allegory for the victory by the sun over the forces of darkness.) Certainly Delphi's most important festivals came to be those held in May and which celebrated the genial influence of the sun in restoring warmth and life to the earth and sea, especially to the dolphins, which were highly esteemed. Having killed the monster which guarded the ancient site of Mother Earth and having learned the secret of prophecy from Pan, Apollo proceeded to install his own oracle, Pythia, and by the eighth century B.C. was referred to by Homer as "lord of Pytho."

"In Apollo," writes Patrick Anderson in *The Smile of Apollo,* "sublimest clarity and the darkness of death face one another, perfectly poised and equal, on a border line."

The original site at Delphi was said to have been selected by two eagles which met there after being released by Apollo's father, Zeus, and charged with finding the center of the world. The cone-shaped stone known as the Omphalos, which stood in front of the temple and marked the earth's navel, is now in the Delphi museum.

Plutarch tells us that a shepherd named Kouretas first discovered the strange powers of the sanctuary when he noticed his goats leaping around irrationally after being exposed to fumes from the chasm. There are curious connections between Delphi which Apollo founded, Delos where he was born, and Crete where in the Minoan capital of Knossos inhabitants once worshiped a dolphin Apollo. The Cretan priesthood was called the Kouretes and the ancient Cretan town of Elyros, like Delphi, used coins bearing the image of a goat. At Delos, as we have mentioned, an ancient altar was constructed from the horns of goats.

After the shepherd Kouretas' discovery of the shrine, peasants flocked to Delphi to sample the fumes and the inevitable trance and gift of prophecy which followed. Many visitors were so carried away with ecstasy that they threw themselves into the fissure, and finally a woman was appointed to sit on the shrine (upon a bronze tripod) and do all the prophesying.

Frederick Poulsen in *Delphi* speculates:

> The Delphian prophets had to know their way well in the politics of that age and have at their disposal a great personal acquaintance with the knowledge about even the districts which lay outside the horizon of the Greeks as a whole . . . they had to actively follow all the important events that took place even in far-off barbarian countries. That in spite of all precautions the oracle was not always lucky in its predictions is well known, but it was strange if the priests did not find a way out of their difficulty afterwards, assisted by the obscurity of the answers themselves.

The various oracles, understandably, offered different degrees of reliability. The Athenian Nicias, for example, told by an Egyptian oracle that he could subdue Syracuse, soon found his expedition in retreat. To make matters worse, an eclipse of the moon occurring about that time was interpreted by his soothsayer as being a sign he should wait three times nine days—a disastrous period in which all Nicias' fleet was wiped out. The popular verdict back in Athens was that Nicias' troubles stemmed from his employment of an ignorant soothsayer. A good one would have known that "when the moon hides her face it is propitious for an army to retreat."

The Delphic oracle's predictions, invariably wise, were also capable of easy misinterpretation. Seeking advice about his childless state, for example, the Athens' king Aegeus was told: "Loose not the jutting neck of the wineskin, great chief of the people, till you have come again to the city of Athens," but instead of accepting this as a prohibition against sex until he got home, he was persuaded by the king of Troezen to mate with his daughter. But all was well: there was an offspring from this union, the famous Theseus.

On another occasion, Phalanthos of Sparta was told while campaigning that as soon as he felt rain fall from a clear sky he should seize the town. Although he later invaded Italy, he had failed to capture any towns until one night, discouraged, he laid his head in his wife's lap. Sympathetic to his troubles her tears fell on him, whereupon enlightenment dawned: her name Aithra meant "clear sky." The next day he attacked and captured Tarentum.

There are innumerable similar examples: Epaminondas, told to fear death from the sea, died in a wood at Mantineia which happened to be called "the sea wood"; Nero, warned to be careful of the seventy-third year, was vanquished by the seventy-three-year-old Galba; and, best known of all, the advice to Croesus that if he went to war with Persia he would destroy a great empire (which turned out to be his own).

On other occasions the message could hardly have been clearer: Chaeremon was informed that his friend Socrates was "the wisest man in the world"; the ambitious and jealous Cleisthenes of Sicyon was told "Adrastus is king of Sicyon and you are merely a stone-throwing bully"; Cicero, seeking fame, was advised to mark his own nature "not the opinions of the multitude."

Sometimes the medium was the message. Plutarch reveals in his *Life of Alexander* that the great general arrived on an unpropitious day to seek the oracle's advice about his expedition against the Persians. The Pythia refused to come to the temple at this unlucky time and impulsively Alexander tried to drag her there by force. "You are invincible, my son," the Pythia told him, and Alexander chose to interpret her rebuke as his fortune.

It would be a mistake to think of the oracle as being merely manipulative, except in the most socially-conscious way. The equality of rich and poor before the gods and the concept of forgiveness for a crime were but two of the principles that successive generations of soothsayers managed to establish. Within the temple were inscribed texts composed by the Seven Sages, ancient Greek philosophers, and among the texts were spiritual admonitions, including the famous "Know Thyself."

Even though he tended to be suspicious of oracles, Plato, whose teacher Socrates believed him to be one of the illuminati (because Socrates had dreamed of a white swan the night before they met), was a devotee of Delphi. Plato felt that a kind of intuitive knowledge bubbled to the surface "when reason and commonsense are in eclipse—the state induced by the mystery cults, poetic inspiration, exaltation of being in love, and prophetic madness." Such a state might be regarded as a prerequisite for the prophet or practitioner of magic today.

At first the oracle spoke only on the seventh day of the month of Bysios (corresponding to today's mid-February to mid-March), which was Apollo's birthday, but the crush of visitors sailing through the Gulf of Corinth, landing at Kirra (near today's port of Itea), and walking up the hillside became so great that monthly consultations were arranged. In the three winter months when Apollo was away, his brother god Dionysus, who was regarded as a son of Zeus, acted as caretaker.

Plutarch wrote that the worship of Dionysus among country folk was an occasion for rural merrymaking. The Dionysian cult probably loosened things up a great deal because its adherents believed that getting drunk was a holy thing to do—an event symbolical of liberating the soul from the body and allowing the god to enter and take possession of the worshiper. At first Dionysian or Bacchic rites were welcomed, but as they spread through Greece they quickly got out of hand with bands of drink-crazed worshipers carrying out rape and terror. Almost disintegrating "the most perfect civilization in the world's history," says Charles Seltman in *Wine and the Ancient World,* the rites struck at quiet, sophisticated seventh-century Greece with something terrible and terrifying. "Orgy and mysticism—the words are interchangeable—came near to disrupting growing Hellenic balance."

The worship of Dionysus later spread to Rome where, according to Theodor Mommsem in a nineteenth-century history of that pagan center, "spreading like a cancer it propagated itself over all Italy, everywhere corrupting families and giving rise to heinous crimes: unparalleled inchastity, falsifying testaments and murdering by poison. More than 7,000 were eventually sentenced to punishment, most of them put to death."

There is no suggestion that the Pythia, either under the direction of Apollo or Dionysus, partook of any intoxicating beverages (although references were occasionally made to those ever-present fumes). In fact several chroniclers mention rather specifically the pure water of the Castalia Spring at the foot of Mount Parnassus. Pythia, before ascending the tripod, is said to have washed her whole body in the Castalia Fountain and drunk large drafts of the water that inspired her to prophesy.

Extra consultations, which didn't need to involve one of the fulltime Pythias directly, could be made by casting lots for yes-or-no answers. Indeed the holiness of Delphi and the reputation it had acquired soon developed a minor local industry in consultation and prophecy and many people were able to find answers and obtain advice from neophyte priests around the town without waiting for an appointment with the oracle.

Cutting off the hair and dedicating it to some river god was often a preliminary to a pilgrimage to Delphi, according to Aeschylus. Then, petitioners to the Pythia, after bathing in the waters of the Castalia Spring ("very good and cool; fit to quench the thirst of those hot-headed poets who in their Bacchanals spare neither God nor man," wrote Sir George Wheler in 1682), waited until a goat had been sacrificed and its entrails examined. If the results were favorable, each paid his fee—four obols (two-thirds of a drachma) for an individual or seven drachmas and two obols for a city—and entered the presence. Favored visitors obtained priority tickets called *promonteia,* others drew lots for who got to ask questions first. Women were obliged to ask questions through a male intermediary.

Preceding the ceremony a goat was prepared for sacrifice by sprinkling it with cold water and no subsequent oracle was pronounced, Plutarch informs us, "unless the whole body of the victim trembles and shudders. That she should twist her head about as at other sacrifices will not suffice; she must tremble all over and her limbs must twitch, otherwise they will say the oracle is not functioning and they will not bring the Pythia to the temple."

Originally consultations were arranged after studying the flight of birds and Plutarch also has some comments on this practice which he describes as the most ancient and most important method of predicting the future. "Thanks to their speed and intelligence, and to the precision of their movements with which they respond to everything impinging upon the senses, birds are the veritable instruments of divining power. It is the gods who determine the variety of their movements and elicit from them their cries and twitterings. Sometimes they hold them suspended in the air, sometimes they hurriedly despatch them to hinder the acts or purposes of men or to assist in their fulfillment. That is why Euripides speaks of them as 'messengers of the gods.' "

In ancient times birds were considered to be the creatures closest to Zeus and Apollo, some being naturally propitious, others of ill omen. The crow, raven, vulture, and eagle were most esteemed for prophetic significance, but the owl, though claimed by Athenians as their special token, was not considered a good omen by others. The Greeks, more subtle than the Romans, according to Robert Flaceliere, "even distinguished between the various degrees of energy and poise (hedra) a bird displayed, although it is difficult to understand precisely how they interpreted this."

But sacrifice being the supreme religious act, the killing of goats, lambs, and calves followed by the reading of their entrails, soon predominated, although in the early days the smoke of incense and the crackling of laurel wood and barley in the flames was closely watched by the priests.

At first the Delphic Pythia was always a young virgin, but after a man named Echecrates from Thessaly caused a worldwide scandal by abducting and raping one of them it became customary for a woman of fifty years or over to be appointed Pythia.

However simple the question, the Pythia's answer was likely to be obtuse: it was not for nothing that Apollo was sometimes nicknamed Loxias, "the ambiguous one."

Plutarch explains this ambiguity somewhat:

> It was not just a question of some individual person consulting the oracle about the purchase of a slave or some private matter but of very powerful cities, kings and tyrants with mighty ambitions seeking the god's advice on important issues. To anger or annoy such men by harsh truths that conflicted with their desires would have had its disadvantages . . .
>
> For this reason Apollo, though not prepared to conceal the truth, manifests it in roundabout ways: by clothing it in poetic form he rids it of what is harsh and offensive as one does with a brilliant light by reflecting it and thus splitting it into several rays.

One of the permanently unresolved questions about the Delphic oracle, of course, is just how credible it was. Herodotus reports that to his knowledge on at least one occasion the Pythia took a bribe, and its equivocations were legendary. But, as Peter Hoyle has suggested, the Apolline priests often had to be mediators who could "appeal to reason above the passions of angry men," and another reason for what seems like extraordinary tact, was that before major battles the oracle's indispensability was such that it was frequently consulted by representatives of both sides. The famous reply to King Croesus: "When a mule shall be king of the Medes, then O Lydian flee and have no shame for your cowardice" brought the oracle into ill repute when it transpired that his victorious enemy Cyrus was, like a mule, of mixed parentage. The priests, says Frederick Poulsen, "had to exert all their sharp wits to explain away this event."

It was particularly unfortunate that Croesus was the legatee of this shrewdly-phrased prediction because it was he who had lavished great wealth on Delphi. Originally a skeptic, he had some years before sent messengers to the oracles at Delphi, Dodona, Abae in Phokis, Amphiaros, and Trophonios, and to Brandidae in Milesia and Ammon in Libya, to ask the same question—what would he be doing in his capital at Sardis one hundred days hence?

Right on the mark was Delphi's reply which read: "I count the grains of sand on the beach and measure the sea; I understand the speech of the dumb and hear the voiceless. The smell has come to my sense of a hard-shelled tortoise, boiling and bubbling with lambs flesh in a bronze pot. The cauldron underneath is of bronze, and of bronze the lid."

Croesus, impressed at this accurate prediction, sent magnificent gifts to Delphi, including a lion made from a quarter of a ton of pure gold. The relationship prospered until his fatal war against the Persians.

In ancient times Croesus' gift, though generous, was not unusual, the shrine being the recipient of treasure from many lands. Long before Delphi was destroyed by fire in 548 B.C. and rebuilt at great expense, the tiny island of Siphnos was rendering as tribute one-tenth of the annual produce of its goldmines. And often it seemed to bear a charmed life. When Xerxes sent a plundering army in 480 B.C. the Delphians, consulting their own oracle, were advised to leave the treasures unguarded, for Apollo "could, with help, protect his own." And so, leaving some of their sacred armor on the ground, the Delphians watched the enemy approach—and retreat, as rocky crags suddenly split off towering Mount Parnassus and rolled down on the attackers.

Again, in 279 B.C. when Brennus, king of the Celtic Gauls, attacked Delphi we are informed that fire came down from the heavens, thunder rolled, and the rocks were rent causing the immediate flight of the invaders.

But in the fourth century B.C. the Roman emperors Nero, Sulla, and Philomelus all plundered Delphi and escaped retribution. Nero stole 500 bronze statues and abolished the oracle after it had rebuked him for the murder of his mother. It was reopened by Hadrian.

By the time that Flavius Claudius Julianus, later to be Emperor Julian, was born at Constantinople in A.D. 331, the old gods were in disrepute and Julian's uncle, Constantine, had embraced Christianity as the semi-official religion of the influential Roman state. Julian, however, was a throwback, a believer in miracles and magicians who restored the ancient shrines and who, according to some hostile sources, imposed taxes on all his citizens who declined to make sacrifices to the pagan gods. His own beliefs were quite clear, as can be seen from a letter he wrote to the Christian bishop Cyril of Alexandria, a letter suppressed for centuries and brought to attention only in 1809 when it was translated and privately reprinted.

"Are you insensible of the splendor that follows the sun?" he asked. "Are you alone ignorant that summer and winter are produced by him? Do you not, also, perceive the great advantages that accrue to your city from the moon, from him and by him, the fabricator of all things? Yet you dare not worship either of these deities but this Jesus whom neither you nor your followers have seen."

Delphi, having been the most famous of the ancient oracles, was naturally on Julian's priority list, and he sent his doctor friend Oribasius there to see if the temple could be restored. "Tell the king," the answer came, "that on earth has fallen the glorious dwelling and the water springs that spake are quenched and dead. Not a cell is left the god, no roof, no cover. In his hand the prophet laurel flowers no more."

For Delphi it was a last chance that in any case would not have given much of a reprieve, for Julian was murdered the following year. "To be sure," writes Giuseppe Ricciotti, "Julian may be regarded as a knight with an ideal, that of restoring paganism; but unless an ideal has a serious connection with contemporary reality it is simply an anachronism."

The Greek playwright Euripides once described the ideal prophet as "a man skilled in conjecture," but Apollonius of Tyana may have been nearer the mark when he admitted that his own "secret remedy" was to take very little food, which retained his senses fresh and unimpaired, freeing them from rust and shadow and enabling him to see present and future as a clear mirror. The sage, he explained, need not wait for the vapors of the earth or the corruption of the air to foresee epidemics. He must know them later than the gods but earlier than the people. "The gods see the future, man beholds the present, sages appreciate what is about to happen. This mode of life makes the senses so acute that one may accomplish the greatest and most marvellous achievements."

Because the practice of magic and the belief in oracles is unfashionable in much of the world today, there is a tendency to dismiss the magnificent remains of Delphi as representing nothing more than a stage for the tricks of fraudulent priests. But to make this assertion is to say that mankind was duped for a period of three or four thousand years. The nineteenth-century translator Thomas Taylor, whose work influenced William Blake, Emerson, and the Transcendentalists, was moved to add a footnote in his *The Arguments of the Emperor Julian against the Christians.* Taylor asks:

How is it possible, even if these priests had been a thousand times more cunning and deceitful than they were supposed to have been, that they could have such a secret so impenetrable in every city and province where there were any oracles, as never to have given themselves the lie in any particular? Is it possible that there should never have been one man among them of so much worth as to abhor such impostures? That no man should ever have explored the sanctuaries, subterranean passages, and caverns where it is pretended they kept the machines? That they should never have had occasion for workmen to repair them? That only they should have the secret of composing drugs proper to create extraordinary dreams? And lastly that they should have perpetually succeeded one another and conveyed their machines and the juggling tricks to all those that were to follow them in the same employments from age to age, generation to generation, and yet no man to have been ever able to detect the imposition?

Besides who were these priests that, as it is pretended, were monsters of cruelty, fraud and malice? They were the most honorable men amongst the heathens and as such were most esteemed for their piety and probity.

Plutarch informs us in one of his treatises that in very old age he presided over the oracle at Delphi—depraved as the age is will anyone be hardy enough to assent that a man of such probity, of such gravity, of manners, of such penetration, learning and judgement, was a cheat and impostor by profession?

Taylor's conclusion is that in certain periods of human time when a society falls out of step with the rhythm of the natural order, "as at present and which has been the case ever since the decline and fall of the Roman Empire, then divine influence can no longer be received tho' the illuminations of divine natures continue immutably just the same."

The Delphi that we visit today, usually by motor coach from Athens 100 miles to the southeast, is an inspiring sight, sprawling across perhaps an acre of rugged, steep hillside which appears suddenly out of the lonely, barren landscape. The landmarks that have been famous for centuries line every yard of the paved path of the Sacred Way, along which the modern pilgrim still walks to reach the fourth-century B.C. temple of Apollo, about 2,000 feet above sea level. All is ruins, but what ruins! Here is the reconstructed portico of the Treasury of the Athenians, there the nondescript-looking Sybil's rock from which the first prophecies were uttered. Further down the hill, just as in ancient days, stands the Castalian Well, the jagged peaks towering behind it—those same ones from which Aesop was thrown to his death for daring to question the wisdom of the priests.

Surely it must be every visitor's dream to stumble across some treasure that has lain undiscovered for twenty-five centuries, but even the most obscure fissure in the rocks appears to be the repository only of contemporary candy wrappers. There are treasures aplenty, but most of them repose in the adjoining museum, whose beauties include the famous bronze statue of the charioteer (c. 470 B.C.) as well as the marble statue of the Caryatids, or three young ladies carrying on their heads a tripod (lost), which dates from the same period as the charioteer. Outside the museum the ground is covered with a Roman mosaic that dates from comparatively "recent" times—about A.D. 500.

Part of Delphi's wealth can be attributed to the fact that for successive generations the Greeks built on top of it. In 1892 what was then known as the village of Kastri was removed and excavations begun. Almost the first discovery was a series of marble fragments, mostly hymns to Apollo, which proved to be a key to early Greek musical notations, the manner in which the Greek letters were tilted forward, sideways, or upside down indicating different notes. One such hymn, dated 280 B.C., and translated by A. C. Swinburne, begins:

> Thee, the son of God most high,
> Famed for harping song, will I
> Proclaim, and the deathless oracular word
> From the snow-topped rock that we gaze on hears . . .

Commenting on this three years after its discovery, Reginald Lister wrote that the melody "has a certain stern grandeur of a distinctly melancholy and religious character."

The modern town of Delphi, a four-hour drive from Athens, sits overlooking a steep ravine that provides one of the most awe-inspiring views in Greece. Most of the hotels (and they range from very cheap to quite luxurious) are on the southern side of the tiny town, so that sitting on their restaurant terraces offers an undisturbed vision of the valley below and the blue waters of the Gulf of Corinth about five miles away. From here, centuries ago, pilgrims made their way on foot up the mountain to where you are sitting. It is a journey that you will probably make yourself as the tour bus proceeds back to Athens via the village of Krisso and by ferry from the nearby port of Itea across to the Peloponnese. Whatever you pay will be a bargain. When the temple to Apollo was being built, more than twenty-five centuries ago, a certain Xenodoros charged 420 drachmas to carry a delicate piece uphill from the port—almost twice what he was paid to transport it from the Corinth quarries where it was mined and shaped.

9

Malta

ANCIENT TEMPLES AND
MEDIEVAL KNIGHTS

Nobody has ever been able to explain the ancient temples of Malta. According to radiocarbon dating, they are the oldest free-standing stone monuments in the world and yet they seem to have no link with any other civilizations. The oldest of the temples date back to before the construction of the Egyptian pyramids. They were built by a race that left no written records, for writing was yet to be invented. And they have survived because they were buried and forgotten. Through centuries of occupation by one invader after another, they remained deep under the earth, rediscovered only in the last century.

Lying between Sicily, fifty miles to the northeast, and the North African coast, the islands of Malta have always appeared to be a strategic base for nations using the western Mediterranean, and it is hardly surprising that the Phoenicians, Carthaginians, Romans, Arabs, and Normans—to name but a few—all in turn coveted and dominated the islands. All left minor traces, although nothing as impressive as the megalith builders, but modern Malta owes little to these early conquerors. In fact no single nation ever shaped and developed the islands as

Illustration: Maltese Cross. Ancient symbol of Malta, originally the emblem of the crusading order of St. John.

much as that body known as the Knights of St. John who accepted Malta reluctantly as its headquarters (after losing a former base in Rhodes) in the sixteenth century and who did not leave until 270 years later.

The Order of St. John, like their better-known contemporaries the Knights Templars, grew out of a handful of knights who formed themselves into a protective force to succor the Crusaders. It became an international order whose predominantly upper-class members took vows of poverty, chastity, and obedience, and who owed their allegiance to the Pope. The Knights built themselves into a superb fighting force whose only major setback came when they were outnumbered by the Turks and forced out of their headquarters on Rhodes. At first reluctant to accept the grant of Malta, and for a long time unwilling to develop it, they eventually took over its administration and fortification and governed and held it superbly through the rule of twenty-eight successive Grand Masters. They left both their genetic and their cultural impress on the islands.

The capital of Malta, Valletta, named after the sixth of the Grand Masters, Jean de la Valette-Parisot who served from 1557 to 1568, is a charming town on a scale just small enough to get around on foot. Its main street, Kingsway, is a permanent pedestrian mall somewhat reminiscent of Dubrovnik, and the visitor quickly learns to relish the evening walk along it when the shops stay open, and the whole town turns out for the casual promenade.

Evenings, in fact, are when Valletta is at its best with churchbells ringing, candles flickering in windows, and the hazy air of the back streets permeated with a rich mixture of countless cooking smells. Like many Mediterranean lands, Malta lives much of its life in the open, and most places on this small island offer views of the sea. Valletta itself, dominating a hilly peninsula, offers picture-postcard views from its outer battlements, particularly over the Grand Harbor. Any number of small, inexpensive hotels line the picturesque steps of St. Ursula Street (try the friendly Grand Harbour Hotel), all looking out over this deepwater bay which has provided a storm-free shelter and an almost impregnable stronghold since the days of the Knights.

Even today, almost two full centuries after their departure, reminders of their presence abound on all sides. Before Valletta was founded, Fort St. Angelo, built by the Moors across the harbor to the east, was the center of their power. Successive Grand Masters strengthened and extended the defenses here, consolidating their power for an assault that never came, once the siege of 1565 was over. The fort is now a Royal Navy base, its formidable bastions infiltrated with all the accouterments of paranoia and panoply that a modern military establishment possesses. Visitors are unwelcome, unless they book for the regular Wednesday morning tour via the tourist office. The officer on duty has total authority to bar all others, and rumor has it that even retired admirals have been unable to gain admittance.

But Valletta, and Malta generally, is replete with ancient buildings and ancient memories: St. John's Co-Cathedral, built in the sixteenth century by the Order's chief engineer, Gerolamo Cassar, with its richly decorated walls and canvases by Mattia Preti and Caravaggio, both member-knights. In the crypt are tombs of several of the Grand Masters. Different sections of the fortifications were defended by different groups of knights, divided into "tongues" roughly representing their different nationalities. They lived in various inns around town, the best preserved of which is the charming Auberge D'Aragon, a white building with a spacious patio at the foot of Archbishop Street where it now serves as the headquarters of the Ministry of Education and Culture.

The flavor of those siege-conscious times, when every day might bring invasion, can perhaps best be recaptured by visiting the armory of the magnificent palace, in the center of town, where a vast hall is lined with pikes, guns, lances, suits of armor, and all the other trappings of battle. It isn't hard to imagine these holy knights turning themselves into superbly equipped men of war when the occasion demanded.

Many knightly artifacts can be seen in the basement of the Fine Arts Museum on South Street: more armor, a seventeenth-century robe, ancient bells, anchors, cannonballs, guns, and swords. There are stone models of the proposed additions to the St. Angelo fortifications—made by a Spanish military engineer in 1680 at the request of Grand Master Gregorio Carafa. Some indication of what these regal knights looked like can be gleaned from the plates and paintings bearing their portraits. Upstairs there are more paintings by Caravaggio, Tintoretto, and other sixteenth-century masters.

A vast amount of valuable art, treasures which the Knights had been collecting for 300 years and which were distributed throughout the churches of Malta, were plundered by Napoleon in the late eighteenth century and were later lost when his fleet was sunk by Nelson during the Battle of the Nile.

Grand Master Emanuel Pinto, whose metal measuring cups are displayed in the museum as well as his portrait in an oval frame, was possibly the best known of his line, and certainly the longest in office (1741–1773). His very longevity gave credence to rumors that he and his friend Cagliostro had achieved the age-old quest for the *elixir vitae,* the secret of eternal life. In 1758 after reading his premature obituary in a French paper he is reported to have exclaimed, "Aha, it is the shadow of Pinto, not Pinto, who rules in Malta." But he continued to rule with an iron hand—"he was haughty, severe and implacable" writes Roderick Cavaliero—and in his final years set up a laboratory in which Cagliostro worked. A secretary to the subsequent Grand Master, Emanuel De Rohan Polduc, wrote that Pinto "dissipated immense sums" in his unsuccessful search for the philosopher's stone, a quest that preoccupied numerous great minds of that century and the previous one.

Although the Order's compatriots, the Knights Templars—both were founded in Jerusalem for similar purposes in the twelfth century—were heavily involved in occult practices, there are only a few tantalizing hints that the Knights of Malta shared similar interests.

During the rule of La Cassière (1572–1581) there were allegations that "heresy" was rife throughout the Order, but nobody has chronicled the specific details.

Count Cagliostro, born as Giuseppe Balsamo in Palermo, Sicily, always insisted that his real birth (i.e. spiritual *rebirth*) took place in Malta after he had been initiated into the Order. "This accession came to him through the mysteries of St. John: tradition, the esoteric language of the Apocalypse, the intuitive methods of visionaries, the revelation of the cabala, the mystique of supernatural interventions on the fringe of doctrine admitted by the Church, and the call of the sublime," is how François Ribadeau Dumas puts it in his book, *Cagliostro, Scoundrel or Saint.* Dumas adds that the Grand Master taught young Balsamo "the inner meaning of occultism: the discovery of the transcendent lying behind tangible reality, the ceaseless search for a way to control forces acting upon all mankind."

As a child in Sicily, a country where in the eighteenth century the sorcerer was as common as the priest, Cagliostro had already achieved an awesome reputation. One day while playing with friends he answered a query about where some little girl was by drawing a square on the ground, making some mysterious passes with his hands, and producing an image of the child within it.

On leaving Sicily he traveled widely, visiting Rhodes (where he sold hemp and silk), Egypt, and Rome. While in London he studied Egyptian magical rites and back in Malta at first made a precarious living selling beauty creams and elixirs for long life, before establishing a friendship with Grand Master Pinto.

His renowned "recipe for perpetual youth," which appears translated from a German treatise (published at Munich in 1919) in A. E. Waite's *Lives of Alchemistical Philosophers,* outlines a forty-day retreat to be made "once in every fifty years beginning during the full moon of May." During this period, Cagliostro explains, the participant must fast, partaking only of May dew and certain herbs. Toward the end of the forty-day period, most of which is to be spent in bed, a few grains of what he terms "the Universal Medicine" will help the hair, teeth, nails, and skin to be renewed.

At his later trials (Rome in 1790, Zurich in 1791) Cagliostro was accused not only of possessing the secret of prolonging life, but also of practicing alchemical gold-making, teaching cabalistic arts, and pretending to call up and exorcise spirits. How much of this activity he conducted while on Malta was not established. In his final years he sought asylum to live on the island, but this was denied him.

There is no doubt that the Order, and especially its all-powerful Grand Master, was in an ideal position to explore some of the arcane (and heretical) occult knowledge of the day. Rich and almost invulnerable, Malta was the total master of all it surveyed, virtually an independent island kingdom theoretically answerable only to the Pope, who maintained a representative on the island in the form of an Inquisitor. This post often marked a man for promotion and twenty-five Inquisitors later became Cardinals, two became Popes.

It may be only because of this ambitious spy in their midst that so little evidence of the Knights' secret practices has come down to us. But the evidence is undoubtedly there, possibly in some of the thousands of books and manuscripts in their decaying leather bindings which fill the cavernous, twenty-foot-high shelves in Valletta's public library, the last building to be built by the Order before its departure from Malta in 1798. There are scores of books of handwritten letters in Italian, the brown ink faded but still clearly legible, an almost-complete record of all the correspondence between Malta and the Vatican for the centuries of the Knights' rule. There is a letter from Henry VIII to Grand Master L'Isle Adam, dated November 22, 1530, and manuals of signals containing neatly-drawn flags for the use of the Knights' sea-going galleys.

Another of the *auberges,* or "inns," in which the Knights were quartered is now Valletta's National Museum on Kingsway. There is little here from "recent" times when the Order held sway, the displays being devoted mostly to the era 1650–1450 B.C. when Malta reached the highest point of its prehistoric development. Burnished pottery and giant vases from the so-called Tarxien period demonstrate the ingenuity of craftsmen whose work preceded the invention of the potter's wheel, all their products being laboriously built up from one successive coil of clay after another.

From the Tarxien temples come the "fertility symbols"—small plaster penises and breasts as well as slabs bearing representations of both. There are also casts of a bull and a sow that are easier to identify than the well-worn originals still at Tarxien itself, a few miles south of Valletta. The museum also contains the immense stone slab with its recessed "cupboard" in which a flint knife and goat's horn were found, and about which Dr. David Trump writes in the official catalog: "Romanticism must always be guarded against in archaeology, but surely here the romantic explanation must be the correct one: that the sacrificial knife, with the horn of one of its victims, was put away carefully in readiness for a later celebration which never came. What prevented it? We wish we knew."

There is nothing that explains the mystery of the temples—to whom they were built, and why—but scale models of the major ones demonstrate how similar was their design for a period of about six centuries, dating from as far before the Christian era as we have come since.

The extraordinary subterranean temple known as the Hal Saflieni and Hypogeum ("under the earth") may offer the most clues to what this early pagan religion was all about. In this intricate series of elaborately carved and decorated caves, which had lain hidden for centuries until building workers accidentally cut through the roof in 1902, mysterious oracular rites were performed. Possibly some devotees came to the temple to sleep, subsequently having their dreams interpreted by priests. One of Malta's most famous ancient relics, a terra-cotta statue of a sleeping woman lying on her side, is barely five inches long, and in the three-quarters of a century since it was found, has prompted more speculation than many a major work. What is the cause of her serenity, her apparently blissful dreams?

The descent into the Hypogeum from the street-level museum is via a spiral staircase into a small cave bearing faint traces of red paint. The temple's interior was probably painted originally and in some rooms the decorated spirals and pentagons are still visible. Ingeniously the ancient builders carved pillars and lintels out of the solid rock to form the entrance to the main hall, and indeed the whole subterranean temple closely resembles similar edifices above ground. One room leads into another, up, down and around—the whole elaborate structure going down to forty feet below ground, representing who knows how many thousands of man-hours expended with antler picks and flints by a race whose gods are no longer known.

Passing out of the Oracle's room, where a recessed niche transforms a deep, male voice into a resonant, awe-inspiring echo (particularly in the darkness or possibly dim light of an oil lamp), we come first to a decorated chamber and then to what is believed to have been the holiest room, with its five carved pillars and semicorbeled ceiling. Here animals for sacrifice may have been tethered, the rope fastened through two interconnected holes in the floor. Stone plugs capped these holes when the site was first excavated and under one of them was found a pair of sheep's horns.

"It is evident that after a burnt sacrifice a portion of the animal was stowed away in [one of] the recesses so numerous in these temples," reported Sir Themistocles Zammitt, then director of the Malta Museum who was conducting the excavations. "That a burnt sacrifice was offered before the statue of the divinity worshipped is beyond doubt, for not far from the altar the pavement is deeply eroded by the action of the fire, which has likewise reddened the stone by its intense heat."

In 1913, while Zammitt was working on the Hypogeum dig, he was approached by a farmer who said that huge blocks of stone blocked plowing beneath his field and asked the diggers to investigate. A sample trench uncovered the top of two uprights which were joined in a manner suggesting a great megalithic circle. There was no time for further exploration that year and the following year, 1914, was the beginning of World War I, so it was not until 1915 that the work began at Tarxien, now generally accepted to be the last of Malta's temples to be built and representing, therefore, the absolute flowering of this particular culture.

At Tarxien was found a huge stone statue representing the lower torso of a woman who must originally have been nine or ten feet tall. All that remains are the feet and hem of a skirt, of the same type worn by the sleeping woman and other figures. Most writers have speculated that fertility was the principle worshiped by these ancient people; they prayed that the land remain rich and productive and that the women, represented by figures with immense breasts and pregnant stomachs, would continue to give birth to workers to harvest it. Many of the figures found here, and now displayed in Valletta's National Museum, stand with one hand resting on an extended belly, the other pointing downward to the earth.

The approach to the Tarxien temple is through a garden filled with cabbage, potatoes, and flowers, but once past the perpendicular stones that form the entranceway it opens up into the series of interconnected semicircular chambers that are a familiar feature of all Malta's ancient temples. There are the usual spherical stones which appear to have been used as rollers to transport the heavy blocks around, numerous altars, and stone slabs decorated with spiral patterns. One slab, also since removed to Valletta, depicted a procession of six animals: a pig, a ram, and four animals looking a bit like Moorish goats, which don't exist on Malta today but whose horns were similar to those discovered at ancient sites. Another slab, still at the site, depicts reliefs of a sow with thirteen suckling teats and a bull. The bones of all such animals were found in niches adjoining the sacrificial altars.

Zammitt, who for an archeologist appears unusually open-minded about magic, suggests that this early Neolithic population had in addition to its artistic achievements "elaborated a religious system of a type which we usually attribute to much later generations." In his book *Prehistoric Malta,* a record of his meticulously documented excavations, he adds:

> The building of sanctuaries, the sacrificial offering of animals slaughtered and burnt before an image or symbol, the consultation of oracles in special oracular chambers, the rites of divination by incubation and interpretation of inspired dreams as suggested by the chambers and figurines of the Hal Saflieni and Hypogeum point to a high moral development and a complicated system of worship such as have never hitherto been attributed to a people who had not yet become familiar with metals and with the ideas supposed to have been introduced into Europe along with them.

He pondered on the limestone "rolling" balls and the stones shaped like cones which "must have played an important part in some magico-religious ritual" and posed an original theory to explain the 10 foot by 10 foot block of pavement inset with five deep pits. These, he suggests, might be "divination blocks" into which stones from a pile nearby were thrown: "lot-casting based on the different ways in which the ball was holed."

Other writers have explained the holes as receptacles for the blood whose life-giving properties invested it with a peculiarly important symbolism in such ceremonies. It was the practice to cover the bones of the dead with red ochre in ancient times, a symbolic reinvestiture of the bones with life, and this paint could also be found on many temple walls. Professor J. D. Evans observes that workmen who discovered some such bones lying in a partly waterlogged well tomb reported they were covered in "fresh blood."

In his book *Malta,* Evans tells of the amulets found at Tarxien which were covered with abstract signs ("probably with magical or talismanic significance"), one, a piece of greenstone with a sign like a three-legged Greek "pi" was encrusted with red stones and gold, both imports to the island. Another small figurine was penetrated all over with sharp fragments of shell while the clay was still wet—a fruitful subject for speculation ranging from sympathetic magic or black magic to some sort of acupuncture technique. Most of these little figures, Evans suggests, might be evidence of a healing cult and were deposited in temples to effect cures or to give thanks for them.

Musing about whether or not the original temples had roofs, something that has been debated inconclusively since their first discovery, he points to the absence of central pillars but also observes that signs of fire on the walls of one temple would suggest that a wooden roof was burned. As to the temples' purpose, he adds: "Collective rock cut and megalithic tombs of Western Europe . . . are all in some degree shrines where rites for propitiation of ancestor spirits were carried out." The religion, he thought, probably grew out of the cult of the dead (the Hypogeum was not only a temple but a burial ground—the bones of almost 6,000 people were found there).

Evans pondered on whether the bulls, horns, and snakes which came to be depicted in the latter phases of Maltese prehistoric culture might have been due to influences from Crete and whether the ancient Maltese could have been known in the prehistoric world as "great magicians, healers, men of spiritual power generally." He draws no final conclusions.

A tiny museum at the entrance to both the Tarxien temples and the Hypogeum (both are within half a mile of each other in the sleepy town of Pawla, southeast of the peninsula on which stands Valletta) displays some of the flint, obsidian, and bone tools used in their construction, also necklaces of beads and fish vertebrae in use by the worshipers. Scale models give an overall grasp of the temples' shape. The model of the Hypogeum is especially revealing with its intricate honeycomb of caves, all sitting calmly under a deserted Victorian house whose florid, peeling wallpaper can still be seen.

A mile or two further southeast, in the barren, rock-strewn valley which adjoins the pretty fishing village of Marsaxlokk (good bathing) are the Ghar Dalam caves whose prehistoric mammal occupants, by comparison, make the temple worshipers seem like our contemporaries. The hippopotamuses and elephants that once lived here up to a quarter of a million years ago may have walked over on what was a continuous land bridge between Sicily and the Maltese islands, gradually becoming extinct as the land receded and left them trapped. The main cave is enormous, high enough to drive a double-decker bus into it, and stretching back for several hundred yards. In the adjoining museum are thousands of bones, tusks, and teeth of these extinct mammals as well as a few bones from much-later human cave dwellers.

What are probably the most impressive megalithic sites on Malta are also the most inaccessible because of bad roads untraveled by local buses. These are the twin temples of Hagar Qim on a cliff overlooking the sea just past the southwest town of Orendi, and the temple of Mnajdra, a few hundred yards below it and nearer to the sea.

Both these temples predate Tarxien, but what they lack in sophistication they more than compensate for with their towering majesty at this lonely site. Hagar Qim's front wall is formed from massive slabs, topped with horizontal slabs which give it the solid appearance of an impregnable fortress. But inside there are the familiar semicircular chambers, altars (some mushroom-shaped ones have a raised rim around the top —possibly to collect blood), niches, carved apertures through which oracles may or may not have spoken, and immense stones stippled with innumerable dots and grooves. It was at Hagar Qim that the famous "fat ladies" were found, statues that can now be seen in the National Museum in Valletta.

Walking around the earthern floor of this temple and inspecting the numerous interconnecting inner rooms, it is impossible to guess who may have worshiped here almost 3,000 years before the Christian era. There is nothing remotely like these temples outside the Maltese islands, in the view of Dr. David Trump, "so we cannot use foreign influence to explain them away." But there's no doubt that they were temples erected to worship some deity. The so-called oracle holes and the fact that the temples were divided into what appear to be public and inner sections would seem to imply a privileged priesthood.

"The increasing evidence [for this] could be quoted as a possible cause for internal revolt," says Dr. Trump, a former curator at Malta's National Museum whose book *Malta: An Archaeological Guide* is both fascinating and comprehensive. The excessive temple building, he says, in an attempt to explain the culture's demise, "might imply neglect of the precious soil of the fields. It could have depleted dangerously the local timber resources, again encouraging soil erosion. To the unprovable 'mights' and 'perhapses' we could add drought, plague, religious hysteria even, or foreign invasion."

Mnajdra's rooms and niches are as numerous as those of its companion temple up the hill, and just as baffling. The solid walls, towering up to fifteen feet high, have preserved the interior of this sheltered spot perhaps better than elsewhere. "In this temple, perhaps more than any other," says Trump, "we come tantalizingly close to the beliefs and rituals of its builders while remaining aware that further progress in understanding is probably impossible."

Because of the location of these temples, with an impressive view over the sea and of the tiny rocky islet of Filfa, moonlit nights make an especially impressive time to pay a visit. Until the enclosing wall is completed, both these temples are open at all times.

Margaret Murray quotes a tradition in her book *Excavations in Malta* that Hagar Qim was built solely by women, but she gives no evidence for this. At Tas-Silg, east of Marsaxlokk, she says another legend concerns the eight-foot "Saracen woman" said to be buried with a spinning wheel of solid gold. There's long been a local belief in the tale of the poor farmer who many years ago dug up a solid gold sheep with his plow and broke it into pieces before selling to the goldsmith for a pension that kept him the rest of his life.

On the cliffs in this region around Tas-Silg, in Roman times, was a temple dedicated to the Syrian goddess Astarte, known to the Greeks as Hera. This may have been the Temple of Juno (Hera's Latin name) which historians report was despoiled about 73 B.C.

The ancient walled city of Mdina, once known as Melita, is much richer in the antiquities of the Christian era than in those of prehistoric days. A Roman villa just outside the city moat (which was dug by the Arabs in the ninth century) has a remarkable tiled floor whose patterns offer the kind of eye-catching perspective still popular today. Other relics of the villa/museum are various funerary monuments "dedicated to the gods of the underworld" as well as a pedestal bearing a dedication to Apollo and the notation that local citizens contributed 110,792 sesterces for its erection.

Mdina's "modern" suburb of Rabat is also interesting but not half so fascinating as the walled town itself, with its cathedral clock noting the day, month, and year, and its excellent museum of natural history with explanatory plans of the island's geology, rock strata, and flora and fauna.

Much of Malta is monotonously barren, strewn with rock and stone-fenced fields, few bigger than the average suburban backyard, but the view from Mdina's city walls is splendid, especially to the northeast where St. Paul's Bay is supposedly the site of Paul's landing back in the first century A.D. The cave in which he is said to have lived adjoins the cathedral in Rabat.

Southwest of Rabat, on the Dingli cliffs, is one of the best examples of the mysterious "cart-ruts" which innumerable archeologists have tried to explain, leaving the inescapable conclusion that there is not only more here than meets the eye but conceivably evidence of strange magical practices, too.

The ruts are deep grooves in bare limestone rock which must have been cut while the rock was still covered with soil, for limestone hardens too much to cut when it has been long exposed to air. The tracks run in parallel lines often for long distances, sometimes up sheer slopes, and occasionally disappearing into the sea. Most historians seem to have decided that they couldn't have been made by wheels (some of the angles of turn are too sharp) and must have been made by poles, loosely tied together, with the burden resting between them.

"By themselves the cart tracks tell a story of immense activity on the part of a considerable population evidently engaged in the transport of a heavy material on hundreds of carts for hundreds of years," Dr. Zammitt writes. "There could be no idea then of road building in the Roman sense of levelling and metalling rough surfaces; the carts were evidently pushed over any rocky surface in the direction desired, whether smooth or hummocky, flat, slanting, hollowed or raised."

Dr. Trump tells us that the commonest pattern is for tracks of this nature, which are the result of wear not deliberate cutting, to climb from one cultivated valley to the next, often by the most convenient route, which is why they are so often found paralleling the roads of today. On the average the parallel tracks are about fifty-five inches apart and sometimes several inches deep. Most could be explained, he says, by regular agricultural activities.

On the Dingli cliffs, just south of Buskett Gardens, the tracks are so numerous, crisscrossing each other, that the spot has been colloquially termed "Clapham Junction" by some writers. On the face of it, there seems to be little explanation for their concentration at this point. Another good selection can be seen at the Naxxar Gap below St. Paul and Targa where ruts approach the ancient defense wall known as Victoria Lines and sweep across the Mosta Road.

The island of Gozo is smaller than Malta and less barren. Its fertile valleys have traditionally produced much of the food to feed its sister island to the south. Gozo is reached by a ferryboat that looks a bit like a Mississippi River steamer: a half-hour ride across calm waters after the pleasant drive up Malta's coast to Marfa, the embarkation point.

Getting around Gozo is very easy: the island is only about ten miles long by four or five miles wide, and buses run to most places. Victoria, the somewhat olde-worlde capital, has two movie theaters, one hotel with a good restaurant, and a main square whose thickly-foliaged trees shelter so many birds that their raucous shrieking can be heard all over town. Only unwary tourists park their cars under the trees in the square, and locals rarely walk through without a hat.

Victoria's major place of interest is the hilltop castle, part of which comprises a museum containing fertility symbols and a finely-dressed block of stone with a snake carving from the Ggantija temple a few miles to the east. There are also numerous Roman relics, such as stone-carved inscriptions and various gods, coins, and vases, many of them recovered from the wrecked Roman vessel found at Xlendi Bay. This little fishing harbor, incidentally, is a delightful hideaway, virtually deserted out of season when self-contained apartments on the harbor can be rented for next to nothing. Some of the best lace comes from Gozo and Xlendi is a good place to buy it.

Ggantija, which is among the oldest of the Maltese temples, dates back to as early as 2600 or 2800 B.C. It was first excavated in 1827, in times when excavation meant little more than uncovering the site, saving the main items and leaving everything else to the elements. Fortunately it became a popular subject for numerous artists, one of whom, the German Brocktorff, painted a series of watercolors which depict details of features long since destroyed. The pictures can be seen in the Valletta library on Malta.

In the nineteenth century few thought of such sites as prehistoric, although the first description of Ggantija to appear, published by L. Mazzara, Paris, bore the curious title of *Temple Anti-Diluvian des Geants.* The temple is very similar to the ones we have already seen on Malta itself, and although one of the earliest visitors made passing reference to a subterranean temple similar to the Hypogeum, this has never since been discovered.

Two of the problems that have troubled most archeologists since Ggantija was first uncovered (the excavations at Hagar Qim and Mnajdra came twelve years later) are, given how small the Maltese population must have been in prehistoric times, how were the temples first built and paid for? In his *The Story of Malta,* Brian Blouet comments: "It has been suggested that Malta was a 'magic island sanctuary' with a great part of the religious paraphernalia being paid for by gifts or fees extracted from pilgrims coming from other lands." But this theory is open to objection, he says, because if such pilgrims did come to Malta they left no traces of their presence, nor have relics from this Maltese temple era been found in other lands.

In a later era Malta built up a considerable export trade in cotton and citrus fruits, but these crops were introduced during the Arab domination of the islands which lasted from A.D. 870 to 1090.

The region around Ggantija is scattered with other sites, none as impressive as the main temple, but it's worth paying a visit to nearby

Xaghra (where a painted clock on the church announces a never-changing 11:47). Weird, rambling underground caves sprawl under the village, their antiquity emphasized by the Victorian houses above them. Access is usually via a carved stone staircase into what would ordinarily be a kitchen cellar—except that some of these "cellars" stretch for hundreds of feet and are filled with stalactites and stalagmites.

10

Rome

PRESERVING PAGAN PRACTICES

Of all the ancient cities there are few that preserve so well the memory of pagan times as that preeminently Christian capital, Rome. The monuments are all around. Tucked away between the cathedrals and the churches are the temples and the shrines, the pillars and the statues erected to the glory of earlier gods. Rome is a living museum, an ageless reminder of the days when man feared Nature and appeased her representatives with treasures looted from the entire known world.

In this city of lunatic drivers, wanted and unwanted serenades, noise, antiquity, and pasta, strolling the streets can be endlessly rewarding. There is history at every corner, but there are also open-air markets that fold up and disappear as suddenly as they arrive, newsstands and flower stalls, peddlers and pickpockets, and everywhere the curious but cautious cats. Romans live their lives out in the streets amid the remnants of twenty-five centuries of civilization whose artifacts clutter the landscape in all directions. It is a titillating experience to join them.

Because of the Roman Empire's impact upon the ancient world, the saga of Rome has been meticulously documented by any number of

Illustration: Mithras, god of the sun, light, and truth; symbol of the Roman Legions. From an amulet, first century, A.D.

historians. And while much of its pre-Christian history is as ambiguous as that of any other nation, especially in that murky area where men and gods seem interchangeable, there is a certain amount of unanimity about the broad outlines.

One of Rome's earliest kings—this was at least eight centuries before Christ—was named Annulius, a man who had usurped the kingdom by murdering his nephew, Numitor. To ensure that his daughter Rhea could not threaten his line of succession, Annulius appointed her a vestal virgin. But Rhea broke her vows (legend credits her with being the wife of Mars) and gave birth to the twins, Romulus and Remus.

Rhea was put to death and her sons tossed into the River Tiber, but instead of drowning they were washed up in their cradle at the foot of the Palatine hill where they were suckled by a wolf, brought food by a woodpecker, and raised by a shepherd.

Romulus wanted to found a city on the Palatine, Remus along the Aventine, and both agreed to let the gods decide. They waited on a hill and watched for a sign. Remus saw six vultures, Romulus spotted twelve. And although each claimed the augury, shepherds decided in favor of Romulus.

Yoking a bullock and a heifer to his plow, Romulus dug a furrow around the Palatine hill in 753 B.C. and built a wall, declaring this to be the city. He killed Remus, the story goes, because the latter jumped over the wall.

With a pressing need to inhabit his city, Romulus at first proclaimed asylum there for criminals and escaped slaves. Later he organized the most famous mass kidnapping in history by inviting the neighboring Latins and Sabines to a festival, during which his men carried off all the visiting wives and daughters. The subsequent battles might have gone on indefinitely were it not for the Sabine women themselves who entreated both sides to collaborate and form one nation.

Romulus ruled for thirty-six years until one day he disappeared, carried off by Mars in a fiery chariot during an eclipse and while a fierce thunderstorm was raging. Later he appeared in a vision to Romans bidding them to worship him as the god Quirinus.

So goes the story about the founding of Rome, and it brings us to the reign of King Numa (715–673 B.C.), who apparently was the first to arrange some kind of order out of the daily life of his citizens. Numa reformed the calendar, encouraged agriculture, built a temple to the two-faced god Janus, instituted the offices of pontifices (sacred priests) and augurs (about which more later), and marked out the boundaries of property which he placed under the protection of another god, Terminus. During his reign a shield was said to have fallen from heaven and Numa, anxious that it not be stolen, had eleven replicas made of it and installed them all in the temple.

Perhaps Numa's most far-reaching decision, and one that did the most to institutionalize religion in the Roman state, was to inaugurate the office of flamen, a priest devoted specifically to one god. At this time the pantheon of gods was not as large as it would eventually become. Janus, whose domain extended over rivers and seas, symbolized the opening day of the year and the beginning of things, and was addressed in every prayer.

But Jupiter, whose Greek name Zeus signified the radiant light of heaven, was the supreme ruler of the universe and the most glorious of divinities. His priest, the flamen dialis, was subjected to many taboos. He was forbidden to ride a horse or walk under a vine; he could not touch dogs, raw flesh, goats, yeast, ivy, or beans, or even name them. He could not go near a corpse or a grave or have a knot in his clothing or wear an unbroken ring. When his hair was cut it had to be buried and iron was attached to his bed to ward off evil spirits.

By the time King Numa died, his books of philosophy comprised the secret mysteries of the state religion and when they were later discovered in his tomb they were burned, at a special ceremony, to avoid the risk of them falling into ignorant (i.e. nonpriestly) hands.

Numa was followed in office by Tullius Hostilius (673–642 B.C.), who was said to be so warlike that finally Jupiter "smote him and his whole house with fire from heaven. Thus perished Tullius."

For hundreds of years more, the supposed wishes of the gods (which they made known through various omens) determined the actions of Roman rulers and their citizens. The aurora borealis, thunderstorms, fallout from volcanos—all were seen as meaningful signs by superstitious Romans.

Lucius Tarquinius Priscus, who became king in 616 B.C. and who during his thirty-seven-year reign constructed the Circus Maximus and the great *cloaca* ("subterranean sewers"), both of which have survived to this day, received an early sign.

One day while he was walking on the Janiculum hill an eagle flew off with his hat and then returned and placed it on his head. Priscus' wife, an Etruscan diviner, had no doubt that this incident was a sign that her husband was meant for high honors. And so it proved to be.

It is time, however, to put aside the history books and make our way into the Rome of today in search of the Rome of yesterday. In no city is there so much of the past still to be seen. Relatively few monuments, it's true, are completely intact; it is more common to find a single column standing straight and stately, guarding its fallen companions that lie in a crumbled mass nearby. But in Rome, to an eye-popping degree, the ancient and modern are inextricably tangled. A city whose major highways are apt to suddenly contract in order to squeeze through the narrow confines of a 2,000-year-old marble archway, is not easy for a motorist to negotiate, and you'd probably do best avoiding the automobile.

Rome is a big and beautiful city, in some respects as chic and modern as cities come. But although any one of a hundred guidebooks offers provocation for weeks of sightseeing the magical tour may be confined to a comparatively small area. This is bordered by the remarkable pyramid of Caius Cestus, a ninety-eight-foot edifice erected over the tomb of the first-century praetor at the Porta S. Paolo, and that preeminent building of the pagan world, the Pantheon, just north of the Corso Vittorio Emanuele. (The enclosed base of the pyramid is currently used as an open-air cat shelter and is rapturously fascinating. You might want to take food to give to the cats.)

Although the distance between these sites is only just over one mile, you will need two or three days to savor it fully, if only for the joy of meandering around the various landmarks to be seen along the way. The forum and the hill that adjoins it need a full day in themselves, and in addition, diversions should be made to the Capitoline Hill, the Colosseum, and the Mithraic temple in the basement of Santa Prisca Church just off the Via Labicana. All these are part of our pagan story, and only a relatively small proportion of it.

It is fitting that the journey start at the magnificent Pantheon (143 feet high and with sixteen 47-foot columns of solid granite), for no other building in the world demonstrates so splendidly the tribute that was paid to ancient gods. The building was commissioned by Agrippa in 27 B.C. and dedicated to Mars and Venus. ("Agrippa" was the term for a baby who came into the world feet first.) The inscription carved over its front portico implies that it was built by Agrippa, but closer investigations during the last century revealed that bricks throughout its entire structure are marked with "brick stamps" (a bit like postmarks) bearing dates between A.D. 120 and 125. This clearly places the structure in the time of the emperor Hadrian (A.D. 118–138), and it is he who is now believed to have reconstructed the Pantheon from its original foundations. (Among Hadrian's accomplishments was his gaining acceptance for the enlightened view that owners of slaves should no longer have the right to kill or torture them.)

Although the Pantheon itself is astonishing enough, what usually fills the visitor with awe is to gaze upward and see the sky through a minuscule (it is actually thirty feet) circular opening which is the massive building's only source of light. This is best seen when the sun is directly overhead at midday.

Very little information has come down to us about the Pantheon's specific purpose or function, although there is a certain irony in the fact that its excellent state of preservation is almost certainly due to its usurpation by the Christians. Speculation that its original shape might have been different is quashed by the Italian historian Giuseppe Lugli, who explains that a fundamental principle of Roman religion was that the gods would not allow any change to be made in the form of temples when they were rebuilt.

"The round shape of the Agrippa Pantheon is most fitting for the mystical nature of the cult," Lugli says, "which, though having Mars and Venus as its chief divinities as well as Julius Caesar, comprised all the gods of Olympus, and was connected with the astral world through an astronomical concept of oriental inspiration."

From the Pantheon we head due south toward the bend in the Tiber, veering east there to the magnificent Capitoline Hill, once the site of the temple to Jupiter, renowned throughout the entire pagan world.

The hill is dominated today by a square which was designed by Michelangelo in about 1550 and in which sits an equestrian statue—the only bronze one remaining from ancient Rome—of Antonious, better known as the great pagan emperor Marcus Aurelius (A.D. 161–180). The explanation for its survival through those early Christian centuries, when the memory of so many pagan heroes was erased, is that for many years it was thought to represent the emperor Constantine. The statue stands, appropriately, on a block of marble that Michelangelo took from the temple of Castor in the Forum at the bottom of the hill.

The top-ranking Roman god was Jupiter, believed to be responsible for the weather. Anything struck by lightning was especially dedicated to him, as were the ides (full moon days) on the thirteenth or fifteenth of the month. The enormous temple dedicated about 509 B.C., not only to him but to his wife Juno and his daughter Minerva, was the most magnificent building in Rome and took nearly a century to build. It dominated the southern side of the Capitoline Hill and its polished stucco surface (made by mixing burned marble and the whitest lime with milk) reflected light like a mirror, reported Vitruvius.

To the Roman temple, 180 feet across and 200 feet deep, came the worshipers of Jupiter and Juno before each harvest, the supplicants offering a lamb at the start of the vintage season. Barefooted magistrates and matrons followed the pontifices carrying the cyclindrical stone (*lapis manalis*—"rain stone") from the temple of Mars.

Before leaving for the wars, consuls came here to pay tribute, and on their victorious return arrived to place a laurel wreath of victory in the lap of the earthenware image which bore a thunderbolt in its right hand and stood in the center of the temple. A white ox was sacrificed in gratitude, and if a white animal could not be found, then another was artificially whitened with pipe clay.

Besides supervising the weather and other natural events, Jupiter watched over truth and justice. He was ever-ready to reveal the truth to augurs, without whom, in ancient times, no public or private transaction took place. The will of the gods was always believed to be revealed to men through signs, and the augurs, wearing state robes with purple borders and carrying the curved staff *(lituus)* of their office, were the ones who interpreted them.

There were five types of auspices:

1. *Ex caelo*—the observation of thunder and lightning, which coming

from the left was lucky, the right, unlucky. (Greek augurs interpreted lightning the opposite way because Italy faced south, Greece north.)

2. *Ex avibus*—birds such as eagles and vultures proffered auguries by their flight and were known as *alites*. Ravens, crows, and rooks did so by their voice and were known as *oscines*. Woodpeckers and owls were both *alites* and *oscines*.

3. *Ex tripudis*—the feeding of chickens with a kind of pulse porridge which was scattered outside their cages. It was a favorable sign if they ate greedily, unfavorable if they refused to emerge, cried, beat their wings, or flew away. This type of auspice was much favored by armies in the field who were often accompanied not only by cages of chickens, but also a special functionary, a *pullarius,* who looked after them.

4. *Ex quadrupedibus*—interpreting the movement of four-footed animals across one's path, used only privately.

5. *Ex diris, signis,* etc.—all other "signs," including sneezing, stumbling, something falling in the temple, or anything that interrupted the *silentium* (which can be interpreted as a state denoting the absence of anything faulty, including noise).

The augurs were not confined to the temples, and certain permanent spots were consecrated for taking auspices. These had boundaries that could not be altered and within which no buildings could be erected to block the view. Such observation posts served much as meteorological observatories do today, with auspices being specially taken before major events such as battles, the founding of new colonies, sittings of the Senate, or the drawing of lots. Augurs were elected for life and could not be deposed.

On the day of the auspices, between midnight and daybreak, the augur used his wand to delineate a division in the heavens called a *templum,* beneath which he took his observations. Then pitching his canvas or leather tent on a bit of ground that was solemnly marked out and consecrated, he took up a position facing south, watching the skies through the single opening onto the *templum.*

In the later years of the empire, auspices began to be abused, and the flashes of lighting that once filled the people with awe of Jupiter were used as an excuse by any magistrate to put off that day's hearing. His observation, though "constitutionally unassailable," as one historian puts it, was not always shared by other citizens, and in time the lesser diviners especially (haruspices) fell into disrepute.

But back in the days of Jupiter's greatest glory, when the purple-robed dignitaries annually climbed on the roof of the temple to repaint in scarlet and gold the glorious terra-cotta images of the god in a chariot pulled by four fine horses, the message of the god, relayed through the augurs, was final.

In the year 83 B.C. the temple burned down, was rebuilt containing a magnificent gold and ivory image of the god, burned down again before the century was out, and while being rebuilt was again destroyed by fire in A.D. 80. This time Domitian constructed it, with a magnificence even greater than before. The poet Martial jokingly wrote that Jupiter himself would be bankrupted, even with all the resources of Olympia behind him, if called upon to pay for his new temple. But the money was raised: Pentelic marble was imported from Greece and golden tiles estimated by John Dennie (writing in 1900) to have cost twelve million dollars were placed on the roof.

Dennie's book, *Rome of Today and Yesterday,* documents with extraordinary precision the pre-Christian history of "the pagan city" and has been an invaluable reference for this chapter.

No traces of this early temple of Jupiter remain today, except for fragments in museums. Its gold was plundered by vandals and later Pope Honorius, who in an early example of the Christian take-over technique, transported the ruins across town for the construction of St. Peter's.

The buildings on the Capitoline, however, which long ago extended over almost the entire hill, are products of such repeated desecration that undoubtedly parts of the temple of Jupiter still rest there.

In a closely guarded vault beneath the Capitoline temple of Jupiter were once kept the renowned sibylline books, which were consulted by the college of priests on the occasion of earthquakes and other disasters. History records that the Apollonian sibyl who dwelt by the spring at Cumae (one of many sibyls known to the ancient Romans) originally offered Tarquinius Superbus (534–510 B.C.) nine books of oracular utterances in Greek hexameters. The price being too high, Tarquinius rejected the offer, only to learn that she was burning the books of wisdom one by one. When the sibyl shrewdly offered the remaining three books for the same exorbitant sum as the original nine, he paid the price, and the books were preserved until the disastrous fire which incinerated the Capitol in 83 B.C. After that disaster the Senate sent envoys to various oracles to collect similar prophecies, assembling a collection that survived until 405 B.C. when it was reportedly destroyed by Stilicho. Virgil is said to have quoted the sibylline oracle forecasting the coming of Christ.

If you walk down the terraced slope at the southeastern side of the Capitoline Hill, you will come almost immediately to the nine remaining pillars of what was once the Porticus Deorum Consentium, built in A.D. 367 as one of the last temples to Rome's major pagan gods: Jupiter, Neptune, Vulcan, Apollo, Mars, Mercury, Juno, Minerva, Venus, Diana, Vesta, and Ceres. The porticus itself was a late example of a Greek idea which the Romans had earlier adopted with enthusiasm: a long, straight arcade whose roof was supported by rows of columns, allowing the cooling air to circulate.

The principal temples of the early Forum were those to Saturn, Castor, Janus, Vesta, and Concord; only a few tall columns remain of the first two and fewer traces still of the latter two. Remains of the temple of Janus may still lie uncovered on the northern side of the Forum.

The temple of Vesta, uncovered late in the last century, was dedicated to the Roman goddess of the hearth and the protectress of the nation. She was said to have spurned both Neptune and Apollo, preferring to remain single. The round temple, according to tradition, was built by King Numa, the successor to Romulus in the eighth century B.C., and the man reputed to have introduced worship of this goddess to Rome. It stood at the eastern end of the Forum, with the building housing the vestal virgins behind it, and the official residence of the chief pontifex nearby.

The goddess Vesta was worshiped under the symbol of eternal fire, rekindled every March 1 from the sun with a burning glass or by the friction caused by boring into a piece of wood from a fruit tree. The half-dozen vestals (originally four) chosen by the pontifex from among the young (between six and ten years of age) daughters of free, respectable families, were charged with keeping alive the flame. If it went out, the guilty vestal was scourged.

The girls, selected by lot from twenty virgins nominated by the pontifex, were obliged to serve for thirty years and few were allowed to avoid the honor. Shorn of their hair, they were obliged to be chaste and were confined to apartments in which no men were allowed. For ten years they learned their duties, for ten more they continued to perform them, and for a final decade instructed their younger colleagues. At the end of their period of service they were granted leave to quit the office, although few took advantage of it. Despite the onerous nature of their duties—any who violated the oath of chastity was beaten with rods and buried alive; their seducer executed—the office carried many honors. Dressed in white beribboned headband, a purple-bordered gown, and a white veil for sacrifices, they were preceded everywhere by a lictor bearing the fasces (bundles of elm or birch rods tied with a red strap) as symbol of their authority. The vestals sat in a place of honor at public games, were entrusted with important legal duties, escorted people (who were thus rendered free of attack), and were protected from assault by the death sentence imposed on any who injured them. Any criminals they happened to encounter while on their missions were automatically pardoned.

The worship of Vesta, especially during the July festival when women walked barefoot to the temple to implore the goddess' blessings on their husbands and when all millers and bakers and others dependent on the hearth fire for their livelihood took a holiday, was well established in Rome and lasted for more than one thousand years until A.D. 382 when it was abolished by Gratian.

In addition, the goddess Vesta was worshiped at the close of other religious services, prayers at the opening being devoted to Janus. He, the oldest of Roman gods, was reputed to open the gates of heaven each morning and was represented as a porter with a staff and key, and two bearded faces looking in opposite directions. In the year 153 B.C. Janus really came into his own when, during a reform of the calendar, January was made the beginning of the year, the first day of which being declared a public holiday when gifts were exchanged, greetings for good omens proffered, and quarrels avoided.

This calendar reformation incidentally undermined much of the authority of the pontifices who up to that time had retained the secret knowledge of how to bring the drifting calendar into line with the actual seasons. They did this by inserting intercalary days or months, often on a random basis that played havoc with anybody trying to make plans for dates far ahead.

The college of pontifices, whose chief as we have seen nominated the candidates for vestal virgins, were charged with many similar duties. Livy says there were originally four, Cicero five, but in any case in the year 300 B.C. the number was raised to eight or nine, of which four had to be plebeians. Sulla raised the number to fourteen, Julius Caesar (who appointed himself Pontifex Maximus and lived in the Domus Publica behind the temple) raised the number to fifteen.

Responsible for supervising the overall worship of the gods and guarding against the neglect of ancient customs or the introduction of strange foreign rites, the pontifices also handled such chores as appeasing the souls of the dead and interpreting signs.

An ancient guidebook to Rome, published in the middle of the fourth century A.D., mentioned the existence of 424 temples, 304 shrines, 80 statues of gods made from precious metals, 64 statues of ivory, and more than 3,700 bronze statues. Sir William Smith who quoted from this guidebook observed that it had been said that in the old days Rome had two populations of equal size: one alive and one of marble. The last century was a particularly rich period for discovery, with more than 1,000 such marble statues having been discovered in the twenty-five years prior to the author's book *A Smaller History of Rome* in 1898. More than 30,000 pagan tombstones had also been uncovered up to that time and archeologists estimated that ten times as many were still hidden in the ground. One tomb was inscribed with the admonition: "Whoever steals the nails from this structure may he thrust them in his eyes."

When the site around the temple to Vesta was excavated in 1883, several statues were discovered (mostly now in the museum in the Diocletian Baths) which indicate that the vestal dress was a long gown fastened by a short cord, knotted in front, and topped by rolls of linen which might have indicated rank according to the number of twists. Certainly the senior vestals held great influence; they were the only women in the Roman state allowed to hold property or make a will.

The complex hierarchy of pagan Rome included other priests, among them the previously mentioned flamen who, because of his emblematic role signifying divine freedom, could not look upon, touch, or even name anything suggestive of bonds or imprisonment. Nor could he work or watch others working, and he was preceded by a lictor who made sure everyone stopped work while he passed. He wore a white conical hat, topped by an olive branch with a woolen thread, and if this fell off his head at any time, he was obliged to resign his office, which he also had to do if his wife died.

A flamen, forbidden to leave Italy, had to spend every night at home (in later times he was allowed two nights off each year) and carried a special staff to keep the public away and a knife to perform his daily sacrifices.

The task of reading the entrails of the sacrificed animals was often left to the haruspices, a salaried class founded by Romulus. Cicero says the art was taught to the Etruscans by the dwarf Tages, who sprang from a stone turned over by a peasant who was plowing. The Romans originally sent twelve sons of nobles to Tuscany to learn the art which later fell into such disrepute that Cicero, who opposed their admission to the Senate, quoted Cato as saying he wondered that one haruspex didn't laugh whenever he saw another.

Sacrifices, which in Roman times could be anything from burning incense to offering food, drink, or cakes but was rarely a human, were performed in reverent silence. The worshiper usually faced east while the animal victim was led to the altar. Male victims were offered to male deities, female to goddesses, and the horns would sometimes be gilded and wrapped with a sacred band of white wool. All movements of the victim were carefully studied as it was led to the altar; it was important that the animal go willingly, and preferably with bowed head, in a straight line and with no sense of fear or unease.

Before the ritual killing, one of the lobes of liver was allocated to those performing the sacrifice, the other to the enemies of the state. Then, after the fatal stroke with an ax or knife, the animal was disemboweled, its blood collected in a basin and burned on the altar, and the entrails examined. Great prosperity and success were forecast if the liver was unblemished, bright red, and not oversized. Heart, spleen, gall bladder, and lungs were also examined before being consigned to a fire whose flame, ideally clear and undivided, was also carefully studied. If the sacrifice was totally consumed by the fire, it was taken as an indication that it had been successfully accepted.

Sacrifices were made to most of the deities, but Mars, the Roman god of war and legendary father of Romulus, stands out because of the elaborate combination of bull, ram, and boar which were usually proffered. The emperor Augustus, having cleared four acres of land for a new Forum in 42 B.C., erected a temple to Mars Ultor, the immense pillars of which still stand today adjoining Via di Tor de' Conti. Sacrifices were made to Mars before and after battles, and a horse was sacrificed in his temple on October 15, the blood being then saved and kept in the temple of Vesta. On certain days in March, once the first month of the Roman year, the priesthood performed a war dance and sang ritual songs. When war was to be waged, it began with this festival, ending with the consecration of arms at the October festival when the campaign was over.

Festivals of one sort or another filled most of the Roman year: sacrifices were offered on April 15 to Tellus, reputed founder of the Delphic oracle and thought to be the first creature born from primeval chaos. As a mother-earth goddess sometimes known as Gaia, she was closely associated with earthquakes, and when one struck Rome in 268 B.C., its citizens made haste to erect a temple to her. On April 19 the celebration was for Ceres, the Roman grain goddess whose Greek equivalent was Demeter. The temple to Ceres, built along the Aventine in 490 B.C., was constructed by Greek artists in typical Greek style. Also, in April, on the twenty-first, which was deemed to be the anniversary of the city's founding, was a festival dedicated to Pales, the goddess of shepherds. It was to promote the fruitfulness of the flocks and to purify the sacred groves and fountains. Cakes of millet were offered to the goddess, houses were purified with sulphur and incense, and shepherds ritually leapt over bonfires of hay and burning straw.

"The Romans used religion as an instrument of social order," says F. J. Gould in *A Concise History of Religion*. "They readily voted the gods of conquered nations into their list of legal divinities so long as the forms of worship were documented in accordance with state policies." And the list was endless: Argentarius, god of silver coins; Cloacina, goddess of the city sewers; Puta, god of beekeeping; even the Etruscan Norcia, goddess of truffles. Every Roman could worship any god he chose, but he also had to honor the state gods and all priests were subordinate to the secular government. The state also appointed the College of Augurs, whose divinatory skills had been passed down from the Etruscans.

Rome borrowed not only art and literature but also her magic from Greece, wrote W. H. Davenport Adams in his *Dwellers on the Threshold*. "Numa was the great prophet of the old Roman magic," he explains, even though the occult science did not really penetrate until nearly two hundred years before the Christian era. Previously there had existed Etruscan sorcery comprising divination, the worship of the dead, the evocation of their lemures (spirits), and the mysterious rites of the Mana Genita, "a nocturnal goddess of terrible character. . . . The influence of the Etruscan augurs passed away when the polished philosophy of the Greeks commended itself to the Roman mind and the Chaldean soothsayers reigned in their stead."

Festivals celebrated the beginning of spring and the harvest; they honored the shortest day of the year and the longest. There were mariner festivals celebrating the sea gods, art festivals, fertility festivals, and a three-day ghost festival (Lemuria) to propitiate the souls of the departed. Instituted by Romulus, this was celebrated on the nights of May 9, 11, and 13, and in silence. People avoided getting married during May and on the fateful three days tried to prevent the ghosts of the dead from coming back to bother the living by beating drums, uttering magical words, and burning beans (sacred to the underworld powers). Beans were also thrown on graves and over the shoulder by the wary who walked barefoot around the house and ritually washed their hands three times.

Odd days of the month were lucky to the ancient Romans. On even days nobody would start a campaign or begin a journey. Astrologers were especially in vogue in Tiberius' time (A.D. 14–37), and while emperors consulted the Delphic oracle the man in the street visited one of the temples where he could get his questions answered by drawing lots from a box made of wood from the sacred olive tree.

Juno, the wife of Jupiter, according to Livy, merited six temples of her own, and was honored on March 1 at a festival known as Matronalia. Money was coined in the temple of Juno Moneta on Capitoline Hill. (*Moneta,* the Latin for "mint," is the source of our word *money.*) Saturnalia was, obviously, the festival to Saturn, and began on December 17 with sacrifices and an open-air banquet. Senators left off their togas, substituting a looser garment known as a *synthesis.* Schools had a holiday, the law courts closed, all work was stopped, no criminals were punished for six days, slaves were entertained at a banquet, gifts were given, and people gambled for nuts (a symbol of fruitfulness)—not quite the sexually licentious picture that the word *saturnalia* usually conjures up. Saturn, god of seedtime and the harvest, is usually shown with his symbolic sickle, and his temple occupied the first consecrated site in the Roman Forum. It also served as the public treasury and both gold and senatorial decrees were kept there. Even today several of its pillars are standing, its ruins being among the most impressive in the Forum.

Saturn's worship has survived the centuries, as can be seen from this injunction found in Raphael's *The Familiar Astrologer* for 1833. "Let the character of Saturn be engraved upon a magnet or piece of loadstone in the time of the moon's increase, and being worn on the right hand no enemy or foe shall overcome the wearer."

Adjoining the Forum at its northwestern end is the gloomy cavelike Marmentine prison where the gallant hero of Gallic resistance, Vercingetorix, was executed in A.D. 51. His memory is still honored in France's Auvergne, which we shall visit later. At the northeastern edge of the Forum is the magnificent Colosseum, which certainly needs no description here.

Only three hundred yards from the Colosseum, on the Via S. Giovanni, in the cellars of St. Clemente Church (named after the third Pope, who died about A.D. 100) are well-preserved traces of the Mithraic religion, a Persian creed that the Roman legions spread widely throughout the empire. Mithras, born of a rock, received a raven-borne command from the god Apollo to trap and spill the blood of some animal that possessed life to the full. This turned out to be a robust bull from the region of the moon.

Mithraic altars, including the one here, usually depict a fight whose participants also included a scorpion (personification of evil), a hound, and a snake. Because the rites of Mithras were especially celebrated at the spring equinox, it has been assumed that the contest is an allegory of the zodiacal bull Taurus being banished from heaven in the daytime by the sun and at night by Scorpio, the constellation in opposition. Mithras was a representative of the Persian sun god Mazda, who carried on a constant combat against the powers of darkness and evil.

The outcome of the battle, Mithras slaying the bull and fertilizing the world with its blood (notwithstanding the evil brought to the world by the scorpion's spilling of some of it), was celebrated with a banquet by Apollo and Mithras. The pair then ascended together into heaven in a golden chariot. The Mithraists' sacred meal of bread and wine memorialized this banquet on December 25, a festival known as *Dies Natalis Solis Invicti:* the birthday of the unconquered sun. At winter solstice the days lengthen and promise the return of spring.

The militant and heroic nature of Mithraic beliefs held special appeal for soldiers, and Alexander the Great's legions had adopted the cult, introducing its disciplines to Rome about 67 B.C. Initiates were required to undergo seven or eight strict and exacting rituals, each more demanding than the previous one. The trials were calculated to purify a spirit that remained undaunted and unsubdued through fire and water, hunger and thirst, scourging and solitude.

Mithras is hailed in a hymn in the *Zend Avesta* as "Lord of the light, god of the sun, whose chariot rolling on one wheel is drawn by white stallions, and is God of truth to whom none must lie, neither lord nor householder." In his *Concise History of Religion,* F. J. Gould speculates that Mithras' association with caves may be a reference to the sun rising from the cave of night.

Sunday was sacred to his worship and Mithraic initiation ceremonies took twelve days, during which time a ram or lamb was sacrificed. Mithras devotees (women were banned) underwent baptism, being marked with a holy sign on their forehead, and partook of bread and water. They were given capes marked with the signs of the zodiac and sent into subterranean caverns to conquer their fears and weaknesses.

The rites were invariably celebrated in a cave or grotto, which represented the universe; in the third-level basement of St. Clemente, this grotto also has a star-studded ceiling, representing the constellations of the zodiac. A carved figure to one side of the altar, Cautes, holds aloft a flame, symbolizing the sun's activity between December 21 and June 21; on the other side, Cautopates, with a lowered torch, represents the sun on the wane.

The lowest cellar of St. Clemente dates from the second century A.D. and is a fascinating anachronism much visited by today's tourists. The Mithraic grotto, lined with stone benches carved out of the rock and now illuminated by a weird green light, is relatively small and probably held no more than thirty or forty worshipers at a time. At the time of Mithras' greatest popularity there were many Mithraea serving Rome's million inhabitants, but increasing pressure from Christianity, which it resembled in many respects, led to the cult's total decline by the fourth century.

The Christian Church (which adopted so many Mithraic customs and celebrations) managed to get it banned in both Rome and Alexandria by about A.D. 376. In Constantine's day coins were still being struck in honor of the invincible sun god, but Julian (A.D. 331–363) was almost its last official supporter. Half a century earlier, Diocletian had ordered a mass assembly of the Roman armies for a pagan festival of sacrifice to renew their "waxing fervor" for the pantheon of Roman gods. But it was what one historian calls "an inevitable reaction against violence under Diocletian rule" that hastened the downfall of paganism in ancient Rome.

So far we have barely strayed from the Forum and neighboring areas such as the Capitoline and Palatine hills. But temples to the various pagan divinities sprang up all over Rome, especially in the trio of new forums built by Trajan, Augustus, and Vespasian to supplement the Forum Romanum. Livy and other classical authors mentioned more than fifty temples, not only to the major deities of Jupiter, Juno, Janus, Venus, and Fortune, but to such minor gods as Valor, Fidelity, Modesty, Hope, and Intelligence. Down by the river, in what was once the Forum Boarium ("cattle market"), two temples stood which still stand fairly complete today. They are believed to have been dedicated to Hercules and to Fortuna, the goddess of luck. The Herculean is circular and particularly impressive. It is believed to date from about the beginning of the first century. The nearby Fortuna temple is barred, but you can look through the gate and see remains of panels on the walls, inscriptions, and fragments of carved stones.

Not far from here, in the Tiber, is Rome's only island and this, too, could hardly be overlooked by the temple builders. Here, twenty-two miles before it empties into the sea, the sluggish Tiber flows past a present-day church and hospital, which seems particularly appropriate because the island housed Rome's very first "hospital," a shrine to Asclepius. How Rome came to adopt the Greek god of healing is recounted in an old tale, when, in the midst of a serious plague, the Romans were told by an oracle to fetch the god Asclepius from Epidaurus and mandated ten senators to the task. When the senators arrived at the temple in Greece, so the story goes, a serpent came out and crossed the city, settling down in their boat, and when the boat returned to Rome the serpent went to live on the island in the Tiber. So the temple was built there, a raven devoted to it for divination purposes, and regular sacrifices made to the god.

Asclepius, incidentally, was usually represented as an old man with a long beard, wearing a laurel wreath, with a dog or an owl at his feet, and carrying a wooden staff full of knots and around which a serpent was entwined. The serpent, whose worship has been universal throughout the world at various times, is often thought to be a symbol of life and recovery because of its habit of sloughing off its old skin and beginning anew.

The island temple had its annual festival on February 13, but, as in Epidaurus, welcomed the sick at any time. They were assigned to quiet rooms, sent to sleep on the fleeces of sacrificed lambs, and (although the historians are silent on this) may have been given something to encourage dreams. The supplicants were often put to sleep by gazing into mirrors on the surface of a fountain. Priests were constantly on call to interpret the patients' dreams, which were popularly supposed to be messages from the god telling how to recover from the ailment in question.

In the confusing way that the names of the old gods overlap, Asclepius is sometimes referred to as Faunus, the good spirit of the forests, plains, and fields who prompted fruitfulness in cattle.

No traces of the temple remain on the island today, although it is an extremely pleasant place to rest on a sunny Sunday afternoon. Though technically private property, the island is relatively accessible. Don't, however, be tempted to bathe in the filthy waters of the Tiber which lap its banks; it's doubtful if even Asclepius could cure the resulting sickness.

In recent times the Tiber has been described as "too large a stream to be harmless and too small to be useful," but in ancient times its sudden floods, or freshets, created disasters. Horace wrote about one, and more than thirty others occurred in the period up to the nineteenth century when bridges and banks were sufficiently strengthened to eliminate such floods. In ancient days building bridges over the Tiber was one of the tasks of the pontifices, who were the possessors of the mysterious magic concerning measures and numbers.

As the Roman legions fanned outward across Europe, their magical heritage traveled with them, and soon there were few parts of the Continent to which this arcane knowledge had not been spread.

Roman civilization, in effect, codified magical lore, refining and organizing it in the efficient manner it dealt with everything else. And when Roman civilization began to collapse, sapped by Christianity and other ills, magic disappeared along with it. There are those who maintain that civilization's "progress" has been downhill ever since.

11

Nemi

DIANA'S MIRROR LAKE AND THE CUMAEAN SIBYL

Two of the most fabled places of the ancient world are within an afternoon's drive of Rome, more or less in the same direction to the south. The nearer is what remains of the temple to Diana, built on the shores of a volcanic lake just outside the charming village of Nemi.

The pleasant two-hour drive to Nemi is a popular one with Romans, who take the opportunity on Sunday afternoons to stock up on salami and various other foods which are sold more cheaply there than in the city. South of Nemi is Pompeii, which we will talk about in the following chapter.

The route south is best made via the Appian Way, alongside which are crumbling tombs, domes, and columns that date back as much as 2,000 years. The road was once lined with huge villas, and in ancient times Romans delighted to be buried here because a law prohibited their burial within the city itself. Huge trees now alternate with decaying tombs, some massive, shading the road with memories. Gypsies find it a satisfactory place to pitch tents and peddle their wares, as they have doubtless done for centuries.

The road to Nemi eventually passes near to another shrine, the lake-

Illustration: Diana's White Roe. From a tapestry. Italy, sixteenth century.

side villa called Castel Gandolfo, which serves as the Pope's summer palace. Close by is what remains of the ancient town of Palestrina. This was said to have been founded when a poor peasant went into the nearby woods and found a tablet on which was engraved the future town's history. A temple was built in which the tablet was concealed in a statue representing the goddess Fortuna nursing Jupiter and Juno. In the place where the man found the tablet a tree began to pour forth honey, and diviners read into this event fortune and glory for Palestrina. The emperor Sulla attempted to destroy the town in the first century B.C., but after that a new and bigger temple was built on the ruins. This housed an oracle that people came from afar to consult. The oracle was outlawed when Rome became Christianized and the temple was destroyed, its ruins rediscovered but a couple of centuries ago.

In the hilltop village of Nemi itself, locals sip coffee at sidewalk cafés along cobbled streets. Beside the central fountain, from which villagers fill jugs of water pouring from the carved lions' heads, is a spectacular view of the lake and surrounding countryside. The air is wonderfully fresh.

A narrow, winding road leads down from the village, around the hillside to the rim of the volcanic lake, beside which Julius Caesar once built a villa whose ruins now lie under the water. It is a beautiful spot. Birds sing, grapes hang heavily on the vine, and there is greenery all around. At the end of the narrow road, signs point to the ruins of the temple in whose precincts a large family enjoying a lavish antipasto sits around a folding table. Everyone is cheerful and gestures vaguely in the direction of the ruins.

The temple at Nemi, discovered in 1871, was first excavated in 1885 by Sir John Saville Lumley. He maintained that in addition to being a place of worship and devotion it had also served as a hydrotherapeutic establishment whose healing waters flowed from springs in the lava rock. A marble pillar, three feet high, discovered in the temple, served as an inventory to its contents and listed various statues, a head of the goddess Diana, various bronze altars, and silver images.

The volcanic lake, beside which the temple used to sit, has receded now, and the distance between its shores and the temple's remains overgrown with orchards. During the 1930s, Mussolini ordered the lake to be dredged and the remains of two large ships were discovered, preserved in the freshwater mud. They were Roman vessels of a type very similar to sea-going ships and were housed in a specially-built museum at one end of the lake. This was closed for "renovations" some years ago and nobody seems to know if and when it will be reopened. Also in the museum are some stone anchors of a kind that once held definite symbolic significance; similar anchors have been found in Greek temples on Delos and at Delphi to which there are references in classical texts.

Usually such stone anchors have holes in them through which was threaded rope or fiber to attach them to the boat. Anchors of this sort were also found in the palace at Mallia, Crete, and at Malta's Tarxien temple, where one example was triangular and carved from soft limestone.

What remains of the temple to Diana at Nemi now has to be searched for diligently; only a semicircular arched wall built into the hillside like sculptured caves and almost covered by trees and foliage is what can be found. The concave stone archways are about twenty feet high and remain only at this one side. Conceivably the temple was quite wide and overlooked the lake; this is now several hundred yards farther down the valley. The lake was always called the Mirror of Diana and it seems reasonable to suppose that the temple stood on its shore. The first priest was, according to legend, a runaway slave named Varbius, and subsequent priests always obtained their position by killing their predecessor. There is a reference to this tradition in Ovid.

The goddess Diana, who "inspired men with enthusiasm and madness, and dreaded the sight of men so much that no man was allowed to enter her temple," was not only regarded as a goddess of the moon but as the personification of the teeming life of nature, both animal and vegetable. This goddess of the woodlands played a major part in early Roman worship. Sometime in the sixth century B.C., Servius Tullus, the sixth king of Rome, founded a temple to Diana along the Aventine which was shared by the Romans and their neighbors, the Sabines. At one time the diviners and soothsayers predicted that if a beautiful cow was sacrificed in the temple the country would benefit. Sabine worshipers took along such a cow to the temple, but before it could be sacrificed, a crafty Roman priest insisted that no sacrifice could be made unless the people concerned washed themselves, and as the Sabine priest went off to wash his hands in the Tiber, Roman priests instead sacrificed the cow.

Tullus (578 to 534 B.C.) was reputedly born of a mother who was a slave and Tarquinius, the king. Livy and other Roman historians have indicated he was of noble birth. Tullus' name is closely associated with other pagan deities, to whom he paid tribute, notably Fortuna the goddess of chance, good luck, and prosperity, who reputedly used to visit him secretly in his chambers for sexual dalliance. After Tullus' death, his statue was placed in her temple and despite a severe fire which subsequently destroyed the temple, this statue remained undamaged.

Plutarch wrote that when Fortuna first entered Rome, "she put off her wings and shoes because she planned to stay." Her major worshipers were newly-married women who prayed to retain their charms.

But back to Diana. Although it is not known when her temple was founded, her sacred day, long regarded as a holiday for slaves, has always been August 13, when annual sacrifices were made and tendered.

Sir James Frazer in his classic exposition *The Golden Bough* points out that a deity of the woods is naturally the patron of the animals and that "the crowning of hunting dogs on Diana's day was probably a purification ceremony to cleanse them from the guilt of having killed game, the creatures of the goddess." The "Golden Bough" of Frazer's title refers to mistletoe, a parasitic plant that claims many kinds of tree as host but is regarded as sacred only when it adorns the oak.

Frazer referred to Nemi as the famous grove of Diana where a priest named Rex Nemorensis, or "King of the Woods," held office by virtue of his vigilance. He could be succeeded as king by anybody who could pluck a bough from the sacred tree and slay him. Unless he was slain, the tree spirit, like the man, would die of old age and weakness, causing the doom of crops and herbs. So of necessity the kingship had a certain built-in obsolescence. Once in the temple here, was a bas-relief demonstrating the priest lying down wounded, holding his stomach to stop the bleeding, while nymphs claim victory for his adversary. This bas-relief is now in the museum at Palma de Majorca.

The first mention of the golden bough that lent such powers to its owner is in Virgil's *Aeneid,* in which he declares: "None may reach the shades without the passport of that golden sprout."

Virgil then goes on to write about the Cumaean sibyl (the one who offered the sacred books of knowledge to Tarquinius), to whom Aeneas pays a visit in her cave barred by bronze gates, beside gloomy Lake Avernus. As Virgil describes her, this priestess of Apollo must have appeared a forbidding creature when she offered a response to a consultant. "She changes her features and the color of her countenance; her hair springs up erect, her bosom heaves and pants, her wild heart beats violently, the foam gathers on her lips and her voice is terrible." And when she was possessed, Virgil added, "she paces to and fro in her cave and gesticulates as if she would expel the gods from her breast."

One of the Cumaean sibyl's peculiarities, moreover, was that when consulted she would write her predictions on oak leaves and lay them at the edge of the cave, from which they were blown hither and yon by the wind and often confusingly mixed up, making them all but unintelligible to their readers. The Cumaean sibyl, declared one historian, never sat on her tripod to give answers without first swallowing a few drops of the juice of the bay laurel.

This then was the lady to whom Aeneas came from Troy after Ulysses invaded the city and caused him to flee. Bidden by his father's ghost to visit him in the Elysian Fields (Hades), Aeneas stopped off here beside Lake Avernus and was told by the sibyl that he would find the key (the golden bough), and after visiting Hades would triumph over his foes and land in Latium with a new bride.

The remains of the ancient town of Cumae, and the adjoining caves, can still be inspected on a deserted hilltop between the main coastal highway and the sea. It is chockablock with antiquities, including the remains of a temple to Jupiter and the ruins of a temple to Apollo. There is also a majestic acropolis. The town was founded by Greek colonists in the eighth century B.C. and was captured by the Romans four centuries later. It declined steadily from Christian times until it was abandoned around the tenth century A.D.

Lake Avernus, filling the crater of an extinct volcano, is about half a mile wide, circular, and very deep. It is surrounded by high banks which in Virgil's time, says Charles Gayley in *The Classic Myths,* were covered with a gloomy forest. "Mephitic vapors rise from its waters so that no life is found on its banks and no birds fly over it." Very eerie.

It was here that Aeneas offered sacrifices to the infernal deities, Proserpine (Persephone), Hecate, and the Furies, and after rumblings from the earth and the great howling of dogs, the gods announced their presence. "Now," said the sibyl, "summon thy courage, for thou shalt need it." And she descended into the cave with Aeneas following. Immediately there were Furies, horrors, hissing hydras, and no end of other frightening sights. And when they reached the underground river, beside which some spirits had been waiting for 100 years to cross because they lacked the fare for Charon's leaky boat, they were confronted with the ferryman's three-headed watchdog Cerberus, his neck bristling with snakes. He barked with all three of his throats until the sibyl threw him a drugged cake, which he devoured. He then went instantly to sleep.

Eventually the pair reached the Elysian Fields where everybody looked blissfully happy, some playing sports and games, others dancing and singing. The region had a sun and stars all of its own and everything was bathed in a strange purple light.

Aeneas and the sibyl got a chance to chat together on the trip, and the seer confided that she had once been proposed to by Apollo. She had turned him down, thus losing her chance for eternal youth. But Apollo had promised her as many birthdays as there were grains in a handful of sand. She'd had 700 of them so far, she said, and had at least 300 still to go. "As my body shrinks up as the years increase in time, I shall be lost to sight; but my voice will remain and future ages will respect my sayings."

Wandering around this weird volcanic region, it is hard not to believe, even today, that the entrance to another world might be nearby. The whole coastline of this peninsula is steeped in mysteries; classical scholars have speculated for centuries on matching the landscape with ancient texts. The small valleys below Mount Miseno were believed to have been the site of the Elysian Fields and Lake Miseno was thought of as the mythical Stygian marshes where Charon plied his boat. From Lake Avernus a tunnel, more than 1,000 yards long, leads to the bleak and now-empty cave in which the Cumaean sibyl lived.

The cave is rather remarkable, consisting of a long tunnel narrower at the top than at the floor. It stretches a long way and has many fissures and clefts opening from it toward the sea. There are also minor tunnels and a large room in which the oracle was presumably housed.

The nearby city of Naples was reputedly founded by Virgil, to whom many magical exploits were once attributed. It was common during medieval times for scholars to transform an ancient poet or philosopher into a master of the black arts. Virgil was said to have covered his garden with an umbrella of air that kept out the rain, to have built an enchanted bridge which could transport him anywhere, and to have placed the bronze image of a fly above the city's gates which kept out noxious insects for eight years.

According to a Renaissance source, Virgil was the son of a wealthy Roman senator who noted "extraordinary portents" when he was born. He was sent to study magic at the University of Toledo, where he quickly acquired a background in the occult arts. While Virgil was still at Toledo his father died, involving him in a dispute over the estate with the emperor from whom at first he could get no satisfaction. Patiently Virgil waited until harvest time and then "shrouded the whole of his rightful inheritance with a vapor so dense that the emperor's men were unable to approach it. Under its cover Virgil's workers gathered in the entire crop with perfect security. This done, the mist vanished."

Apparently Virgil made amends with the emperor, for a later account tells of him building in Rome a stately palace for his imperial majesty whose four corners corresponded to the four corners of the city. Whenever the emperor chose to stand in any one of these corners he could overhear all that transpired in the corresponding corner of Rome.

Another of the apocryphal stories told about the young Virgil is how he once extinguished all the fires in Rome. This was in revenge for a humiliation he suffered at the hands of a young lady who made a fool of him by hauling him halfway up a tower in a basket and then leaving him dangling. Once all the fires were out, Virgil insisted that the only way they could be restored was for the young lady to stand nude in the center of Rome for three days and for anyone who wanted a light to go and get it from her. "This was the most popular of the legends relating to the magician Virgil," wrote Thomas Right, early in the last century, "and is frequently alluded to in old writings. The story itself is generally told with coarse details better suited to those times than the present."

Virgil was buried at Pausillipo, near Naples, with which he is still closely associated, and where he was also said to have built a tower on which he set an intricately balanced series of objects, including an egg. "When the egg stirreth so should the town of Naples quake, and when the egg break then should this town sink."

Naples is no longer the beautiful city it once was. It has suffered numerous cholera epidemics, owing mainly to a polluted water supply, and is noticeably poorer and more decrepit than many other Italian cities. Its major attraction in recent times has been as a sort of way station for visitors en route to the ruined city of Pompei. Even passengers aboard boats making brief stops on the way to Piraeus or Marseilles are whisked out to the ruins for a rapid tour. Pompeii is too important to miss if one gets that close.

12

Pompeii

RELICS FROM THE ASHES

IDEALLY, Pompeii should be visited at night, for in the daytime the clattering of tourist feet tends to dispel any romantic visions of its ancient life. To see the moon rising over the ruined city and to conjure up the chariots and the toga-clad citizens going about their business requires the kind of contemplation and imagination that is best exercised in relative peace and tranquility.

But don't be led into believing Pompeii remains open at night. The wishful thinking of the Michelin Guide to the contrary, the enclosed ruins are, with infrequent exceptions, closed at 5 P.M. Occasional theater performances are given in the open-air stadium on summer evenings. If there is a chance to attend one of these, don't miss it.

The first thing that astonishes visitors is the immensity of the place. This is no mere batch of ruins, but literally an abandoned city that needs time to be fully appreciated. Official guides recommend about three hours for even a quick tour, which would cover only the main highlights. These would certainly include the public bath with its decoratively carved panels, the immense amphitheater and adjoining stadium, and the civil forum which, as befitting the center of public life, is as

Illustration: Dionysus bringing the vine across the seas. From a Greek bowl, about 535 B.C.

spacious as present-day Times Square.

Off this forum is the museum, which offers a good introduction to the ruins. It displays gold and turquoise rings, vases, fragments of pottery, and grotesque models of human and animal victims caught on that fateful August night when Vesuvius erupted without warning almost 1,900 years ago, covering the city with a layer of lava and filling the sky with smoke and dust. "Now it was day elsewhere," reported Pliny the Younger, "but there night darker and denser than any night."

Because of the stunning swiftness of this first-century eruption, Pompeii's day-to-day life was interrupted in midstream, so to speak, preserving commercial life and pagan temple side by side, just as it was.

The macabre figures displayed in the museum, animal and human, are plaster reproductions of the victims caught up in the attitudes in which they died and were made by pouring a quick-setting liquid into identations in the earth which marked where the bodies were discovered. Other relics in the museum, all uncovered during the excavations, include pots, charred cloth, marble statues, bone needles, bronze oil lamps, cooking stoves, and gold earrings and bracelets as well as other jewelry. The walls are covered with fragments of decorated pottery from the temple of Hercules and the famous ROTAS, OPERA, TENET, AREPO, SATOR symbol which has been found in many other places and which is known to have had magical significance.

Outside the museum is the central avenue which connects the plaza with the arena at the far end of town. In between are an amazing succession of shops, homes, temples, all easily identifiable.

It is surprising to see how much modern town planning has followed ancient concepts. The main street of Pompeii leads out of town to the sports stadium where the crowds could gather without interrupting traffic, just as today. The wide, cobbled streets are regularly crossed by large stepping stones, which are separated by grooves through which chariots could pass abreast at regular intervals; carved stone wells or springs, often lavishly sculptured, slowed traffic at certain points to one way. Houses and shops line both sides of nearly all the streets, stretching back to gardens with tiled walls, patios, altars, and pillared courtyards. Here and there, some frescoes or wall paintings are covered by glass or by canvas drapes to prevent the sun from fading them any further.

The largest building in Pompeii stood at the southwest end of the forum and was a basilica dedicated to Orpheus, the legendary singer first glorified by Pythagoras and his followers. The term Orphic rites usually refers to Pythagorean themes, and after this famous school at Crotona, on Italy's southeast coast, was disbanded in the fifth century B.C. its members became Orphists. Orphists wore white robes, believed in the transmigration of souls, abhorred bloody sacrifices, and abstained from meat, fish, eggs, and beans. Uneducated and superstitious women also were especially attracted to Orphism, we are told, prompting a class of religious beggars who roamed around with books and sacred utensils offering expiation to all who would pay for it.

Plato mentions Orpheus more than any other writer, for he was greatly influenced by Pythagorean doctrines, and "Orpheus" seems to have been used as a sort of collective pen name by poets dealing with these themes and as a touchstone for magical practices. What is known as Orphic literature comprises miscellaneous verses, hymns, and the collection known as *The Rhapsodies.*

Orpheus is often considered to have been a mortal, yet he had such extensive musical gifts that when he played his tortoise-shell lyre the creatures of the wild gathered around and quietly listened. He descended once into Hades to rescue his wife, Eurydice—his singing having gained him permission from Pluto and Persephone to lead her back to life. Contrary to instructions, however, he looked back before they were home free and she was lost to him forever. Orpheus is often associated with Dionysus, or Bacchus, and one tale of his death is the familiar theme of him being torn to pieces by Thracian bacchantes.

It was at the basilica to Orpheus that the bankers and merchants of Pompeii met to discuss business. Here also judgments were made.

There were other temples around the forum, notably those to Jupiter and Apollo. But the temple of major interest in the city today is that of Isis. It sits on a high podium in its own garden not far from the smaller, triangular forum. In its southeast corner is a small room which leads to an underground cavity, and there was kept the water from the Nile.

Isis, whose cult first developed in Egypt at least twelve centuries before Christ, came to be widely worshiped throughout the ancient world as a goddess of the earth. She had been associated with love, healing, magic, and the moon. The ancient Greeks identified her with their own Demeter and erected shrines to her in Athens and on Delos. The Romans equated her with their grain goddess Ceres. Sir James Frazer explains that she is described in a Greek epigram as "she who has given birth to the fruits of the earth" and that both Greek and Roman artists depicted her carrying a sheaf of wheat.

The Pompeian temple of Isis was built during the turn of the first century B.C. and was destroyed by an earthquake in A.D. 63. It had barely been restored when the city was devastated by the volcanic eruption sixteen years later. The Isis cult in Rome, at first unrecognized by the state, finally gained acceptance, and became a rival of the emerging Christian faith.

Worship of the Earth Mother had undergone remarkable change during the rise of the Roman Empire. First-century B.C. devotees of Isis observed a strict regimen of atonement in prayer and penance for past sins. The cult abstained from flesh meat and sensual pleasures. Votaries were called to the faith in a dream and after a period of preliminary training were admitted to "the Mysteries," which held the promise of "a true perception of divine light." Apuleius in *The Golden Ass* describes the rites of initiation into the mysteries of Isis but concludes: "Now you have heard what happened but I fear you are still none the wiser."

Although Apollo, Orpheus, Jupiter, Juno, Fortuna, and Isis were honored at Pompeii, we are soon made aware that the city belonged to another—the god of many joys—Dionysus. His symbols are everywhere: on the walls, floors, and in the gardens of private homes. In mosaic tiles, paintings, and sculptures are Dionysian dolphins, goats, leopards, masks, grapes, amphoras, blackbirds, and depictions of the god himself. The tributes to Dionysus culminate in what is probably the most admired building in Pompeii: a house on the outskirts of town known as the Villa of the Mysteries. Its walls still retain excellent frescoes, which probably date back to the first century B.C. and which illustrate themes that even today have not been fully explained. It is a fairly long walk from the ruined town to the villa, along a road lined with tall cypress trees. The villa closes early (officially it is 5 P.M.), as the guards seem unreasonably anxious to get home. At night it is guarded by an angry watchdog which wanders around discouraging trespassers. There are numerous rooms and halls, but the fragmentary wall paintings of the great hall are surprisingly less clear than in the official booklet (sold at the site), which reproduces them in much more vivid color than the originals have retained.

Professor Vittorio Macchioro, in his book *The Villa of the Mysteries,* suggests that what once served as a dining hall was adapted to the purpose of initiation into the Dionysian mysteries and that the scenes depicted on its walls detailed the ceremony.

The initiate, a young woman, appears in each of the eight episodes illustrating the various stages of the rite. Almost life-size figures, costumed as Greeks of the fifth century B.C. and painted against a red ochre background in a manner reminiscent of the same period, dominate the room.

In the course of the mural's story the mystic bride of Dionysus dons the ritual veil, is instructed in the sacred nature of her vow, partakes of a purifying repaste (the lustral agape) and then celebrates an allegorical rebirth corresponding to that undergone by Dionysus. Symbolically in communion with the deity, the neophyte now faces terrible tests of her faith. She is made aware of how the god, as a child, beheld his future in a magic mirror—and it is a future in which he is killed and reborn. The final frescoes portray the ritual flagellation symbolizing death and her rebirth as a semidivine figure, dancing wildly, imbued with the spirit of Dionysus.

Other characters take part in the painted pantomime. Silenus, the drunken old fat tutor who was associated with Pan as well as Dionysus, is represented playing a lyre. Dionysus appears in his goat form called Zagreus; Ariadne, the Cretan princess who became beloved by the god, is the winged figure witnessing the revelation of the symbol of fertility —the phallus in the sacred basket. Numerous priestly attendants, wearing myrtle crowns, and satyrs with pointed ears observe the proceedings. The high priestess carrying the *thyrsus* (the pine-cone-tipped staff) who is present at the height of the drama may be a portrait of the villa's owner, a member of the Istacici family.

The various ceremonies known as "the Mysteries" honored many deities, took place at a variety of sites, and were similar in content if not in form. Professor Macchioro conjectures that with a series of ritual acts the participants attempted to reproduce "the gestures and actions attributed to the Divinity." As, for example, in the later Christian ceremonies the eating of bread and the drinking of wine symbolically joined the partaker with Jesus.

Macchioro believed that in the beginning "the mystery was a purely magical ceremony but with time it acquired a spiritual and moral content." Which is to say the magical rites were absorbed into a religious philosophy.

According to Greek myths, Dionysus was torn to pieces and eaten by the Titans—sent by the jealous Hera—and Macchioro explains: "Mankind had birth from the ashes of the Titans smitten by the thunderbolt of Zeus in punishment for their crime. This is why all men bear the burden of the Titans' crime; but as the Titans devoured Zagreus, man has within him also the nature of Dionysus. Theologians said that it was the Titanic nature innate in the body from which man must free himself to reunite with the Dionysiac nature through the agency of the mysteries." More simply put, the Dionysian aspect of man, i.e., the wild part of human nature, can be denied only at peril. It must be given an outlet.

Greek drama originated with Dionysus and its forms, comedy and tragedy, were related to his ritual. The word *tragedy* comes from the Greek *tragōidía,* meaning "goat-song." Worshipers of Dionysus sometimes substituted a goat for their god, sacrificed the animal, and sacramentally drank its blood. The *tragōidía* may refer to a dirge sung at the ceremony.

The violent death and dismemberment of Dionysus parallels not only the Egyptian Osiris myth (his murder and dismemberment by Set and subsequent regeneration through Isis), but also the resurrection theme of the Christian faith.

Hesiod is the first to call wine the gift of Dionysus, and in Thrace and Phrygia the god's worshipers sought to become possessed by/assimilated with him through drinking and wild dancing. "By consuming as much wine as possible, the followers of the god thought they themselves could become divine," writes C. A. Burland in *Secrets of the Occult.* They would race through the woods, tear people and animals apart, and return home happy "with the glorious memory of having danced with the god."

According to Greek mythology Dionysus was born under unusual circumstances at Thebes. He was the son of Zeus and a mortal woman, Semele, the daughter of Cadmus. Zeus, in the form of a man, had fallen in love, courted, and married Semele. Unfortunately, his passionately jealous wife (and sister) Hera continually thwarted all Zeus' happy unions with other mistresses and wives. Hera caused Semele to request Zeus to reveal himself as a God, knowing that this would result in Semele's death. As Zeus revealed himself, Semele, who was carrying their child, was consumed by lightning and died instantly. Zeus snatched the unborn Dionysus from the ashes and implanted him in his thigh, where he grew into a full formed baby. Hera's hatred was not abated by Semele's death and she stalked Dionysus for the rest of his life despite Zeus' efforts to protect his child.

Dionysus possessed the gift of prophecy and at Delphi came to be on equal terms with Apollo, taking over in winter when his brother vacated the shrine. It was as if the myth-makers were saying that moderation must have a respite of abandon. Eventually, too, the god took his place at Eleusis, joined with Demeter in whose honor the rites had been founded. Both being deities of the earth, it seemed a natural association. Representing the grain and the vine, both reflected the resurrection theme and the capacity to rise from the dead. It became the custom to bury the dead with Dionysian hymns, which it was believed would guard the deceased in the underworld.

The mathematician Thoen of Smyrna said there were five stages to the Dionysian rites: (1) baptism in the sea for purification; (2) instruction; (3) the scene of beholding; (4) initiation; and (5) the condition of bliss. Herodotus avoids using the god's name (It is "forbidden to speak of the death of the god who is the life of the world.") when he describes the five-part ritual as containing the sacrifice, mourning, search, discovery, and resurrection. What began as a rural worship of regeneration evolved into a creed of wisdom. The mysteries were revered by the best minds of an era regarded by many as the ultimate in human achievement.

Pompeii preserves that moment in time when the gifts of the Greeks had degenerated into empty ceremony. The ascetic, life-denying adherents of Isis had replaced the joy of living implicit in the worship of Demeter and Dionysus. The mysteries of the earth deities were celebrated secretly in a remote villa. And although Pompeii had at one time revered Dionysus, or Bacchus, the ruins suggest that it was only in his capacity as the god of wine. The old truths were lost.

There is no doubt that Pompeii is totally fascinating. In addition to the haunting Villa of the Mysteries, other houses have decorative contents, many of them delightfully placed around interior courtyards with pools, fountains, and statues. In summertime the streets are crowded with tourists from all over the world clutching cameras and guidebooks and pausing at crossroads to study their maps. It is easy to miss some of the subtleties such as the tiny statuettes which line the walls above head level on many streets and the occasional entrances through city walls to the sewer which ran under the streets and for centuries efficiently carried away the refuse.

Now and then you will pass something labeled a taverna with a marble table, a bakery with its mill and oven, or a shop with an amphora still marked with the name of the fish sauce it once contained. The setting is beautiful, with mountains on two sides and the domes of nearby churches and houses lying outside the walls in the foreground.

But, however much time we allot to it, Pompeii will always retain its undiscovered secrets and eventually we must move on. Paganism did not die when Pompeii died, but it was already under pressure and within a century or two there was no wish by the new rulers of Rome, the Christians, to dig under the ashes for traces of an alien cult. Excavation of Pompeii finally began in 1748.

When paganism died in Rome the old gods were forgotten, and Europe began to bow to different creeds. It was not until the eighth century that magic began to stir again and that was when the Moors swept across the Mediterranean and set up their outposts in Spain. It is there our quest takes us next.

II

13
Toledo

PORTALS OF MOORISH WISDOM

SPAIN'S OFFICIAL AND POLITICAL CAPITAL is Madrid, but its artistic capital, and for almost 1,000 years the center of its cultural life, is Toledo, a mere forty miles to the southwest.

For centuries visitors have exclaimed over its glories. "Toledo," wrote Théophile Gautier, "has something of the convent, of the fortress and also of the harem—memories left there by the Moors who passed that way."

The majestic, brooding grandeur of this fortress city, so high above the winding Tagus River it seems to be of the clouds, was described by Cervantes as "that rocky gravity, glory of Spain and light of her cities."

Its winding streets, its soaring towers and domes, its crests and coats of arms surmounting portals that have remained unchanged for centuries, invest Toledo with a regal splendor that is unmatched anywhere else in the country. The whole city has been declared a national monument, and indeed it is.

The Romans, who arrived in 200 B.C., were the first to take advantage of its strategic position and fortify it. A few scattered remains of their presence can still be found. But after the collapse of the Roman Empire,

Illustration: Moorish Astrologers. Medieval woodcut.

the Spanish peninsula was wide open to invaders and first came the Vandals, then the Visigoths. Their court at Toledo became the capital of the fifth-century Christian world, their last king the greedy and ambitious Roderick.

But in A.D. 711 came the Arab invasion from North Africa and with the capture of Saragossa in 714 the Moors began an occupation of Spain that lasted for four centuries. They governed well, built extensively, and were tolerant to both Christians and Jews. The schools of medicine and philosophy that the Moors established in Toledo included judicial astrology and other occult lore, bringing to the European continent all that residue of magic and mystery that had made Egypt's Alexandria famous for what came to be known as "the Black Arts."

Yet what was for Europe "the Dark Ages" was a time of great triumph for the Moors. There lived among them Geber, one of the earliest alchemists; Ben Musa, who invented algebra in the tenth century; and Avicenna, the eleventh-century physician, author of half a dozen works on the philosopher's stone and whose encyclopedia of medicine was the fullest codification of the subject since the Roman Galen, nine centuries earlier.

Despite the undoubted benefits the Moorish civilization had given Europe, their dark-skinned presence was regarded as an insult and was feared as the spearhead of an invasion that would overrun the Continent with African hordes. Until the Moors were driven out, which finally happened in the twelfth century, there was constant plotting by the European powers to get rid of them. Granada became their main center, and they lasted there for two centuries after their other Spanish strongholds—Seville, Cordova, Ronda, and Toledo—had fallen.

It was at Toledo, however, that their coming was clearly forecast, if the old legends are to be believed. Here at Toledo once stood the renowned tower of Hercules, built by a king "who was mighty and wise beyond all men who had ever lived" and who had foreseen "that the kingdom of the Goths" would eventually be ruined by a ruler whose pride and lust would come ahead of his people's welfare.

John Lomas, recounting the story in *Travelling in Spain,* says: "And so he had built this palace of jaspers and richly colored marbles, and himself sealing up the door had ordained before his unaccountable disappearance from the earth, that each successive monarch should add another seal within a few days of his accession to the throne, and should sacredly forebear from seeking out the mysteries of the building."

All went well for many years until the accession of King Roderick, "the ill-fated and ill-natured [king] who cared nothing for any custom, religion or rite nor suffered these things to stand between his lust and himself." The legend tells how Roderick ransacked the enchanted palace:

... and what awful confirmation he met there ... how, as he was grasping at the goodly things he had come upon they turn to veriest ashes and how, as he and his companions fled terror-stricken from the scene a tongue of fire darted out of the lurid blackness that had gathered around him and the whole edifice crashed down into a heap of half-buried ruins is well-known to those who are willing to sit at tradition's feet.

Then the Arab hosts speedily made their appearance in the south. Swiftly they overran Andalusia, scattering the puny force which the Gothic viceroy opposed to them. Within two years the whole of Spain lay bleeding at their feet.

The now-inaccessible Cuevas de Hercules, which once stood below the tower, is buried behind a wall that forms part of St. Gine's Street in Toledo.

The reputation of the University of Toledo as a center of magic spread far and wide and long outlasted the Moors. There are innumerable references to some of its more famous students. Virgil, of course, and it was here in 1217 that the Scottish magician and scholar Michael Scot translated Arabic texts to take back to Oxford. And half a century later, the famous Portuguese Dominican monk known as Blessed Gil of Santarem took Toledo's statutory seven-year course under the guidance of a stranger who offered to teach him magic in return for signing his soul over to the devil and sealing the pact with blood. Eventually Gil repented of his decision, burned his *grimoire,* and returned to Santarem in Portugal where he died, apparently without further consequence, in May 1295.

Johannes Faust may have visited the occult university at Toledo, and among those who studied there was the French magician Nicholas Flamel, who sought help from the Cabalists in translating a twenty-one-page book made from tree bark which he had picked up from a bookstall for two florins. Every seventh page of the book was free from writing but inscribed with a serpent swallowing rods, a serpent crucified on a cross, or an arid expanse of desert. The more Flamel studied it, the more mystified he became: it was obviously an alchemical text of some sort. At his wife's suggestion he went to consult the Spanish rabbis on how to read it. His two-year stay was fruitful, because on returning he was able to transmute mercury into silver and gold, and although he failed to discover the *elixir vitae* he reputedly lived to the age of 116, taking the secret of the book with him when he died in 1417. His wealth was distributed to churches and hospitals.

By the fifteenth century Toledo's magical fame was widespread enough for the Italian poet Luigi Pulci to comment:

> The city of Toledo erst
> Fostered the lore of necromancy
> Professors there in magic versed
> From public chair taught pyromancy

Or geománcy; or rehearsed
Experiments in hydromancy.

The compactness of the hilltop city, with its resultant lack of space, has produced a curious jumble of architectural styles. Many of the older buildings have been demolished to make way for newer ones, but others survive side by side as chronological anachronisms. The only Moorish building that remains intact is the pleasant but fairly small tenth-century mosque of El Cristo de la Luz, with its horseshoe arches and beautifully shaped domes. According to legend, the Christians profaned this mosque by celebrating the first Mass there when they reconquered the city. The adjoining Puerta del Sol is also Moorish, built in the twelfth century by Arab labor after the city was once again in Christian hands.

Many of the artistic treasures of Toledo are to be found in the amazingly impressive cathedral, built between 1227 and 1497. "Sumptuous without gaudiness, austere without gloominess, it is one of the noblest specimens of Gothic architecture the world affords," according to one historian. And it is an astonishing place with its innumerable grottoes and chapels, elaborately decorated stone works, immensely high stained-glass windows, statuary, and fenced-off nooks and corners. The paintings, sculptures, stained glass, and wrought-iron work make it more of a museum than anything else. It is also gigantic.

Three other museums should also be noted: The Hospital de la Santa Cruz, a fifteenth-century building that is as splendid as any of the valuable (mostly religious) paintings it contains; the adjoining Archeological Museum, and the charming house in which the sixteenth-century painter El Greco is said to have lived and in which some of his paintings are now displayed. Under the house are some caves in which a later tenant, the Marquis of Villena, is believed to have conducted a school of magic and alchemical experiments.

Just as Toledo was the geographical center of Spain, coveted because of its strategic position where major routes converged, so was the main plaza the center of Toledo. And the name the Arabs gave to it, Plaza de Zocodover ("market"), prevails to this day.

In this square the Arabs held their markets and traded rare spices from Malaya, tapestries from India, and the finest silks from Damascus. The market is still held in the plaza each Tuesday, but the products of today seem less exotic. The Alcazar soars above the square, at the city's highest point, but to get there we must pass the famous Posada de la Sangre, in one of whose rooms Miguel de Cervantes, author of *Don Quixote,* stayed and wrote. The Alcazar—"that immense pile, the irregular in a picturesque line of buildings at least one half of them convents each with its tower and terrace and hanging gardens," as Henry D. Inglis, an English traveler noted in 1831—dates back to Roman times. There is very little to be seen today of earlier periods and all the emphasis is upon the Alcazar's role in the Spanish Civil War when it served as a refuge for Franco's forces who successfully withstood an epic siege. Today the Alcazar serves as a Civil War museum.

The vast square which adjoins the Alcazar at the top of the hill is used as a bus terminal but is spacious enough for private cars to park. For transients in VW buses, it is well-nigh perfect, offering excellent views, public toilets, and no parking attendants until mid-morning. Even then the fee is minimal and it is advisable to leave the car and negotiate the narrow cobbled streets on foot, taking care to acquire a map first. The streets, lined with souvenir shops and cafés, are extremely confusing and it is easy to find oneself going around in circles and getting lost, particularly as it is impossible to see over (or between) the towering buildings.

The winding river Tagus, "which circles the town like some green viper in its gorge," says V. S. Pritchett, is crossed by three bridges. One, the Puente de Alcantara, stands on the site of an Arab bridge built in the ninth century and swept away by a flood in 1257. Although rebuilt by King Alfonso X (the Learned), it is now considered unsafe for all but pedestrian traffic. Automobiles use the new bridge further down the stream. The third bridge, also attributed to Alfonso, bears a sculptured head over the central arch and is reputedly a likeness of the wife of the original architect. Legend maintains that the architect made an error in building and was worried that when the scaffolding was removed the bridge would collapse. Supposedly his wife set fire to the wood during the night and the bridge fell, concealing the "error," because it had to be rebuilt.

Not far from this bridge is an ancient keep known as Baño de la Cava, which owes its name to having been the bathing place of Florinda, the daughter of a local count in the days of Don Rodrigo, the last of the Gothic kings. Rodrigo—that same Roderick we have encountered in connection with the tower of Hercules—reputedly fell in love with Florinda, but finding his love unrequited, raped her, thus bringing down the vengeance of her father who joined the invading Moors in bringing about the king's downfall.

On the riverbank near the Puente de Alcantara, in the northeast part of town, once stood the Palace of Galiana. Only crumbling ruins remain today of the palace where once the Moorish king of Guadalajara and Charlemagne fought for the hand of Galiana, the only daughter of King Galafre and "the most beautiful Moorish lady of Moorish lands." The Frenchman won the fight and whisked Galiana away, but it is said that on moonlit nights one can still see the flash of the swords and hear the cries of the combatants as the fight is endlessly reenacted in ghostly pantomime.

Overlooking the ruins is the ninth-century Castle of San Servando, once occupied by the Knights Templar whose task it was to guard the entrance to the city.

The southwestern portion of town, on the banks of the Tagus, has always been known as Judería and has been the Jewish ghetto since the early Christian era. The Jews are said to have given Toledo its name, from the Hebrew word *toledoth,* meaning "city of the generations." King Peter, often known as "the Cruel" favored the Jews and this favoritism led directly to his murder and a massacre of the Jews in 1350.

Jews were living in Toledo as early as the sixth century, according to the *Jewish Encyclopedia,* which adds that they assisted the Arabs with their conquest of the city in A.D. 715. Although they were later granted full equality with the Christians when Alfonso X retook the city, their position later weakened and anti-Semitic feeling twice culminated in riots and massacres.

In 1260, however, the Jewish community was granted permission to construct "the largest and most beautiful synagogue in Spain," which today (as the Church of Sta. María la Blanca!) is a national monument.

It was about this time in Toledo (during the thirteenth century) that the mystical form of thought known as the Cabala came to be studied and practiced. Its origins were attributed to a second-century rabbi named Simeon bar Yochai, said to have escaped persecution from the Romans by hiding in a cave. Actually the real author of the most important cabalistic work, *The Zohar,* was the thirteenth-century writer Moses de Leon, who incorporated numerous earlier teachings.

The name Cabala, with its variant spellings, is derived from the Hebrew *qabbalah,* meaning "the received lore," and according to the occultist S. L. MacGregor Mathers, "refers to the custom of handing down the esoteric knowledge by oral transmission and is nearly allied to 'tradition.' "

Oral tradition though it may have been originally, the Cabala came to be written down as an exceedingly complex, multileveled form of thought involving among other things numerology, astrology, magic squares, and cosmic images. "Natural magic depends largely on man himself," says the *Jewish Encyclopedia,* "for according to the Cabalah, all men are endowed with insight and magical powers which they may develop."

Moving south, in the opposite direction of the river's course, we come to the magnificent synagogues, the chief of which—the one now called Sta. María la Blanca—was where the Jewish community assembled all through the thirteenth and fourteenth centuries to hear the reading of the sacred books. After another violent racial clash in 1405 in which many Jews were slain by newly converted Christians, the building became a Catholic church and then a convent. It was restored as a synagogue and designated a national monument in the past century.

Its exterior is modest, but the snow-white beauty of its interior—

from which it derives its name—is punctuated with thirty-two octagonal pillars whose graceful symmetry is awe-inspiring.

Not far away, adjoining the house of El Greco where the great Cretan painter lived in the sixteenth century, is the Synagogue of the Transito, built around 1366 by Samuel Levi, personal friend of and treasurer to King Peter I. Expense was no object, according to history, and today the synagogue is admired as an architectural marvel.

A magnificent ceiling, constructed of cedar wood, envelops a vast rectangle—78 feet by 32 feet—whose four walls are covered from top to bottom with exquisite filigree work as elaborate as fine embroidery.

It was already old by the year 1577 when El Greco (Domenikos Theotokopoulos) first arrived at Toledo to be enchanted by the city's magic and mystery. He remained there to paint, and to ponder, and when he died he bequeathed to the city many of his best works, which can still be admired in the house and museum that bear his name.

El Greco was born on Crete in 1541. He lived in Toledo for thirty-seven years. The city itself was uniquely suited to his style of painting. His curious but effective manner of elongating forms doesn't seem especially exaggerated when one compares today's Toledo with the El Greco masterpiece *View of Toledo* in New York's Metropolitan Museum of Art. The rocky landscape rises sharply, dramatically within narrow limits, thrusting into the lightning-shot clouds.

Long before the famous Greek painter's arrival, however, his beloved city had relinquished its Moorish rule and was retaken by the Christians. It was another "El," the legendary El Cid, sometimes regarded as "the King Arthur of Spain," who was the eventual conqueror of the Moors. El Cid's reputation rests mostly on a 3,700-line epic poem, a compilation of ballads written around A.D. 1200, about the real-life Rodrigo Diaz de Bivas (born c. 1030).

After a bitter seven-year siege, Toledo was retaken in 1085 by El Cid, and the Moslems retreated to Granada. But they never quite abandoned the idea that their time would come again. "They still preserve with care the keys of their old houses," reported Henry Blackburn after a visit to Algiers in the middle of the last century. "They have waited for centuries and still wait (it may be) for some kingly summons from the walls of the Alhambra. But the long-awaited messenger makes no sign; the Moors and their Spanish paradise are yet divided. Years pass on, the pattern of the key is now of a past age and the Mediterranean rolls between them still."

Although the Moors were finally driven out—"the total collapse of Moorish civilization remains one of the mysteries of history," writes Cecilia Hill in *Moorish Towns in Spain*—the legacy of superstition and mysticism with which they infused Spain lives on. By the late fifteenth century, as a result of the furor over the infamous Torralba case, the Grand Inquisitor, Don Alfonso Manriquez, felt obliged to issue an edict enjoining all good Christians to report to the tribunal any instances of their fellow citizens practicing magic. Specifically he asked for reports on persons invoking spirits for divination purposes; persons reading or keeping *grimoires* or other magical manuscripts; persons making mirrors, vials of glass, "or other vessels in order thereby to control or therein to contain some spirit who should reply to his inquiries and aid his projects." And not only the practice of astrology was banned, but also a formidable list of related divinatory arts including geomancy (earth), hydromancy (water), aeromancy (air or weather), pyromancy (fire), anthroposcopy (facial features), theomancy (oracles), cleromancy (dice or lots), cheiromancy (hands), oneiromancy (dreams), capnomancy (smoke), tephromancy (sacrificial ashes), necromancy (communication with spirits of the dead), "or any other magic craft."

The main event that brought all this about, the Torralba case, had been concluded in 1528 when a man named Zugriga confessed to the Inquisition that he had copied from an occult text a magical formula that had brought him success at gaming. The book had been handed to him, he said, by his friend Eugenio Torralba, a man who while in the household service of the Bishop of Volterra had studied medicine and acquired a spirit named Zequiel who kept him informed of various plots against church officials and taught him palmistry and the casting of horoscopes.

Zugriga told the Inquisition that Torralba had instructed him to copy the magical formula from the book in his own hand, and to do it on a Wednesday—the day dedicated to Mercury, god of sharpers and thieves. Torralba, he said, had also boasted of being conducted to Rome by some magical aerial transport that flew him there and back with great speed. (Michael Scot, incidentally, had made similar claims three centuries before.)

Denounced by a repentant Zugriga—possibly his gaming luck had declined—Torralba was arrested and examined. He was condemned to make a public abjuration of his heresy and magic and had to wear the heretic's *san benito,* a yellow garment emblazoned with a cross.

But the most far-reaching effect of this notorious case was the Grand Inquisitor's edict, which in addition to the prohibitions already listed also denounced those who entertained familiars and flies. This last reference is the clearest possible reminder that Moorish magic was still prevalent, it being an ancient Arabic belief that three million flies had once been imprisoned by Solomon in a bottle of black glass and kept safely in a well near Babylon until locals in search of treasure broke the bottle and released them.

14

Granada

MOONLIGHT MAGIC AND
GYPSY LORE

THE WAY BETWEEN THE TWO CITIES OF TOLEDO AND GRANADA is the fabled route of Don Quixote, the Man of La Mancha. Most of the provinces of Ciudad Real and Albacete, as well as wide stretches of Toledo and Cuenca, lend their varied geography and scenery to make up this historic mosaic, and with its windmills and huge pottery jars it constantly reminds the traveler of that lovable knight.

Spaniards have a penchant for selecting strategic sites on hilltops, especially those jutting up dramatically from the midst of flat plains, and erecting on them enormous plywood advertisements ten times larger than life. These figures—a jolly Michelin man with igloo-shaped suit, an exotic bird advertising Perdiz, a huge black bull for some sherry, a nose-diving airplane, occasionally giant figures gazing admiringly at billboards—are invariably on ridges, presenting an eye-catching perspective that dominates the horizon for miles. From time to time the plywood images of man or beast will be supplemented by the natural fringe of a wooded slope looking for all the world like a giant hairbrush or bread knife against the skyline.

It is nearly always hot and one is tempted to stop and doff one's

Illustration: Detail from a tile mosaic in the Alhambra, thirteenth century.

124

clothes to run among the water sprinklers that dot the fields of olive trees and, occasionally, watermelon. The road is narrow, a two-lane highway for most of the way, but the scenery is varied: flat, arid desert is succeeded by mountains, their sharply projecting outlines etched against the white sky. As the road twists and turns, the notches in the mountains ahead shift their perspective like the sights of a giant gun. Spain is a country of black and white: dark shadows, bright sunlight— *todo o nada,* "all or nothing."

"In Spain," wrote Somerset Maugham, "you are seldom out of sight of mountains. They rise before you, arid, gaunt and austere; blue on the far horizon, they seem to summon you to a new and magic world."

It is hard to go astray: follow the route from Toledo to Orgaz, thence to Ciudad Real, and on to Almodovar del Campo. The next stop is Granada, last stronghold of the Moors in Spain.

Throughout the journey so far we have searched for evidence of magic; we have rarely been bold enough to define it. But with Granada's magnificent Alhambra palace we must make an exception. Before our own first visit we were lucky enough to have read nothing about it. And when we arrived we were even luckier, for it was night time and there was nothing, and nobody, to distract our attention as we wandered through and made our first discovery of what, to us, is surely one of the world's most enchanting wonders.

The Alhambra, sprawling across the spine of Granada's highest hill, has a compelling mystery that pulls like a magnet. Room after beautiful room leads one on a seemingly endless journey through a fantasy world in which time appears suspended. The visitor enters a dreamlike trance in which he or she loses all sense of direction, knowing only that the next arched doorway will lead to fresh wonders hitherto unimagined.

Words are inadequate to describe the spell, the feeling of wonderment that possessed us. The Alhambra appeals to the very depths of one's subconscious, evoking a feeling of tranquillity that we have rarely experienced before or since.

The entrance at night is through an immense rotunda, open to skies and flanked by sweeping staircases leading to a gallery which circles the building. The ceiling is a perfectly symmetrical sky, a navy blue globe with twinkling dots of light for stars.

A flight of stairs leads down to the wondrous enclosed gardens and courtyards which do so much to evoke the unforgettable atmosphere. Stone lions guard gently splashing fountains, languishing in moon-lit splendor amid towers of gold mosaic and filigree plaster. Walls are intricately carved in elaborate patterns whose symbolism can only be guessed at. Ceilings are recessed, patterned and embroidered with graceful sensuality.

The sound of fountains draws one constantly onward, from one delight to the next. Perspectives become distorted, inverted; a glimpse of finery through a hedged arch tempts one into an apparent diversion, but this route has been subtly anticipated. The night perfume is heavy, sensuous. Is it real or imaginary? Captivated by the spell, lost in a gilded kaleidoscope, one no longer knows or cares.

The Alhambra and the gorgeous gardens known as the Generalife that adjoin it were first conceived and laid out in 1248 by Al Ahmar, first of the Nasrid kings. They were later enlarged and modified by Abul Hachar Yusuf I and his son and successor Mohammed V. After the fall of Granada in 1492, this magnificent landmark was all but abandoned until early in the nineteenth century. When the American writer Washington Irving arrived in Granada in 1829, restoration was underway.

Irving, both of whose parents had emigrated from Britain, lived for a while in England; the mystic theme of his famous story "Rip Van Winkle" is right out of English folklore. He had originally studied law but turned to writing to support himself when his brother's business, in which he was a partner, went bankrupt. The success of his writing allowed him to travel throughout Europe and he first settled in Spain in 1824, staying for a while at the home of the U.S. consul in Madrid. Then, in the chance-of-a-lifetime, the forty-six-year-old writer was privileged to take up residence in this unsurpassable palace, and his *Legends of the Alhambra* reveals how clearly he sensed the magic with which it was (and is) permeated. With rich, intoxicating, and evocative language he savors its luxury and mystery, and his stories are so spellbinding that today's visitors to Granada are sometimes advised not to read the book until after they have seen the place for themselves.

Every room, every fountain is lovingly detailed by Irving. He learns from Mateo Jiminez—a "son of the Alhambra," now a guard who could trace his family back for centuries—of the tradition of the Gate of Justice. This is adorned with a gigantic hand and a huge key which are, according to Mateo, "magical devices on which the fate of the Alhambra depended." It is said that the builder was a magician who declared that the Alhambra would remain intact until the day "the hand on the outer arch should reach down and grasp the key, when the whole pile would tumble to pieces and all the treasures buried beneath it by the Moors would be revealed."

The tale reminds us of Pythagoras and his laws of visual harmony. It seems likely that he would have delighted in the beauty of the Alhambra. Arches and columns create intricate patterns of light and shadow. The geometric mosaic designs on the walls and floors combine with calligraphic panels of stucco to form a masterpiece of harmony and logic. The Alhambra is perhaps the ultimate structural expression of the magic of mathematics.

The city of Granada, whose lowest point is still more than 2,000 feet above sea level, has much to offer the stroller, apart from the beautiful Alhambra. It is a city of flowers, hidden patios, dreamy squares, and the evening sound of gentle convent bells. Although the architecture is still predominantly Moorish—more so than in Toledo—the seesawing fortunes of the city's different occupiers are illustrated by the history of its religious shrines. The site on which the cathedral now stands belonged to, until 1227, a mosque, which in turn had been erected in 712 atop the ruins of a sixth-century church.

Everywhere there is style and elegance; even the people in the streets, with the languor so characteristic of hot countries, seem to reflect the passive dignity of the architecture among which they live. Yet there are startling contrasts. Not all are well dressed and well fed: Granada, too, has its poverty.

Up on the hillsides of Sacro Monte to the north of the city, clustered in shabby quarters near the wretched caves in which they used to live, are a tribe of Gypsies renowned for their music and dance.

The Spanish call the Gypsies *gitanos,* a shortened form of *egipcianos.* When the dark-skinned wanderers arrived in Europe during the late fourteenth century, it was popularly supposed that Egypt was their homeland.

The Gypsies of Sacro Monte are unique in that their tribe settled in Andalusia centuries ago, breaking the roving tradition. The art of flamenco was not originated by the *gitanos* but rather preserved by them from Moorish themes and seventeenth-century music and dance of the countryside. No one could deny that the Gypsies have developed, embellished, and perfected the style.

But the tribe in Granada and their music strengthen Charles Godfrey Leland's theory that Gypsies are not originators but rather custodians of magical lore. Leland's book *Gypsy Sorcery and Fortune Telling* is a marvelous potpourri of western folk magic collected by Gypsies from every corner of Europe and the British Isles. Their oral tradition has managed to keep alive skill in divination, herbal knowledge, and an almost mystic ability in training animals.

Gypsy attitudes reflect an old wisdom of mystical life and arcane practices. "We fall back upon Nature," a Gypsy told author Vernon S. Morwood, almost a century ago. "We are contented with the light of the sun, the moon and the stars; we love the woods, the trees, the fields, and the flowers and to listen to Nature's own music in the songs of the birds, in the murmuring stream and in the breeze . . . Nature is our altar and even in the green lanes, on the mountainside, in the forest recess, or anywhere else we can raise our shrines of devotion."

Some historians claim to have traced Gypsies back to the Jats or Yats, a pastoral race that lived in the foothills of the Himalayas in northern India until some of them were invited by the king of Persia to relocate in his country. Eventually they became lazy and the king expelled them from Persia, thus starting their wanderings. Other historians have suggested that Gypsies were a mixture of Arabs and Jews who escaped from the slavery of pyramid-building in Egypt and headed eastward through Arabia into northern Hindustan, and thence throughout the world. The Gypsies themselves are ignorant of their origin but do call themselves the Rom, their language—Romany. About 40 percent of the words they speak are said to be traceable to Sanskrit.

The area of Sacro Monte, beside the caves, is not especially pleasant today. Gypsies and tourists crowd the single-track road around the hillside. From the clubs and bars pour waves of sound, more tacky than traditional, and on all sides are the evidence of poverty and exploitation. The atmosphere discouraged our search for a particular cave of occult significance.

It was in a cavern here, carefully sealed with great blocks of stone and guarded by a solitary stone pillar, that a bizarre discovery was made. A dozen skeletons, dating back to Neolithic times, were found sitting in a circle around the skeleton of a woman wearing the remains of a leather tunic on which were incised complex geometric patterns. Also in the cave archeologists discovered such signs of ritual magic as amulets and inscribed clay discs of the type usually identified with sun worship. The floor was covered with beads and seeds of the opium poppy, which was known in the earliest times as *nepenthe,* a narcotic.

Anthony Roberts in his *Giants in the Earth* theorizes that the woman must have been an adept and spiritual guide who led the initiates into an astral state of contemplation. "The people who made this magic trip," he says, "had never returned from its mystical revelations, and this was quite possibly by choice."

The Moorish presence in Spain, which left so rich a legacy of art, magic, and occultism, was centered in Granada for almost five centuries, and became an actuality only after Spain itself—formerly a mélange of different kingdoms (Barcelona, Galicia, Aragon, Castile)—had become unified. The driving force behind the Arab invasion was the new-found militancy and sense of identity instilled by Mohammed (born about A.D. 571). And by the time of his death on June 8, 632, the Moors themselves, once a group of warring tribes, had become a nation.

Musa, the governor of Barbary, crossed the Mediterranean to capture Saragossa in the year 714, and within 100 years of Mohammed's death Islam controlled an empire which, expanding east and west from Alexandria, stretched from the Bay of Biscay almost to China. Greece and Asia Minor eluded their control, but most of the Mediterranean was under their sway and the rest of Europe trembled with anxiety about this dark-skinned, distinctly non-Christian race and knew no peace until they were eventually ousted from the Continent in the thirteenth century.

But long before this, the Arab's doctrines and beliefs had become well established. From Alexandria, the intellectual center of the known world where Greek, Egyptian, and Jewish traditions combined, they flooded Europe with a stimulating mix of alchemy, astrology, and the Cabala. Arabic numerals and Arabic science and philosophy were propagated, and the works of Plato, Aristotle, and Pythagoras were disseminated as well as Greco-Egyptian mysticism and Gnostic thought.

The essence of Alexandrian magic is contained in what is called the Hermetic literature: its importance in ceremonial magic is supreme. Thoth was the Egyptian god of wisdom, numbers, the moon, magical knowledge; he was also the divine scribe and patron of intelligence. In Greco-Roman times Thoth became associated with Hermes (Mercury), and it is Hermes Trismegistus (Hermes three times the greatest) who is credited with the authorship of the body of work known as Hermetic doctrine. Although it was no doubt authored by many, a belief sprang up that an adept-king had written the books. And as many as 36,525 volumes (reduced to 20,000 by Iamblichus and 42 by Clement of Alexandria) were credited to Hermes Trismegistus. Today only fourteen short texts survive. The most famous is called "The Emerald Tablet." Some sources state with certainty that this credo of magic was written in the eleventh century by Syrian alchemists, but the discovery in 1828 of a copy of it in the eighteenth-dynasty tomb of a magician at Thebes testifies to the text's antiquity. From "The Emerald Tablet": "True it is, without falsehood, and most real: that which is above is like that which is below, to perpetuate the miracles of One thing. And as all things have been derived from one, by the thought of one, so all things are born from this thing, by adoption." Ponder that.

Gnosticism (from the Greek *gnosis,* "knowledge") comprised several sects that were active in Alexandria and had always been considered a threat to the growth of Christianity. Some sects were actually Christian but did not accept all of the doctrines set down by Rome. Some Gnostics claimed to possess divine revelation, consisting of intuitive knowledge and esoteric truths reminiscent of the Eleusinian mysteries. (In fact, the Eleusinian mysteries had flourished in Alexandria under the early Ptolemaic rule.) Gnostics were declared heretics and Gnosticism, along with other divergent philosophies, was suppressed. Feelings would run so high that in A.D. 415 a beautiful woman, a Neo-Platonic philosopher named Hypatia, who graced Alexandria with her loveliness and intelligence, was attacked and torn to pieces by a mob of Christian fanatics.

Tokens of the Gnostics may be found today in most museums. These are the so-called Gnostic gems or amulets. The art of gem engraving reached a height in Alexandria during the early centuries of our era and many beautiful examples of it are extant. Stones of carnelian, jasper, and onyx bear the sacred name of Abraxas (from which is derived the mystical word *abracadabra*) and his personification: a strange figure with the head of a cock, a human torso, and two serpents for legs; his human hands hold a shield in the right, a whip in the left. This bizarre creature is associated with the number 365 and seems to have been invented by

Basilides, chief of a Gnostic sect in the second century A.D. Other gems are engraved with Serapis, combining the Egyptian Osiris with the sacred bull Apis, a form of the ancient Ptah, and worshiped as the god of time. Another common design is the goddess Isis holding the baby Horus in her arms. Such representations were often mistakenly identified as the Virgin Mary and the Christ Child.

It was through Arabic translations of the collected wisdom secured at Alexandria and carried by the Moors on their historic thrust into Europe that the fire of the Renaissance was sparked. The universities established by the Arab conquerors in Italy and Spain were instrumental in awakening European thought from its long medieval slumber.

Gnosticism would emerge again after ten centuries of complete Christian domination in Europe when the Cathars (also called the Albigenses, from Albi, a town in southern France) became strong enough for Pope Innocent III to mount a Crusade against them. From 1140 to 1208 Catharism had spread rapidly through France, Italy, and into Germany, particularly Cologne. The Papal Crusade of 1208 (the first inside Europe) began an agonizing war and a brutal Inquisition in the Languedoc region of France. The stronghold of the Cathars at Monsegar held out for ten months and finally, rather than surrender or renounce their faith, the 200 survivors threw themselves on an enormous funeral pyre in the year 1244.

The Cathar philosophy was dualistic; the universe was thought to contain two opposing principles of good and evil. They denied the supremacy of Christ, rejected the authority, sacraments, and priests of the Roman Catholic Church, and maintained that the god of the Old Testament was actually a demon. They thought of themselves as akin to the early Christians before the dominance of the Roman church. The Cathars were ascetics and renounced the material world. They denied the eating of flesh meat and the drinking of spirits and frowned on sex. They trained themselves to endure torture. They withstood half a century of indescribable massacres and atrocities. Paintings of the period often depict the burning of the books of the Cathars; the nonheretical volumes rising unsinged from the pyre. It is said that the last of the Cathars at Monsegar hid their books and a treasure of gold in a secret cave. Despite the brutal suppression, the Cathar heresy would surface again and again.

The proximity of the Languedoc to Spain and its Moorish universities suggests that the Gnostic themes may have arisen from the teachings of the Arabic scholars.

"The intellectual avenue leading from the portals of Toledo through the Pyrenees," writes Philip K. Hitti in *The Arabs*, "wound its way through Provence and the Alpine passes into Lorraine, Germany and Central Europe and across the Channel into England."

But the forces of Christianity, which had been seething through these past centuries, finally got together. Toledo fell in 1085; Cordova and Seville followed in 1236 and 1248 respectively, and by the middle of the thirteenth century the reconquest was completed.

From thence, with the Christians once more in control, a darkness descended on Spain which has never entirely lifted. Many of the themes of art and letters which underlie Spanish philosophy and culture today are traceable to the influences the Moors instilled so many centuries ago.

But though Spain itself languished, and the Moors retreated back to their African strongholds, the wisdom and skills they had so brilliantly synthesised moved onward—up through Europe and in particular to the intellectually fertile universities of southern Germany.

15

Southern Germany

FAUST, PARACELSUS, AGRIPPA VON NETTESHEIM, AND OTHERS

EARLY IN THE SIXTEENTH CENTURY a man named Faust, or Dr. Faustus, lived somewhere in what is now southwestern Germany. What that man was and the facts of his life—and death—are still disputed, but the basic legend of how he sold his soul to the devil in return for surpassing wisdom is one that has never failed to grip the imagination in the succeeding centuries.

Since a Protestant pastor, Johann Gast, preached a sermon about Faust's supernatural powers after dining with him at Basle in 1548, the legend has continued to expand and grow. Johann Spies' *Faustbook,* published in Frankfurt in 1587, was ostensibly a biography, and even though some of its tales had appeared elsewhere, attached to such earlier magicians as Merlin and Albertus Magnus, the book was received with enthusiasm. Dr. Faust had been immortalized.

During the next few centuries one writer after another developed the admonitory theme that to search in the black arts for supernatural knowledge inevitably led to eternal damnation. It was a theme, much reinforced by the strict Christian ethics of the day, that was soon to be current in the literature of many nations. Christopher Marlowe, the

Illustration: Magical talisman in Hebrew, from Agrippa's Occult Philosophy *(1531).*

131

English playwright, was among the first to deal with the Faust theme, and Goethe was also impressed enough to comment.

The sixteenth century was a time for astrologers, adventurers, and illusionists. Itinerant preachers wandered about Europe peddling their theories and in Toledo and Cracow the universities were turning out students schooled in magical lore and practice. Faust himself is said to have studied at Cracow. But after his pact with Mephistopheles his future had a lien on it with a cut-off date twenty-four years ahead. And from this there was no appeal.

The most likely claimant for Faust's hometown is the pleasant hamlet of Knittlingen, about thirty miles northwest of Stuttgart on the edges of the Black Forest where on Walpurgis Night (April 30) farmers shoot their guns into the air, light a bonfire, or hide some elderwood in the barn as an antidote to the witchcraft they still believe to be present.

Founded in the ninth century, Knittlingen is a lovely town of cobbled streets (one called Mozartstrasse) lined with old houses whose steeply sloping, rich red roofs overhang the narrow sidewalks. By eleven o'clock at night almost everyone is abed, the only signs of life come from the teen-agers hanging around the pool room opposite the Rathhaus, or city hall, and from a bar down a side street. A bronze statue of a robed Faust by sculptress Hanne Schorp-Pflumm stands beside the fountain in front of the Rathhaus, its neatly carved inscription reads (in rough translation): "He wanted to fathom all the secrets of heaven and earth."

Inside the Rathhaus a small collection devoted to the doctor-magician occupies a pair of adjoining rooms on the second floor. Mostly it consists of copies of the various books, opera scores, scripts, manuscripts, and paintings executed since Johann Faust was born in the town around 1480. Knittlingen boosters say proof that this was Faust's hometown is to be found on the title page of one of the doctor's works, *Dreyfacher Hollenzwang,* in which he reveals his alchemical recipes for making gold. This title pages carries a picture of Faust bearing the name D. Faustus Magus Maximus Kundlingensie. Kundling is the old name for Knittlingen.

In September 1951 lectures on Faust "as a historical personality in legend and fiction" satisfied local authorities that Knittlingen was definitely his hometown, and the decision was made to accumulate material for a museum. There are plans to convert a timbered house adjoining the parish church into a repository for these books and artifacts. The house in which he is said to have been born—ostensibly the illegitimate son of a rich farmer named Gerlach—was bombed during World War II. Recently, in a timber joist in what was its cellar, a small leather bag was found containing parchments bearing magical figures and formulas. One of them was the famous SATOR, AREPO, TENET, OPERA, ROTAS formula, which has turned up in places as far apart as Pompeii, Hadrian's Wall in the north of England, and on Coptic papyri discovered in Egypt. In

Asia Minor it was identified on a bronze charm dating back to the fourth or fifth century, in Austria on a sixteenth-century coin, in France on a Bible pendant in the Abbey of St. Germain de Prés.

S A T O R

A R E P O

T E N E T

O P E R A

R O T A S

The formula has been translated variously. SATOR seems to mean "a sower" or "to sow seeds; AREPO possibly comes from *arrepo* ("I creep to") and refers to a plow; TENET means "a belief"; OPERA means a work; and ROTAS refers to wheels. From this we might roughly translate the sentence as "The sower is at the plow; the labor occupies the wheels" or more loosely as "Creative power holds the wheels by a thread." Neither of these explanations seems entirely satisfactory, but whatever the efficacy of the magical square its adherents were certainly widespread.

The square and its accompanying leather bag found at Knittlingen are being preserved with other memorabilia for inclusion in the town's new museum. Also carefully guarded is a strange, star-shaped cabinet covered with signs and symbols of the four elements. It was found in the cellar, and speculation is that it was actually Faust's magic cupboard. At the top it bears the symbol for quicksilver and in the middle the letters ELOHIM, an ancient Hebrew name for God.

An old legend reports that Mephistopheles, who had earlier appeared in the form of a dromedary-like horse and carried Faust around the world for fifteen months, returned to fetch the magician from a weathervane in Knittlingen and that Faust haunts the spot to this day.

Faust is supposed to have studied magic, astrology, chemistry, and medicine at Cracow and at various German universities (Erfurt, Wittenberg, and Ingolstadt), supporting himself with a legacy from a rich uncle. Among the earliest reports on Faust is the mention by Trithemius, the famous abbot, with whom he stayed at Gelnhaussen in 1506 and who wrote that in 1507 Faust got a job as a teacher in Kreuznach but had to give it up because of lewdness with the boys.

Trithemius, later Bishop of Würzburg until his death in 1516, felt that Faust was a charlatan and seemed shocked by the doctor's blasphemy that he could reproduce the miracles of Christ. On his visit to Gelnhaussen, the abbot said in a letter dated August 20, 1507 that Faust had described himself with "pompous and exotic names."

But Trithemius himself, author of books on sorcery, geomancy, and alchemy, claimed to have had traffic with an evil spirit by name of

Hudekin and was reputed to have become rich through his alchemical discovery of the philosopher's stone.

In the archives of Heidelberg University for January 15, 1509, mention is made that a brilliant scholar named Johannes Faust had completed his studies to the standard of baccalaureate, obtaining a degree in theology. He came in first in a class of sixteen. In 1513, Zachanas Hogel wrote that Faust had come from Wittenberg and was giving lectures at the University of Erfurt. Faust's lectures on Homer and mythology at this university were reported to have been accompanied with side effects so realistic that the students were terrified. Not every professor had the assistance of a supernatural stage manager who could cause the appearance of Trojan heroes right in his classroom.

Once, it is said, Faust climbed by means of a ladder into the Archbishop of Salzburg's house, accompanied by some of his students, and proceeded to drink up the cleric's wine. He was disturbed by the butler whom he calmly conjured high into the branches of a tree to await rescue while Faust left with the drunken students.

A letter dated 1513 from the humanist Conrad Mutianus Rufus, Canon of Gotha, describes the charlatanry of one Georgius Faust at Erfurt who had been heard boasting of his skills as a sorcerer while drinking in local taverns.

By 1519 Faust's reputation as an astrologer was widely known. On February 12, 1520 in Bamberg, he was paid ten florins, a high fee at that time, for the horoscope he cast for the prince and bishop Georg III Schenk von Limburg. But, as with so many intellectuals of the time, the spiritual currents of the era—Catholicism, Protestantism, and humanism—were pulling him in different directions, and his abilities as a medium and his occult talents made Faust a suspicious figure to many. By 1525 his behavior in Wittenberg was reputedly so untenable that civic authorities ordered his arrest. He escaped arrest by fleeing to Ingolstadt, from which he was then banished on June 17, 1528.

His reputation followed him. About 1530 tradition has it that he had a protracted stay in Prague where the astrologers at Rudolf's court jealously prevented him from getting a secure post. In 1532 he attempted to settle in Nürnberg, one of the empire's most important cities but was refused permission by the authorities (as reported in the city records) for being a "sodomist and necromancer."

It was while on a visit to Nürnberg in 1534 that Faust predicted that Bishop Graf von Waldeck would capture the town of Münster from the Anabaptists on June 23, 1535, and the fact that this took place gave credence to his gifts as a seer but made the authorities even more wary of him.

There are tales of him inviting the prince of Anhalt to dinner at a five-towered castle he'd built overnight by magic and which he caused to disappear when the meal was over. At Innsbruck, Charles V asked him to conjure up Alexander the Great and Faust was happy to oblige. It was while at this court also that he made fun of a knight by tying antlers to his head. Later the knight waylaid Faust on the highway, but the wily magician conjured up an illusion of marching troops coming to his aid and the knight was forced to surrender his horse and sword. Faust gave him a new horse—which promptly plunged into the river and disappeared, leaving the knight soaking wet and greatly rueing the encounter.

One day, out in the countryside, Faust was said to have stopped a wagoner to ask if he could eat some hay, and the peasant tolerantly agreed. But the magician ate, or appeared to eat, so much of the load that the peasant begged him to stop. Of course, when he arrived home with his load he found it to be intact. On another occasion Faust asked a peasant for a ride and, on being refused, magically caused the wagon wheels to fly away and the horses to sit down.

Living in a time when belief in sorcery was very strong—thousands of men and women were hanged or burned alive for witchcraft—Faust apparently spared no efforts to perfect his art. He is said to have supplemented his studies with visits to numerous other places, always anxious to extend his reputation as a magician and healer. At one period he apparently spent some time at the royal court in Paris, serving the Elector of Brandenburg there.

Various of his contemporaries, including the writers Johannes Weyer and Joachim Camerarius, described Faust as a cheat. Weyer (1515–1588) refers to Faust in his occult study *De Praestigiis Daemonum,* as a pseudomagician who practiced "with unspeakable deceit, many lies and great effects." Weyer, a Protestant doctor, dismisses Faust as a drunkard who himself invented the story of his relationship with the devil to add to his self-importance. But Weyer does agree that Faust was strangled by Satan after a tremendous noise had been heard coming from his house.

In his *Encyclopedia of Occultism,* Lewis Spence writes: "From other evidence it is pretty clear that Faust was a wandering magician or necromancer whose picturesque character won him wide publicity or notoriety."

Whatever the truth of Johann Faust's capabilities as a magician, he appears to have been sincere in his intentions. In a book published in Wittenberg in 1524, he describes how as a youth he experimented with conjuring up spirits, following the directions he learned from a book of magical formulas. "At first I had little faith that what was promised would take place," he confessed. "But at the very first invocation which I attempted, a mighty spirit manifested himself, desiring to know why I had invoked him. His coming so amazed me that I scarcely knew what to say, but finally asked him if he would serve me in my magical investigations."

Faust goes on to explain how, in his ignorance, he had not taken precautions to protect himself with the correct magic symbols and thus was at the mercy of the spirit who demanded that he sign a pact. "I did not dare refuse his request and resigned myself to the inevitable, considering it wisest to turn my mantle according to the wind."

What followed next, according to a biography of Faust published at Toledo in 1594, was an immense tumult in the depths of the wood in which he stood.

> It seemed as if the whole forest was peopled with devils, making a crash like a thousand wagons, hurrying from left to right and before and behind in every possible direction with thunder and lightning and the continual discharge of a great cannon.
>
> Hell appeared to have emptied itself to have furnished the din. There succeeded the most charming music from all sorts of instruments and sounds of hilarity and dancing. . . . Then a griffin and dragon came to the edge of the circle, then a pillar of fire with red-hot globes and finally the devil appeared as a gray monk.

The spirit, Asteroth by name, then proceeded to introduce Faust to lesser spirits, two of which the magician thought too slow for his needs. The third spirit, when asked how quick he was, replied, "I am as swift as a human thought." Faust found this entirely satisfactory and thus formed a partnership that lasted for some time.

Much of the rest of the sixteenth-century book is devoted to repeated assertions that many spirits are willing to be invoked by man, and it gives specific instructions about how to draw the circles, prepare the parchment with the correct symbols, and read off the sacred invocation to the appropriate spirit. "You must also note the day and hour," the writer adds, "for each spirit can only be invoked at certain times."

Like most magicians of his day, Faust soon turned his attention to the alchemical search for the philosopher's stone. "During the Middle Ages alchemy was not only a science but also a religion," writes the noted occultist Manly P. Hall. "Those who rebelled against the religious limitations of their day concealed their philosophic teachings under the allegory of goldmaking. In this way they preserved their personal liberty and were ridiculed rather than persecuted."

About 1516 Faust was at the monastery in Maulbronn, supposedly making gold for a boyhood friend, the abbot Johannes Entenfuss, to pay the monastery's debts. Evidence of his sojourn there can be found in the register of the abbots of Maulbronn monastery, now preserved in the Public Records office at Stuttgart. Traditionally it is said that Faust, finding the monastery wine too sour, sneaked out by an underground passage on several occasions to go on drinking bouts in Knittlingen. The beautiful ivy-covered abbey is today one of the best-preserved medieval monasteries in Europe.

Although the alchemical search for gold is often regarded as an allegory of man's search for his own soul through laborious and repetitive processes of purification, there are many books containing specific directions for actually making gold. Many stories exist of magicians who have accomplished it; many more are ambiguous. But the recipes remain and, assuming some of the more obscure ingredients could still be obtained, there is nothing to stop contemporary alchemists from experimenting in their own back-room labs.

Fred Haas, commenting on the vast amount of literature "proving" that the alchemists did not make gold, says it is useless to argue about whether or not it was made (although if the General Electric company can make diamonds . . .). "The important thing about alchemy is not whether or not gold was made, but whether or not man's spiritual nature could become gold-like. Alchemists agreed that this was possible. By a unification of opposites and a purification of his nature, man transcends duality and becomes golden. The Golden Man is the theme of alchemy."

For those interested in metallic rather than spiritual gold, however, the author of a *Treatise on Philosophical and Hermetic Chemistry,* published in Paris in 1725, explains that it is first necessary to distill "from the interior of mercury" a fiery spirit which was not solid like metal or soft like quicksilver, but between the two. This concentrate was acquired by purging ordinary mercury with salt and vinegar, subliming it in various acids and distilling it.

> This is the first operation in the grand work. For the second operation: take, in the name of God, one part of gold and two parts of the spiritual water, charged with the salammoniac; mix this noble crystal in a vase the shape of an egg; warm over a soft but continuous fire, and the fiery water will dissolve little by little the gold; this forms a liquor which is called by the sages "chaos" containing the elementary qualities—cold, dryness, heat, and humidity. Allow this composition to putrefy until it becomes black; this blackness is known as "the crows head" and "the darkness of the sages," and makes known to the artist that he is on the right track. It was also known as "the black earth."
>
> It must be boiled once more in a vase as white as snow; this stage of the work is called the "swan" and from it arises the white liquor, which is divided into two parts—one white for the manufacture of silver, the other red for the manufacture of gold. Now you have accomplished this work and you possess the Philosopher's Stone.

Was this where Faust's studies led him? There are insistent reports of his experiments with the making of gold and he was supposedly engaged in manufacturing quantities of it for Baron Anton von Staufen of Freiburg on that fateful night in 1540 when the devil came to claim his due. It is said that a flame rose out of the chimney, a hellish stench of sulphur filled the house, and when neighbors rushed to investigate,

Faust's corpse was found with a blackened face. Further embellishments to this simple tale have been added by more than 200 chroniclers over the years.

One of the other versions of his death is that it followed a farewell supper at the Lion Inn, Staufen-im-Breisgau, at which the magician entertained his students and revealed to them how he had acquired his powers.

"They one and all expressed the deepest sorrow," writes William Godwin in his *Lives of the Necromancers*, "and regretted exceedingly that he had not been unreserved in his earlier communications. They would have had recourse in his behalf to the means of religion and appealed to pious men, desiring them to employ the power to intercede with heaven in his favour." Faust assured them it was all in vain and that his tragic fate was inevitable.

Sometime after midnight a great storm arose in the little town with gusts of wind almost strong enough to shake the inn to its foundations. The students were frightened but did not venture from their beds, even when they heard the doctor's voice calling for help. The next morning Faust was discovered either in bed with a broken neck or, depending on which account is believed, on a dung heap in the yard with all his limbs mangled. His "accidental death" was reported in the *Zimmersche Chronik.*

While the character Faust dwells somewhere between fact and fiction, there is no doubt about the existence of Albertus of Cologne, Albertus Magnus.

Albertus was born of a noble family in 1206. He joined the Dominican order and taught at several German universities before moving to Paris in 1245, where he acquired great fame for his scholarship. With boundless intellectual curiosity Albertus investigated Arabian, Jewish, Neoplatonic, and Aristotelian sources. His interests ranged from the natural sciences of zoology and botany to medicine and metaphysics. Appointed Bishop of Ratisbon in 1260, he departed two years later to resume teaching at the University of Cologne. Until his death in 1280, Albertus lectured on the works of Aristotle and Plato despite the fact that both philosophers were viewed with suspicion by the Dominicans. Albertus Magnus was finally canonized by the Roman Catholic Church in 1932. It took over six centuries to dispel the doubt about his devotion to the wise men of antiquity.

Another factor may have been his reputation as a master of the black arts. Just as Virgil's memory acquired a host of mysterious legends, Albertus Magnus became renowned as a magician.

One of the wondrous tales about Albertus is that he spent thirty years working on the making of what sounds like the world's first robot: a bronze figure that could speak and perform simple tasks. Getting it to answer questions was supposedly the hardest part and it is said that when it eventually did speak it spouted such nonsense that Thomas Aquinas, Albertus' assistant, knocked it on the head in a rage and it never said another word.

Albertus Magnus' reputation for being able to "change the seasons" may have rested on nothing more than a brilliantly conceived midwinter dinner party which was made to appear as if it took place in summer. The occasion, New Year's Day in 1249, came about when Albertus Magnus wanted some land on which to build a monastery near Cologne and its owner, William, Count of Holland, didn't want to sell it. Persuaded to be his guest for dinner on a cold, bitter day when the Rhine was frozen and its banks were piled high with snow, the count arrived, and as he took his seat, "the dark clouds rolled away from the sky, a warm sun shone, the cold north wind veered around and blew a mild breeze from the south, snows melted away and the trees put forth their green leaves and fruit. Flowers sprang up beneath their feet while larks, nightingales, blackbirds, thrushes, cuckoos and every sweet song bird sang hymns from every tree."

How had Albertus managed it? One explanation may be hypnotism, another that he had built the first known winter garden. At any rate, the chroniclers inform us that after the dinner, the winds blew cold, the songbirds dropped dead, the leaves and fruit withered and fell from the trees, and the count and other guests all huddled around the fire in the kitchen to warm themselves. Impressed with the scholar's talents, the count sold him the coveted piece of land.

Albertus' fame increased apace when his works were published in the sixteenth century. Treatises on the sacred and healing properties of plants and stones as well as texts about alchemy and astrology seemed to confirm what was already suspected—here was a man in league with the devil. The infamous occult textbooks or *grimoires* titled *Lé Grand and Lé Petit Albaërt,* in the rare book collections of many European libraries, are culled from the writings of Albertus Magnus.

According to Albertus, "The alchemist must be silent and discreet. To no one should he reveal the results of his operations." Another recommendation warns the alchemist "to avoid all contact with princes and rulers." As we shall see, his followers did not obey the rules Albertus Magnus set down.

The celebrated Paracelsus (1493–1541) is said to have died of what he thought to be the elixir of life, which was actually an immensely strong distillate of alcohol. (Rumors persist, however, that he was actually poisoned by jealous medical colleagues at Salzburg where he died in St. Stephen's Hospital in 1541, about the same time as Faust.) Paracelsus (born Theophrastus Bombastus von Hohenheim at Einsiedeln, near Zurich, the son of a doctor) is a key figure in the history of magic if only because he appeared at a time when medicine was being redefined and alchemy was on the road to becoming chemistry.

Paracelsus may have been referring to the deeper meaning of alchemy when he declared: "That man no other man shall own who to himself belongs alone." More directly, he explained that "The object of chemistry is not to make gold but to prepare medicines. Medicine is an art and requires practice."

Tradition has it that he studied at Würzburg under Bishop Trithemius and met and became friendly with Agrippa von Nettesheim in the same town, though there is no concrete evidence of this latter meeting. Certainly his travels were numerous (his father's comment that "a rolling stone gathers no moss" was met by his son's retort, "I have no wish to gather moss") and his unorthodox ideas and theories offended the medical establishment almost everywhere he went.

"My accusers complain I have not entered the temple of knowledge through the legitimate door," he once commented, "but which one is the truly legitimate door? I have entered through the door of Nature; her light and not the lamp of an apothecary's shop has illuminated my way."

He was a willing student wherever he went. Captured by the Tatars during their invasion of Russia, the nomadic Swiss was treated well and took the opportunity to study the curative effects of his captors' occult healing methods, which he later said were dependent on "absolute faith and resolute imagination." He visited Italy, Crete, and Egypt, and in his later books made references to Nile physicians and certain "magical instructions" imparted to him there.

In the preface to his first *Surgery Book,* published in 1536, he spoke of commencing his studies at universities in Germany, Italy, and France but not being content with their teaching, he wandered farther. "And in all those countries and places I was diligently investigating and enquiring into the certain and true art of medicine. This I tried out not only with learned doctors, but also at the hands of barbers, bathkeepers or shearers, and with experienced surgeons; even with old women, with necromancers . . . with the alchemists, and in monasteries; with the nobles and the common people, with the cleverest and with simpletons."

The conclusion he reached, after all this study, was that magic and medicine were not only related but that "The first requirement for the study of magic is a thorough knowledge of nature—magic is the power which teaches the true nature of the inner man as well as the organization of his outward body." Magic was, he said, "the power that ruled over the world's fate."

In his book *Bygone Beliefs,* H. Stanley Redgrove comments: "Until Paracelsus, partly by his vigorous invective and partly by his remarkable cures of diseases, demolished the old school of medicine, no one dared question the authority of Galen (A.D. 130–205) and Avicenna (980–1037)."

Paracelsus' views, says Redgrove, were based on his theory (undoubtedly true in a sense) that man is a microcosm, a world in miniature. "He also held the Doctrine of Signatures, according to which the medicinal value of plants and minerals is indicated by their external form, or some sign impressed upon them by operation of the stars." Examples of this were the mandrake, symbol of fertility whose root resembled the human form, and eyebright, a plant with a black pupil-like spot in its center, used for complaints of the eyes. Good health in man, Paracelsus thought, was due to the right proportions, and he likened the salt, sulphur, and mercury that he believed present in all things to be equivalent to spirit, soul, and body.

Paracelsus wrote more than 100 books in all, half of them on medicine and 33 on magic or alchemy. He lived in so many places it is difficult to keep track of them all. One of his homes, however, was in the old fortress town of Esslingen, southeast of Stuttgart, where, less than a century ago, the roof of his cellar workshop was found to be covered with astrological signs and cabalistic characters. The owner had the cellar blocked up but had a life-size portrait of the doctor-magician painted over the gable end of the house.

The cellar was only 13 feet long, 10 feet wide, and 13 feet high, but Paracelsus apparently had built into it a furnace and a full-scale laboratory. He once wrote: "The skilled alchemist achieves the highest results with next to nothing, while the unskilled always attributes his failure to lack of a great store of the newest, most expensive and impressive-looking utensils."

Alchemy's history, according to John Henry Pepper, began 200 years before Christ with Hermes Trismegistus, said to be the inventor of arts and sciences. The historian Diodorus Siculus, a contemporary of Caesar, attributed the invention of chemistry to Hermes, and the Syrian writer Iamblichus noted that it was the custom to attribute all books of science, or magic, to Hermes, the result being that there were 20,000 books said to be written by him.

Pepper, in his *Play Book of Metals,* says that the early alchemists guarded their secrets jealously and "the punishment of the peach tree" was the fate of those who betrayed the arcane knowledge. This is taken to mean poisoning by prussic acid, which can be acquired from a distillation of the stones and leaves of the peach tree.

Be that as it may, sixteenth-century Germany fairly bristled with students of alchemy—Faust, Trithemius, Paracelsus, Agrippa von Nettesheim, and the Scotsman Alexander Seton. A row of old houses in Prague (where Faust is also said to have lived and worked), still exist on Golden Lane, and they are known locally as "the alchemists' homes."

Agrippa von Nettesheim, who was born in Cologne on September 14, 1486, was said to have been "accompanied his entire life by his familiar, a large, black dog, banished by the magician on his deathbed when he renounced his magical works." Heinrich Cornelius Agrippa von Nettesheim began his career as a soldier and then was a teacher, but turned to magic very early and wrote several occult books. The main work, *De Occulta Philosophia,* was published in Antwerp in 1531, about twenty years after he had written it. In this work he declares that arithmetic and geometry are part of the first principles of magic, describes the means of discovering the occult virtues in things, explains divination by means of auguries and omens, and makes the astonishing claim, "I have learnt to make glasses by which anyone may see what he pleases at a very great distance." Presumably he is talking about a kind of early telescope.

Agrippa's philosophy in general managed to alienate most of the people with whom he came into contact, especially the monks who denounced him as a heretic. He was persecuted, deprived of his salary, denounced, and jailed and, according to some sources, ultimately regretted his "youthful errors."

Of the many stories told about his misfortunes an especially memorable one concerns the time a young lodger in his house persuaded Agrippa's wife to let him enter the magician's laboratory when Agrippa was away. The youth, immersed in a book of conjurations, failed to hear a knocking at the door, until a demon entered and demanded to know why he had been called.

"Fear stifles the youth's voice, the demon his mouth and so he pays the price for his unholy curiosity," an old chronicler noted. Meanwhile, Agrippa returned, found the youth dead and summoned the spirit to breathe life back into the corpse in order for it to be seen walking in the marketplace before collapsing. "It was long thought that this youth had been seized with sudden death but signs of suffocation first begat superstition, afterwards time divulged all."

Other strange tales are told of Agrippa's exploits, notably of his capacity for being in two places—Fribourg in Switzerland and Pont-à-Mousson in Lorraine—at the same time. He was reputed to receive secret information about matters all over the world from his familiars (more likely from his widespread network of correspondents) and to pay for his lodgings at foreign inns with money that later turned into seashells.

There have been suggestions that Agrippa met Faust in Cologne and certainly the two renowned seers must have known of each other. Trithemius, of course, knew both (in a letter to Agrippa dated April 8, 1510, he asks to see more of Agrippa's writings). And another friend of Agrippa, Dr. Johannes Weyer, makes reference to Faust in his book *De Praestigiis Daemonum.*

Faust's stay in Cologne is mentioned briefly in a report from the papal legate Minucci to Duke von Bayem on April 4, 1533, and Agrippa who was born there forty-seven years before might well have been around. Some historians have even made the curious suggestion that Spies' *Faustbook,* from which most of the later tales derived, was based on Agrippa's own life, the character of Faust actually being a fictional composite. Their lives did have many parallels—Agrippa's major work, *De Occulta Philosophia,* the three-volume compilation of the occult wisdom of the ages—was written at Knittlingen, the "home" of Faust, in 1510.

Agrippa, like Faust, traveled from one European country to another for most of his life, finding and losing patrons because of his beliefs and activities. During a brief sojourn in Metz, where he had been appointed public advocate, he defended a woman accused of witchcraft and secured her release. As a favor to a friend he then publicly debated a theological point with the reigning clergy, presenting his arguments with such sound logic that they had no alternative but to ask him to leave. Married three times he acquired a large family but lacked the business ability to stay out of debt.

Early in his *De Occulta Philosophia,* Agrippa states that, in his terms, magic has nothing to do with the devil or sorcery but rather with certain occult abilities to which all may aspire. He holds that imagination is the beginning of all magic and if humans can but learn the harmonies of nature, they will be able to attain their highest potential. In his words, "though man is not an immortal animal, like the universe, he is nonetheless reasonable, and with his intelligence, his imagination and his soul, he can act upon and transform the world." The magus must study nature to increase his wisdom: "Through the study of stones, he will learn the essence of the stars." Agrippa published *De Intercertudine et Vanitate Scientiarum (The Vanity and Uncertainty of Knowledge)* in 1530. On the surface, at least, it would seem to contradict his earlier premise. Yet while he maintains conscious knowledge alone brings disillusion, he urges a return to a primitive faith in which intuitive forces are recognized and honored. Another book, *De Nobilitate Feminei Sexus (The Nobility of Women),* is usually dismissed as nothing more than a ploy to gain the patronage of Margaret of Austria, to whom it is dedicated. But from what we can discern of Agrippa's character, it seems quite unlikely that he would stoop to flattery. The theme of the neglected importance of the subconscious mind runs through his writing and leads one to consider that he believed what he wrote. Women, reputed custodians of hidden knowledge and intuitive power, probably held a high place in his esteem.

His death in 1535 in Grenoble is reported in two ways. One source insists that he died in abject poverty, lamenting his occult involvement and begging forgiveness of Christ. The second account says his last years were spent in luxury, surrounded by those who loved and respected him.

Despite an increase in the number of charlatans, interest in alchemy continued to grow over the next couple of hundred years. More than half a century after the time of Faust, Paracelsus, and Agrippa, a Scotsman named Alexander Seton arrived in Cologne on what began as a triumphant tour because of his ability to change lead into gold by means of a mysterious black powder. He traveled through Holland, Italy, Switzerland, and then went to Germany where he visited Strasbourg, Hamburg, and Cologne. In the latter city he produced six ounces of gold which withstood all tests, making such an impression upon the skeptics that a book published in 1604, *Historiae Aliquot Transmutationis Mettalicae,* records the incident.

As so often happened, greed then entered the picture, but not on the part of Seton, who appears to have behaved honorably and honestly from beginning to end. Unfortunately news of his magical skills reached the ears of the ruler of Saxony, Christian II, who commanded the Scotsman to attend his court, satisfied himself of the validity of his claims, and then demanded the alchemical secrets. These Seton refused to divulge, and threats and promises being equally unable to persuade him, he was horribly tortured. A local chemist, Michael Sendivogius, next entered the story. Tempted by dreams of wealth he thought the alchemist's secrets would bring, he contrived Seton's escape, but even then was unable to obtain the formula for the magical black powder. Seton explained, as he had previously maintained all throughout his torture, that he could not reveal such secrets to the uninitiated. He did, however, give his rescuer the rest of the powder before he died from his injuries, and Sendivogius used it first to make gold and then, when it was gone, dishonestly got money on the strength of his earlier successes. He died in 1646, still ignorant, and Seton's formula remains a secret.

But just as Agrippa was said to have publicly recanted his earlier interest in magic, there is a curious echo of this in Seton's last testament. "The extraction of the soul out of gold and silver by what vulgar way of alchemy soever," he wrote, "is but a mere fancy." Disillusion, an attempt to protect family and friends from hostility, or perhaps a device used by later historians to tidy up the record?—the passage of centuries obscures and distorts biographical details.

On the whole, though, it was an age of intellectual exploration. The doctrines of Paracelsus and the alchemists were carried one step further by the Rosicrucians, a mysterious body said to have been founded in the fifteenth century by the German philosopher Christian Rosenkreuz. While traveling in the Holy Land he picked up the seed of this new belief from some Arab philosophers, and gathering disciples in Europe, enjoined them not to reveal the order's secrets for "six times twenty years."

When this period ended, it was another German scholar, Johann Valentin Andreä, born near Würtemberg in 1586, who first wrote about the Rosicrucians and revealed their disciplinary laws. These included adhering to such injunctions as the following: they should, without fee, cure all diseases in their travels; they should adopt the customs of the country in which they resided; they should meet every year; and that every brother should appoint a successor before he died. The password by which they recognized each other was to be the words "Rose Cross." They insisted on absolute purity in morals and actions by their members, a restriction that failed to prevent their critics from accusing them of being hostile to the Pope and blaspheming the Church. They were also said to "turn invisible for lustful purposes" and work their miracles with the aid of demons.

The Rosicrucians themselves believed chastity to be the highest of virtues, maintaining that if a man subdued his carnal passions he could become aware of the undines that dwelt in the water, the salamanders in the fire, and the gnomes in the earth; all spirits of great power that could warn him of approaching danger through dreams or omens.

It was not long before this whole area of southwestern Germany, which had become "the region of the magicians," could more accurately be described as the "region of the witches." In 1477 a coven of witches had been routed from the city of Heidelberg, and twelve years later publication of the infamous *Malleus Malificarum* in Cologne gave the witch-hunters a bible with which to persecute the innocent for centuries to come.

The lovely city of Heidelberg today, at whose university (Germany's oldest) Johann Faust studied more than four and a half centuries ago, offers delightful walks along the banks of the River Neckar or on the grounds of the medieval red sandstone castle on the hill. Not far from the old town hall, built in 1701, is the Market Place with its charming eighteenth-century fountain. The cheerful fruit and vegetable market, held in the open here several times a week, obscures the past history of this square, which is where witches were once publicly burned.

In the worst years of the witch persecution few of the small towns and villages around here, or elsewhere in Germany, were free from the investigation of witch-finders. The chronicler of Treves recorded that the diocese was so "scourged, scoured and purged" of sorcerers in 1586 that in two villages only two women were left alive. In the village of Lindheim on the banks of the River Nidder, not far from Hesse, the Witch Tower is a grim reminder of the trials that took place in the seventeenth century when men and women were hanged inside and burned alive. Today the tower of Lindheim sits in a lovely flower-filled park, but a writer who examined it a century ago described it as "supremely horrible. It is impossible to gaze into the shadows without a shudder."

The controversial Montague Summers, in his *Geography of Witchcraft*, says that even in the late 1920s there were certain regions, particularly the mountainous regions of central Germany, where the witch was still hated and feared. "On certain days such as Walpurgis Night, St. Thomas' Eve or Midsummer, the sorceress will make her way into a neighbor's house and try to borrow some trifle or else filch it unobserved. Misfortune will fall on the homestead when she has succeeded in her quest."

On these days, too, Summers says, cattle were protected by the sign of the cross and bunches of sweet herbs such as marjoram and gilly flowers, "which the foul crew loathe and warily shun." On Walpurgis Night in Bohemia the peasants lit huge bonfires in which they burned effigies of witches and strewed brambles and thorns around to discourage the night riders from effecting a landing.

Summers is a puzzle to contemporary occult historians. They can't take him to task for his scholarship—it is impeccable and often from primary sources—but his credulity offends them. There can be no doubt that he firmly believed in the power of witchcraft and its threat to Christianity.

An earlier chronicler reported that one Walpurgis Night in the Kreidenburg Mountains near Würzburg, more than 3,000 sorcerers and witches assembled to dance and drink gallons of wine stolen from the local bishop's cellar. There were little girls as young as ten years old among the witches, twenty-seven of whom were later convicted and burned.

Walpurgis Night is often spoken of in hushed tones, producing a shivery feeling. Actually the May Eve festival was named for a Christian saint to lessen its pagan reputation. Traditionally the joyful holiday was celebrated in Germany by an ascent of the Brocken, the highest peak in the Harz Mountains. The Brocken heights became so well known as the meeting place of witches that map makers of the eighteenth century always added a few flying over on broomsticks. (Brocken figures in Moussorgsky's *Night on Bald Mountain*.)

Long before the Middle Ages when the mountain became especially linked with witchcraft and devil worship, it had been a sacred place, associated with pagan myths. Undoubtedly the high god of the Anglo-Saxons, Woden, was worshiped at the place before the emergence of Christianity. Woden, the god of victory, death, and magic power (his Scandinavian name is Odin), was also known as Grim, "the masked one," and in that form makes an appearance in various earthworks (such as Grim's Dyke) across the Channel in Wiltshire, England.

Today the Brocken is in East Germany and less accessible, but for those who have ever lived or even visited there, it holds an unforgettable fascination. In the 1930s a special train used to bring the Walpurgisnacht celebrants to the mountain and a woman who used to live there in those days recalls that many of them dressed as witches or devils, like the participants of a fancy-dress ball. Whether or not they were merely dressing up for fun, she says, the Old Religion was at that time still taken seriously in the region, even though most of the local population was ostensibly Lutheran.

The woman, Gisela von Steuben, who now lives in New Mexico, says she has visited few places in the world that gave her such a sense of solitude and yet "you get the impression you are not alone, that you have invisible company."

Ignoring the shorter tourists' route, Ms. von Steuben used to make the climb through the woods dotted with thick patches of mushrooms and blueberries. "The higher up towards the top," she says, "the smaller the vegetation grows. The pines become shorter and gnarled. During the winter months snowdrifts of up to twenty feet will pile up, making the icy trees look bizarre. On clear days one can see for miles around, but if it rains you may walk through the clouds and sit above them, looking down on the turmoil of their boiling. Once in a while they will part and allow you a glimpse through. Often in winter the top is hulled in clouds for weeks at a time."

At the Brocken's summit a mass of huge granite blocks have for centuries been known by such names as "the Sorcerer's Chair" and "the Witches' Altar." A nearby spring is "the Magic Fountain" and the anemone which grows here and there on its rugged slopes is known locally as "the Sorcerer's Flower."

16

The Basque Country

WITCH WAYS AND CAVE ART

THE WITCHES OF SPAIN congregated mostly in the Basque Provinces, a rugged terrain stretching from the foot of the Pyrenees along the Bay of Biscay, an area that even today is alive with legends and long-held customs. The region has always had a reputation for independent thinking and in this century has often been the nursery for liberation movements influencing events far beyond its borders. The Basques successfully withstood domination by the Romans, Visigoths, Franks, and the Moors. They bowed to Christianity only after a long and fierce struggle and, then, on their own terms.

The Basques are possibly the most singular people in Europe. The seven Basque Provinces—four Spanish, three French—claim a population of about 900,000, and share a language that is unrelated to that of either Spain or France. In fact, Basque (Eskuara) is unlike any Indo-European language. Philologists have been baffled for a long time by the Basque tongue, claiming that it may be a survival of paleolithic speech or a derivative of an obscure Phoenician dialect. Links to Gaelic, Finnish, and even Japanese have been suggested and rejected. No one knows.

A proud and forthright people, the Basques are remarkably intuitive,

Illustration: Detail from a medieval woodcut depicting a Witches Sabbath. Dover Collection, Bodleian.

which may be because of their early education and training. A child is taught to avoid speaking of (i.e., giving birth by thought) any kind of ill-tidings with the admonition: "Thoughts are things." The ailing child is advised to visualize its desired goal: "Close your eyes and see yourself well." Imagination is encouraged, as is independence of spirit: "There is but one of you in all of time"; "Rely upon yourself"; and "Only you know what is good for you."

The Basque country—a splendid region of sparkling seas, distinctive mountains, and perpetual sunshine—is part of both France and Spain, but the Spanish Basques are apt to consider themselves superior to their French counterparts. The more attractive scenery, however, is on the northern side of the border. Here you'll find such lovely towns as Mauleon with its charming riverside chateau, and Pau with its flower gardens and terraces overlooking the river and offering sweeping views of the tree-covered mountains. "I know of nothing more pleasant or charming," writes Maurice Barres, "than the series of walks stretching along the south side of this town [Pau]." And of this famous Boulevard des Pyrenees, Lamartine adds: "Pau is the most beautiful landscape, as Naples is the most beautiful seascape." Pau calls itself "the royal city" by virtue of its having been the birthplace of two kings: Charles Jean Bernadotte, King of Sweden, and Henry IV, King of France.

On June 14, 1610 at the very moment when Henry IV was assassinated, it is said that the king's shield fell from the front wall of his chateau in Pau and broke into pieces. Simultaneously the cows of the royal herd lay down on the ground and the royal bull jumped into the moat and broke his spine.

Over to the west of Pau, in a region where ancient legends live and folklore groups still cling to centuries-old dances, are gorgeous little towns like St. Jean Pied-de-Port, surrounded by fields of fruit, flowers, and grain. Cows and goats graze happily and the handsome white-washed buildings are dappled by sunlight. An old citadel, now a school, dominates the town, whose pleasant outdoor cafés are filled with travelers bound for Spain. On the coast nearby, in a region that prides itself on its gourmet cuisine (local specialties include pheasant, young wild boar, duck, salmon, asparagus, lamprey, fresh-water prawns, and turtle dove), is the quaint harbor town of St. Jean-de-Luz, a resort popular with Napoleon.

Some say the fishermen of St. Jean-de-Luz were Europe's first whalers and even today they cast their nets far afield, usually setting off in November for a six-month voyage along the coast of Africa to follow the schools of tuna.

Once across the Spanish border the scenery changes very quickly, for this part of Spain is predominantly industrial. Endless factories belch smoke into a sky of spectacular sunsets and whose clouds appear as gold-edged islands in a clear, blue sea. A broad superhighway with an entrance at San Sebastian whizzes the visitor from Bayonne to Bilbao, bypassing most of the towns and allowing peek-a-boo glimpses of rugged seacoast and fascinating hillsides, lush and fertile. One of the Basque country's most characteristic features is its mountain peaks whose brooding promontories seem to take on the characteristics of individual personalities.

During the Middle Ages the Basque witches became renowned for their magical skills. The first historical reference may be in 1466 when a proclamation from the Spanish court deplored the presence of men and women on the shores of the Bay of Biscay who practice black witchcraft to the despair of their neighbors. They could, according to the royal edict, raise storms, blight crops, damage property, and cause sterility in men and beasts. The strongest condemnation was that they denied the divinity of Christ and practiced a pagan worship of dead souls.

Around 1500 Archdeacon Pedro Fernandez de Villegas, in an essay on Dante's *Inferno,* placed the center of Spain's witchcraft in the Basque country. In the mountains of Amboto was a cave where a deity called *la Dama* lived, the Archdeacon recorded. To her the witch sect paid homage and in her cave their holidays were celebrated. The motif of a divine lady who dwells in a cave of gold is found in Basque folk tales.

The annals of the Spanish Inquisition detail confessions obtained under torture of the witch meetings where participants denied the Christian faith, indulged in sexual orgies, and worshiped the Devil in the form of a black goat. By 1500 the witch-hunter's guide to judicial procedure, *Malleus Maleficarum,* was in use throughout Europe and trial records reflect its dictums. Martin Antoine Del Rio's *Disquisitionum Magicarum,* published in 1599, reinforced the rules with the warning: "judges are bound under pain of mortal sin to condemn witches to death who have confessed their crimes; anyone who pronounces against the death sentence is reasonably suspected of secret complicity." Yet, surprisingly enough, Spain dealt more kindly with witches than any other region. Exile or ducking and flogging were more often than not the harshest punishment imposed.

Trial records do provide glimpses of the true nature of Basque witchcraft. A woman named Maria, from Ituren, described the ingredients of the "flying ointment" that enabled her to ride the winds. Her formula combined an herb called in the Basque tongue *usainbelar* (water plantain) with the skin of a toad. Another of the accused witches described the custom of collecting wild plants when they came to blossom to be made into amulets and philters. Another tradition that is still observed forbids witches to die before passing on their knowledge to someone else.

One of the most infamous of all witch persecutions was that suffered by the French Basques during the seventeenth century. A magistrate named Pierre de Lancre (1553–1631) was sent to investigate rumors of a startling increase of sorcerers in the region called Labourd. In his capacity as King's Councilor, De Lancre proceeded to indict so many witches that the jails lacked space to hold all the accused.

Although De Lancre did not understand the Basque language and seems to have harbored a personal resentment toward the natives of Labourd, he spent over a year interrogating, recording confessions (translated into French), and sending vast numbers to the stake where they were burned alive.

Pierre de Lancre proudly reported the success of his mission in *Tableau de l'inconstance des mauvais anges* (Description of the Inconstancy of Evil Angels), published in 1612. Unfortunately, this text provides the major source material for most discussions of Basque witchcraft. And it is, in fact, little more than a vain effort to justify the inhuman cruelty in which De Lancre indulged.

Obvious errors in translation along with a natural Christian bias— Basque witchcraft had to be a form of devil worship endangering the true faith—weaken the validity of De Lancre's report.

Yet we find, scattered through the text, references that may possibly shed light on certain old customs. The witches, De Lancre states, were usually initiated as children, having been introduced by their mother or another woman who undertook to act as their guide, or *maraine.*

Every Wednesday and Friday night were set apart for the sabbats, and according to De Lancre, the assembled witches found a jug in the center of the meeting place out of which their god rose in the shape of a goat.

Margaret Murray noted that the Basque word for sabbat is *akhelarre* ("field of the goat") and for the god, *Jaincoa* ("he-goat"). Dr. Murray's *Witch–cult in Western Europe,* published in 1921, provided the subject of European witchcraft with its first scientific investigation. Her theory, based for the most part on trial records, holds that medieval witch practices were survivals of ancient religious expressions. Relying heavily on De Lancre's *Tableau,* Dr. Murray remarked the likeness of the Basque sabbat celebrations to Dionysian revels. Both centered about a deity in goat form and practiced ecstatic entry by means of frenzied dance.

Despite originality of thought and sound scholarly procedure, Dr. Murray's work is discredited by the majority of contemporary academicians. A strong argument against her thesis is that many of the witch-hunters, De Lancre, and the Jesuit Del Rio, were scholars acquainted with Roman history and Latin verse. Might they not equate the new enemies of the Church with those of the ancient world? Yet the god of the witches bears little resemblance to the Greek version of Dionysus. From De Lancre and the annals of the Spanish Inquisition we can draw a composite picture of *Jaincoa,* or Janicot.

The devil had large round inflamed eyes, the beard of a goat, a black face, the body of a man and goat combined. His fingers were hooked like talons, his toes webbed. He received his followers in the center of a heath enthroned on a chair of gold, his brow wreathed with a crown of myrtle. Around his head a light shone illuminating the whole assembly.

The Spanish painter Goya undoubtedly drew upon this description when he created "Scène de Sorcellerie," now hanging in the Prado in Madrid.

The modern view that witch persecution of the Middle Ages was a kind of ecclesiastical hysteria, a delusion, and fraud is currently undergoing a reappraisal. It is far more likely that witchcraft was practiced by the Basques. If not as a religious expression then certainly as an art. Ancient secrets of mind control, knowledge about animals and herbs— traditions as old as mankind—combined to form a body of knowledge passed down from one generation to the next. The atmosphere here with its rugged seacoast and brooding mountains seems to be exactly the kind of place custodians of occult doctrines might choose to live.

And in Basque country it is possible to travel even further back, to a time when man and magic were new. Santillana is a spectacular movie-set village in pastoral surroundings where cars vie for space on the narrow roads with horse-drawn carts spilling out sweet-smelling grass. Santillana, a village (population 800) of sleepy dogs, melodic churchbells, and cobbled streets, is filled with flowers. Its alleyways twist and turn past old stone houses, arched wooden doorways, and inhabitants leaning over their carved balconies to call down to their neighbors. There is a charming hotel here, the Los Infantes, which though expensive is a worthwhile touch of luxury in these relatively primitive surroundings. There are also cheaper places to stay.

Six or seven miles away, at the far side of the undulating velvet hills, is the unsophisticated coastal town of Suances with its white-sand beaches, but our quest takes us the other way—to Altamira where a 900-foot cave, discovered accidentally by a hunter in the last century, contains artwork executed as long ago as 14,000 years.

The bumpy ceiling of the cave is covered with paintings of bulls, bison, and boars, whose bodies and shapes conform to the irregularities in the rocky surface. Using brushes of animal hair and wooden palette knives, the unknown artist or artists created—in smoky black, sepia, red, and yellow—pictures which can still be admired today, although they are seen to better advantage when the modern lighting system is extinguished and the light provided by candle-power is more equivalent to that known by the original artists.

Because of the vulnerability of this ancient art, admission to the caves is now strictly limited; parties of only about a dozen people are allowed in at any one time. It is not unusual to arrive there early in the morning and be behind a line-up of people who had slept in their cars or buses in the spacious car park in order to be the first in line for the day. Some of the flints, primitive painting materials, and animal bones found in the cave when it was first rediscovered are on view in the attractive museum beside the car park. Color movies about the Altamira paintings are shown in several languages throughout the day.

Once inside the cave's narrow entrance, the passageway opens up into a vast underground network of many separate rooms whose ceilings range from seven to twenty feet high. Some sections are big enough to drive a bus through, in others stalactites and stalagmites fill the cramped space. The guide punctuates his commentary (in Spanish) by lighting up consecutive sections of the cave and pointing to isolated scratched drawings separate from the main "art gallery" where a canvas cover over a hummock of rocks enables the visitor to lie back and study the roof paintings from a reclining position.

The cave is quite spacious, with many twists and turns, and hollowed-out spaces may well have accommodated a substantial family or group of people at one time. The original discovery of the paintings was met with great skepticism initially, but similar cave discoveries, particularly in the south of France and northern Italy, helped to convince the experts of the paintings' authenticity. Altamira, however, is regarded as by far the finest of its genre and has been referred to as "the Sistine Chapel of prehistoric art."

"What mysterious force encouraged paleolithic man to congregate, as if in a wild flock, so many recollections of his most proximate preoccupation, which was hunting?" asks Miguel Guinea in his *Altamira: The Beginning of Art.*

> Was the bison about to disappear in the beginning of an emigration and did man try to create a fantastic world which would bring out, as if by magic or enchantment, the possibility of a reproduction so strongly desired? Did the tribe shelter itself in its mysterious conception of the world and life under the symbolical totem of the bison? Was the cave a center of rites or an occult sanctuary of a mythological incipient?
>
> Nothing, although much has been theorized upon it, can certify the reason for which rupestrine painting was provoked. An unknown relation between the hunt, magic, mystery and rites is certain, although the organized thought is hidden from us, the thought which could have explained the metaphysical or substantial worry, which as a consequence would have impelled man to the marvel of art.

Dr. Guinea suggests that it is the repetition of the animals—"pawing the ground, nodding their heads, tossing their manes or galloping in the prairies"—that is the most impressive.

Caves were used as dwellings, sanctuaries, and tombs from the earliest times and Mithra was among the earliest gods who was worshiped in them, having supposedly been born from a rock. The name of the Asia Minor earth goddess Cybele actually means "place of caves."

In his *History of Magic,* Joseph Ennemoser says:

Cybele, the goddess of all that is earthly, bears a tower on her head and a key in her hand because she bears and cherishes the towered cities and because she locks up her treasures in winter and then unlocks them. She is drawn by lions to show there is nothing so wild and untamed that may be subdued by diligence and humanity and made serviceable. Although in all temples a certain degree of silence prevailed this was most strictly observed in the worship of Cybele. "We honor man by speaking," says Plutarch, "the gods by silence."

Perhaps the Basque *la Dama*, divine lady of the cave, is a dim folk memory of Cybele retained by Phoenician seafarers swept by storms into the Bay of Biscay to settle beside the Pyrenees.

Or does the essence of Basque magic spring from a far older source than Asia Minor? The sensitivity and skill of the cave art at Altamira completely refutes the historic view of the West's Stone Age as uncivilized.

17

Chartres

IN THE STEPS OF THE DRUIDS

Driving along the highway from any direction the magnificent cathedral of Chartres with its twin spires can be seen from miles away, towering above the flat, barren plains that surround it. The cathedral itself dates to the twelfth century, but a Christian church has existed on the site since the fourth century and hundreds of years before that, at what was then known as Carnute, religious ceremonies were performed.

For 400 years preceding the birth of Christ Celtic tribes of central Europe swept across the continent ranging east to Asia Minor and west to Ireland. In 390 B.C. Celtic warriors sacked Rome. The year 279 B.C. found one of their raiding parties attacking the shrine at Delphi. But by the first century B.C. the migration impulse of the loosely knit tribes was spent and Roman legions captured this region of France called Gaul, a Celtic stronghold. Most of what we know about the Celts of Gaul was recorded at this time. Roman commentators, as the Greek geographer Posidonius before them, were especially impressed by their highly organized social structure dominated by a hierarchy of priests known as Druids.

Julius Caesar tells us that the Druids used to meet at Carnute, and

Illustration: The labyrinth in Chartres Cathedral.

Aventinus adds that when they were expelled from Gaul by the emperor Tiberius (early in the Christian era) their sacred groves were cut down. But Carnute retained its significance as a place of power and the Christians were determined to absorb it. So the site of Chartres was chosen by its unknown architect for a cathedral of surpassing beauty. Thrusting up the gray stone vaults to a height never before attained, he countered their considerable pressure with the addition of spectacular flying buttresses, reinforced by small columns arranged like the spokes of a wheel.

The effect is magnificent, even to those who neither know nor care about the intricacies of architecture, and its style inspired many a subsequent builder, notably the architects who fashioned the cathedrals at Amiens and Rheims, which were constructed in the following century.

But just as spectacular are the cathedral's 160 stained-glass windows —a fantastic mélange of yellows, reds, blues, and greens depicting tales of saints and sinners, biblical parables and early Christian emperors. There is a zodiac window depicting the astrological signs in circular medallions.

In his book *The Mysteries of Chartres Cathedral,* Louis Charpentier makes much of one of these windows through which on June 21 (summer soltstice) at midday the sun's rays shine onto a gilded metal strip set into one of the flagstones of the floor. It started him thinking about who built this magnificent cathedral—and how. Where the money came from to finance it and why Chartres itself had always been a place of pilgrimage. Charpentier discusses the subterranean currents known to the ancients, which we today call "telluric," explaining that where they were most active they were localized and condensed by tall stones used as markers. Animals and humans both prospered better in such a place, for these were fertility stones accumulating "the fertilizing properties of earth and sky."

"If the Druids gathered here," he says, "if men accepted the discomforts and dangers of pilgrimage it was because they knew they would find in this place a 'spirit.' . . . If you prefer it in modern terms let us say that this Mound on which the cathedral stands is a place where a particular telluric current comes to a head."

The cathedral's historian, Suchet, said that ancient records showed a sacred wood had once stood on the present site of the cathedral; other historians have supported this view. The Druids in fact clearly preferred woods over buildings. Pliny commented that they held nothing in greater sanctity than the oak "and of themselves they select groves of oak trees and do not celebrate any religious rites without oak leaves." Strabo added, "Groves abounding with trees of great age and extraordinary height, whose thickly interwoven boughs excluded the light of day, seemed to be more majestic than temples reared with human hands."

Some writers have suggested that they smeared the trees with the blood of victims of their gruesome sacrifices, and the Roman historian Diodorus Siculus gives us a picture of what supposedly took place on these occasions. "When they have under consideration certain matters of great consequence they have a custom which is strange and incredible. Having persuaded a man into compliance they strike him with a sacrificial knife on the part above his midriff and when he falls under the blow they divine what the result of their enterprise will be by the way in which the man falls and his limbs are scattered about as well as from the gushing of the blood, putting faith in an old and long-protracted observation of these signs." Strabo agrees with this, but says it was the back and not the breast that was struck.

Maximus Tyrius who averred that a lofty oak was "the Celtic image of the deity" wrote about where some of these sacrificial victims came from. "In war if their ranks anywhere seemed to waver they would massacre those warriors as an offering to the war god or if they suffered under any public calamity they would devote a separate victim to each of the deities under whose displeasure they imagined themselves to have fallen." Confirming this, Siculus, like Caesar, wrote that they preferred criminals to innocent people, burning them alive in huge bonfires. "For the religion of the Druids since it was characterized by revolting cruelty, since it admitted customs that were strange and incredible, since its devotees at savage altars worshiped frightful deities not without blood offerings of a most horrible kind, according to the accounts transmitted to us, was an abomination of such a nature that the cultured Romans never at any time ceased from laboring to suppress it."

Siculus added that the Druids subscribed to the doctrine of Pythagoras, believing like him that souls were immortal and entered another body on the death of one subject.

Looking around the precincts of Chartres today, with its thousands of sightseers and a whole industry having grown up around the sale of Christian souvenirs, it is hard to visualize most of these alien practices. And yet this hilltop was always a sacred place, and from all accounts, the transition from one religion to another was relatively smooth.

Many historians have commented upon the affinity between Druidism and other beliefs such as Brahmanism, Judaism, and the religion of the ancient Persians: all had sacred fires, open-air worship, and no idols. The Greeks also danced around altars, venerated the oak, and studied entrails.

And some claim to see a similarity between Druidism and Christianity. In *Written Records of the Cymri,* J. W. Arch remarks: "When a Druid instructor was persuaded of the general truth of Christianity he had fewer prejudices to surmount than any other civilized heathen of the ancient world. . . . Druids held many of the tenets inculcated in Christianity including the doctrine of immortality of the soul, a belief in miracles, reincarnation and baptism."

In the translation of rare book called *A Dissertation Upon the Druids* ("printed at Gouda by the Widow Heyne, 1650"), M. Esaias Pufendorff says that traces of the reverence this sect reserved for the mistletoe plant still remained in Gaul, notably in Burgundy where at the beginning of the year people visited their friends and invoked blessings with the words *au guy l'on neuf* ("new year of the mistletoe"). Mistletoe, he explains, could not be planted, being reproduced by passing through the stomachs of wood pigeons or thrushes, and when it was made into a dough with acorn oil took fast hold of the wings of birds unlucky enough to touch it and thus was used as a snare. The Druids believed mistletoe was a panacea and that a potion distilled from it would make sterile animals fertile. He quotes Ovid's description of the ceremony in which a Druid priest in a white robe climbed the oak tree and cut the mistletoe with a golden sickle. Beneath the tree was the altar on which two white bulls, their horns wreathed in oak leaves, were sacrificed.

In Gaul, as elsewhere, the Druidic priests exercised considerable authority. They were exempt from military service and taxes and expected their wishes to be obeyed. Pufendorff declares that they interdicted "with direful curses such refractory and obstinate offenders whether they were petty chiefs or great princes or fire and water. When the offenders had been terrified into submission the Druids endeavored to reclaim them to a better life. This interdict was indeed the greatest and severest in punishment they could inflict. For those on whom it was laid were classed with the impious and the reprobate. All men forsook them, avoided going near them or talking with them. They obtained no redress when they appealed before law and no mark of honor was paid them."

An old well just behind the Chartres cathedral, now covered over with metal grating, is said to be a Druidic well, one from which they may have studied the heavens or practiced divination rites. For, in addition to making auguries from the neighing or prancing of white horses attached to a consecrated chariot, and from the turnings or windings of a hare let loose from the arms of the diviner, Druids also practiced divination from the bubbling of water when stirred by an oak branch. The anonymous author of a book called *Thaumaturgia, or Elucidations of the Marvellous* suggests that in some of their practices the Druids had much in common with the Persian magi. Both believed in the efficacy of certain herbs, which were cut with a specially consecrated knife.

At any time of the year Chartres cathedral is crowded with visitors. They take a conducted tour of the crypt (disappointing), admire the soaring architecture, and bathe themselves in the soft light filtered through the thirteenth-century stained-glass windows. But—even on the infrequent occasions when a service is not taking place—few do more than glance casually at the elaborate maze, forty feet across, which covers the floor between two of the aisles. Formed of blue and white stones, its path is about 150 yards if followed to the center, and has the same pattern as two similar mazes at Rheims and Amiens, both now destroyed. Discussing the symbolism of such creations, Louis Charpentier points out that the path in such labyrinths is not random but fixed, implying that it was followed in a specific route for some now-unknown purpose.

"Reflect on it," he writes. "We are now in a place that was chosen for human utilization of a telluric current that surfaces and must have close analogies with currents that are magnetic." Could it be, he suggests, that the intended participant should create his own current by moving through the maze? "This is in fact the way electricity is made, by causing a rotor to revolve in a magnetic field, natural or artificial."

And British occultist Anthony Roberts adds: "The maze may possibly be linked with the geodetic currents running through the earth, more easily definable at sacred sites."

In many cases church labyrinths were once known as the road to Jerusalem and following their path "became a deed equivalent in spiritual worth to making a pilgrimage to the sacred city," explains geomancer Nigel Pennick. He adds:

> The Freemasons, inheritors of much ancient lore, traditionally dating back to the Temple of Solomon, were responsible for the design and execution of the churches and cathedrals of medieval Europe. Guided by mystical schemata they created the shrines which, in mutilated and colorless form, still survive now. Among these schemata was the labyrinth, a mystical symbol almost impossible for the uninitiated to draw, which was placed upon the correct point, the omphalos [center] of the church.
>
> The treading of it was done barefoot, or on the knees, so that the properties inherent in the omphalos might not be shielded from fulfilling the functions for which the labyrinth was originally laid out.

A century-old book about pagan Rome explains that the labyrinth is symbolic of human life. At the time of the Crusades, church labyrinths began to serve a practical purpose for the faithful who would traverse them on their hands and knees murmuring prayers. The maze at Chartres used to be 666 feet long and took one hour to complete. Later, the book says, labyrinths lost their religious meaning and became "a pastime for idlers and children."

We now head northwest, but it seems appropriate to note, while in Gaul, the legendary connection between Druidism and witchcraft to which many writers have alluded. Certainly both were prevalent in these regions, if several centuries apart. But the continuity of Druidic traditions was probably noticed only at times of specific persecution. On most other occasions historians failed to take note of it as being outside the normal fabric of day-to-day life.

As early as the eighth century, however, a council at Soissons warned the Christian bishops to be on guard against sorcery and pagan rites, and under Charlemagne a law was passed which forbade interpreting dreams, consulting with wizards, invoking storms, or even the tying of witches' knots.

In the year 1022 a band of Manichaean heretics was discovered at Orleans and burned at the stake for sorcery. In the same century and in the one that followed, two archbishops and a duke were rumored to have been killed by witches burning wax effigies. By the fourteenth century the scandal crept higher and in 1308 at Troyes, the Bishop himself, Guichard by name, was on trial accused of having bewitched to death Queen Joanna of Navarre. (He was later transferred to Avignon, examined by Pope Clement V and acquitted.)

The fourteenth century, of course, brought the scandal of the Knights Templars, with their allegedly black magic rites, and less than one hundred years after that came the international debate over another accused witch, Joan of Arc, but we shall learn about both of these stories later on at the palace of Chinon.

18

The Auvergne

MERCURY ATOP THE
MOUNTAIN

THE HEART OF FRANCE is the beautiful region of the Auvergne, a series of lovely towns set amid the tree-covered lava slopes of a score or more of extinct volcanoes. Hauntingly captivating songs, timeless folk customs, and mysterious caves and grottoes all help support the belief that magic exists here, and has always existed, in one of the most unusual areas of Europe. Fairies, witches, and werewolves people the old legends, and as elsewhere, Druids are associated with the numerous dolmens and menhirs that stand guard over lonely glades.

Somber forests, volcanic lakes, and noble waterfalls abound among the highest peaks of central France and the pleasant towns and sleepy hamlets seem to pass life as unhurriedly as they did centuries ago.

A good central destination is that curious mountain known as Puy de Dôme, supposedly the sanctuary of the ancient sun god Lug. In medieval times it was celebrated for its witch sabbats, but hundreds of years before that the Romans worshiped at its summit.

The logical entrance to the Auvergne region from the north is at the lovely town of Moulins, where one should park in the tree-lined Place

Illustration: Mercury, worshipped by both Romans and Celts as the God figure of the city. Detail from a woodcut in Wirkungen der Planten, *about 1470.*

d'Allier, bounded at the bottom end by the magnificent cathedral of Nôtre Dame, at least long enough to sit outside the Grand Hôtel or Hôtel Le Dauphin to sip a coffee and watch the hustle and bustle of the nearby market. There are two excellent museums of folklore and archeology here which offer a helpful introduction to the region, and the interesting Jacquemart, or bell tower, is renowned for its jack-o'-the-clock figures which strike every quarter hour. The town's most prized possession is a magnificent twelfth-century manuscript, the Souvigny Bible, bound in red velvet and gold, and preserved along with 40,000 other volumes in the municipal library.

Souvigny itself, seven miles to the west through countryside filled with the beautiful white cows of the region, is a sleepy little town dominated by the priory church of St. Pierre, outside which stands an ancient stone market cross and a rusted iron pump. The church, some of which dates back to the eleventh century, is famous for its amazing cloisters, in which, spotlighted, is the renowned Calendar Stone, a tall pillar of the twelfth century covered with delicately carved signs of the zodiac and such mythical beasts as griffins, unicorns, and manticores. Obviously Christianity and astrology were not always strangers to each other, as we shall again see when we visit the church of St. Austremoine at Issoire further south.

Around the Calendar Stone in this underground crypt at Souvigny are innumerable other treasures, including tombs made from worn rock, statues with no heads, apparently awaiting repair, and an occasional head gazing stony-eyed at the calendar.

Not far away is the village of St. Remi, centered around an enormous, well-lit square bounded by cafés and opening onto narrow back streets whose houses retain the character of centuries past. The Van Gogh Hôtel is a reminder that the celebrated artist once committed himself to an institution here. A native son of St. Remi was the celebrated astrologer Nostradamus, born here in 1503. Nostradamus studied at the University of Montpellier, whose school of medicine was said to have been founded by Arab physicians forced out of Spain in the twelfth century.

Nostradamus was fond of saying that the perfect knowledge of medicine was unattainable without the help of astrology. Henry II and Catharine de' Medici, who were among his earliest patrons, thought him a genius and endowed with supernatural powers. Among his predictions were Henry's death in the tournament of St. Quentin and his subsequent posthumous popularity; Napoleon's exile to Elba; the dates of the Great Fire of London and the French Revolution; and the capture of Marseilles by the Spaniards.

On one occasion, while accompanying Lord Flounville, Nostradamus saw a black pig and a white pig and forecast that his companion would eat the black pig and a wolf would eat the white one. To confound his prophecy Lord Flounville had his cook roast the white pig, but before it could be served a tame wolf sneaked into the kitchen and devoured it.

His prophetic method was a marvelous mélange of plays on words, anagrams, and puzzles—put together in magnificent verse. He went through the centuries ahead predicting a wide range of events, including his own death on July 2, 1566.

The road southward into the Auvergne proper enters a magical region of haunted castles, mysterious stones, springs with legendary properties, and magnificent chateaus. Gold was found here in abundance in Gallic times, and the workers' pickaxes of today still occasionally unearth some ancient artifact. The chateaus, all gloriously majestic and most of them open to the public, are everywhere, especially within sight of the slow-moving river in the fertile Loire valley. A tourist board leaflet lists more than 200 different chateaus in this part of France.

Once you get accustomed to the washboard nature of second-class roads which make driving in France somewhat akin to riding horseback, you'll be able to appreciate the distinctive beauty of the Auvergne landscape. By day selective mists hover over certain fields as though they had been celestially selected for mysterious ceremonies; at night it is as if a soft velvet curtain had been drawn across the cloudless sky to close out the day. The lush green land is dotted with red-tiled cottages, sleepy villages, and amiable cows. It is made-to-measure country for the traveler with, say, a VW bus in which to stay. One can stop overnight in any of a score of villages with tree-shaded squares for overnight parking beside the public toilets and awaken to the sound of church bells, fresh running water from the village fountain, and delightful cafés for hot croissants and coffee.

The road leads to graceful Riom with its unhelpful tourist office and folklore museum (closed Mondays). Then onward through the industrial city of Clermont-Ferrand, nominal "capital city" of the Auvergne, before ascending the 5,000-foot Puy de Dôme, one of the most famous mountains in France, and certainly its most mysterious. Last stop before the summit is at the elegant spa town of Royat, where for 2,000 years the thermal waters have been regarded as healthful. A pleasant park in the center of town houses the up-to-date thermal baths, and scattered around surrounding hills are the somewhat faded grand hotels that made Royat so much more fashionable a century ago. The area is riddled with mysterious caves and grottoes, some with petrifying waters, and every second shop sells postcards and souvenirs.

The drive to the summit of Puy de Dôme, seven miles away, is steep, and the view is spectacular, looking out for miles over barren hills and moors. At first it is sunny, the bright rays forming curious patterns of light and shade on the surrounding landscape; but, as often as not, the familiar mist will descend cloaking everything in a hazy gauze. It is as if the pockets of mist from the surrounding fields were suddenly gathered up and spread over the hill to hide its secrets. And how many secrets must this ancient hill conceal! For centuries it was the meeting place for all the witches of the district who assembled here to celebrate their sabbats.

Much of the information about these meetings has come down to us through the confession of "la femme Boisdeau," a witch named Jeanne Boisdeau who was tried for sorcery in 1594 and later burned at the stake.

"On the night of Midsummer's Day," reads her confession (quoted by Henri Pouvrat in *Gaspard des Montagnes*), "witches came there from Auvergne, Limousin, la Marche, Velay, Vivarain, Geraudan, even from as far as Languedoc. For they only had to mount their broomsticks and they were taken there in the twinkling of an eye by the winds of the night. Satan was their master, in the form of a he-goat. He received them at the middle of a circle braced in the turf at the summit of the mountain. Each of them came to light his candle from the black candle he wore on his horns and to kiss his rump devoutly. To start the sabbat, the devil said mass in his own manner with a slice of radish by way of a sacrament. Then he meted out the tricks of witchcraft for their New Year, generously distributing charms against fire, wolves and wild animals and breathing on his henchmen to give them the power to predict the future."

According to popular tradition, at the spot on Puy de Dôme known as *le Cratère du Nid de la Poule* ("the crater of the hen's nest"), an enormous black hen with three tails appeared during this black mass, laid three black eggs, then disappeared into the flames of the fire. The witches broke the eggs and found Satan's orders for the coming year.

"Sitting on the bare grass," continues Pouvrat, "these accursed creatures made a meal of bread, wine and cheese—all provisions laid out together to show that they were brothers. Then, until the time when the air turns from pale to red, their ceremonies continued with debauchery, atrocities and lewdness which are not worth recounting."

According to Boisdeau's confession, however, one of the ceremonies was the following of a black goat in a back-to-back dance, the oldest person present holding his tail and the remainder of the company holding hands. This, says Margaret Murray in *The Witch-cult in Western Europe*, is the earliest known type of dance, and was usually associated with fairies. It was regarded as "a sinister ceremony" by those charged with stamping out the Old Religion in the Middle Ages. The ring usually moved to the left and where the dancers faced outward, as in France, the movement was *widdershins* ("against the sun").

Witchcraft was at one time a part of daily life in the Auvergne just as in many other regions of France. Most people had experiences, direct or indirect, and even the author Pascal had dealings with witches. Jacques Chevalier, in *Dictionnaire des Auteurs,* writes: "Between the ages of one and two, his niece relates, something extraordinary happened to him; he could not bear the sight of water, nor the sight of his father and mother close to one another. In order to exorcise the spell cast on him by a woman it was necessary to transfer it to a black cat which died, and to apply to the child a poultice of nine leaves and three blades of grass picked before sunrise by a child less than seven years old."

At Languedoc, from whence witches were said to have come to the Puy de Dôme celebrations, a horrible story circulated in 1321 that sorcerers had poisoned the wells and streams with a ghastly paste made from a distillation of blood, urine, and herbs, mixed together with the holy sacrament stolen from churches. One woman who was arrested was found in possession of a gruesome paste made from the head of a snake, legs of a toad, and strands of human hair. Horrified by the public outcry, King Philip V commanded that all the guilty be burned alive: 600 accused witches went to the stake.

Nine years later, at Carcassonne, three shepherds and eight women were convicted of killing cattle and flocks by evil spells; in 1335 at Toulouse 63 people accused of witchcraft confessed to regular attendance at sabbats and having intercourse with the devil in the shape of a black goat. The Inquisition at Carcassonne sent 200 witches to the stake between 1320 and 1350; at Toulouse during the same period 400 more witches were burned alive.

Nor had any of this been a recent phenomenon. A law passed under Charlemagne in 800, according to Montague Summers in *The Geography of Witchcraft*, forbade consultation with wizards, interpretation of dreams, taking omens. "Enchanters, diviners, mediums, those who brew philtres, invokers of storm or hail, those who tie a witches' knot—all are to be shunned. Let them amend their ways or they will be cast into a close prison. Fairy trees, pagan monoliths, haunted wells, the rendezvous of witches are to be destroyed and demolished utterly."

The he-goat, incidentally, is only mentioned in accounts of continental witchcraft. Links with Pan and Dionysus possibly influenced the medieval French to choose the goat as a symbol of lewdness. When the Romans controlled the Auvergne they did not honor a sylvan god on the heights of Puy de Dôme but rather the urban Mercury, god of commerce. A magnificent temple to Mercury dominated its summit.

The fabulous remains of this temple, a series of well-preserved stone terraces sweeping up a central platform inset with semicircular chambers, can still be seen today and are amazingly impressive, especially considering how long it must have taken to transport the stones to the top of the hill. The temple is believed to date to the first century A.D., and some pottery fragments discovered during excavations in the eighteenth century are preserved in the nearby museum. This museum is very disappointing, devoted much more to the meteorological observations taken atop the hill than to the extraordinary Roman remains that stayed covered for so many centuries.

Although the museum (admission: 1 franc) displays an artist's reconstruction of what the impressive temple must have looked like originally with its five Parthenon-type columns, it is otherwise hardly worth visiting. Bronze statuettes and inscriptions to Mercury originally found at the site are now preserved at Nîmes (whose own Roman ruins are surely the most impressive in France, and well worth a visit).

Mercury, whose solitary temple on the Aventine hill in Rome was built in 495 B.C., was never the most popular of the Roman gods and derived his origin from Greece, whose equivalent god was Hermes. The son of Jupiter and Maia, a daughter of Atlas, Mercury is said to have invented the lyre from a tortoise shell. He gave this to Apollo, who rewarded him with with the caduceus, or "magic wand," he is always depicted as carrying, and which could reconcile all conflicting elements.

Mercury was regarded as the god of eloquence, speed, rain and wind, and the special patron of travelers, shepherds, and thieves. Appointed messenger of the gods and given winged sandals and a winged cap, Mercury's major function, according to Homer, was to conduct the souls of the dead "that jibber like bats as they fare down dank ways, past the streams of oceans, past the gates of the sun and the land of dreams, to the mead of Asphodel in the dark realms of Hades, where dwell the souls, the phantoms of men outworn."

Just beside the temple, at a spot where the view is at its most magnificent (on days without fog), is a curious machine which for one franc yields a tape-recorded commentary in any of four languages. Pointing out that on a clear day Mont Blanc can be seen 300 kilometers away, it advises staying on the summit until sunset, when the sun "setting with tongues of fire" can be seen gently sinking behind the mountains. Further down the hill, beside the car park, a cavernous snack bar sells ash trays of enameled lava rock. Until 1926 a steam railway ran to the top of Puy de Dôme; it was replaced by the present toll road.

Not far away is the hill of Montjuset, which originally took its name from another Roman temple, this one dedicated to Jupiter. According to a century-old book by the Abbé Delarbre, the temple was served by women named *fatuae* ("fairies") and *fatidicae* ("diviners") who initiated and indoctrinated young girls who were called *bonnes filles* ("good girls") into their mysteries and ceremonies.

Fairies seem to have been prevalent in the whole region. In a field near the road between Champeix and Ludesse is a fourteen-foot menhir known as *Pierre des Fées,* or "fairy stone"; nearer to Ludesse is a logan stone and some early Roman remains known as *cabanes des fées,* or "fairy huts." At St.-Floret-le-Chastel, just south of Champeix, the fairies were reputed to inhabit the pool in a grotto whose water was thought to cure sick children. It was the custom after washing, to throw the wet linen used against the roof of the grotto; if it stayed there the child would be cured. In the chateau of Saint-Floret thirteen surviving frescoes out of the original thirty depict episodes of the Tristan romance, notably the hero's fight with thirty-six knights led by the fairy Morgan le Fey.

At Ronzières a chapel was built by St. Baudine on a site supposedly consecrated to the fairies, with a statue to protect the spring. Over the years the chapel was demolished and the statue disappeared, but according to a local folktale, a farmer plowing his fields noticed that his bullocks always stopped beside some bushes and refused to go farther. Investigation of the spot revealed the statue hidden in the bushes.

Clermont-Ferrand (population 200,000), now one of the major world centers of the rubber industry, preserves interesting Roman remains in its Historical and Fine Arts museums. In the town center, the Place de Jaude, from which Puy de Dôme can be clearly seen, stands the statue to Vercingetorix, a brave young leader of the Gauls who fought against Julius Caesar. The freedom-loving, independent Gauls, whose major pursuits were hunting, rearing cattle, and collecting gold jewelry, resisted fiercely when Caesar was made their governor in 57 B.C. and Vercingetorix, barely out of his teens, became their champion when his father was killed by men friendly to the new Roman overlords. With a hastily assembled army, Vercingetorix massacred the Romans in what is now Orléans, burning a score of towns in the path of the oncoming legions before being besieged and captured in Alesia. He was taken to Rome and imprisoned for five years before being forced to march in Caesar's triumphant homecoming procession and brutally executed in the cramped Marmentine prison adjoining the ancient Roman forum.

Some altar stones found under Nôtre Dame in Paris and that are now in the Cluny Museum give us some information about the ancient Gauls. The Gallic gods are described as "thickset, heavy men, bearded and with blazing deep-set eyes." Among them was Esus, the god of summer and an incessant demander of sacrifices, men nailed to oak trees and burned on oak fires (a custom made familiar to us in Roman accounts); and Cernunnos, the stag-like horned god of the moon, and death.

In the older section of Clermont-Ferrand can be found the twelfth-century church of Nôtre-Dame-du-Port with one of its exterior carvings representing Adam and Eve and showing the tree of life as a "Y"—a symbol used in alchemy and known as the *Yggdrasil* in Nordic myths.

The area south of Clermont-Ferrand is ruggedly beautiful: deep valleys with jagged rocks jutting from all angles high above the road. On these cloud-shrouded peaks ruins of forts or castles can often be seen. Auvergne sunsets are spectacular: clouds turn orangey-red in the silver-blue skies, all dazzlingly reflected in the ponds which spread languidly beside the road. The fields are full of oversized sunflowers, left to die for the harvest of their seeds.

There are traces of what may have been an Isis cult at Chambon-sur-lac, to the east, in the rotunda of the local cemetery, and at Massiac, south of Issoire. The *Guide de l'Auvergne Mysterieuse* talks of a curious custom that used to be celebrated every Midsummer Day. *La vache de la St. Jean* ("the cow of St. John's Day," or Midsummer's Day) was purchased at the market on June 9, covered with multicolored ribbons and marched through town to the accompaniment of music. Before being killed for the feast on June 21, this creature had the right to graze in all the meadows of the valley and none should prevent it. Only one man in the town's history dared to chase the cow from his pastures, the guide adds, and this farmer, a certain Gaspard d'Epinchal, was stricken with a crick in his neck which would not heal until he made amends. The custom may have been a relic of an ancient ceremony, for the cow was the symbol of Isis, goddess of the moon. At summer solstice when the sun retreated, the moon was welcomed to rule in his stead.

The church in the little mountain town of Issoire must surely be one of the most impressive in France. Graceful arcades sweep up the outside to the central bell tower, ornate and somber at the same time. Inside, the atmosphere is one of contented contemplation. Religious associations aside, the beauty and general feeling of tranquillity transcend traditional Christianity. The columns, painstakingly painted in vivid reds and rich golds and surmounted with carved figures, lead skyward to a high dome whose paint is now beginning to peel. If you are lucky the organist will be playing, filling even the darkest corner with rich chords and causing the whole church to swell and solemnly pulsate with unfathomable mystery.

One reason to visit this twelfth-century church, the largest in the Auvergne, is to inspect the carved signs of the zodiac gracefully adorning the upper walls of the church on the outside. They must be looked for carefully, however, because the church is covered with centuries of dirt. All the carved stone medallions are original except for the ram of Aries, which was remade in the last century.

A fabulous treasure is said to be buried under the old abbey, now the local lycée, hidden there by the Catholics when the town was pillaged by Protestant invaders in 1575. The fortune was never found when the town was recaptured, although unhappy times are prophesied for anyone "lucky" enough to discover it.

19

Chinon

ST. JOAN AND THE KNIGHTS
TEMPLARS

THE BEAUTIFUL TOWN OF CHINON, southwest of Tours, is totally dominated by the magnificent chateau towering over the sleepy community. From the sandy walls of this spacious castle, the gray stone houses beside the river hundreds of feet below present an enchanting picture relieved as they are by patches of trees and the roofs of fourteenth- and fifteenth-century houses among more modern buildings. Innumerable bakeries and flower stalls dot the narrow streets of the town. An equestrian statue of Joan of Arc, in the fields beside the winding river, shares the attention of visitors with a Delacroix portrait of the celebrated author Rabelais, a native son, in the town hall.

The hilltop castle itself, on the site of earlier forts dating to pre-Christian times, is solidly built of limestone. Magnificent towers and bulwarks adjoin spacious, green lawns, and gazing down from the ramparts through the pleasant haze of a summer's afternoon, it is easy to imagine the kings who have stood here and admired this panorama. For Chinon was a royal palace from the twelfth to the fifteenth century, and both English and French kings left their mark upon it.

In the eighty-foot-high tower of Coudray castle, one of three which

Illustration: An early graphic form of the fleur-de-lys often found on French bearings.

comprise the fortress and together cover the hilltop, the Knights Templars were imprisoned after their arrest in 1308, and in this same tower a century later Joan of Arc stayed, while the advisers of the future King Charles VII checked out her claims.

The fourteenth and fifteenth centuries were times of great turmoil and confusion for France with control of the country seesawing back and forth across the Channel. In 1347 the English conquered the port of Calais, and although their successes in France varied, they managed to retain this beachhead for the next two centuries. By 1420 with a mad king (Charles VI) on the French throne, civil war ravaging the country, and the future Charles VII officially disinherited by his mother, Queen Isabella, the English occupiers controlled much of the country.

The disinherited heir, Charles, apparently had no future. Beset by doubts and surrounded by sycophants, he lived a life of indolence in the palace of Chinon. So notorious was his mother, Isabella of Bavaria, so scandalous her conduct, the young Dauphin was uncertain of even his parentage. One tradition has it that Charles VI dabbled in magic, and when he went mad unsuccessful incantations had been offered for his recovery.

It was into this scene on March 9, 1429 that Jehanne la Pucelle ("Joan the Maid") intruded. For years she had been hearing mysterious "voices" while living at Domremy, the tiny village on the Meuse at which she had been born seventeen years before. This part of France—the Lorraine—had long been steeped in mysticism, and it was here that only a century before the Synod of Trèves had met to condemn what it described as "all kinds of magic, sorcery, witchcraft, auguries, superstitious writings . . . and the illusions of women who boast that they ride at night with Diana or with Herodias and a multitude of other women."

Boulourmak wrote that at her birth "an extraordinary and unaccountable exultation" was manifest throughout the village. The people ran from house to house rejoicing, although they did not know why. "The cocks crew," he recorded, "with unusual vehemence on this occasion."

Was Joan of Arc a witch? It is a question that is still debated inconclusively to this day. Margaret Murray theorizes that Joan was voluntarily a "divine victim," a sacrificial victim in whom the spirit of God resides until the appointed time "when no hand may be outstretched to save him."

In *The God of the Witches,* Dr. Murray comments: "If Joan were a pagan and in the eyes of her pagan following a substitute for the king and therefore God Incarnate for the time being, much of the obscurity which surrounds her life and death is cleared away." Joan came from a pagan area—hundreds of witches from surrounding districts were executed in the following century—and had first reported hearing her "voices" near what was known locally as the Fairy Tree. Even her title, La Pucelle, was significant in witchcraft circles where the Maid is a person of high rank in the coven.

The twelfth-century historian Geoffrey of Monmouth records a prophecy by Merlin that "a marvellous maid will come from the Nemus Cenutum for the healing of nations," and at the time of the Maid's triumphs this came to be identified with the Bois Chenue, a wood near Domremy. The so-called Fairy Tree, an oak, was there—the children regularly hung garlands on it—and it was supposed to be there that, in an ancient tale, Pierre, Lord of Bourlemont, had met his fairy love.

One allegation eventually made about Joan was that she had been in the habit of attending the regular Friday night witches' sabbat at the fountain near this oak. Joan's confessor, Pasquerel, later said that it was while she was on her way from Domremy to Chinon that she encountered a man on horseback who swore at her. "In God's name, why do you swear, and you so near your death?" she was reported as saying. And scarcely one hour later the rider fell from his horse into a moat and drowned.

Tradition has it that Joan waited two days at Chinon for a royal audience and then was shown into the castle's great hall where Charles waited, hidden among the 300 nobles and courtiers, one of whom was dressed in the royal garb. But the Maid did not hesitate. Advancing directly to the young Dauphin she knelt at his feet and declared: "The King of Heaven sends word by me that you will be anointed and crowned in the city of Reims, and you will be the Lieutenant of the King of Heaven, who is the King of France."

The great hall of Chinon still exists today, empty and barren of furnishings, and so does the adjoining Château of Coudray in whose tower Joan was lodged while she was being questioned by the bishops surrounding the Dauphin. Eventually she satisfied her examiners about her sincerity and gave instructions where a certain sword could be found behind the church altar in the little town of St. Catherine-de-Fierbois. It was by some mystical divine revelation, she explained, that she knew of the whereabouts of this sword; it had five fleurs-de-lis engraved on each of its sides. With this weapon, she told Charles, and the aid of his good soldiers, she would raise the siege at Orléans and bring him to his coronation at Rheims where previous kings had been crowned.

After choosing as her patron and protector a rich knight from her own province, Gilles de Rais (who, nine years later, was tried and executed for witchcraft), she told the king: "I shall only last a year; take the good of me as long as it is possible"—a significant remark that indicated her awareness of her fate. Then donning the suit of white armor inlaid with silver given to her by the queen of Sicily, she set off on April 27 on what was to become a triumphant campaign.

"The English hated her lustily as a witch casting spells and enchantments so that the strength was sucked out of a man's arm and the courage from his heart," writes Mrs. Margaret Oliphant in *Jeanne d'Arc.* And many on both sides believed her to have supernatural powers. Some saw white butterflies forever dancing around her standard, a white flag depicting lily fields and angels.

But whatever the source of her strength, it triumphed—at least for the year that she had predicted. "I fear nothing but treason," she told visiting peasants from her native village. And after a series of successful battles she was able to fulfill her promise and accompany Charles to Rheims, where he was crowned on July 17, 1429. Although she fell at his feet and said her task was finished she was prevailed upon to continue, later being wounded during the attack of Paris, a city where the return to French control was so strongly resisted that Charles finally called off the attack and retreated.

The following year Joan was captured by the Burgundians at Compiègne, the gold-embroidered, crimson tunic she wore over her armor making her an easily identifiable target. Despite her services to king and country, none in France made a move to ransom her during a long imprisonment. She tried unsuccessfully to escape from prison (or kill herself) by jumping from the sixty-foot tower in which she was held. She was sold to the English who immediately began to make preparations for her trial.

"It is evident that in this frightful pause of fate," Mrs. Oliphant explains, "Jeanne had become to France as to England the witch whom it was perhaps a danger to have anything to do with; whose spells had turned the world upside down for a moment. But these spells had become ineffectual or worn out, as is the nature of sorcery."

At the lengthy show trial that followed, much was made by the prosecutors about Joan's background and her visions. She was asked if she owned a mandrake, a root popularly supposed to possess magical qualities, and Joan denied it. She was asked about her "voices" and named four saints, Gabriel, Michael, Marguerite, and Catherine, as the bearers of her tidings. Margaret Murray says her description of the voices "shows that they were certainly human beings" and suggests that whoever guided her in her answers to the court "guided her to her doom."

The mere possession of a mandrake was regarded, at one time, as prima facie evidence of practicing witchcraft, and three women were put to death in 1630 when mandrakes were found in their homes in Hamburg.

The mandrake's magical associations go back at least 2,500 years to a time when it was also believed to have aphrodisiac attributes. Hippocrates said it would relieve depression and anxiety. Six hundred years later, the first-century Greek physician Dioscorides wrote that a patient about to be operated upon was given mandrake and became "overborne with dead sleep" so that the surgeon could conduct his operation pain-lessly. The diluted juice of the root, at that time, was commonly used to produce a dreamlike sleep that could last for days. Sometimes people who were to be crucified were given a sponge soaked in the mandrake juice, to produce insensibility.

According to legend the mandrake was a dangerous thing to dig up and unless the digger covered his ears he was liable to go mad on hearing the scream it made as it was pulled from the ground. On the other hand, if he failed to dislodge it, he was likely to disappear forever, pulled down into the earth by the fiend that guarded it.

Joan's "voices," said her critics, were the result of delirium caused by the juice of the mandrake, the root of which she was alleged to have kept in her bodice. Academicians and clerics joined to pronounce her "Sorcière, devineresse, fausse prophète, invocatrice de demons, conjura-trice, superstitieuse remplie et entierment adonnes a la magie . . ." The opinion of the savants at the University of Paris was that Joan was "a woman of Belial, Satan and Behemoth."

History records that she was burned at the stake in the city of Rouen on May 30, 1431, but Dr. Murray questions this, quoting the *Journal d'un Bourgeois de Paris* to the effect that "someone else had been burned and not herself." Five years after the trial Joan's brother visited Orléans to declare that his sister was still alive and in July 1439 turned up accom-panied by a woman who claimed to be Joan, by then married. Yet in 1456 when an inquiry into her earlier trial resulted in an official Sen-tence of Rehabilitation, the family apparently accepted it on behalf of the Maid who had been burned to death by the English in 1431.

In his *Trial of Joan of Arc*, Scott Donceaur comments that it is hard to draw any firm conclusions about Joan's actual capacities as a witch. "That she had some very extraordinary abilities—adolescent virgins often attract mystical vibrations by their 'innocent' auras—is certainly without question."

The common people believed her to be saintly, setting up representa-tions of her in shrines and carrying metal images of her about their person. According to written records of the period, Joan cured the sick by her presence and her followers constantly assembled to touch her garments as she passed. A long-time pagan festival that took place in Orléans was, after her time, celebrated as the *Fêtes de Jeanne d'Arc*. But, as Dr. Murray explains, many of Joan's comments were ambiguous, and "she utterly refused to acknowledge the authority of the Church" and declined to say the Lord's Prayer—"a refusal which in later times would have been tantamount to confessing herself a witch."

Although there is an interesting Joan of Arc museum in the clock tower of the fortress, complete with weapons and armor of the period and maps depicting the Maid's fifteenth-century campaigns, no trace of her residence remains in the cylindrical, three-story Coudray keep where she is said to have passed her time in captivity.

But there is much graffiti on the walls of this tower which popular legend attributes to the Knights Templars, sixty of whom, including the Grand Master Jacques de Molay, were imprisoned here in 1308. They were examined by a commission of cardinals and then taken to Paris to be tortured and executed.

The graffiti on the walls of this circular, ground-floor room with its vaulted arches, include the name *Molay* scratched above a rough drawing of a stag chased by a hound. Other markings include heraldic banners, crosses, kneeling figures, and an enigmatic sign composed of a cross with a rounded base supporting a slightly flattened sphere girded by two wavy, curving lines. This bears a resemblance to a cabalistic symbol for movement and life. In addition, the graffiti include three examples of an open hand—an emblem much used during the Middle Ages as a talisman against evil spells. It is related to the little amulets of metal, coral, or ivory known among the Arabs as the "hands of Fatima," used to drive away malevolent spirits. The Moors of Spain carved them on the doors of the Alhambra in Granada, and Gautier in his *Voyage in Spain* explains that it was believed these hands had the power to ward off the evil eye.

The Knights Templars, founded in the eleventh century to protect Christian Crusaders to the Holy Land, soon became a power in their own right and as the Crusades declined, the Templars became the bankers of the Mediterranean, holding huge tracts of land in Paris and in other European cities. It was even said that they possessed a flotilla of bizarre ships which traveled to unknown parts beyond the ends of the earth.

Although one of their early symbols was two impoverished knights sharing one horse, riding together, the Templars soon became very prosperous. They took their name from the so-called Temple of Solomon, adjoining the royal palace in Jerusalem. Their rules were secretive, never divulged to anyone outside the order, and novices were initiated at night behind closed doors. "Their uniforms were white, their spurs of solid gold, and their image was pride." The French king, Philip IV, at one time sympathetic to the Templars, eventually became greedy for both their power and possessions, and when his application for membership was refused he laid elaborate secret plans to stamp out the order.

They were said to have first been denounced at Toulouse by a Templar, who lay in jail under sentence of death, and word reached the Prior of Montfaucon who accused them. The trials took place over five years in various countries and confessions were so commonly obtained under torture that it is difficult today to determine what statements were actually true.

Thomas Wright, in *Narratives of Sorcery and Magic,* says one of the charges made against the Templars was that they worshiped the head of an idol which they were told was their god, their Mohammed. Many Templars confessed to having seen this head, but described it differently. Some said it was of frightful appearance with a long beard and sparkling eyes, others that it was a man's skull or had three faces. It was said to be of wood, of metal, of gilt. The one belonging to the order at Paris was described as being of silver with two faces and one beard.

Although their "crime" was probably the fact that they controlled vast sums of money and the king needed funds, there seems to be no doubt that the Templars did practice curious rites with Gnostic and cabalistic overtones, and that they brought back with them from the Orient more or less occult doctrines from many different heresies, most of which had their origins around the beginning of the Christian era and were in direct competition with Christianity.

One such "heresy" was Manichaeism which, by recognizing the principle of twin gods—"good" and "evil"—gave recognition to the power of Satan. The third-century Persian prophet and philosopher Mani, crucified and flayed alive by the Zoroastrian Magi under Bahram I in A.D. 277, had taught Gnostic dualism. This was a belief that the powers of light and darkness represented good and evil and that man was a mixture of both; his spiritual side was represented by God and his body (especially his sexual passions) was governed by the devil. The Manicheans repudiated Judaism and Catholic Christianity as false doctrines. The sect enjoyed a relatively brief spell of popularity in Rome from A.D. 208 until 440, when it was outlawed by Pope Leo I. The Templars' beliefs were akin to those of the Bulgarian Bogomils and the Cathars of southern France; both were contemporary with the Templars and both suffered a similar fate.

Some averred that the Templars' vast wealth accrued through the practice of alchemy, their knowledge based on a long-lost manuscript known as "The Key of Solomon," the most celebrated and feared work of ancient times.

"The Templars' trial," says journalist Craig Copetas, "was one of politics and not really one of blasphemous actions. Their occult wisdom was renowned throughout Europe and they were greatly feared by monarchs because they were consolidating both occult power and vast financial wealth. The mass slaughter in 1307–8 only made their ranks stronger and their practices more secret. Although they were Christian in name, their foundings and tenets were quite definitely shrouded in the mysterious working of Arab occultism."

Grand Master Jacques de Molay, after a sequence of confessions, withdrawals, torture, more confessions, and a final protestation of innocence, was burned alive in front of Paris' Nôtre Dame on March 14, 1314, in the presence of the entire royal family of France. While covered in flames he pronounced a final curse on Pope Clement, King Philip of France, and his minister Nogart. Molay said: "I summon you to appear before the Tribunal of God before a year is over."

Clement V died forty days after the Templars were sentenced, his last words: "I'm burning up." Soon after, Nogart died, a similar statement on his lips. And finally, one month after the death of Nogart, Philip himself died in the Forest of St. Maenxe while chasing "a mysterious stag or boar." (Remember Molay's drawing on the walls of the Coudray tower?) Philip's last words, as his companions rushed to his side, were, "I'm very hot, very thirsty."

The Templars' sins were allegedly more sacrilegious than criminal. Occult books all discuss the allegations made against them in some depth, concentrating especially on the infamous kiss bestowed on the deity, and emphasizing its similarity to what was confessed in a later age when so many French witches admitted they had "kissed the goat's backside." It is probable that the infamous kiss of the Templars inspired the inquisitors to, with leading questions, extract one more shocking detail from the accused witches.

In the secret archives of the Vatican, inspected recently by Copetas, are documents which refer conclusively to the Templars' homosexual proclivities and to their experiments with psychedelic drugs, a practice they had learned from the Arabs. Under torture, in most cases more obscene than their alleged crimes, individual Templars confessed to worshiping an idol with a dead cat's head, spitting on the cross, and carrying out sodomic practices.

The persecution of the Templars was most cruel in France, more lenient in England where the order was suppressed with no executions. In Spain the severity of the judges varied: members were pronounced innocent in Castile while reduced by force in Aragon because they attempted to resist with arms. In Germany the Templars gave up their own order only to be admitted into others. The Pope was offended at the leniency shown to the order in England, Spain, and Germany, although in all these places it was abolished and its memory branded with disgrace.

Some of the Knights were said to have remained together, later forming their own secret societies. Even today this rumor is still heard and the modern Freemasons are often thought to be descended from the Templars' traditions.

20

Brittany

STONES OF POWER

Apart from being extraordinarily beautiful the province of Brittany in northwest France is one of the most magical areas of Europe. Skirted on three sides by the sea and populated by a Celtic people who share many of the ancient beliefs of other Celts (such as the Welsh, the Irish, and the Cornish), Brittany is a repository of all the myths and legends that have long disappeared from more sophisticated regions. From the westernmost tip off Brest, where on the island of Sena dwelt nine virgin witches with the power to raise winds and storms (according to the Roman historian Pomponius Mela), to the northeastern island of Mont-Saint-Michel, on the Normandy-Brittany border, where once roamed giants, the area is steeped in the kind of thinking that always has a supernatural explanation for the inexplicable.

The Héloïse who loved Abélard is still regarded as a Druidess in these parts, and strange ballads extolling her magic powers are part of the region's folklore which maintains that fairies built the Druid monuments. Breton proverbs recall the exploits of necromancers and enchanters, and many tiny villages and hamlets were said to be the dwell-

Illustration: The triskelion, a common Celtic magic symbol. From a shield of the La Tène period (500 B.C.–1 A.D.)

ing places of witches not much more than a century ago.

Memories of old customs live on in the rural rites of the Catholic Church, whose feast days embody many pagan customs. Water that flows from the wells on Easter Day is believed to have especially magic qualities and the Feast of Les Brandons, on the first Sunday in Lent, when villagers rush through the fields after sunset brandishing lighted torches, is likely a survival of an older custom of nature worship.

"This ceremony is in conception magical; fire and song are to consecrate the crops and drive away spiritual and mortal forms of evil," writes Andrew Lang in the *Folk Lore Record* for 1878. He refers to the rural novels of George Sand. "There the curious can read about *fées,* or fairies; the *grande-bête*—a shapeless flying terror of the night; the spectres who wash dead men's bodies by moonlight; the werewolves and *le meneur des loups,* a wizard whom the wolves follow in his darkling walks; the *herbe qui égare* [whose] fragrance turns the traveler from his path." The reader also learns, he says, "how to guard your health from witchcraft, how to see a vision of your future husband, where 'Arthur's hunt' " may be met and "where to see the Druid stones dance around the Virgin Mary."

It is not always easy to delineate where paganism ends and "modern" religion begins. What are we to make of the curate of a Breton village who leads his choristers in a solemn procession on St. Anne's Day to burn the prow of an old boat in which a serpent is tethered? Or the custom in some places of burning at a crossroads the mattress of someone who dies and examining the ashes next morning for footprints in case the deceased has returned to seek the prayers of his friends?

There are other interesting beliefs. Animals are supposed to have the power of speech on Christmas Eve and a new house is exorcised, by the family taking possession, with the sacrifice of a cockerel and similar rites.

Until the last century the Abbey of Poissy held an annual mass with the sole purpose of protecting the nuns from the power of the feys, or fairies, notes Joseph Ritson in *Folklore & Legends.* He adds helpfully: "The fairy may be defined as a species of being, partly material, partly spiritual, with a power to change its appearance and be to mankind visible or invisible according to its pleasure."

In Brittany the classic manifestation of this spirit is the *korrigan,* or "fairy," who haunts the glades and forests and who is believed to possess powers of enchantment to lead men to their doom, where they perish from hopeless love. Outlawed by the church, along with other relics of paganism, *korrigans* are said by some to be pagan princesses of Brittany who refused to submit to Christianity when it encroached on their terrain and have remained outcasts ever since, hating all who approach them.

According to A. Lang, writing in the last century:

So widespread was this primitive supersitition, this belief in the deadly lore of the spectral forest women, that a friend of mine declares he knew a native who actually died, as he himself said he would, after meeting one of the fairy women of the wild wood.

Looking back on the field of French folklore we seem to detect more of primitive practices and superstitions than in England; France escaped the full force of the Reformation and the Catholic church has always been more tolerant of the earlier rites, which she sanctified, while puritans persecuted even the dances of May Day.

The coastline of Brittany, raggedly indented with sudden harbors and sunken valleys now inundated with the sea, juts into the Atlantic like the prow of a ship. One is never far from the ocean, yet the interior— once an impenetrable tangle of oak and beech forests—is a world of its own. Yellow broom and purple heather cover the moors which alternate with fields and woods.

It is a land in which one is rarely far from some physical manifestation of magic. Near to the town of Ploermel, on the main highway between Lorient and Rennes, is a fountain long known for its prophetic qualities. Within living memory seamen's wives used to throw bread into this fountain to ascertain whether or not their husbands would return safely to harbor.

This is but one of a number of fountains and springs that are reputed to cure a wide variety of diseases and afflictions and possess similar powers of divination as well. Such places, as we have seen, have been adopted by the Catholic Church, which holds annual ceremonies consisting of a mass and a feast, usually under the auspices of a locally popular saint.

One that seems to have eluded the Church's attention in recent years is the renowned Fountain of Barenton in the nearby Forest of Broceliande. This is where the wizard Merlin, believed by some to have lived his life backward, is said to have met the fairy Vivienne, fallen in love with her, and deliberately allowed himself to be enslaved by her. A typical *korrigan* legend. The forest is dense and mysterious, much as it must have been centuries ago, in the days when King Arthur's knight Lancelot reputedly had a tryst with his queen Guinevere beside the Bridge of Secret.

The forest almost encircles the tiny town of Paimpont, which owes its origin to a seventh-century monastery at the site, and the location of the bridge is recalled today by the Auberge du Pont du Secret, a charming inn on the main national highway between the towns of Beignon and Plelan-le-Grand, south of the forest. The river, crossing under the road, passes through the grounds of the inn where now stands a rustic wooden bridge on what could well be the site where the two lovers pledged their love.

The whole region, dominated by the extensive forest which fans out on both sides of north-to-south highway N. 773 and is also crossed by other roads, is still pleasantly rural and almost completely uncommercialized. A small café in Paimpont called Le Mazelet offers a rough map of the region which is so vague as to be almost useless, but a walk in the woods takes one into a lovely, sleepy, timeless land populated only by rabbits, birds, and deer. Thick foliage obscures all thought of the outside world and almost all sound save the distant pealing of a church bell.

In ancient times the forest covered a vast area extending from Carhaix to Rennes, almost eighty-five miles away, but the cutting and clearing that have continued for centuries has reduced the forest to an area of twenty-five square miles. Although a shadow of its former self, the forest still offers many chances to get lost and in recent years extensive replanting of coniferous trees has been undertaken.

Small signs along route D.141, east of Paimpont, mark the route into the forest where the Fountain of Barenton, sacred to the Druids, is to be found. But once inside the forest the signs disappear, and the visitor must rely on intuition or good luck to locate the site. Actually it isn't too hard to find, once in the wood, if you stay straight on the path after the last sign. Not far into the wood beyond that, the path widens into an L-shaped clearing with a wooden gate. This point is as far as a car can get and the fountain is 1,250 paces ahead. The pathway, muddy and rutted because of frequent rain, inclines leftward and winds gently uphill. It is entirely deserted and hares and other forest fauna scurry away at the visitor's approach.

Eventually the path peters out and takes a sharp left which opens into a small isolated clearing in which, sitting alone, is a stone-sided spring of fresh water. This is the Fountain of Barenton and an excellent spot it is for quiet meditation and an attempt to summon the spirit of Merlin. Modern-day lovers have carved their initials on nearby trees.

It was while Merlin was resting beside this fountain that Vivienne first appeared and asked him what he was studying. Merlin told her that it was the magic arts and randomly traced certain mystical characters in the grass. Immediately the glade was filled with a magnificent castle completely populated with maidens and knights. Understandably Vivienne was delighted and at her request Merlin retained the castle grounds—naming them "Joyous Garden"—when he dismissed the rest of the visions. The pair made a vow to meet one year later on the Vigil of St. John, and after going to England for the wedding of Arthur and Guinevere, Merlin returned to Broceliande to keep the appointment.

Enchanted by Vivienne, Merlin willingly revealed to her the magical knowledge that bound him to her forever, and while he slept she walked around him nine times muttering the mysterious words he had taught her. In such a way, according to the Breton version, Merlin at the close of his life, but appearing forever younger, withdrew from the world. In another version of the tale, favored by the Arthurians, the enchantress Vivienne is sometimes alluded to as Nime, or Dyones, the sea goddess. As the lady of the lake she is the foster mother of Lancelot and is classed as water spirit.

Merlin supposedly lived in the sixth century and was known among the Welsh as Myrddin, but according to Funk and Wagnall's *Standard Dictionary of Folklore,* "no authentic effusions of Myrddin have survived and it is only in obscure poems of the eleventh and twelfth centuries that the legend built up." It was Geoffrey of Monmouth in his *Prophetia Merlini* in A.D. 1135 who first introduced the Merlin saga, mingling authentic Welsh lore with his own imaginative theories. From Nennius' ninth-century *History of the Britons,* he lifted the story of the red and white dragons fighting below the foundations of Votigern's tower and the fatherless boy who solved the problem "coolly identifying the prophetic boy with Merlin," as the *Standard Dictionary of Folklore* puts it. Later Geoffrey credits Merlin with transferring Stonehenge from Ireland— clearly anachronistic as the famous landmark, by the sixth century A.D., had already stood on Salisbury Plain for at least 2,000 years.

It was also Geoffrey of Monmouth, an entertaining writer if not a reliable historian, who identifies Merlin's supposed cave at Tintagel. There seems to be little other evidence except Geoffrey's word for this and his "spurious etymology" crediting the Welsh town of Carmarthen as his former home. But the *Dictionary* is suspicious of other Merlin legends, too, as for example the wizard's two reputed "graves": at Drummelzie on the Tweed in Scotland and in the Forest of Broceliande.

"According to a tradition of doubtful antiquity," the reference work adds, "the magus was born on the Isle de Seine off the Breton coast, and to it he conveyed the wounded Arthur." The island is the same one referred to at the beginning of this chapter which the first-century Roman historian Pomponius Mela averred was the home of witches who could raise storms. Mela made no mention of Arthur for the obvious reason that the king hadn't by then been born. (As to Arthur's last resting place, there are almost as many claimants for that site as there were Knights of the Round Table, which incidentally pops up in yet another romance about Merlin, this one by the twelfth-century Burgundian poet Robert de Boron, who was probably the first writer to introduce the story of the sword embedded in the stone.)

There are numerous Breton folktales about Merlin, who was a notable figure on both sides of the Channel by the Middle Ages. And the Fountain of Barenton, too, became sanctified at that time when the Catholic Church, in its inimitable style, incorporated its magic in ceremonies during which the local priest would dip a cross into its waters to bring rain in barren years.

A thirteenth-century writer says of the fountain that if a drop of its water is dropped onto the Stone of Merlin beside the spring "the water changes to vapor and the air becomes thick with shadows and the muttering of thunder." There are further legends of travelers beholding other marvels with similar rituals beside the spring.

On our own recent visit rain poured down in sheets, obscuring everything but the soggy path a few steps ahead. It would have been impossible to check the accuracy of Wace's assertion (in *Histoire des Ducs de Normandie*) that

> In the forest and around
> I wot not by what reason found
> There may a man the fairies spie
> If Breton do not tell a lie.

According to Lewis Spence's collection of folktales called *Legends and Romances of Brittany*, a certain knight of the Middle Ages, Sir Roland, on his way to the Holy Land, spent the night in the Forest of Broceliande. He had taken a vow to give up the company of women, a vow which must have been known to the *korrigans* who infested the forest.

> In Broceliande is gathered all the rich and haunting mystery of the remote magic of Breton lore, and whether the fairies of Brittany be the late representatives of the gods of an elder day or merely animistic spirits haunting the glades, it is certain that the strict ban imposed by the church on all things magical in this peninsula has incurred their enmity and today they are enemies.

With this kind of hazard, Sir Roland, it would have appeared, didn't have much of a chance. But the story continues, although lured into an enchanted chateau and tempted by a *korrigan* he managed to resist her charms and next morning the enchanted chateau became once again the trees and banks of the forest and the lovely maiden a hideous old hag.

What may have brought Sir Roland to Broceliande, and reputedly many of the Knights of the Round Table before him, was the legend of the Holy Grail. That holy relic of the Last Supper was supposedly in the possession of one of the disciples, Joseph of Arimathea, when he paused here on his way to Glastonbury. But it has never been found.

Brittany treasures other famous legends, among them that of the tragic lovers Tristan and Iseult, immortalized by Wagner's opera. Tristan, prince of that legendary land of Lyonesse now lying somewhere under the Channel, was sent by his uncle Mark, King of Cornwall, to bring back the Irish princess Iseult whom Mark was pledged to marry. But on the boat the pair unknowingly drank a magic love philter which bound them instead to each other. In one version of the legend Mark kills his nephew, in another he dies at his castle in Brittany.

An even earlier tale centers upon the lovely town of Quimper where two rivers meet, the Odet and the Steir, whose numerous footbridges remind one of Venice. Set in beautiful countryside in which nestle orchards rich with cherries and apples, Quimper still pays tribute to the sixth-century king Gradlon whose statue stands between the towers of the medieval cathedral.

King Gradlon's daughter, the gorgeous Dahut, was supposedly tempted by the devil to steal the king's key and open up the sea gates, which of course flooded the town of Is where they lived. Escaping on horseback with Dahut behind him, King Gradlon was informed that he would be saved only by casting his demon daughter into the waves: she is said to dwell still in the drowned city as a mermaid luring sailors to their doom.

The lost cities that lie under the waves are a part of folklore in Brittany and have their parallels in the Atlantis-like legends that permeate the south and west coasts of Britain. Certainly there has been erosion over the centuries and traces of sunken forests, and occasionally walls, have been discerned at low tide on both sides of the Channel.

Bretons believe that the mist-shrouded islet off Tregastel is none other than the fabled Isle of Avalon to which King Arthur was borne after his last battle. He would recover from his wounds and await the day when he would be called again to fight for the forces of right.

But we shall leave Brittany's north coast temporarily to explore an even older mystery, the eleven long avenues of standing stones at Carnac on Quiburon Bay in the southwest. The plethora of stone structures that dot the countryside from one end of the province to the other are perhaps Brittany's most curious features. There are literally thousands of these mysterious menhirs and dolmens, in fields, on hillsides, and in particular on the fringes of the south coast.

Nobody has ever satisfactorily explained their purpose, although their age—even the most conservative estimates date them back at least 3,000 years—would seem to rule out the far-fetched speculation that the Romans erected the huge stones to protect their encampments from the wind. In any case, the Romans were driven out as their empire collapsed (by a mass migration of settlers from Britain) and if the stones were an integral part of their armed occupation it seems likely they would have been vengefully destroyed.

The visitors-from-other-worlds theorists have suggested that they were built as navigation beacons, either by people from other planets or for such outer-space visitors to use as landmarks. In his *Legends of the Sons of God,* T. C. Lethbridge says that Carnac stands in a similar position to Scotland's Callanish, with drowned land surface in the sea in front of it. He discusses the Greek gods who "flew" in their chariots from Mount Olympus, and adds: "If you had an apparatus in a flying machine set to the right wave length, you could pick up the rays from the stored energy in the stones and hone in on it like a moth to its mate."

Theories have proliferated in abundance over the centuries and range from suggestions that the stones are immense plugholes that prevent vast underground springs from bubbling up and inundating the land, to the perennial, and universal, folktale that the upright pillars are the bodies of soldiers turned to stone through magical powers by someone they were pursuing. Concurrent with the latter belief is the familiar legend that at certain times the stones return to life and hold dances, go to the nearby spring for water, etc. Invariably the story carries the admonition that the unwary onlooker must be careful not to be crushed in the headlong rush as the phalanx turns back to stone!

The most prominent group of stones, eleven parallel rows stretching for more than 1,000 yards and culminating in an impressive semicircle just outside the town of Carnac, does indeed look like an army "fatal, invincible, eternal, marching—and growing as it marched," as Gerald Hawkins puts it in *Stonehenge Decoded*. Hawkins, whose impressive books would seem to establish that Stonehenge was undoubtedly a sophisticated astronomical observatory, suggests that the menhirs at Carnac plus those to the northeast at Kermario and Kerlescan may have formed one colossal system. But apart from indicating that all are oriented northeast-southwest he declines to speculate on their purpose.

There is no doubt, though, that the concentration of upright stones in the Carnac area is one of the most impressive sights in Europe. Not even advance knowledge of what is to be seen quite prepares the visitor for the extent of the system. Carnac itself, a pretty seaside town dotted with enticing crêpe restaurants and all the souvenir shops and flotsam and jetsam of any resort, is conventional enough, with a predictably glorious beach. But less than a mile north of the town, right beside the road, the rows of stones begin at Menec.

Here are the tallest of the stones, some as high as thirteen feet, but as the rows stretch away to the northeast the stones get gradually smaller until many of them are only three or four feet high. Grass, yellow gorse, and shrubbery abound and at any time of the year there are dozens of cars parked along the road and adults and children poking around, taking photographs and checking out the stones' supposed magical properties.

Specific "warm stones" are reputed to have the power to find marriage partners for young women who choose to sit on them, but as the particular stones are not indicated in any way, the mate-hunting young ladies will have to discover which for themselves by trial and error. (The ruined dolmen of Croez-Moken, not far away, gained a similar reputation so potent that the local priest wisely decided to conduct a procession to it every spring so that all the local spinsters could visit it together under the auspices of the Church rather than making solitary pagan pilgrimages to it on their own.)

Other properties attributed to the menhirs are the capacity to make barren women conceive if they rub their bellies against a certain spot: a stone called the "Giant of Kerderf" is credited with this power as is the isolated pillar at St. Cado, a village near Ploermel to the northeast. Just down the peninsula, toward Quiburon, the dolmen at the village of Roh-en-aod was for centuries popular with fishermen's wives who used to go at night with hammers and tap the stone's five cup-shaped depressions to ensure favorable winds for their husbands.

These so-called "cup and ring" markings have also been found on stones in New Caledonia, as well as in Scotland and Ireland, and are usually associated with the concentric and spiral designs of Celtic art. Archeologists have speculated that the stones were a feature of some kind of rainmaking ritual, the grooves being filled with water to typify a country partially covered with rain and, under the principles of sympathetic magic, to induce more of it.

Other highly distinctive markings, seemingly imitating the loops and whorls of an enormously enlarged fingerprint, can be found on stones on the island of Gavrinis in the Gulf of Morbihan to the south. The stones, whose markings of serpentlike figures, axes, spirals, and circles seem to have been carved with metal tools, line a passageway which ends in a square chamber supported by eight menhirs of granite, a stone not found in the area. For what it's worth, granite is a type of rock that was formed underground eons ago and specific varieties seem to have been particularly prized by the ancients.

"Today in modern Celtic folk-belief certain stones are accredited with supernatural powers," says Anne Ross in *Everyday Life of the Pagan Celts,* "and use of stones in black magic and allied practices is still remembered in isolated parts of the existing Celtic world."

The museum at Carnac (open daily in summer to 7 P.M.; in winter by request only) is well worth a visit, if only to inspect more closely casts made from carvings on some of the megaliths. The museum was founded by a Scotsman, J. Miln, and later maintained by the redoubtable Zacharie Le Rouzic who, at his death in 1939, was the acknowledged expert on Brittany's megaliths.

In the museum are the relics excavated from the nearby St. Michel Tumulus, a covered mound more than 100 yards long and 38 feet high, which housed numerous prehistoric burial chambers. But a tour of the tumulus itself is quite an adventure (apply to the Tumulus Hôtel for a guide) being made by eerie candlelight.

In the complex at Menec there are a total of 1,169 upright stones, all but 70 of them in 11 long, parallel rows, the remainder of them forming cromlechs, or circles, and whether in groups or alone—many others, scattered around the countryside, mark tombs, boundary lines, roadways, etc.—are symbolic of "the spirits of the dead," according to a local guide book.

"In the minds of builders of megaliths the dead were beings who continued to exist in another form, or rather, in another state, and who could still exercise influence over the living and inspire in them feelings of awe. The menhir symbolized this state and thus became an immortal divinity to be prayed to and worshiped." And Bretons to this day believe they contain some mysterious power and that to damage one would be a sacrilege bringing misfortune.

Le Rouzic theorized that the alignments were "sacred ways" leading to sanctuaries where priests held rites with the order of the stones (the tallest always stand nearest to the cromlechs) representing some symbolic progression or hierarchy of human or divine beings. Obviously they must possess some magical (i.e. "religious") significance probably related to one of man's primary religious symbols, the sun. Both the sun and the moon played a major role in everybody's life at this time in history (as they still do), and the ability to predict eclipses lent considerable prestige to the priestly orders.

A study of the regions's various stone systems shows that each has a specific solar orientation, relating apparently to the dates November 8, February 4, May 6, and August 8—mean dates of the principal divisions of the agricultural year. Moreover, the numerous dolmens, or tombs, covered over with large stone slabs, were also constructed with entrance passages bisecting the sun's course during the solstice. The dolmens, many of which carry symbolic engravings of fertility goddesses, plows, wheat, ox horns, or axes. One of the menhirs guarding a burial mound at Kermario, the complex of ten rows totaling 1,120 stones, 300 yards northeast of the Menec series, is engraved with five snakes standing on their tails. Nearby were found five votive axes pointing at the sky. These polished stone axes (called *men-gurun,* or "thunder stones," by today's Bretons) were the subject of a special cult and under the principle of sympathetic magic are regarded as talismans to protect houses from lightning. They were made in special sanctuaries by a religious caste of priests or magicians, who perhaps claimed they had fallen from the sky during a storm. In the days of the Roman occupation the cult was exemplified by the practice of consecrating tombs to guardian spirits represented by the same ax-symbol and inscribed *sub ascia*—"under the ax." In medieval times these thunder stones were used for such varied purposes as improving butter yield and relieving congestion in cows' udders, preventing lard from going sour, and endowing water with healing properties while it was boiled with the stone.

These small polished stone axes were often among the objects found in the dolmens along with weapons, jewelry, pottery, and often even horses and oxen, all to accompany the dead to the afterworld. The tombs were undoubtedly the final resting place of persons of tribal importance—chiefs, priests, or celebrated warriors—and there is evidence that people came from far away to bury their religious and military leaders, with the tombs revealing traces of a mixture of races. Le Rouzic likens the whole area to "a kind of Elysian Fields," and numerous writers have emphasized the importance given to the cult of the dead and a belief in the transmigration of souls, reincarnation, or possibly immortality.

Local tradition claims that the dolmens were formerly inhabited by *korrigans* and that a race of strong dwarfs can still be seen dancing and singing in the fields nearby on Sabbath nights by anybody who takes the trouble to cut a corpse's toenails and hang onto the clippings. *Korrigans* are believed to sneak into houses at night and sew people up in shrouds. If the victim wakes up before the sewing is finished, he or she will have a long life; if not, death comes before the year is out.

In his *Geography of Witchcraft,* that indefatigable chronicler of sorcery Montague Summers tells us that the relic of yet another vanished race, the Nain, also lurk around the dolmens. He has "dishevelled locks, a cruel countenance wherein his eyes gleam red as carbuncles with the fire of the damned. His voice is harsh and horrible. He has the legs and hooves of a goat."

The Nains, says Summers, are the inventors of a cabalistic alphabet, the characters of which are engraved on several of the megalithic monuments. "He who can decipher the magic creed will be able to tell where hidden treasure is to be found."

But although the dolmens are probably more revealing of the era from which they date, it is definitely the almost endless rows of the more numerous menhirs that are the most awe-inspiring. Between the 1,169 stones of Menec and the 1,120 stones of Kermario is a gap of 300 yards, just enough space to emphasize the vastness of the project. Then, following on from Kermario and heading farther northeast come 13 more rows comprising a further 570 stones. It is a site, resembling an enormous slalom course or an above-ground minefield, that never fails to provoke the visitor into asking, Why? What could possibly be the purpose of so many stones?

In *The Pattern of the Past,* the archeologist Guy Underwood quotes the speculations of Charles Diot who wrote in his *Les Sourciers et les Monuments Mégalithiques* (1935) that the rows of stones marked parallel underground streams. But this seems to be nonsense; there are just too many rows, and all run in straight lines. A more likely theory is that the stones, as at Stonehenge, are aligned with the midsummer sunrise in some way, but even if this were true, why so many unless it had something to do with the way the sun's energy could be caught and stored, or rechanneled for other purposes?

It seems almost a relief to turn to the local supposition that the megaliths are handiwork of spirits, giants, or fiends who harnessed their oxen to the mighty stones to bring them to the selected sites and then climbed on each other's shoulders to erect them to the necessary height. The dolmens, supposedly, were built to hold the mortal remains of those who had made good use of their lives and when surprised by daylight the fairies were unable to finish their task, hence the many roofless tombs.

Even more currency is attached to the legend that St. Cornelius, a former Pope pursued from Rome by pagans all the way to Brittany, took his stand at Carnac and changed his attackers to stone. Their ghosts wander among the lines at night; the menhirs dance, or make an annual trip to the sea to wash themselves. St. Cornelius' journey, incidentally, was in a cart pulled by two oxen, which has given rise to an ox cult that survives today: every September 13 local farmers lead their herds to the annual "Benediction of the Beasts" at a fountain in the churchyard. The cattle are blessed by the priests after offerings are made of hairs from the animals' tails. The church at Carnac contains a series of frescoes depicting episodes in the life of the saint. A sculpture of him with two oxen stands in the churchyard.

All this is very charming but doesn't explain why over 3,000 menhirs were raised in deliberate patterns to form a stone forest on this lonely seacoast thousands of years ago. Inevitably there are legends that treasure is buried beneath these ancient pillars, but that whoever tries to dig for it will perish.

Breton customs reflect the Celtic heritage they share with the Cornish, Welsh, and Irish. As on the eve of Midsummer Day in Brittany, bonfires used to be lit and huge copper basins beaten with rushes to make a sound audible for miles. Farmers made fires of greenery at the entrances to sunken roads and drove their flocks through the smoke, with the charcoal and ashes preserved for later use as talismans.

Yet in the folklore of Brittany are hints of a much earlier time when the peninsula belonged to the master of the world—a god of death named Ankeu.

A story still circulated locally is of "the good woman Janton of Kerlescan" who, just over a century ago, was working in a field near the village spring when she heard a noise in the sky and looking up saw a fiery cloud in the midst of which she could clearly discern two eyes, a nose, and a mouth. Seven people later died of smallpox in the village because the cloud was one of the manifestations occasionally assumed by "Er Ankeu," the notorious harbinger of death who usually appears as a skeleton in a white shroud and driving a cart with squeaky wheels.

There is no doubt that whether or not the visitor meets with "Er Ankeu," a visit to the Carnac region induces a special feeling. Le Rouzic quotes the writer Anatole Le Braz as saying that his soul was seized by "a kind of religious awe" once he left the pleasant countryside southwest of the town of Auray:

> A frown of sudden severity descended; not exactly hostile, but serious, enigmatic, soaked in mystery . . . Even before we caught sight of the first

silhouettes of the menhirs we felt that we were entering a land dedicated since time immemorial to the redoubtable gods of the dead.

We wind up our tour of Brittany, and of France, back on the north coast, about as far northeast from the forest of Broceliande as Carnac is to the southwest. Despite its name, the cone-shaped "island" (now permanently connected to the mainland) of Mont-Saint-Michel also has associations with Brittany's local saint, Cornelius.

St. Cornelius is credited with installing the ancient site with curative powers. Peasants brought their cattle here to be blessed and made healthy. Such pilgrims, it is said, brought with them the stones and earth that later formed the mound, although if such a story were true it would indicate the existence of more sick cattle than the entire human population of France. Julius Caesar is reputed to be buried under Mont-Saint-Michel, wearing gold boots and reclining in a golden coffin, and stories abound about the gold pieces that can sometimes be seen coming out of the eastern end of the mound and rising into the air.

Possibly there was a Roman temple on the site long ago, but for at least ten centuries there has been a Christian church. The present-day abbey dates to the fifteenth century. Inside the abbey is a statue of St. Michael, but it is not he who is credited with killing the notorious giant who once inhabited the site, but the famous King Arthur himself. The monster, having come from Spain, had holed up atop the mountain with his kidnapped prize—Lady Helena, niece of the duke of Brittany—and found no difficulty in killing the brave knights who had swum to the castle to rescue her.

Arthur and Bedivere, undaunted, managed to climb the mount and after a fierce battle Arthur plunged Excalibur into the giant's brain and Bedivere cut off his head.

Another ancient legend, which purports to explain why the monastery atop Mont-Saint-Michel is not very solidy based and sticks together only by "divine grace," concerns the devil. It seems that Satan (for some inexplicable reason) was helping with the construction and at one point he dropped one of the stones from his bag, finding himself left with only two on which to place the foundations. The third stone, known as *La Pilière,* can be seen sticking up from the ground not far away and is said to still bear the marks of the devil's fingers from when he tried unsuccessfully to lift it back.

None of these stories are repeated to the tourists who visit Mont-Saint-Michel today. Mostly they are interested in the Christian association, the abbey's fame having spread since the Middle Ages. They crowd the narrow, cobbled streets, pausing to eat crêpes or buy souvenirs in the cafés and shops. They walk the winding uphill path to the monastery and climb scores of steps to the ramparts to look out over the protective circle of quicksands and, to the south, the little town of Pontorson about five miles away.

As they stand atop this Great Pyramid, which seems from afar to rise sheer out of the sea, few are aware that across but twenty-five miles of water, in another country, other sightseers, too, are standing atop St. Michael's Mount. Were there giants once, to whom these twin hills were but a few paces apart?

III

21

Cornwall

A RACE OF GIANTS

LEGENDS OF GIANTS cluster about the distinctive island of St. Michael's Mount near Penzance and at such other Cornish sites as Carn Brea and Chapel Porth. Such legends are ubiquitous in the West Country, a relic perhaps of those far-off times when giants ruled Britain before the arrival of the semi-mythical Brutus the Trojan, a grandson of Aeneas. One of Brutus' followers, the Trojan general Corineus, was made ruler of Cornwall and in this capacity he killed off all the giants of the region, wrestling with the last one, Goemagot, and throwing him into the sea. The rock at Plymouth from which the last giant plunged is still pointed out, and official records exist of the giant that was once carved into the turf on Plymouth Ho. No trace of it can be seen today, although other giant figures still exist cut into hillsides throughout southern Britain.

St. Michael's Mount, which also had its giant, was called Dinsul ("mount of the sun") in pre-Christian times, and though connected to the mainland today by a short causeway covered only at high tide, it was once situated many giant strides away. Even in the fourth century, historians say, it was several miles out to sea, and fossilized roots of trees now washed by the tide are evidence of the way that earthquakes

Illustration: Winds from the Four Corners of the Universe. Medieval woodcut.

193

have altered the surrounding terrain.

Atop the Mount is everyone's dream of what a castle should be—lofty, towering, awesome, powerful yet poetic. Rising from a promontory off the coast of Marazion, its hillside presence dominates the area from as far away as Penzance. It is possible to walk to it from the shore at Marazion, but only when the tide is out. When the tide is full, St. Michael's Mount is as aloof and inaccessible as any castle should be. Picture postcards which tourists buy by the thousands fail to capture its intensity; glossy reproductions vulgarize what should be etched or painted. For St. Michael's Mount is, in an odd way, a very personal place. It caters to anyone's fantasies—pirate's hangout by moonlight, grand manor, brooding fortress shrouded in mist, or playground of the giants.

"The ancient people of most countries seem to have possessed in the strongest degree a faith in giantology," writes Edward J. Wood in *Giants and Dwarfs*, "as evidenced by the vast images of the gods and the colossal monuments of architecture." And he points to the giant statues in Egypt at Karnak (52 feet high) and Luxor (38 feet) as well as to the unfinished figures of enormous size in the nearby quarries of Silsileh.

Anybody who cared to make the jump of imagination might suggest that the megaliths, up to and including Stonehenge, would have been all the easier to construct if they had been the work of giants rather than today's puny-sized man. But this is not a theory that has received much credence.

Certainly western England, and particularly Cornwall, is liberally sprinkled with enormous standing stones. Such stones are called variously quoits, dolmens, tumuli, or cromlechs. What they all have in common is immense slabs of stone erected above ground, topped with even bigger ones, sometimes before being covered with earth. That they were used for burials, often as mass graves holding up to scores of people, is beyond doubt, as is the fact that the older ones date back to at least 2,000 years before Christianity.

But occultists, and some historians, suspect they were used for other purposes and only later as tombs. At the very least they may have been infused with a magic that would enhance the survival chances of the soul, and possibly even the body. Coffins were an extravagance that had not been invented at that time.

Many of Britain's hundreds of stone circles, ranging from a dozen feet in diameter to hundreds of feet across, are to be found in Cornwall. (Some stones exist in rows or singly as well.) A few have received attention from archeologists, most are little known outside their own region. To some people the rarely-visited circles appear to emanate powerful, almost tangible currents of energy.

In *Crossing's Guide to Dartmoor,* William Crossing writes:

Suggestions have been made that rows were intended for gymnastic performances, that they were used for solemn Arkite ceremonials, that they were part of serpent temples, that they formed the processional roads of the Druids, that they were race courses, that they were once roofed in and formed shelters, that they represented armies drawn up in battle array, that they were intended to guide people over the moor in misty weather, that they have an astronomical significance and that they are a representation of passages that led to the chamber in a tumulus. From these hypotheses it certainly should be possible for the visitor to select one to his mind.

One unusual aspect of St. Michael's Mount is that the granite rock of which it is composed is traversed by veins of quartz—used as a conductor since ancient times—which run east and west with great precision and regularity. If the Mount was built, and certainly its construction is beautifully symmetrical, perhaps only giants could have performed such a task.

Legends say that long, long ago, when the Mount was part of the fabled lost land of Lyonesse (now believed far below the ocean), the giant Cormoran, its builder, used to share a hammer with another giant who lived on Trencrom Hill, near Lelant to the north. They threw the hammer casually back and forth to whoever happened to need it, but one day Cormoran's wife leaned out of a window at an inopportune moment and took the hammer right in the eyes. Cormoran's anguished cries as she fell dead at his feet caused a storm far out to sea. After he recovered he buried her beneath nearby Chapel Rock.

Cormoran himself came to a violent end, slain by Jack the Giant-killer, an early Cornish (Celtic) warrior who is the subject of many similar tales. Jack dug a hole, covered it with sticks and straw, and blew a blast on his trumpet. He then brutally hewed Cormoran to death when the giant rushed out and fell into the pit.

The Chronicles of Great Britain by the fifteenth-century author John de Wavrin explains that the world was originally populated by giants but that after the flood, the height of men decreased. At the time of Jahir, third judge of Israel after Joshua, he says, Lady Albine and her sisters settled in what came to be called Albion after her. A devil who took the form of a man dwelt among them and their offspring were giants who continued to multiply until the arrival of Brutus.

But what if the word "giant" meant the possession of superior knowledge, surpassing wisdom. All prehistoric ruins are not necessarily tombs, temples, or simple phallic symbols. The standing stones could mark telluric currents or a system of prehistoric alignments named ley lines by antiquarian Alfred Watkins.

It seems obvious that the long stone causeways indicated something and were not just pointless work projects. Archeologist and dowser Guy Underwood speculated that when they bend and twist for hundreds of yards over hillsides and across streams, they may be following the course of some meandering geodesic current.

In the southern portion of Dartmoor, a mile or two north of Corn-wood at Stall Moor, there is such a causeway. A stone circle fifty feet in diameter dominates a remote stretch of heather-covered wilderness, out of which two lines of stones run parallel down the hillside and across the River Erme, continuing up the hill at the other side and fading out just before a burial ground at the 1,500-foot crest of Green Hill. The lines, heading roughly north to south, might well mark some mysterious "highway" above or below ground.

Underwood's book, *Patterns of the Past,* suggests that all ancient sites are situated over blind springs. He comments: "These would be recogniz-able as holy places and their business under divine protection and guidance."

Whatever their original purpose, the stone circles have found their worshipers since. Medieval witches celebrated their rites there and lat-ter-day disciples of magic and witchcraft have also adapted them to their own use. Even in these hard-headed times fires have been seen flickering late at night on remote moors, and occasionally the visitor to such a site will note the presence of ashes in the center of such a circle.

The Boscawen-un stone circle, just north of highway B3283 between the villages of Catchall and St. Buryan, is regarded by some as Corn-wall's most potent megalithic power center. It is charming because of its inaccessability. For the gloriously commanding Stonehenge, one buys a ticket and follows the crowd into a fenced-off enclosure; at Boscawen-un the circle is reached only after a laborious walk across muddy trails in the outlying fields of Boscawen-un Farm. And when the nineteen stones, in a perfect, unbroken circle, are literally stumbled upon, there is a greater sense of discovery—and of magic.

The four-foot-high megaliths with a central menhir at an acute angle are partly overgrown with brambles and surrounded by a circular raised mound of earth. Their purpose? Nobody knows, but the boy at the farm says visitors come from all over the world to probe and ponder.

Within a radius of a dozen miles, there are innumerable other stones: the solitary, ten-foot monolith known as the Blind Fiddler northwest of Catchall; the Pipers and Merry Maidens near Boleigh, which T. C. Lethbridge claims are "charged" with an energy which visitors from outer space could have homed in on; the Hurlers, three stone circles on Bodmin Moor outside Minions. All of these standing (or "tilting") stones share the same legend in local folklore: that they are the petrified remains of people punished for playing or dancing on the Sabbath.

Near to St. Just, on Bossalow Common, is the curious Men-an-Tol, a doughnut-shaped stone about four feet high with a hole in the center big enough to crawl through. It is said to be psychic, possessing fertiliz-ing and energizing properties capable of curing almost any ailment suffered by the visitor who cares to crawl through it toward the sun. The

Men-an-Tol, flanked by a solitary four-foot pillar at each side, is thought to be an instrument for measuring the May-August sunrise line, and in reverse direction, the February-November sunset.

The moors between Penzance and St. Just—abounding with barrows, mounds, stone circles, and hills—are very weird, and numerous legends persist about the spirits of the ancient Celts said to still inhabit this region. The nineteenth-century historian J. T. Blight writes: "The people tell of midnight fights by demons and of a shadowy form holding a lantern to the combatants."

The ubiquitous crosses of Cornwall used to mark the pilgrim's route to St. Michael's Mount, according to the Victorian antiquarian J. T. Blight, who documented his obsession in a book called *Ancient Stone Crosses in West Cornwall.* Blight's specific interest was the sacred relationship of the crosses to the landscape in which they were placed. His other book, *A Week at Land's End,* was published in 1861 and both books brilliantly capture the eerie power of the old stone monuments in their proper setting. Blight never finished his magnum opus entitled "Cornish Cromlechs," because, in the words of John Michell in his recent work *The Old Stones of Land's End:* "The mystery of the past, acting on a sensitive nature, drove him to insanity and prevented the completion of his last work."

Lethbridge maintains that many of the crosses were erected by Christians to negate the magical power of the stones nearby.

The days when a young Cornish girl might aspire to be a witch are not so far in the past, and there are innumerable reminders of such aspirations in the various logan or rocking stones dotting the countryside. The ritual usually involved climbing on top of such stones or rocking them nine times at midnight. Often the stones were so balanced that, enormous as they are, they could be rocked on their axis and not tip over.

Cornish people appear to be natural mystics and being predominantly rural, they have retained a strong belief in supernatural forces. In centuries past scores of ordinary folk practiced magic and extolled the skills of the "cunning man," whose powers included keeping away evil spirits by carving a five-pointed star on the threshold and curing whooping cough by boiling nine quartz pebbles in water dipped from a running stream to be administered to the patient by the wineglassful every morning for nine consecutive days. Many of these cures, because of Cornwall's geographical isolation, are still current—especially the numerous remedies for removing warts: Tie a knot in a piece of string or steal a piece of meat, touch the wart, bury the charm and as it decays, the wart disappears. It seems as if knowledge of magic and witchcraft as evidenced by traditional folklore has survived longest in the areas where the ruins of megalithic culture are found in greatest abundance.

The Witches' Rock at Treen was a popular magical site, as was the nearby granite pinnacle known as Castle Peak, where covens reputedly gathered on moonlit nights to watch the sinking of ships they had bewitched. Treen signifies Cornwall at its finest: the rock, seemingly precariously balanced, hovers over a dark blue sea, brilliantly outlined in white foam. Cliffs are jagged and great fun to climb, either down to the sandy beach or to the Witches' Rock itself. Be sure to have a sandwich at the Logan Rock Inn where a clipping from the *Cornish Telegraph* relates how the rock was willfully overturned in 1824 by a certain Lt. Goldsmith and then replaced (at his expense) in November of that year. There follows a long list of the people who were hired to replace it: fifty-eight of them, all of whom had to be lodged, paid, and transported, for a grand total of £130–8s–6d, almost $700 in the money of those days. The rock itself, now stable, sits on the edge of the cliffs overlooking a magnificent beach. It's a popular spot for picnics.

There is a witch's initiation stone at Zennor, where a carved bench in the parish church recalls the story of the chorister who was lured to sea by a mermaid's singing and never seen again.

At St. Cleer, near Liskeard, the annual ceremony on St. John's Eve, June 23, of "banishing the witches" retains such pagan touches as casting various herbs before a bonfire.

And at Boscastle there's a museum of witchcraft containing hazel wands, magic mirrors, love charms of snail shells, and the skeleton of the famous witch of St. Osyth, Ursula Kemp, who was executed in 1582.

Omens have always been taken seriously in Cornwall, as in any place where elementals are felt and feared. Animals and birds always had messages to convey. Rabbits and hares, the traditional witches' familiars, were especially significant. In a country where mining was prevalent, the appearance of a white hare near the numerous pits presaged disaster. The howling of dogs or the sight of a lone crow foretold a mining accident or a shipwreck. To see a snail on the way to work in the mine was good luck, while if a miner worked underground on Midsummer Eve he could expect misfortune.

Cornish black witches had a malevolent practice of ill-wishing or "over-looking" their enemies. The result of the evil spell could be pain, illness, or death. Dancing around the midsummer bonfire and leaping through its flames or circling one of the ancient stone slabs known to have sacred properties counteracted the witches' curse. A black witch often took the shape of a hare and in that form could be killed only by a silver bullet.

A version of a familiar tale is recounted in Ritson's *Folklore and Legends of England.* There was a witch in Tavistock who would assume the form of a hare and have her grandson alert the attention of the local huntsmen. Paying the boy a good price for telling where he had seen the hare, the hunters would go unsuccessfully in search of it. When the deception had been practiced many times the huntsmen became suspicious and a witness was posted when the boy gave the alert. At a signal from the witness, the hunting party gave chase. When this happened the boy was heard to cry out "Run, run for your life." The hare was pursued into a cottage, where the hunters found an old woman upstairs bleeding from her wounds, and out of breath.

Judging by his contribution to place names—Devil's Bridges, Jumps, Ditches, to name but a few—His Satanic Majesty must have spent a good deal of time in the English countryside, desolate Dartmoor proving to be particularly appealing. It was on Dartmoor, not far from Widecombe that, one day, when he was tired and hungry after a lengthy horseback ride between his lonely parishes, Exeter's famous thirteenth-century Bishop Walter Bronescombe encountered Satan. A poorly-clad peasant appeared suddenly out of the peat bog and offered to share his food, so the story goes, if only the Bishop would dismount from his horse and salute him.

This the Bishop was about to do when, glancing at the stranger's feet, he noticed a cloven hoof. A sudden shock of recognition prompted him to make the sign of the cross. The stranger instantly disappeared in the predictable puff of smoke and Bishop Bronescombe, chastened by his narrow escape, returned to Exeter and lavished most of his personal fortune on rebuilding the place. His elaborate tomb can be seen there today as can a medieval clock relating the earth to the positions of the sun and moon. It bears the inscription (in Latin), "The hours perish and are reckoned to our account."

On October 21, 1638, the devil turned up again at the lovely village of Widecombe, dressed in black, mounted on a black horse, and carelessly displaying the same cloven hoof to the local publican. He asked the way to the parish church, a location he might have been expected to know well, and dragged out one of the congregation (with whom he had had previous contact) by his hair, causing a conflagration, described by witnesses as "a ball of fire," that killed four parishioners and injured scores of others. The legend persists, but a more prosaic explanation points to a flash of lightning.

Not far away, Shebbear in North Devon celebrates an annual ceremony on November 5 to turn over an enormous boulder said to have been dropped by the devil in the village square. Legends maintain that disaster will befall the village if the ceremony is abandoned.

Dartmoor's most potent legend concerns the dreaded Wist or Wisht hounds which haunt the spooky Wistman's Wood near Two Bridges, and which are said to have inspired Sir Arthur Conan Doyle's *Hound of the Baskervilles.* These jet-black hellhounds, accompanied by their ghostly keeper with hunting horn—said to be the god Woden—supposedly roam the moors on stormy nights. They will reputedly bring death within the year to anyone unfortunate enough to meet with them. This, strangely enough, hardly discourages curious visitors, who head on foot up the valley from the comfortable Two Bridges Hotel, past Cravern's Farm, and following the stream northward, eventually reach the eerie wood on the stream's right bank.

It is very still and quiet here except for the constant low whistle of the wind sweeping across the barren moors. The wood, a tangle of gnarled moss-covered oaks interspersed among half-buried boulders, slopes down to the stream where sheep tend to congregate. Here and there a pile of blood-stained bones and tufts of wool indicate that one of the sheep has fallen victim to some predator. Late on Sunday night is said to be the most favorable time to encounter the spectral hounds.

The grotesque wood of ancient oak trees is said to have been the site of Druidic rituals and is one of the few patches still remaining from an era when Dartmoor itself was completely forested. Not far away from the woods are the remains of a prehistoric village which is itself supposedly haunted. But the wood is not the only spot where the glowing Wist hounds have been spotted, for their route takes them in full cry across the lonely moors to the Dewer Stone at Dartmoor's southern tip. Here they are said to disappear over a precipitous crag, sweeping any pursuers along with them.

Since 1677 they have also been seen breathing fire and smoke in the vicinity of Buckfastleigh, where the Lord of Brook Manor, a man of evil reputation named Sir Richard Cabell, was supposedly whisked off to hell on the night of his death. Cabell's body is buried in a pagoda-like building in the Buckfastleigh churchyard, where according to legend one need only insert a finger in the keyhole to feel it being nibbled by the spirit.

Writing about Dartmoor's hellhounds in an article in the *Quarterly Review* of July 1873, R. J. King comments: "The cry of the whish or whished hounds is heard occasionally in the loneliest recesses of the hills whilst neither dogs nor huntsmen are anywhere visible. At other times (generally on Sundays) they show themselves—jetblack, breathing flames and followed by a swarthy figure who carries a hunting pole. Wise or Wish, according to Kemble, was the name of Woden, the lord of 'wish' who is probably represented by the master of these dogs of darkness."

The legend of the wish hounds also persists west of Dartmoor at Buckfastleigh abbey, near Yelverton, where the phantom hunter who sometimes is seen leading the pack along Abbot's Way is reputed to be Sir Francis Drake.

Driving through Dartmoor is an eerie experience. The atmosphere can change abruptly: green rolling hills transform into craggy towering peaks, fertile fields disappear to be replaced by patches of dry, scraggy prairie grass. Suddenly the sun goes behind a cloud, and the mood is one of brooding, forlorn barrenness, sheep braying plaintively in the distance. All this in a manner of minutes can happen on these celebrated moors which cover a large area of both Devon and Cornwall.

22

London

THE DRUIDS AND JOHN DEE

WHETHER OR NOT giants once ruled Britain, statues of two of them still maintain majestic guard over London's glorious Guild Hall. Kilted, bearded, carrying lances, they can be seen standing one on each side of the medieval stained-glass windows in the main hall. Although weighing half a ton apiece, they are but striplings compared to the 14½-foot figures destroyed by German air raids in 1940—and which were replaced in 1953.

The pair are named, curiously enough, Gog and Magog, and first appeared in London in the fifteenth century, at least three hundred years after Geoffrey of Monmouth's reference to one Goemagot being tossed into the sea at Plymouth, thus ending Britain's rule by giants.

Records show that almost ten pounds (a magnificent sum in those days) was spent to erect the pair on London Bridge as a welcome to King Henry V at the time of his coronation in April 1413. Subsequent pageants held in London featured the two giants, although the pair that welcomed Philip of Spain in 1554, and appeared at the Lord Mayor's show of 1605, were called respectively Gogmagog and Corineus (the name of Goemagot's supposed slayer). The Great Fire of 1666 appar-

Illustration: Wheel of Life, defining the influences of the zodiac on the life of man. Medieval woodcut.

ently destroyed the two figures and at some point in the interim Corineus was forgotten and "Gog" and "Magog" became two separate figures, possibly, suggests T. C. Lethbridge, because of the names Gog and Magog appearing in Ezekiel. Lethbridge's book *Gogmagog, the Buried Gods* mentions two giant figures he once uncovered on the turf of Wandlebury Hill outside Cambridge, following a tip from the writings of historian John Hale in 1640 who had attributed their origin to scholars at the university.

According to a pamphlet of the same period, a semimythical figure named Long Meg (immortalized in a megalithic stone circle at Little Salkeld northeast of Penrith in Cumberland) was a giantess who was buried on the south side of the cloisters of Westminster Abbey, a site which was sacred long before the arrival of Christianity.

It's well known, of course, that the elevation on which Westminster Abbey now stands was once a Druidic site, but much less publicized is the theory that a temple to Apollo also stood there. Tot-hill (as it then was) has always been sacred and there are frequent references to it throughout history. In the sixth century it was the scene of the labryinthian joust known as the Troy Game, played on horseback every Sunday in Lent by knights who eventually devised the tilts and jousts which so enlivened King Arthur's court.

Sir Thomas Malory, the fifteenth-century documentor of an Arthurian age he never knew firsthand, writes: "So it befell in the month of May, Queen Guenevere called unto her Knights of the Table Round; and she gave them warning that early upon the morrow she would ride on Maying into the woods and fields beside Westminster. And I warn you that there be none of you but that he be well-horsed and that ye all be clothed in green, either in silk, outher in cloth, and I shall bring with me ten ladies, and every Knight shall have a lady behind him." So-called Troy Towns still exist under that name in some parts of the country, invariably as complex mazes, usually cut in the turf.

Tot-hill was one of four Druidic sites in London, the others being Penton (now the site of a reservoir), the "White Mound" (now part of the Tower of London), and Parliament Hill (then called Landin) at Highgate, atop which since ancient times has been a stone proclaiming the people's right of public assembly there. All except Tot-hill are in a straight line and within a degree or so of the place of the midwinter sunrise.

The white-clad Druids, plus the green-robed philosophers known as Ovates and the Bards ("wearers of the long blue robes"), gathered for their ceremonies in early times to carry out "their sacred and scientific duties," according to Tacitus. The Druids had the care of education, the Roman historian reported. "They alone cultivate knowledge; they conceal from the vulgar the secret doctrines in which their pupils only are initiated. They determine the litigated questions; it is their business to allot rewards and punishments."

Two other legendary figures are associated with the hills we have mentioned. Britain's redoubtable pagan queen Boadicea, who fought the Romans to a standstill in the year A.D. 60 after her husband was killed, is said to be buried on the slopes of Parliment Hill at Highgate, and the head of the Welsh superhero Bran the Blessed, famous in Celtic legends, is said to lie under the White Mound. "No plague could ever come across the sea" as long as it remains there, say the legends.

Mystical creatures are associated with both these people. Boadicea's success in battle was said to be due to her powers of divination by means of plotting the twists and turns of a runaway hare she let from her bosom, and Bran the Blessed has always been closely tied in Celtic folklore to the prophetic raven. Needless to say, ravens have guarded the precincts of the White Tower (built on the White Mound by William the Conqueror) for centuries and the legend has somehow become transformed so that London is guaranteed free from destruction as long as the birds remain.

Also supposedly buried under the White Mound is London's legendary founder Brutus, whose disembarkation at Totnes in Devon is marked by what is known as Brutus' Stone in that town. In London, set into the wall of the Bank of China near St. Swithin's Lane, another stone known simply as "the London Stone" is said to have been Brutus' original temple altar. It is obviously prehistoric, and a sixteenth-century writer said that in that era it was still much venerated and well protected.

Passing through that part of London known as "the City" (and noting the magnificent pairs of red and silver dragons which mark its boundaries), we might hear the chime of the Bow Bells, whose evocative tones called Dick Whittington back to London in the fifteenth century, a summons that ended with his being named Lord Mayor and later founding an elite society of bell-ringers that exists to this day.

The church of St. Mary-le-Bow, its churchyard now a minuscule city park dominated by a statue of Captain John Smith (leader of the Jamestown settlers in America), was rebuilt in the seventeenth century by that indefatigable church architect Sir Christopher Wren (who also designed St. Paul's Cathedral and a host of smaller churches). But it, too, stood on a site that had been sacred since Roman times and probably before.

Those born within the sound of Bow Bells are genuine Cockneys, a tenacious breed of Londoner who take a peculiar pride in their reduced circumstances and barely comprehensible accents. The concept of geographical definition within the radius of bells is thought to date back to the fourteenth-century custom of prohibiting citizens from wandering after hearing the nightly 9 P.M. curfew.

Bells have always been considered to possess magical properties, having served "among almost all people for thousands of years as amulet, fertility charm, summons to a god, prophetic voice, curative agent or purely musical instrument," as Funk and Wagnalls *Standard Dictionary of Folklore* puts it.

Church bells have received most attention, but bells of one kind or another have been used for at least 3,000 years. In the American South and in parts of Ireland it has long been thought that drinking liquids out of bells would cure ailments; some African tribes encourage rain by imitative magic—pouring water onto the ground from the bowl of a bell. Siberian shamans wear bells for incantations and prophecies, and the Bible (Exodus 28:35) tells of priests who wore gold bells in the hem of their garments to keep away the demons. In myths, fairies often appeared to the sounds of bells, and many "little folk" wore them sewn on their clothing.

But we continue our journey across London, past Cleopatra's Needle (removed from Alexandria), past the circular Temple Church built by the fourteenth-century Knights Templars, and past Mayfair where the annual May Fair and dancing around the Maypole celebrated the fertility rites of spring. We are heading for the sleepy Thames-side town of Mortlake, a few miles past the western suburbs of London, where England's last royal magician, John Dee, was occasionally visited by his patron, Queen Elizabeth I.

The preeminent magician of the Elizabethan era and the man whose occult writings undoubtedly influenced Shakespeare, Dee was born in London on July 13, 1527 and died at his Thames-side house eighty-one years later. He entered Cambridge at the age of fifteen and declared that for the rest of his life he planned to spend sixteen hours each day studying magic, two hours eating, and the rest sleeping.

Much of his studying was done abroad, some of it presumably in the service of the queen (whom he first met when her predecessor, Mary, was on the throne). His place in history is confused because some considered him a charlatan while others regarded him as a credulous fool. A third point of view claims Dee's interest in occult matters was a pretext to conceal espionage activity. His scholarship is well-documented. Versed in Latin and Greek, Dee was the acknowledged authority on mathematics, navigation, optics, and astronomy in Elizabethan England.

In 1563 Dee's discovery in an Antwerp bookstore of a rare book called *Stenographia,* written by the German abbot Johann Trithemius almost a century before, excited him enough to complete work on his own magnum opus, *Monas Hieroglyphica.* Both books deal with cryptographs, and are a complicated exposition on the relationship between magic, numbers, cyphers, and symbols, recently described by occultist D. P. Walker in *Spiritual & Demonic Magic* as a telepathic means of acquiring universal knowledge.

As astrological adviser to the queen, Dee selected the date for Elizabeth's coronation and she later visited his home from time to time, on her way to and from the various palaces she maintained. On one occasion she asked to see the "magic glass of which she had heard so much," a presumed reference to the royal astrologer's mirror of obsidian (a volcanic black glass), which he had acquired after Cortes brought it back from his conquest of Mexico in the 1520s. This glass and a *speculum* (a solid sphere of pale pink glass about the size of an orange) now rest in the British Museum along with other discs and devices employed by Dee and his one-time assistant Edward Kelley for their psychic experiments.

From speculation about the content of dreams Dee proceeded to investigate trance inducement by means of scrying, or crystal-gazing. According to his diary, Dee did see spirits on May 25, 1581. Feeling his talent for the art of scrying was limited, Dee hired Kelley, a reputed seer, to aid in the undertaking. The work continued for seven years and in the manner of a scientist, Dee carefully recorded the results of their collaboration.

Although Dee was said by his biographer Meric Causabon to have conjured up only good spirits—"At no point in his occult wanderings did he consider himself to have passed the bounds of Christianity," Causabon writes, half a century after Dee's death, in *A True and Faithful Relation of Dr. John Dee and Some Spirits*—he continually suffered angry opposition. Even before Elizabeth's accession to the throne, Dee was imprisoned as "a companion of hellhounds and a caller and conjuror of wicked and damned spirits." He was once accused of killing children by sorcery but acquitted.

On returning from one of his foreign trips Dee found his lovely home at Mortlake had been ransacked by an angry, probably religiously motivated, mob which had wrecked or stolen his priceless collection of books and damaged his laboratory. Some of the books that were saved are now in Oxford's Ashmolean Library.

Dee presented a claim to the queen for £2,000, and was partly recompensed. But he spent the rest of his life in financial difficulties, constantly importuning the queen for some official position. He was appointed warden of Christ's College, Manchester, but soon returned to London, writing in his diary that the only journey left for him to take was to "that undiscovered bourne from which no traveler returns."

No trace remains of his Mortlake home, although down by the river where it once stood (and where stands an old building called Tapestry Court) the view must be at least as tranquil as in his day. The river passes leisurely by, with no traffic in view, and apart from a few small houses, there is little to be seen along the bank. Across the street is a new apartment building, but adjoining it, as it was centuries ago, is the graveyard of St. Mary's parish church in which the last of England's royal magicians is said to be buried.

23

Glastonbury

SHADES OF KING ARTHUR

THE FABLED KING ARTHUR whose personality and exploits have captured the imagination of successive generations of romantics, may or may not have been a living person. But if he did live, the one place in Britain with the strongest claim to being his last resting place is the lovely town of Glastonbury, less than an hour's drive from Stonehenge in an archeologically and historically rich countryside.

Glastonbury is undeniably Britain's most magical town, the site for centuries of a magnificent abbey which survived the dissolution of the monasteries in 1539 and whose extensive ruins can still be admired today. The earliest Christian church on the site dates possibly to the second century, but Glastonbury was a pagan site for countless centuries before that. Archeological excavations around the ruins of the abbey once uncovered the cemetery of a Celtic monastery that is so old it cannot be dated accurately.

If Arthur lived, and it does seem fairly certain that a British chieftain of that name won some battles against the invading Saxons in the sixth century, he would surely have been familiar with what is now Glastonbury, which in his day was a well-established, thriving community.

Illustration: A twentieth-century rendering of Glastonbury's Tor.

The whole of Britain, and Northern Europe, too, is rife with Arthurian legends, some of them based on Geoffrey of Monmouth's accounts in his twelfth-century *History of the Kings of Britain,* others dating to Sir Thomas Malory's celebrated *Morte d'Arthur* of the fifteenth century or to Tennyson's *Idylls of the King* of the nineteenth century.

The bards of France also dealt with the stories of the Round Table, with the poems of the twelfth-century Chrétien de Troyes being perhaps the culmination of these.

Although Glastonbury has been tagged as that celebrated Isle of Avalon by romantics who need to place it *somewhere,* Arthur himself has been associated with innumerable sites. Among the better known are Cornwall's Tintagel Castle, in a cave near which, according to Geoffrey of Monmouth, Arthur was raised by Merlin; Somerset's Cadbury Castle, said to be Camelot and still haunted at the summer solstice by skeletal horsemen who ride the causeway glowing with spectral light; the northern border town of Carlisle from which, according to a fourteenth-century ballad, Arthur ranged the surrounding countryside fighting magical boars, giants, and fairies; the Cumberland castle, near Kirkby Stephen, of Arthur's reputed father, Uther Pendragon; and a dozen sites in Wales, including the lonely Snowdonia lake of Llyn Llydaw, where Arthur was said to have disappeared after that final, fatal battle of Camlan.

Camlan has also been placed near the River Camel in Cornwall, at Camboglanna in Cumberland, or by the River Cam in Somerset: The sites of Arthur's battles, courts, and encounters are much disputed. There are also many Arthur's stones, quoits, chairs, seats, fountains.

In the castle at Winchester, whose foundations are said to have been laid by Arthur, is what is known as King Arthur's Round Table, a solid oak table subdivided into twenty-five green and white segments which, according to records in the castle, was repaired at a cost of £66 before a royal visit in Henry VIII's time. There is, unfortunately, no record of the table before 1522 when it was said to have been shown to the visiting emperor Charles V.

The oldest surviving Welsh manuscript (c. 1150), *The Black Book of Carmarthen,* refers to King Arthur, and the earliest recorded mention of the Round Table occurs in the poem *Roman de Brut* written by Robert Wace around 1155: the legend's origins are lost in the distant past. History and legend finally fused in 1184 when most of the abbey at Glastonbury was burned down, and in the course of rebuilding, the monks discovered what they claimed to be Arthur's burial place. Arthur's body, and that of his bride Guinevere, were said to have been discovered buried sixteen feet deep, between two stone pyramids which have long since disappeared.

The twelfth-century historian William of Malmesbury said that the pyramids were carved with figures and inscriptions which nobody could decipher and which may have been Celtic. No fragments of these pyramids have been found, but it is possible they may have been incorporated into other buildings and will turn up someday.

The two bodies discovered in the twelfth century were in the trunk of a hollowed-out oak and the flaxen hair of the woman fell into dust when it was touched. The man's bones were described as so large that when his shinbone was measured against the leg of a very tall man "it reached three fingers above his knees." He had ten wounds in his skull.

Near the remains was a leaden plate in the form of a cross, described by the historian Giraldus Cambrensis, and which reads in translation: "Here lies interred, in the Isle of Avalon, the renowned King Arthur." No trace remains today of cross or bones, and there are those, of course, who ask whether they ever existed, and if they did, whether they belonged to King Arthur.

M. R. James was one of the skeptics. Writing in a book called *Abbeys,* he speculates that the date of the discovery fell at a time when the monks were in great straits for funds for rebuilding the abbey, commenting acidly: "That so important an addition to the place as would have been conferred by Arthur's relics would have been most opportune." It has been suggested, James continues, "that the discovery was engineered from headquarters in order to put an end to the belief in a future return of Arthur and to British aspirations which were prejudicial to the reigning dynasty. If that was the hope it failed. The Britons yet [a generation after the discovery] remembered that Arthur is alive and dwelleth in Avalon with the fairest of all elves and ever yet the Britons look for Arthur's coming."

According to old records, the exhumed skeletons were later buried in a black marble casket before the abbey's high altar when it was rebuilt after the disastrous fire in the late twelfth century. No trace of the casket has been found, although a plaque marks the grassy lawn in the center of the abbey's grounds where the two bodies were originally said to have been uncovered.

John Michell, a cult figure in contemporary British occultism, theorizes in his seminal *The View Over Atlantis* that the abbey's original ground plan was conceived as being representative of a solar structure: the canonical units of measurement employed being those to which sacred structures have been built all over the world since the time of the Great Pyramid.

The basis of both Glastonbury abbey and Stonehenge, says Michell, is an ancient figure of natural magic traditionally known as the magic square of the sun. "This consists of the first 36 numbers arranged in a block so that each row column and diagonal adds up to 111 and a total to 666. [See illustration.] Upon this number, 666, Stonehenge was founded. These magic squares were highly valued by the philosophers of antiquity, for they appeared to be constructed according to certain

6	32	3	34	35	1
7	11	27	28	8	30
24	14	16	15	23	19
13	20	22	21	17	18
25	29	10	9	26	12
36	5	33	4	2	31

The Square of the Sun

numerical laws which also expressed the ratios of natural growth."

This system of geometry and numerology by which Stonehenge was built and which some believe survived at least into the Middle Ages, formed part of an arcane tradition which, says Michell, were "known only to those groups of masons and geomancers who preserved the secret of a source of magical invocation inherited directly from a world of unimaginable antiquity." Be that as it may, there is something extremely strange about the vibrations given out at Glastonbury. On one occasion as we were looking around the ruins of the abbey a friend who was accompanying us suddenly felt faint and almost collapsed beside the walls of the old rectory. Later, as we studied local maps, we realized the building was at the exact point at which several ley lines intersected.

As in most places claimed by Christianity for its own, the local ethic is more Puritan than pagan, and the occasional festivals or "fayres" celebrated by the local chamber of commerce tend to become a battleground for differing beliefs. The town's charms, however, have a soothing effect, although there is hardly a visitor who is able to resist leaving its crowded streets for a leisurely climb of the 500-foot Tor, whose brooding mystery tempts one to sit at the top in quiet meditation for hours. Any visit to the Tor will find swarms of people clambering up and down the hillside or sleeping overnight at the top beneath the ruins of an abandoned tower.

"There are certain places around our planet," says travel writer W. Tudor Pole, referring to this strange hill, "which owe their formation and destiny to heavenly influence, and this is one of them. It is a global center of light enveloped in a sacred aura of protection."

According to legend, the surrounding countryside was once covered in water, with the Tor being one of the high points of dry land. The paths to its summit formed a spiral which the renowned occultist Dion Fortune speculated in *Avalon of the Heart* were a processional path used by the pre-Christian worshipers. "Such mounts as this," she writes, "were always sacred to the sun."

The stone tower is all that remains of a church erected to commemorate St. George and wrecked by an earth tremor about A.D. 1000. But archeologists maintain that there has been an ecclesiastical building atop the Tor since at least the fourth century when a group of hermits founded Britain's first monastery.

And even before then, pagan rites were observed, probably around a megalithic circle, some of whose stones were believed to have been built into the abbey in the town below. Excavations on the Tor in 1967 also revealed the remains of a fortified site from post-Roman days, the era of King Arthur.

A few years ago the Pendragon Society, an organization that specializes in exploring Arthurian legends, published a book to coincide with the Glastonbury Fair, and in this there was some speculation about the original Arthur. It was suggested that he might have been a local chieftain who became familiar with Roman methods of soldiering and assembled a well-drilled body of men to take up the slack after the Romans left.

There is evidence that a commander named Arthur, flying a standard depicting a red dragon, took charge of the British armies around A.D. 480 and proceeded to fight the dozen or so battles later documented by the eighth-century monk-historian Nennius. The Saxons' advance was halted for twenty years at Badon (c. 510), but British resistance finally collapsed at Camlan where Arthur was mortally wounded.

Cornwall's Tintagel Castle is traditionally said to have been Arthur's birthplace. Here, around A.D. 460, the Druid magician Merlin assisted Uther Pendragon to impersonate Gorlois, Duke of Cornwall, in the seduction of Igraine, Arthur's mother. Arthur became king of the Britons while still a young man and fought numerous successful battles with the aid of a magic sword, Excalibur, given him by a fairy known as the Lady of the Lake. Arthur's half sister, Morgan le Fay, later managed to replace this sword with a replica and while fighting with the duplicate he was wounded, although later he regained the original.

The famous Round Table, with its specific seats for each of Arthur's knights, originally belonged to Uther Pendragon but was passed on to Arthur on his marriage to Guinevere, daughter of Leodegrance.

The knights were often engaged in the quest for the Holy Grail, an ineffable symbol of enlightenment, grace, and glory. In early Irish legends the Grail was a vessel of plenty, providing whatever food and drink was desired. It also symbolized the Cup of Knowledge, following the traditions of many similar legends about bottomless cups or bowls that could never be emptied. Legends about such vessels appear to exist in virtually every culture in the world.

Later the Grail story was Christianized, thereafter becoming associated with the body and blood of Christ. Joseph of Arimathea, who reputedly visited Glastonbury soon after Christ's death, was said to have caught the martyr's blood in the chalice alleged by some to be the one used at the Last Supper. Joseph is reported to have come to Britain bringing the Grail with him, and it is now said to be hidden in the Chalice Well at Glastonbury. Other legends relate that the Grail was stolen by the Saxons and the first of King Arthur's quests was the search to regain it. The Grail is a magically potent symbol, binding the old myths with the new: a pagan-Christian fusion.

Sometimes the Grail was described as a stone, with the power to ensure longevity and youthfulness. It has also been suggested that the theme of the Grail legends were closely related to earlier pagan fertility rites or with that search for spiritual perfection whose counterpart is the alchemists' search for the means to make gold from base metals.

The reputed hiding place of the Holy Grail, the so-called Chalice Well, is a chalybeate (impregnated with iron) spring of beautifully clear water at the foot of Glastonbury Tor. In 1582, the magician John Dee declared that he possessed the *elixir vitae,* which he had found at Glastonbury. Although little more was heard of that, the water of the Chalice Well has long had a reputation for healing. The spring which feeds it gives an outflow of 25,000 gallons per day and in the eighteenth century much of it was collected, bottled, and taken away by pilgrims who sought its curative powers.

An early excavation of the well revealed the stump of a yew tree near to the foundation stones and after analysis it was declared to be a tree living in Roman times, circa A.D. 300, which would suggest that the ground level at that period was approximately the same as the present bottom of the well and that the water then bubbled out through a surface spring. No trace of the Grail, or anything like it, has ever been found.

John Dee, however, has another connection with Glastonbury, having been the first to point out what he described as "Merlin's Secret." Following his visit to the area, of which he made a map, Elizabeth's royal astrologer wrote: "The Starres which agree with their reproductions on the ground do lye onlie on the celestial path of the Sonne, moon and planets, with the notable exception of Orion and Hercules . . . all the greater starres of Sagittarius fall in the hinde quarters of the horse,

while Altair, Tarazed and Alschain from Aquilla do fall on its cheste
. . . thus is astrologie and astronomie carefullie and exactly married and
measured in a scientific reconstruction of the heavens which shews that
the ancients understode all which today the lerned know to be factes."

What he was apparently revealing was explained three centuries later
by an amazing woman named Katherine Maltwood, who astounded
everybody in the early part of this century with her theories about the
Glastonbury zodiac. This was nothing less than a grandly conceived
plan to build giant constructions representing the symbols of the zodiac
in a circle thirty miles around. Mrs. Maltwood, and many later researchers, claim to see the 552-foot Tor as the zodiac's center, its symbols
represented and outlined by various old tracks, hills, water courses, and
earthworks. Some people recognize these symbols instantly, others are
skeptical, but it is said that an aerial view is most convincing, which
raises not for the first time or the last the possibility that ancient man
may have been able to acquire such a perspective. If, indeed, the people
who constructed such a massive earthwork didn't themselves come
flying in from somewhere else.

The Glastonbury zodiac, says occultist Anthony Roberts in *Atlantean
Traditions in Ancient Britain,* is a perfect example of the way the ancients
moulded the earth "to conform to the harmonies of the terrestrial and
celestial energy patterns," for the effigies on the ground "all tally with
the appropriate star constellations that shine in the sky above them."
Roberts maintains that the Tor was not only the spiritual center of the
zodiac, but also the focal point of the main Glastonbury power center.
In Celtic mythology, he explains, the entrance to the land of the dead,
known as Avalon, was always a high hill surrounded by water, and in
the Iron Age the Tor would have been one of the few places that
towered above the surrounding waters made up of interlinked lagoons.

Mrs. Maltwood, who died in 1961, aged eighty-three, said she considered the zodiacal myths as an allegory of the sun's wandering among
the stars, a myth with origins in Sumarian and Chaldean lore. The
Druids continued this traditional knowledge and in Britain the central
god-figure subsequently became Arthur, perpetuating the real or imaginary king who, like the sun after its nocturnal decline, would return
again.

The reign of the legendary Arthur came to an end at the battle of
Camlan where he fought his nephew Mordred who sought to usurp his
power. Arthur killed Mordred but was severely wounded by him. According to legend, the dying king was carried by boat rowed by six
black-clad queens to the Isle of Avalon, which many people now place
at Glastonbury.

It is a necessary part of the legend—and many similar legends abound
in other parts of the world—that this hero was never actually seen to
die, merely to disappear, and that one day he would reappear bringing

salvation and greatness to his native land. He is said to sleep in a mountain cave awaiting the call.

After Arthur's death, so the stories go, the remaining knights were pursued westward by Mordred's men, fleeing to Cornwall and thence south to the now-legendary land of Lyonesse. There, Merlin caused an earthquake to intervene, submerging Lyonesse and killing the traitors to the Arthurian ethic. Arthur's knights spent their remaining days in the Scilly Islands, which are said to be what remains of this long-submerged land.

24

Wales

MERLIN AND THE MOON
IN A WELL

From the holy city of Glastonbury the trail of the once and future king leads northwest into Wales. Here, the tales of Arthur and his mentor, Merlin, diverge, the king last being seen (if we are to believe some reports) on the lonely lake of Llyn Llydaw, near Llanberis Pass, and Merlin first making an historical appearance at the little town of Beddg-elert (on the A498 north of Portmadoc) a few miles to the south.

Llyn Llydaw is a boomerang-shaped lake, to the shores of which Sir Bedivere is said to have carried the wounded Arthur after his fatal fight with Mordred at Bwich-y-Sasthan ("the Pass of the Arrows") in the surrounding mountains. "Arthur himself, our renowned king," says Geoffrey of Monmouth, "was mortally wounded and carried off to the Isle of Avalon so that his wounds might be attended to . . . this in the year 542 after our Lord's Incarnation."

Geoffrey, whose *History of the Kings of Britain* was written in Latin, is himself a confusing figure who has baffled historians. They are unable to agree about how much of his "history" is fact and how much is the product of his obviously vivid imagination. Geoffrey, apparently born in the town of Caerleon-on-Usk, about twenty miles south of Mon-

Illustration: From Aubrey Beardsley's illustration of Merlin from Malory's Le Morte D'Arthur.

mouth on the Welsh-English border, was an official of the Christian Church and one part of his history, "The Prophecies of Merlin," prefaces a letter to another churchman-acquaintance, Alexander, Bishop of Lincoln. The historian constantly refers to an earlier book, in Welsh, as the source of his statements, and what later historians have never been able to ascertain is whether this book existed or whether it was a figment of Geoffrey's imagination.

One of the tales he tells is of the fifth-century king Vortigern who was attempting to build a castle at Beddgelert only to find it constantly sinking into its foundations. Vortigern's wisest advisers told him that only the sacrifice of a child born of no man would be able to solve this bizarre architectural problem and after a search, a child named Myrrdin, supposedly born from the union of a nun and the devil, was found.

Myrrdin (or Merlin) escaped being the sacrificial victim by telling the king that the reason the castle kept sinking was that a pair of dragons were fighting in a subterranean lake beneath its foundations. Excavations were made which demonstrated the truth of this prophecy (which, incidentally, was an allegory for the manner in which Britain, the red dragon, would drive the Saxons out of Wales), and Merlin started on the royal road that eventually led him to the side of King Arthur.

"Among the British races," wrote W. H. Davenport Adams in 1864, "Merlin occupied the position the Greeks had accorded to Apollo," and it is hardly an exaggeration. Certainly Merlin appears to have been a half real, half supernatural figure to whom was attached many dreams and aspirations.

In Beddgelert today can still be seen the tree-covered hill on which a fifth-century fortress, Dinas Emrys, stood, and recent excavations have proved, astonishingly, that there was indeed a fortress there at the time of Vortigern.

The village of Beddgelert, little more than a narrow, winding street lined with cafés and souvenir shops, is a popular tourist spot today. The surrounding countryside is spectacular, the main road traversing a dramatic valley beside a rushing river whose source lies in the Snowdonia mountains to the north.

The magical history of Wales begins well before Merlin's time, although Merlin has been sometimes described as "the last Druid." On an autumn day in the year A.D. 61, the conquering Roman legions under the command of Suetonius Paulinus reached the island of Mona (now Anglesey) off the northwest coast of Wales and encountered the strangest opposition of their hitherto triumphant tour of these islands.

The historian Tacitus describes the scene: "On the shore stood the opposing army with its dense array of armed warriors while between their ranks dashed women in black attire like the Furies, with hair dishevelled waving brands. All round, the Druids lifting up their hands to heaven and pouring forth dreadful imprecations scared our soldiers by the unfamiliar sight."

But their magic was apparently ineffectual against the disciplined Roman armies, and the Celtic defenders along with their Druid priests were beaten back and the land ravaged. "Their groves devoted to inhuman superstitions were destroyed," says Tacitus. "They deemed it indeed a duty to cover their altars with the blood of captives and to consult their deities through human entrails."

The criticism seems unfair, as does that of Strabo who wrote that "on account of their evil sacrifice . . . the Romans endeavored to destroy all the superstitions of the Druids but in vain." Studying entrails for divination and rites of sacrifice were both familiar practices in Rome, as we have noted. The actions of the Celtic Druids may easily have been misinterpreted by the Romans in the light of their own experience.

Anglesey today is a resort center. An enormous bridge connects it to the Welsh mainland across the Menai Straits, and all the usual facilities await the tourists who are its lifeblood. Ancient sites of all kinds abound: standing stones, cromlechs, megalithic tombs, even a magnificent castle or two. An excellent book to acquire, if you are contemplating a visit, is the comprehensive guide issued by the Ministry of Public Buildings and Works (H.M. Stationery Office, 49 High Holborn, London WC1), *Ancient Monuments of Anglesey.*

Most of what we know about the Druids of Britain comes from Roman sources: there are no writings extant from the Druids themselves. Ammianus Marcellinus wrote that they were "uplifted by searchings into secret and sublime things"; the Stoic philosopher Posidonius maintained that they were knowledgeable about philosophy, theology, astronomy, ethics, and natural science; and Julius Caesar said that "in the schools of the druids they learn by heart a great number of verses, and therefore some persons remain twenty years under training . . . they make use of Greek letters . . . the cardinal doctrine which they seek to teach is that souls do not die but after death pass from one to another." Such was their belief in reincarnation, explained Valerius Maximus, that they even lent each other sums of money repayable in the next world.

Caesar, especially impressed with Druidic disciplines, believed that they originated in Britain and spread to Gaul where, following that special talent possessed by the Romans for absorbing the best their foes had to offer, Druids were employed in tutoring the children of upper-class families.

Tacitus said that they had neither villages nor temples, for "they thought it absurd to portray like a man or circumscribe within the walls of a house the Being who created the immensity of the heavens." Druidical rites were always performed out of doors, usually within a grove or high on a hill. Days were reckoned from nightfall to nightfall, so festivities began at sundown. Many of the places where people gather publicly today date to "places of assemblage" in Druidic times, and the holidays we celebrate, though later Christianized, were originally Celtic festivals. On May Eve, the pagan celebration of spring, the Druids toasted the fertility god Belenos. They called upon his magical rites to encourage the growth of cattle and crops. Bonfires were lit and cattle were driven between them for purification. Also, according to *Larousse,* "The people danced, probably in a sunwise direction, and carried burning torches around the fields, a form of sympathetic magic to aid the sun in his all-important role in an agricultural economy."

The winter solstice celebration when, says Pliny, the sacred mistletoe was cut from the oak tree with golden scissors, became Christmas in the Christian calendar. Other festivals were *Imbolc,* or *Oimelc* which became Candlemas (February 2), the summer Lughnasa (August Eve) when the crops were harvested (still celebrated in Britain as "August Bank Holiday"), and Samhain on November Eve (All Souls' Day), a night of divination and magic when (says the historian Anne Ross) "the correct ritual must be performed to pacify supernatural forces."

More than a few present-day sites of Christian churches were formerly Druidic groves in which were located stone shrines or magic trees, wells or fairy mounds. J. D. Evans-Wentz in *The Fairy Faith in Celtic Countries* suggests that there was a close affinity with fairies and Druids, the early Celtic peoples having drawn much of their fairy tradition from dimly-remembered Druidic rites of divination.

Even such commonplace activities as kissing under the mistletoe, bobbing for apples at Halloween, and decorating the house for Christmas are said to be vestiges of Druidical rites, as is the custom of walking *tuaithiuil,* the Gaelic for "widdershins," or clockwise.

And just as Celtic customs were undoubtedly shot with the threads of earlier beliefs, so Christianity was able to absorb and incorporate established traditions. Wherever a site was already known as sacred, it was either destroyed or reconsecrated to the new faith.

A classic example is the holy well, constructed originally, say some historians, for use as a telescope "to bring the moon down to earth." Long before the tenth century most of the ancient wells bore the name of Christian saints and had achieved a reputation for miracles. Such was the case with St. Winifride's well at the aptly-named town of Holywell, about seventy miles to the east of Anglesey on Wales' northern coast. But although this is the best known and most visited, there is hardly a town in Wales without its ancient well. Often, however, these are now hard to find and in such a shabby and neglected state as to be hardly worth the trouble.

The worship of water, like that of earth and fire, goes back to ancient times and was an attempt to propitiate the spirits that animated or lived in lakes, rivers, pools, and streams. A frequent theme in various folktales concerns the "marriage" of young girls to a river to appease the dragons that caused floods, clearly a "watering down" of the earlier custom of sacrificing victims for the same purpose.

Running water, in particular, was supposed to be efficacious in keeping away evil spirits, which may explain why the Celtic races so often buried their dead on islands or dug channels around tombs into which rainwater would run. We have already noted the tradition in Brittany's Forest of Broceliande that storms could be raised beside Merlin's fountain of Barenton, and a similar tradition prevails at Snowdon's Black Lake, where according to popular belief, if water is sprinkled onto the farthest of a line of stepping stones, rain will fall before nightfall.

As paganism gave way to Christianity water worship at wells began to be more formalized, probably because those people who became the first Christians used them not only for their own domestic purposes, but also for baptisms. A. W. Moore speculates that it was part of their policy to locate themselves close to wells which were already associated with pagan rites "so that the memory of the old beliefs might be obliterated by the practice of the new."

The wells were patronized, Moore wrote in *Folk Lore* (September 1894), for the cure of diseases, protection against witches and fairies, and for good luck in general. "The usual ritual was to walk around the wells one or more times sunways, to drink the water, to wet a fragment of their clothing with it and to attach this fragment to any tree or bush that happened to be near the wells. Then to drop pins, pebbles, buttons or beads into them and to repeat a prayer in which they mentioned their ailments. . . . When the wells were visited for other purposes [than curing diseases] the fragments of cloth were dispensed with."

In a book called *The Holy Wells of Wales*, Francis Jones lists almost one thousand wells, which he classifies according to their locations and associations (near to or associated with churches, megaliths, festivals, saints, etc.). It is widely believed, he explains, that wells containing such elements as *wen* ("white," "blessed," "holy"), *llwyd* ("gray," "old," "holy"), and *ddu* ("black," "sinister," "evil") in their names possess a religious origin.

During pagan times the wells—used for purification, sacrifice, divination, fertility, healing, and forecasting weather—were often associated with local heroes, giants, and legendary figures such as King Arthur. But after Christianity arrived almost all of them became known by the names of saints. An inevitable progression.

Jones says that survival of respect for the wells is due to their actual or supposed healing qualities. "The wells were the doctors of the peasants . . . and what we call 'superstition' in the modern Welshman is, in reality, a survival of the religious convictions of his earlier ancestors. The pagan gods did not die: they were not allowed to."

Wells were sometimes believed to be entrances to the underworld and it is common tradition that fairies lived in or beneath them. The devil is associated with some wells: near Llanarth church in Cardiganshire is a place called Ffynnon Gloch, where supposedly you cannot hear the nearby church bells ringing because the devil once rested at this spot by the well. And more than one well bears the legend that evil spirits take the form of frogs and will jump down the incautious drinker's throat.

We will leave the subject of wells though not of water, and travel to Wales' west coast to discuss some Arthurian legends. Here we recall Arthur in the legend of Llyn Barfogi ("bearded lake"), the lonely loch in the hills behind Aberdovey in which nothing is said to have lived since that day in the fifth century when the king pulled out a hairy monster. Aberdovey itself, a beautiful coastal town and a busy port until the seafaring trade moved elsewhere, is famous for mysterious ghostly bells which peal softly from under the sea off the harbor. These are from the sunken city of Manua which disappeared without warning many centuries ago.

There have long been Atlantis-type legends about villages disappearing under the sea off this coast, and the shifting sands occasionally throw up physical evidence of the ocean's erosion over the centuries. Old tree stumps can still be seen embedded in the sands near Borth. The twelfth-century *Black Book of Carmarthen* recounts the story of a mysterious maiden who abandoned her care of a magic well which caused the entire Plain of Gwyddnen to be flooded.

One of the few survivors of the flood was Taliesin, a bard at the royal court who later turned up around King Arthur. An enigmatic figure (after whom a present-day village is named), Taliesin wrote a book whose first appearance was apparently six centuries after his death and is therefore somewhat suspect with historians who like to have a clearer attribution for their facts.

One of the stories in the *Book of Taliesin* concerns the magic cauldron owned by a witch or earth mother named Ceridwen, who left it in the charge of a certain Gwion Bach. The contents of the cauldron, a rather special brew which bubbled for one year and a day, were capable of offering universal wisdom to whomever drank of it and Gwion Bach was unable to resist sampling three drops. Ceridwen, angered by this breach of trust, followed Gwion through his various evasive manifestations (as a hare, a fish, and a grain of wheat), finally gobbling him up and giving birth to Taliesin.

The story is reminiscent of the legends of the Holy Grail, particularly where it relates Arthur's quest into the Welsh underworld, Annwn, to gain possession of a magic cauldron which is the source of endless food.

F. Marian McNeil, in *The Silver Bough,* calls it "one of the most striking instances of the fusion of Druidical and Christian beliefs, for it derives in part from the magic cauldron of Celtic paganism and in part from the sacred chalice of Christianity. . . . The legend of the Grail," she writes, "has been treated by a succession of poets who developed its ethical and mystical import so that the Grail becomes a symbol of man's loftiest inspirations."

For our final stop in Wales we traverse the lonely moors between Nevern and the busy coastal town of Fishguard (from which ferries run to Ireland) which merge gently into the famous Prescelly Mountains. The village of Nevern itself, center of rabid Welsh Nationalists (who break the English place names off signposts), is worth some attention because the church contains the renowned Maglocunus Stone with inscriptions in ogham, a system used for writing Old Irish. The churchyard also shelters a tall Celtic cross and a "bleeding" yew tree, which has inexplicably been dripping with a bloodlike sap for sixty years. (The village is tiny, sleepy, and has places offering bed and breakfast.)

The Prescelly Mountains, rich in a number of standing stones, are best known among archeologists as the source of the bluestones which form the inner ring at Stonehenge, and there have been some suggestions that before arriving at their present site on Salisbury Plain they stood here in the mountains as a primitive "Bluestonehenge."

The Prescelly Mountains were yet another haunt of King Arthur who is remembered here with innumerable standing stones around the tiny village of Mynachlog-ddu. On the rough track that ascends Talmynydd are two six-foot standing stones called Corrig Meibion Arthur ("the stones of the sons of Arthur"); further north is Carn Arthur, recognizable by the stone poised precariously on top; nearby is Bedd Arthur ("Arthur's grave"); and half a mile to the east, Costan Arthur, a boulder supposedly thrown by the sixth-century king from Dyffryn farm to the Gors Fawr circle of standing stones.

But even these are exceeded in significance by the stones atop Cwm Carwyn, sometimes known as Prescelly Top, which mark the victories of Twrch Trwyth, a horrible boar (a king turned into a boar because of his wickedness) who killed eight of Arthur's men, almost finishing off the famous king himself.

Maybe Arthur never lived, but around Mynachlog-ddu there are plenty of memorials to his name.

25

Stonehenge

THE EARLIEST SOLAR TEMPLE?

There have been hundreds, possibly thousands of books about Stonehenge and very few of them come to the same conclusions. The currently fashionable theory is that the whole place is a sophisticated observatory built to predict solar eclipses, Professors Gerald Hawkins and A. Thom being the major proponents of this viewpoint which has gained wide acceptance as a result of elaborate television documentaries.

The official booklet at the site, gently dismissing Merlin as the architect of Stonehenge, does imply that one man was responsible for planning its construction, although it has no suggestions about who he might have been. It points out, however, that there were three different Stonehenges, each being a progression and a partial rebuilding of the earlier monument.

"All forms of worship require a calendar in order to keep their festivals on the right day," it explains, "man the world over has tried to do this by synchronizing solar and lunar phenomena, a nomadic people using the moon for their calendar, a sedentary people the sun."

Stephen Usherwood theorizes in *Britain, Century by Century* that Stone-

Illustration: Ground plan of Stonehenge according to Inigo Jones (1573–1652).

henge is "an astronomical clock 100 feet in diameter, its huge monolithic columns having been erected in two concentric rings so that the sun's disc can be framed exactly between two of them as it rises above the horizon at the winter solstice."

Of the thirty original uprights, sixteen are still standing, the tallest being about twenty-two feet plus another seven or eight feet sunk into the ground.

Before we proceed further it may be necessary to point out that a visit to Stonehenge will not be the tranquil pilgrimage to a magical site that you might have envisioned. Because of its popularity it is invariably crowded and even in winter you can expect to find a line-up of people waiting to buy tickets before negotiating the underground tunnel that leads from the vast car park to the fenced-off area on the other side of the road which encloses the circles of giant stones. In summertime anything less magical than screaming children, the fumes from arriving and departing buses, and a plethora of discarded ice cream wrappers would be hard to imagine.

It might seem that night would be a better time to visit, but unfortunately Stonehenge is closed after dark. It is patrolled at regular intervals by local police who, it is said, maintain a radar watch on the site from some distance away. (Incidentally, the site is not easily accessible without a car, being situated three or four miles from the nearest town, Amesbury, on no regular bus route and with taxis charging astronomical rates. Be sure, too, to have a hotel accommodation already booked—there are very few hotels—or be prepared to travel many miles after your visit.)

A good deal of attention has been given to a carving on one of the stones of a dagger with a fairly long tapered blade of a kind not found elsewhere in Britain during the Bronze Age (approximately 1500 B.C.). This type of weapon was common to the Mycenaean civilization about this time, so some archeologists have concluded that Stonehenge may have been built by or under the supervision of some architect from Greece who signed the pillar with his trademark. This view, however, has had as many skeptics as supporters.

The idea is unfashionable these days, but in the middle of the last century academics were often to be found writing to magazines suggesting that the word *henge*, meaning "hanging" (and presumed to refer to the way the lintels "hang" over the uprights) should be taken literally, the pagan Saxons having hung up human victims as offerings to the god Woden. A contributor to *Notes & Queries* in 1860 says: "As long as the Anglo-Saxon language is Anglo-Saxon, Stonehenge can mean nothing but "the stone gallows."

The outside circle of stones are known as sarsens and are sandstone blocks found on the Wiltshire Downs. There have been various explanations for the derivation of *sarsen,* among them "saracen," a term applied to Celtic or Roman objects which predate Christianity. But James Waylen's nineteenth-century *History of Marlborough* maintains that "the term Sarsen or Saresyn was applied by the Anglo-Saxons simply in the sense of pagan . . . as all the principal specimens of these mysterious blocks were perceived to be congregated into temples popularly attributed to heathen worship."

Only a few of the lintels atop the upright stones are now still in place, but even when all of them existed they possibly didn't complete the structure. The suggestion that the whole complex was covered over with an earthen roof, once advanced quite seriously, has since, however, been thoroughly discredited by thoughtful historians.

The layout of Stonehenge clearly seems to offer an endless field for speculation to those who enjoy such things. Was it a temple or an observatory? Or both? Was it already more than a thousand years old when the Druids arrived, and if so, did they make use of it? Do any of the fanciful theories of today have any foundation in fact?

"What happens at midsummer," reads one report, "is that the light from the rising sun coming over the hole or Gnomon Stone passes through the central portal which directly faces into the 'horseshoe' of trilithons and shines onto the Altar Stone, now in a prone position. The light therefore goes through this entrance place and into the fivefold horseshoe symbolizing birth."

This is from a mimeographed booklet—one of scores of a similar nature—put out, in this case, by the Order of Bards, Ovates and Druids, a latter-day organization that revived many of the ancient Druidic traditions and attempts to keep them alive through such celebrations as their annual gathering at Stonehenge on the morning of the summer solstice.

In her *Everyday Life of the Pagan Celts*, Anne Ross maintains there is no evidence that the Celtic Druids were ever associated with Stonehenge, and although such modern gatherings as the Welsh musical meeting, the Eisteddfod, have perpetuated an image of the idealized Druid, "it is an essentially false image, based on revival, rather than survival."

Although archeologists state quite categorically that Stonehenge belongs to an era about 1500 B.C. there is strangely no mention of it in early Roman writings nor in the manuscripts of such early Christian historians as Gildas, Nennius, or Bede. Much stress has been laid on the reference by Mecateus, a contemporary of Alexander the Great, in his *History of the Hyperboreans*, to a round temple dedicated to Apollo on their island. The Hyperboreans' island, he explained, was as large as Sicily, lying toward the north, over against the country of the Celts, fertile and varied in its productions, possessed of a beautiful climate and enjoying two harvests a year. It could have been Britain he referred to, but there are many authorities who don't think so.

Amazingly enough, there is then no mention of Stonehenge—if, indeed, this *was* a mention—for another fifteen centuries when Henry of Huntingdon, who died after 1154, mentions it as one of the four wonders of England.

But it was Geoffrey of Monmouth, the twelfth-century historian, with his *Historia Regnum Britanniae* who placed on the record the stories that have caused endless arguments ever since. It is known that Geoffrey added to and embellished the legends that the ninth-century monk Nennius had recorded, but nobody is certain where fact diverges from fantasy.

Geoffrey reports a conversation between the wizard Merlin and Aurelius, who was planning a memorial to the British nobles whom Hengist the Saxon had murdered at Ambresbury. Merlin suggested that he "send for the Giants' Ring which is on Mount Killaraus in Ireland. In that place there is a stone construction which no man of this period could ever erect, unless he combined great skill and artistry. The stones are enormous and there is no one alive strong enough to move them. If they are placed in position round this site, in the way in which they are erected over there, they will stand forever."

Aurelius is understandably skeptical and treats the idea as a huge joke, pointing out that Britain itself has plenty of huge stones.

"Try not to laugh in a foolish way, Your Majesty," Merlin answers. "What I am suggesting has nothing ludicrous about it. These stones are connected with certain secret religious rites and they have various properties which are medicinally important. Many years ago the Giants transported them from the remotest confines of Africa and set them up in Ireland at a time when they inhabited that country. Their plan was that whenever they felt ill baths should be prepared at the foot of the stones; for they used to pour water over them and to run this water into baths in which their sick were cured. What is more they mixed the water with herbal concoctions and so healed their wounds. There is not a single stone among them which hasn't some medicinal virtue."

The tale goes on to record the subsequent expedition to fetch the stones and how Merlin "laughed at their vain efforts" to dismantle the Giants' Ring before beginning his own preparations. "At last, when he had placed in order the engines that were necessary he took down the stones with incredible facility" and bought them to England where they were erected during a three-day celebration, Merlin thereby giving a "manifest proof of the prevalence of art above strength."

Half a century later the story is echoed in the work of another great historian, Giraldus Cambrensis (1146–1223), who writes of some large stones in Ireland's plain of Kildare which had been carried by giants from Africa and later brought to England by Merlin.

Merlin's participation in the building of Stonehenge was still being mentioned in the sixteenth century when John Leland said that the artful wizard had conveyed the stones not across the sea but from a nearby quarry, adding that he'd done it by "art and skill, which the men's strength could not supply."

It has been only within the last 400 years that the old stories of Merlin's magic began to be questioned. In 1627 a Cheshire-born tailor-turned-antiquarian named John Speed said this about Stonehenge: "In this place this forsayd King Aurelius with two or more of ye Britishe Kings his successours have beene buryed with many more of their nobilitye and in this place under little bankes to this daye are founde by digging bones of mighty men and armoure of ancient fashion."

Speed was the first of what proved to be a long line of unbelievers who cast doubt on Geoffrey of Monmouth's history. A more enlightened (?) age was approaching and magical explanations would no longer satisfy. Significantly it was a church historian, Thomas Fuller (d. 1661), who was the first to seriously question the legend. He wrote that the story of Merlin conjuring the stones out of Ireland by magic was "too ridiculous to be confuted." However, his own equally ridiculous explanation was that the stones were artificially contrived out of sand.

From the 1600s on, the sophisticated appraisals of architects, astronomers, academics, and modern-day scientists begin to take over. King James I sent the celebrated architect Inigo Jones to investigate Stonehenge. The seventeenth-century antiquarian John Aubrey plotted the site and discovered the circular ring of holes which now bears his name and which, says the official guide, presumably "had some ritual significance." Aubrey was the first to suggest that it might have been a Druid temple, and a century later William Stukeley agreed with him, averring that Druids built Stonehenge about 460 B.C. Stukeley did some excavating around the altar stone but didn't find anything much, although at this spot in the time of Henry VII a tin plate was found engraved with characters nobody could read. Unfortunately it has been lost.

In his *Worship of the Serpent* (1833), John Bathurst Deane says that "the circle and the horse shoe were both sacred figures in the Druidical religion as may be seen at Stonehenge where they are united, outer circles enclosing inner horse shoes."

Another nineteenth-century author suggests that after the Romans left Britain the natives reverted to heathenism but substituted "groves of upright stones for the oak groves of obsolete Druidism."

The tendency to attribute ancient stone circles to the Celts or their Druidic priests, "under the sanction of whose names we shelter ourselves whenever we are ignorant or bewildered," is referred to by Jacob Bryant in his *Analysis of Ancient Mythology*, Volume 3 (1776). But such places were the operations of "a very remote age," he suggests, adding that he doubts whether there was any monument in the world much older than Stonehenge.

On January 3, 1797, with a crash that was heard half a mile away, two of the largest trilithons fell to the ground after a sudden thaw, following a very deep snow. These were re-erected by the Ministry of Works in 1958, and the following year a radiocarbon determination was made of antler pick tools discovered at the site; their age was said to be about 3,500 years. If this is correct, one part of Stonehenge was built around 1500 B.C. Recent revisions in the system of archeological dating may reveal that the earliest foundations of Stonehenge and other megalithic sites in Britain are hundreds of years older than has up to now been thought.

At one time, people had easy access to the site, which is not possible now. Two young men cycled across Salisbury Plain on a moonlit night in 1870 and used a rope ladder to reach the top of the stones, taking a walk along a lintel 5 feet wide and 15 feet long. Dr. William Stukeley had made a similar climb a century before, and when the Wiltshire Archaeological and Natural History Society made an expedition to Stonehenge in September 1865, one of its members took along a ladder so several of them could climb to the top.

No such adventures are possible today, but there are plenty of people who have visited the site after tourists have gone for the day and sensed mysterious things. One of them, Mollie Carey, writing in *The Ley Hunter,* said she saw an eerie round light around the trilithons one night that kept going on and off. Another time one of her friends who was leaning against one of the stones felt a headache which vanished when he moved away:

> Everyone noticed a strange clicking sound coming from the stones. It wasn't the noise they make as they cool down after a hot day. We had been often enough to be used to the noises that were natural, but this was very different. We started running and as we left the circle a strange whirring noise shot heavenwards as if a giant catherine wheel had gone spinning upwards. . . . As we sat in my kitchen recovering, a figure of a woman materialized by the door, dressed in yellow, having long plaited hair, wearing a headdress similar to ancient Egyptian. She was very tall and was smiling at us. I had the impression there had been some sort of struggle between good and evil that night.

Before Stonehenge was guarded it was not only climbers and mystics who had unlimited access to the place, but also vandals. Stukeley refers to the practice common in his day of chipping off fragments. It was believed that the powder from crushed stones dropped into a well would keep away toads, and over the centuries even bigger pieces have been removed for the construction of walls or buildings. Inigo Jones reported in 1620 that the stones had been "not only exposed to the all-devouring ages but to the rage of men likewise."

Noting in his book *Survey of the Early Geography of Western Europe* that of the original 130 or so stones only 91 remained at that time (1859), Henry L. Long "hoped that the work of destruction is now at an end" and speculates that although some of the damage may have been done by excavators in search of buried treasure, "I am more inclined to attribute their overthrow to the same cause that inspired their construction, namely to religious fervor." It seemed likely to him, that upon the conversion from paganism to Christianity, attacks would have been directed "against the symbols of Druidical superstition."

Writing in *The Wiltshire Archaeological and Natural Magazine* a century ago (1876), William Long noted many other examples of damage to the stones, including that done by a picnic party that had lit a fire against one of the outer stones causing portions to break off. Some of the markings that would undoubtedly confuse future historians, he explained, were of relatively recent origin and he had himself noticed in October 1875 a "broad arrow" chiseled on the large stone behind the leaning stone of the largest trilithon.

Stonehenge has been under government protection for only about sixty years; until 1918 the land on which it stands was sold over and over again, the stone site itself being just part and parcel of grazing land that, at the last sale, sold for £6,000 (about $15,000). Now admission fees alone exceed that sum each year.

The earliest part of Stonehenge, or rather the first of what eventually became three successive Stonehenges, is believed to have been the outer bank and its ditch, the inner circle of bluestones being brought here about a century later. The periods can only be approximated through radiocarbon dating of various organic artifacts found on the site.

The term "blue" for the inner ring of stones can be misleading, being a description of their appearance when wet. Technically the stones are mostly of a type known as dolerite, a variety of crystalline rock often dotted with whitish-pink spots; others are of a hard, flinty type known as rhyolite, or a species of sandstone.

It was not until the 1920s that geologists established that the 4½-ton bluestones that comprise the inner ring were bought from the Prescelly Mountains in Wales by what has been assumed was a route of about 240 miles, mostly over water.

Addressing the Antiquarian Society in 1923 on his discoveries in Wales, Dr. H. H. Thomas commented: "It is probably more than a coincidence that this area, clearly indicated by geological evidence as the source of [the stones], should contain one of the richest collections of megalithic remains in Britain."

And it is not only stone sites for which the Prescelly Mountains are legendary but also age-old folklore concerning lords of the underworld, fairies, and Druids. King Arthur hunted the Welsh boar Twrch Trwyth here, and more than one ancient monument marks the reputed site of their skirmishes.

At least three eminent archeologists have expressed the opinion that the bluestones were already part of a sacred site in Wales before being transported to Salisbury Plain, a move that might conceivably have duplicated or followed the transference of political or administrative power. Dr. V. E. Nash-Williams of the Welsh National Museum suggests that the ancient builders regarded the Prescelly Mountains as a place of special sanctity: "Just as today the builders of American cathedrals like to incorporate stones from the mother church at Canterbury, so builders of Stonehenge were at pains to re-use materials from [such a] highly venerated shrine in Pembrokeshire."

The route that the bluestones followed is generally thought to have been from the port of Milford Haven, on Wales' south coast, and up the Bristol Channel to Avonmouth, thence up the Avon and Frome rivers to near Frome in Somerset, overland to near Warminster and back onto water via the Wylye and Avon rivers to the end of Stonehenge Avenue near West Amesbury. This is the official version, supposedly confirmed by an experiment conducted by BBC television twenty years ago when a concrete copy of a bluestone was slung between canoes and poled up the River Avon by a quartet of schoolboys.

What today is known as the Heelstone, at whose peak (or very near to it) the sun rises at summer solstice, used to be called Friar's Heel from an ancient folktale that the devil threw it at a friar when he discovered the latter eavesdropping. At the time the devil, sent by Merlin, had just returned from buying the stones from an old woman in Ireland for as much money as she could count while they were being removed—one of those bad bargains made by an innocent old lady who didn't realize that removal would be instantaneous. The imprint on one side of the stone, more than 200 feet from the center, was said to be that of the friar's heel as the stone struck him a glancing blow.

Some of the most interesting research at Stonehenge has been done by Guy Underwood, a former British Museum curator who followed up a tip from a colleague, Reginald Allender Smith, an expert on Roman history, that there might be a connection between the location of ancient monuments and the presence of underground water. Smith, a water diviner himself, read a paper to the British Society of Dowsers, theorizing that at the center of every prehistoric temple would be found a spot from which underground streams radiated. Before this, Capt. Robert Boothby and two French archeologists, Louis Merle and Charles Diot, had published their ideas that such streams crossed or surrounded famous stone sites.

Underwood expanded this kind of research extensively, quickly discovering what he termed an "earth force" whose chief characteristics, he said, were that it appeared to cause wave motion perpendicular to the earth's surface; that it had great penetrative power; that it affected the nerve cells of animals whose behavior was influenced by it; and that it formed spiral patterns. He concluded that it was an unrecognized side effect of some already established force such as magnetism or gravity.

In his book *The Pattern of the Past,* Underwood raises some fascinating points, one of which is why modern man still has the ability (with a little training) to dowse successfully for water. Perhaps it's the remnant of a latent talent that he once needed for something else. So far as we know, early man didn't sink wells, but maybe, implies Underwood, he did dowse to find hidden springs or to divine some hidden line of energy —the "old straight track" so beloved of today's ley line hunters?—that existed below the earth.

Underwood took his theories (and his dowsing rod made of bamboo) to Stonehenge and proceeded to come up with some highly original theories. For example, it's always been assumed that when the great circle was complete that lintels stood on top of all the pairs of uprights, whereas only half a dozen remain in place today. But why would thieves, vandals, or later builders take the trouble to erect scaffolding to remove these six-ton lintels, taking them so far away that they have never been found? He suggests that maybe the "missing" lintels were never there at all, particularly since the ones that remain are over the spots where he dowsed underground springs. Maybe, Underwood explains, that's why the existing lintels stand where they do—and also because they would clearly indicate to celebrants specific points for some religious purpose.

All the stones at Stonehenge were long ago officially numbered and Underwood pays particular attention to number 51 (first stone of inner circle on left, after entering from the northeast) because he says that not only is it encircled by underground springs, but also that a hole in the stone is invariably filled with water. And this in a place where there is no known natural water supply within a mile. Underwood theorizes that water—which has always been an essential ingredient in almost all religious rituals—was supplied here by condensation from the top (condensation is a special property of sarsen stones), being led down to the hole by an almost imperceptible groove.

By the time Underwood died, his maverick theories had still not received much acceptance in the scientific world, and as he himself wrote, he would have to be content with merely recording his discoveries because he was unable to reduce them to a mathematical formula. But, he said, "I am in good company. Even when they used it, and marked its presence, the priests and initiates of early days did not profess to understand geodetic phenomena."

Among the modern techniques applied to "solving" the mystery of this monument is that of using a computer to examine the immense number of alignments that the sun, moon, and stars, rising and setting at different times of the year, make with the various stones and spaces between the trilithons. Gerald S. Hawkins, an astronomy professor at Boston University, has spent hundreds of hours investigating this aspect in the past decade. Hawkins reports in *Stonehenge Decoded* that he has found that Stonehenge can be used as an accurate predictor of the movements of the heavenly bodies and to foretell eclipses. This can hardly be accidental, but perhaps it does not yet tell the full story.

So the twentieth-century "scientific" explanations match those of many earlier observers that in one way or another the purpose of Stonehenge was sun worship.

The nineteenth-century antiquarian William Long, in his lengthy book *Stonehenge and Its Barrows,* comments:

> Man, even the most savage and degraded, must have his god or gods. The religious instinct implanted in man and fostered by the constant realization of his own weakness and of the existence of powers above him, around him and independent of him, by which his welfare is more or less affected, must have an outcome. And if he knows not the Creator he will worship the creature. . . . In such a climate as that of Britain, dependent so much on solar influences for its material prosperity, would it be unreasonable to suppose that the solar cults would prevail? It can hardly have been an accident that the stone without the circles at Stonehenge should have been so placed that the sun should ride immediately over it at the summer solstice.

The famous stone circle is not, as we have said, the whole of Stonehenge, although most of the three-quarters of a million tourists who visit here each year don't bother about anything else. A ley line has been plotted as far away as the ancient earthwork of Clearbury Ring, about ten miles to the south, on its way passing directly through Old Sarum and Salisbury Cathedral. But much, much nearer than that are all the earthworks and sanctuary of Avebury, the West Kennet Long Barrow, Silbury Hill, Woodhenge, the earthworks of Windmill Mill and Durrington Walls, and the scores of round and long barrows with which the whole region is dotted.

It is impossible to escape the conclusion that the area around Stonehenge was especially holy and that to be buried there was to offer the greatest possible guarantee of glory in the next world or even possibly a triumphant return to this one. Amazingly enough, historians can't say for certain what the purpose of these barrows was any more than they can explain Stonehenge. Half a mile north of the famous stones, for example, is the Cursus, a rather extraordinary mound almost two miles long and 100 yards wide, most of which has now been destroyed by plowing. There are many similar mounds in Britain, one in Dorset stretching for more than six miles. They are enigmas.

A few hundred yards to the right of the Cursus is Woodhenge, a circular earthwork (about 200 feet in diameter) surrounding what was probably a roofed building. Aerial photographs gave archeologists the first clue and when the area was excavated in 1928 the rotting stumps of posts were found in some of the holes. A circle of concrete posts, somewhat like milestones, now indicate the original plan. There are no clues to the purpose of the building, but the suggestion has been made that magical formulas caused its construction to invoke the influence of Mercury. It is unguarded (a couple were sleeping in a tent at one edge of it when we last visited), and so the magical vibrations may be stronger than at Stonehenge which is tinged with commercialism.

The heaviest concentration of circular mound tombs—"these round barrows that are like the floating bubbles of events drowned in time," as Jacquetta Hawkes colorfully phrases it in *Guide to the Prehistoric and Roman Monuments in England and Wales*—are centered around Stonehenge itself where there are more than in any other area of comparable size in Britain. Most of them are circular and have yielded up large quantities of burnt bones, both animal and human, as well as vast numbers of amber beads. Some of the skeletons in the long barrows were of victims who appeared to have been killed with stone axes for ritual burial, along with the chief who had apparently died naturally.

About fifteen miles north of Stonehenge is the impressive village of Avebury, impressive because the entire village is scattered around and within an enormous circle of sarsen stones which nobody has ever satisfactorily explained. It was constructed, say the pundits, "for unknown religious purposes" sometime around 2000 B.C. John Aubrey, among the first to discover it in modern times, commented that it "doth exceed Stonehenge in grandeur as a cathedral doth an ordinary parish church."

A couple of centuries ago the circle's basic features were much clearer and Dr. William Stukeley, who visited the site early in the eighteenth century, affected to see there what looked to him like a mystical serpent formed by two avenues of stones stretching for more than a mile to the southeast and southwest. Traces of the southeastern avenue can still be seen, culminating in a stone circle known as the Sanctuary atop Overton Hill. The southwestern avenue has long since disappeared.

Stukeley's 1724 engraving of the site can still be inspected in Avebury's charming museum, which also contains interesting artifacts from ancient earthworks at Windmill Hill, a mile or two to the northwest. This site, say archeologists, dates back as far as 3700 B.C., and the carved chalk objects and human bones found there "testify to the performance of rites and ceremonies connected with fertility and the harvest."

It was not until 1930 that serious excavations began at Avebury, by which time much destruction had taken place. The massive circular bank, once a full 50 feet higher than the ditch which adjoins it, had crumbled away in parts, although its shape and outline were still clearly visible. More important, scores of the stones which once marked the site had been broken up, removed for building purposes, or in some cases deliberately buried as if to defuse their suspiciously magical powers.

Considerable restoration work followed and the site now has great charm. Cows graze around and between the deeply pocked stones, many of them up to 12 feet tall, and the tranquillity is disturbed only by camera-toting tourists.

The countryside around Stonehenge is relatively flat, which makes the sudden eminence of Silbury Hill, a flat-topped mound that towers 130 feet above the adjoining London to Bath highway even more impressive. Archeologists who have probed into this mound of 12½ million cubic feet of earth—the equivalent of every man, woman, and child in present-day England adding a bucketful to the pile—have found nothing to explain it. They say that it is the largest man-made hill in Europe and that it must have taken the equivalent of 700 men building for almost a decade to erect it. Why? Nobody has been able to say, although explanations have ranged from a burial mound for ancient (and possibly mythical) King Sil who was supposedly entombed underneath on horseback, to the intriguing suggestion of Moses B. Cotsworth, around the turn of the century, that the hill acted as a giant sundial. He suggested that it had been topped with a ninety-five-foot sighting staff which provided a shadow long enough to give accurate measurements prior to various solstices and equinoxes.

The hill, which originally must have been considerably bigger but has eroded through the centuries, covers an area of more than five acres at its base and definitely predates the ancient Roman road which swerves to avoid its foot.

Another curious site we can scarcely afford to overlook in southern England are the massive hill figures which are a fairly common part of the landscape, at least in Wiltshire. The nearest to Stonehenge is a relatively small one known as the Cherhill Horse, said to have been cut into the chalky earth of the downs beside the Avebury to Bath highway, by a Cherhill doctor late in the eighteenth century.

But the best-known example is the fabulous 360-foot-long figure known as the White Horse of Uffington, sprawling over a gentle slope of the Berkshire Downs southwest of Oxford. At one point it is as deep as 130 feet, and its white, chalky outlines can be seen as far as fifteen miles away. Truth to tell it resembles more a dragon than a horse, a resemblance made sharper by the adjoining flat-topped mound known as Dragon Hill. Here, legend goes, St. George slew a dragon, and the two bare patches of ground on which no turf will grow mark the spot on which its blood was spilled.

The official notice at the site attributes its construction to the first century, but there have been endless contradictory explanations of why it was carved. It has been said that it is a Celtic shrine connected with worship of Epona the horse goddess; a prancing white horse that represented the battle standard of Alfred, Hengist, or some other Saxon ruler;

a symbol of the once-prominent cult of stag worship; a series of spirals to mark underground springs; a representation of the Norse hero Wayland the Smith, the legendary god whose long-chambered barrow lies close to the Icknield Way less than a mile away.

Until the middle of the last century it was a rural custom to "scour" the horse (or dragon) every seven years, the whole village turning out for the ceremony of cutting away the turf that had grown over its outline and enjoying the festival that accompanied it with two days of feasting paid for by the local squire. These days, the figure is maintained by the Department of the Environment which keeps a fence around it to discourage vandals. An old superstition maintains that to stand in the figure's eye and revolve three times is to ensure the success of any wish.

One of the curious aspects of the older hill figures, like the Westbury White Horse, south of Devizes, which is 176 feet long by 113 feet high, is that they often adjoin ancient earthworks or hillforts from the Iron Age. Possibly they were sacred enclosures in which fertility rites were practiced to maintain the productivity of the land and whose rituals gave rise to the festivals and fairs which were a feature of rural life until recent times.

John Michell suggests that many of these figures originally depicted dragon legends and says that in every continent of the world the dragon chiefly represents the principle of energizing fertility. "The places associated with the dragon's death," he writes, "the nerve centers of seasonal fertility, appear always to coincide with rites of ancient sanctity. Churches on old mounds, flat-topped hills, holy springs and wells are pointed out as the scene of the dragon's life or death. And the processions at the beginning of winter that seasonally mark the dragon's death are invariably preceded by rites and festivals of the sort that always appear to have taken place on or near hill figure sites."

The one other hill figure which should be noted is the notorious Cerne Abbas Giant, an immense figure almost two hundred feet high, with shoulders forty-four feet wide, which has stood for centuries overlooking the tiny village of Cerne Abbas on route A352 in Dorset. In the giant's hand is an upraised club, 120 feet long and ominously knobbled, but more striking is the figure's erect penis, measuring almost 30 feet, on which childless couples from the village sleep if they wish to improve their luck.

As elsewhere the figure is supposed to be a fertility symbol, and this conclusion is strengthened by the presence of a rectangular earthwork enclosure on the hillside above it in which for centuries were held maypole dances around a freshly-cut fir tree.

One local legend suggests that it may have been carved as a joke to anger the abbot and monks of a nearby monastery that existed until the sixteenth century; another legend suggests that the villagers found a real giant sleeping on the hillside one day, and after killing him, carved his outline on the spot. The thirteenth-century historian Walter of Coventry says the sun god Helith was once celebrated in the district and William Stukeley, writing in 1746, commented that the giant was known locally as Helis.

When Stukeley addressed the Society of Antiquaries later that year, however, he had another suggestion: that the giant was a representation of Hercules—not the original god but the Roman emperor Commodus (emperor, A.D. 180–192), who regarded himself as a reincarnation and gave himself the title of Hercules Romanus when he appeared in public as consul and gladiator.

Commodus, the nineteen-year-old son of the great Roman emperor Marcus Aurelius, was certainly enough of an egotist to prompt such a monument. He had already replaced Apollo's head with one of his own on a colossal statue that stood in Rome's Imperial Forum. But in his short twelve-year reign, before being murdered in his own palace, there is no evidence he ever visited Britain.

26

Scotland

PROPHETS, FAIRIES, AND THE
LOCH NESS MONSTER

ANY JOURNEY in search of magic takes one inevitably to Scotland where the ancient Pictish stones with their magical (and largely indecipherable) markings are physical reminders of a race that left no other written traditions. Pictish symbol stones feature unidentifiable figures, sometimes described as elephants but resembling much more prancing horses with horns. Other animals are also carved upon them, including serpents, bulls, boars, wolves, stags, fish, and bears. But their best-known markings are less understandable: triple discs, crossbars, crescents, and V-rods.

These stones are found all over Scotland but chiefly in the northern Pictish strongholds where, in the remoter regions, it is still the custom to celebrate *samhain,* the ancient Celtic festival of November Eve when the sun fell under the sway of the evil forces of winter.

Sir James Frazer speculates, in *The Golden Bough,* that the fire practices of samhain were a form of imitative magic "to ensure a needful supply of sunshine for men, animals and plants by kindling fires which mimic on earth the great source of heat and light in the sky." In addition to worshiping the sun, the Celtic Druids also paid homage to the moon,

Illustration: A twentieth-century rendering of Loch Ness.

a symbol found frequently on the Pictish stones.

"Picts were pagan," writes J. Cameron Lees in *A History of the County of Inverness*, "and the Druids among them dwelt at the residences of kings and exercised great power in national affairs. They appear to have been magicians, soothsayers and enchanters—workers of spells and charms —their influence with the king founded on the belief that by their necromancy they could aid those who sought their assistance or injure those opposed to them."

Lees explains that their favorite methods of divination included natural events such as sneezing or interpreting the song of a bird in a tree. He quotes an old poem attributed to St. Columba:

> Our fate depends not on sneezing
> Nor on a bird perched upon a twig
> Nor on the root of a knotted tree
> Nor on the noise of clapping hands.

Many traces of paganism survived until Lees' time, almost eighty years ago, "in the belief in charms, in fairies, in witchcraft, in the power of the evil eye which still lingers in many of our Highland glens. We have relics of the old Celtic heathenism still existing in the midst of our present civilization."

The stately city of Inverness, impressively located at the head of sea-girt Moray Firth on one side and Scotland's biggest lake, Loch Ness, on the other, has many claims to fame as a center of magic. Home of numerous fairy legends and the Loch Ness monster, it was also one of the happy haunts of the twelfth-century magician Michael Scot, who is reputed to be buried in Melrose Abbey to the south.

Scotland gave birth to many renowned magicians, among them the astrologer Simon Forman and the alchemist Alexander Seton, but Scot was probably the most famous, spending much of his life abroad in the service of the emperor Frederick II. Renowned as mathematician, alchemist, and physician (his recipe for making gold includes such ingredients as "the blood of a ruddy man and the blood of a red owl," also saffron, alum, urine, and cucumber juice), Scot also wrote a trio of celebrated books on astrology, the best-known of which are *Liber Introductorius* and *Liber Particularis*. His extensive knowledge of magic led Boccaccio to describe him as "a great master of necromancy" and for Dante to list him in his *Inferno*. His fellow countryman Sir Walter Scott wrote about him in *The Lay of the Last Minstrel*.

Scot's alchemical studies led him to believe that "gold grows and is born underground by the combination of heat and sulphur," an observation that may have been the basis of some of his experiments. After studying at Oxford and then at the Sorbonne in Paris, Scot learned Arabic in the occult academy of Toledo and at the same place gained the reputation of being able to harness demons in his service, especially for building purposes. Sir Walter Scott once commented that most of the works of antiquity in southern Scotland were credited either to the devil or to Michael Scot. In the Inverness area he is remembered for many bridges built north of the city, one of them an immense bridge right across the Moray Firth, which local merchants eventually persuaded him to demolish (leaving the spur that still projects into the water above Portrose).

Scot was reputed to have acquired his magical powers after killing a mystical serpent while he was walking across the Grampian Hills. On arriving at a nearby inn and telling his landlady, a witch, of the encounter, she instructed him to go back and fetch a portion of the snake which she was then to use as the principal ingredient of one of her magical spells.

Watching her through the keyhole, Scot acquired second sight, seduced "some thousands of Satan's best workmen into his employment," trained them as architects, and proceeded to erect bridges at stupefying speed. His satanic workmen kept demanding more and more tasks until he was able to keep them occupied only by commanding them "to manufacture me ropes that will carry me to the back of the moon," using as ingredients only "miller's suds and sea sand."

In the threescore years of his life (1175–1234) Scot wrote about many subjects, including aeromancy—the art of divining from aerial phenomena such as clouds, fog, lightning, thunder, and falling stars. "Cloud formations in the shape of dragon, horse or man," he warned, "betray the presence there of demons and it is a good time to invoke them with conjuration."

Scot's biographers explain his aerial maneuvers variously: some say he rode the skies astride a demon steed, others that he constructed "flying machines" and flew to Paris and Rome on a mechanical "horse."

Five centuries after Scot wrote about trickster, sorcerer, and sage (illusor, maleficus, sapiens), along came Coinneach Odhar who may have been all three. Known as the Brahan Seer, he achieved a considerable reputation in the seventeenth century for his supposed gift of second sight—a doubtful blessing, as it happened, because it led to his being burned alive on the Black Isle (the land between Moray and Cromarty firths). The place of his execution (he was thrown into a blazing tar barrel) is marked by a stone just east of the road leading from Fortrose to Fort George ferry, in the desolate sandy dunes near the lighthouse.

There are differing versions of an incident that happened to Coinneach while still in his teens, but most of them boil down to the fact that he took a nap while out cutting peat one day, and awoke to find a small stone on his chest. On looking through a tiny hole in the stone's center, he saw a vision of the farmer's wife bringing him a meal which had been poisoned. When the meal arrived he fed it to a dog which promptly died. This confirmed his feeling that by means of the stone he had acquired a degree of second sight.

He became renowned for his prophecies, and people traveled from all over the Highlands to consult him. Like most prophets, he may have made some shrewd guesses about future developments, observing the changing coastline and guessing that canals would bring ships ashore, or that railroads would enable horseless carriages to be seen at some unlikely places.

But he also predicted some events which nobody could possibly have had advance knowledge of: a loch bursting its banks and flooding a nearby village (although it was 300 years before this happened), or an eight-ton stone being carried out to sea, or most dramatic of all, that a certain bleak moor "shall, ere many generations have passed away, be stained with the best blood of the Highlands." The moor he referred to, as he walked across it, later became known for the bloody battle of Culloden.

One of the Brahan Seer's predictions concerned Tomnahurich, the fairy hill of Inverness, which he said "will be under lock and key and the fairies secured within." More than a century later this famous hill was turned into a cemetery and secured with a fence and a gate, pad-locked each night at sunset.

What led to Coinneach Odhar's undoing was his success. Isabella, Countess of Seaforth, heard of the accuracy of his prognostications and sought a consultation with him concerning the whereabouts of her husband who had long been absent in Paris. Assuring her that Lord Seaforth was in good health, the seer was reluctant to say more, but when pressed revealed the lord's dalliance with another lady. This news made the countess furious and she promptly had the unfortunate Brahan Seer condemned and executed for witchcraft.

But Coinneach had the last word. He told the countess that the Seaforth family would come to an end, the sons all dying before their father who would become deaf and dumb. And then he threw his "seeing" stone away—it was never found—and went to his execution. It hardly seems necessary to add that things came about exactly as he had predicted, almost the last piece of Seaforth property passing out of family hands when the Isle of Lewis was sold to Sir James Matheson more than a century ago.

One of the Brahan Seer's successful prophecies, as we have said, concerned Tomnahurich, the fairy hill in Inverness which is now a fenced-in Christian cemetery. These days it is famous locally not so much for its fairy associations but for its very distinctive shape, which everybody refers to as "an upturned boat." Fairy hills are not particu-larly uncommon—other celebrated ones include the Blackdown Hills in Somerset; Cnocnam Bocan in Monteith; and the Gump at St. Just in Cornwall—but Tomnahurich stands out in folklore because of its as-sociations with yet another Scottish seer, Thomas the Rhymer, who was chosen as a lover (the ancient tales say) by none less than the fairy queen herself.

Not knowing, or maybe not caring, about the belief that a garment turned inside out would break a fairy's spell, Thomas allowed himself to be carried off into fairyland, which he found to be "darke as at midnight" with the sound of a great flood in the background and water up to his knees. Wherever this actually was, legend attributes it to Tomnahurich, on the side of which Thomas found himself when released from the queen's embrace seven years later.

The fairies, we are told, "were wont to assemble on good occasions to do homage to Cynthia and celebrate her revels in the autumn months under the silvery moon's pale ray." That is how the anonymous author of the *Sixpenny Guide to Inverness* described it in 1872. And in *Tales of the Heather*, published locally in 1892, Emma Rose Mackenzie recounts the story of another of the fairy hill's involuntary visitors, Donald the Fiddler, a lazy fellow who much preferred to play rather than pursue his trade as a tanner, and thus fell asleep near Tomnahurich one day after a heavy bout of drinking. He awoke to find an old man in a velvet cloak, trimmed with fur and tied with a crimson sash, bending over him. Seeing him awake, the old man invited Donald to come and pluck the fiddle for his friends at a party. Accepting, Donald soon found himself in a magnificent mansion, playing the fiddle for hours in a sumptious ballroom where he was enchanted by the gaiety, good food, and heavenly music. The only problem was that the guests danced and danced without stopping. Donald came to believe that they were superhuman, and he called out in consternation, "Holy Saint Mary, help me. What shall I do?"

At these very unpagan words everything suddenly vanished and there was Donald back lying on the river bank near his home. But as he walked toward the town it looked somehow bigger and less familiar, the people strange and unable to understand his questions. He came to realize that somehow his night in the hidden mansion under the hill had actually lasted 100 years.

In alarm he made his way to a nearby chapel, St. Mary's, where his antiquated clothes and manners made worshipers laugh, but not for long. Because as the first words of the service rang out, Donald collapsed in a heap of decaying flesh and bones. He was quickly buried.

Tomnahurich, though a Christian cemetery for a century, still retains a somewhat untamed appearance. Towering more than 220 feet above sea level, its lower surface is covered with tombstones, but the remainder is densely wooded and unkempt. A narrow road spirals up the hill, sometimes almost obscured by the overgrowth.

The view from the top of Tomnahurich is of the neighboring Caledonian valley, the River Ness flowing into Loch Ness which lies at the foot of majestic 2,300-foot Mt. Meanfourvonie. We shall shortly pay a visit to this romantic loch.

The author of a curious collection called *Superstitions,* a nineteenth-century minister named John Gregson Campbell was much interested in the subject of impish fairies. "A common belief is that they existed once though they are not now seen," he wrote. ". . . According to Scoto-Celtic belief [they] are a race of beings the counterpart of mankind in person with its occupations and pleasures but unsubstantial and unreal, ordinarily invisible, noiseless in their motions and having their dwellings underground, in hills and green mounds of rock or earth. They are addicted to visiting the haunts of men, sometimes to give assistance but more frequently to take away the benefits of their goods and labours and sometimes even their persons. They may be present in any company though mortals do not see them. . . . Men cannot be sufficiently on their guard against them."

Fairies, seen most at dusk and during wild and stormy nights of mist and driving rain when streams are swollen and "the roar of the torrent is heard on the hill," were said to come always from the west where blood-red skies combined with deep blue hills, gray clouds, and the greenish light which was sometimes known as fairy fires. They invariably dressed in green robes, were fond of music (there are numerous legends of villagers being given green violins and taught to play tunes which the untutored could not duplicate), and dwelt in regal palaces under the hills and within domed mounds. They worshiped Truth, Justice, and Equality—a parallel here with the Druids—and celebrated magical rituals with endless festivities.

The unfortunate mortals who stumbled upon fairy celebrations, often by catching a glimpse through an open door in the hillside, lost all count of time if they accepted an invitation to participate. And if they were rash enough to sip magical drinks or sample fairy food (which left one as hungry as before), they might stay for years without knowing it. Often the fairies, not content with enticing the occasional passerby, would steal a baby from its cradle, replacing it with a changeling. The mother's only recourse when this happened was to stand in a running stream at dusk and toss the bundle in, whereupon her own child would reappear at home, looking none the worse for this unsought adventure.

Leaving the city of Inverness and heading south, there is a fantasy that, contradictory as it sounds, sometimes takes a more tangible form, the Loch Ness Monster. Is it an occult phenomenon or an anachronistic throwback? A physical manifestation of the viewer's subconscious or a living, breathing specimen that has somehow outlived its prehistoric saurian cousins for thousands of years?

Victorian lecturers were fond of drawing parallels between the dragons of medieval repute and the gigantic monsters that roamed the earth in its earliest days—the winged pterodactyl, for example, with its long neck, big head, scaly body, and two-legged birdlike stance. Lord Lindsay summed it up when he wrote (in his *Sketches of Christian Art*): "The dragons of early tradition, whether aquatic or terrestrial, are not perhaps wholly to be regarded as fabulous. In the case of the former, the race may be supposed to have been perpetuated till the marshes or inland seas left by the Deluge dried up."

Dragon legends persist throughout Britain, the authentication of their one-time presence is living on in innumerable place names and marked by dragon stones and carvings in cathedrals and churches, among them York Minster and Fountains Abbey. The Sockburn "Worm" (from the Norse word *ormr,* "dragon") is said to have provided the inspiration for Lewis Carroll's "Jabberwocky." "With eyes of flame, came whiffling through the Tulgey wood and burbled as it came." Carroll presumably heard the local folktale when he lived near the tiny Northumbrian village of Sockburn.

At Lyminster in Sussex, a "bottomless" pond behind the church is still called Nucker Hole, the name a supposed corruption of *nicor,* the Anglo-Saxon word for "sea serpent." Such beasts or monsters were traditionally supposed to lie at the bottom of lakes and wells guarding treasure.

One of the most famous of North Britain's dragon stories concerns the Lambton Worm, a fearsome serpent fished out of a Durham river not far from the Scottish border sometime in the fourteenth century. Tossed carelessly into a nearby well, it soon outgrew its cramped watery quarters and for years terrorized the surrounding countryside. Many a brave knight sought to vanquish it, but the creature had the formidable habit of reunifying itself every time it was chopped apart. One day a brave knight, acting on the advice of a local witch, donned a suit of armor studded with razor-sharp spikes and tackled the monster in the middle of a fast-flowing river, which instantly carried away the severed head. However, the story has a sad ending: The witch had extracted a promise that after his victory the young knight would kill the first living creature he saw or else "for nine generations no Lord of Lambton shall die in his bed." Unfortunately, the hero's father rushed out to congratulate him, and unable to make the necessary sacrifice, the knight stayed his hand with the consequence that the prophecy was fulfilled.

Writing in his *Notes on the Folklore of the Northern Counties of England,* William Henderson reveals that old family manuscripts identify the slayer of the Worm as a certain Knight of Rhodes, Sir John Lambton, and that nine generations after him Henry Lambton died in his carriage while crossing the River Wear on June 26, 1761. The previous eight squires had all died away from their homes, many violently in far-off wars.

Discussing dragons in general, Henderson comments: "Such tales come before us in widely separated countries, among people of different races, interwoven with almost every form of religion. They are the inheritance of every branch of the human family, and the question recurs again and again to the thoughtful mind: how are we to account for the firm hold they possess over the heart of man?"

Some authors, he continues, consider legends of dragons and sea serpents to be merely figurative, mere allegories of good versus evil, while others believe them to be a corruption of beasts that once existed. "For myself, I would ask whether both points of view may not be held together. Believing as I do that the ancient dragon myth embodies and has helped to uphold in the world a belief in truth victorious over error, holiness triumphant over sin, yet it does appear perfectly clear to me that the outward form and presentment of evil as thus set before us is borrowed from those monstrous forms of animal life which were more familiar to our ancestors."

And so what are we to make of the "dragon" of Loch Ness (the "monster" is a newspaper tag dating from the 1930s)? There is no doubt that *something* exists; there have been too many independent sightings, photographs, and even films for it to be a myth.

But are we to deal with it in concrete terms, summarizing its numerous physical appearances and documenting the methods and increasingly sophisticated equipment deployed in searching for it during the past half-century? Or should we concentrate on its magical associations —the obvious similarity between the elusive monster and the legendary kelpies, or water horses, which have haunted the Scottish lochs and rivers from the earliest times? St. Columba's biographer, Adamnan, recounts the story of Columba who crossed the River Ness and came upon a group of people burying a man who had died after being bitten by a "water monster."

Sending out a man to retrieve the rescue boat, St. Columba suddenly saw the beast rising to the surface in search of this potential victim, and raising his arms to form the sign of the cross, commanded it: "Go no further, nor touch that man; go back at once!" To everybody's amazement the monster obeyed.

Incidentally, in St. Columba's time—the sixth century—a Druid priest named Broichan is reputed to have astounded the Christian saint by invoking magic to cause darkness and a storm to cover the loch. After that, the monster seems to have laid low for several centuries, although the desolate nature of the area around the loch, coupled with no effective means of communication, may have had a lot to do with the public's lack of awareness of the possibility of its existence.

Loch Ness exudes the kind of atmosphere that makes one want to believe in sea monsters. Long and narrow, the loch winds out of sight from almost any point. It is one of the biggest of Scotland's lochs, and easily the deepest. The water is murky, always covered with odd and exotic shadows from the nearby trees, and because sunshine is not exactly one of Scotland's outstanding features, usually shrouded in mist which weaves back and forth into the many inlets and crevices.

Because the loch is so winding, there are many secluded lagoons and ponds, all luring the visitor into dark corners seemingly unexplored. And until the relatively recent popularity of monster-hunting, Loch Ness was considered too far north to warrant much attention from tourists. Much of this attitude still prevails: most of the loch's shoreline is free from buildings, and indeed from visitors, and calls a wild, primitive welcome.

Sightings of the mysterious creature began to be reported on a continual basis in the 1930s when a new road was built along the loch's northwestern shore. Workmen and local residents checked in with reports, and a story in the *Inverness Chronicle* on May 2, 1933 first used the phrase "The Loch Ness Monster." Newspapers and radio took up the story, and outsiders began to arrive in search of the elusive creature.

One is Frank Searle who managed a store in London and gave up his job to take up a lonely vigil beside the lake. Living in a tent just south of Dores Village he is constantly looking for opportunities to photograph the monster. His pictures have appeared many times in Fleet Street papers and are reproduced on postcards sold in local stores. London's sensation-seeking tabloids treated the monster as a joke at first, seemingly unconcerned about distinguishing hoaxes and genuine sightings. But an impartial group known as the Loch Ness Investigation Bureau, which was formed in 1965 to coordinate relevant information, reported that by the 1970s the loch's thousands of annual visitors were increasingly sympathetic toward the monster's existence.

There have been no reports of any attacks since the one recounted by Adamnan, but superstition attaches to the fatal crash of speedboat racer John Cobb on the loch in 1952. Witnesses hinted at a sudden turbulence in the water ahead of the boat, which for some reason capsized and exploded.

Understandably there is no shortage of literature about Loch Ness, an inevitable spin-off of what might be termed "the monster industry." One handbook sold in local stores screams: "Amazing Facts: Improve Sighting Chances!" and lists a score of preferred "sighting viewpoints" from which the monster might best be seen.

A comprehensive history of developments in the story from 1933 onward can be read in Tim Dinsdale's excellent paperback, *The Story of the Loch Ness Monster,* in which he charts the various sightings, photographs, films, recordings, and expeditions. Dinsdale himself has made more than a score of expeditions to the loch, once spending more than eleven weeks living on its surface in a 16-foot boat. He, too, has taken photographs of some creature that's hard to explain away.

Since Dinsdale's book, the expensive and elaborate (but largely unrewarding) expedition by Japanese promoter Yoshio Kara has taken place.

Kara promises to make a return visit soon with his high-powered staff of researchers and electronic equipment. Monster-hunting equipment needs to be pretty elaborate because the peaty water of the loch frustrates normal underwater photography. Better results have been obtained sonically by bouncing signals through the murky water, occasionally discovering an uncharted obstacle that can't be explained. Is it the monster? Nobody knows for sure.

Although seven rivers flow into Loch Ness, there is only one outlet: the fast-flowing River Ness, which swiftly rises as much as two feet in times of heavy rain. The twenty-five-mile loch itself is almost 1,000 feet deep at its deepest point, and because of the nature of the water one can see only a few feet below the surface.

So the hunt continues. On our visit to Loch Ness in the summer of 1974, we parked in a pretty spot where daisies, wild roses, and strawberries lined the bank beside the eight-milestone marker on the road at the loch's northern side. Our nearby companions, vacationing photographers in a car marked Granada Television, said that the frequent "No Overnight Parking" signs at most of the favorable viewing spots were undoubtedly the result of pressure from the owners of campsites, and might safely be ignored. They said that they had already spent two days at this spot, keeping a vigil for the monster, and that although they hadn't seen anything believed it is there. It was the night of the full moon and assuredly a magical place in which to stay. We saw nothing but the moon shimmering beautifully upon the choppy water.

What might be down under Loch Ness has intrigued many people who have never been within a thousand miles of the place. Giant seals or eels, some extinct creature from the sea which has gradually adapted to fresh-water conditions—even the legendary kelpie has been suggested. This, wrote a Scottish minister named A. M. Macfarlane, is "the personification of the sudden blast of wind or of a whirlwind which sweeps over the surface of the lakes and pools."

Writing in *Myths Associated with the Mountains, Springs and Lochs of Scotland,* Macfarlane further explains: "The latter strikes the water suddenly, leaves behind a ripple like the wake of a living creature swimming beneath its surface, and then halting for a moment raises, a few inches above the surface, a dark crest of little waves which bear a remote resemblance to the back and mane of such a creature."

The loch's fame does not rest solely on its reputed monster. The Picts are said to have had a castle at its head centuries ago, a statue of the Jacobite heroine Flora MacDonald looks up the Great Glen, and at the turn of the century the area achieved some renown as the home of the magician Aleister Crowley. He lived in Boleskin House, now owned by members of the rock group Led Zeppelin.

27

The Western Isles

SKYE, LEWIS, IONA

HUNDREDS OF BREATHTAKINGLY BEAUTIFUL ISLANDS fringe the west coast of Scotland like random pieces of a jigsaw puzzle that has come apart along one side. Almost all of them retain traces of life that has more in common with previous centuries than this one. Like most communities away from the mainstream, what they offer, preserved in the amber of isolation, is a dark mixture of tradition and legend that hint of mysterious forces.

Three islands in particular are essential to any magical tour. Two are accessible from Inverness by heading southwest along the shores of Loch Ness and then westward to Kyle of Lochalsh. Here, ferries run regularly across to the first of these islands, the Isle of Skye. Then from the port of Uig, at the upper end of Skye, ferries run across to the northernmost island, Lewis, which shelters one of the remotest and most awe-inspiring stone circles in the world, the Callanish Stones.

The third island is Iona, off the southwest coast of the island of Mull farther south, and to get there it is necessary to backtrack, driving down along the mainland to Oban and taking the ferry to Mull. For those with

Illustration: The Agishjalmur, *an ancient Norse amulet. It was used in most homes for protection against the elements and to bring good luck.*

ample time it is just possible, by a complicated series of maneuvers, to island-hop down the Outer Hebrides from Lewis to Uist and thence across to Mull. To do this means keeping a careful eye on ferry schedules. (You can get a current copy by writing to Caledonian Mac-Brayne Ltd., The Pier, Gourock PA19, Renfrewshire, Scotland.)

Skye

Fairy legends are ubiquitous on Skye. The little people are believed here to venture often from their subterranean palaces to cause mischief and sometimes to accept the offerings of food that people lay out to appease them. Fairies were the original inhabitants of the country, according to Scottish lore, and they were driven into hiding when invaders came. They have assumed responsibility for watching over the cattle and crops.

The doors of their enticingly-lit underground homes are often left open to attract unwary mortals who, if lured inside with food, drink, and revelry, may find themselves lost to the world for many years to come. Among the ways to enter fairyland, according to popular belief, is to walk widdershins (that is, clockwise, against the sun) nine times around certain hills, but the cautious visitor should take the precaution of wedging any open doors with a knife or fish hook to ensure departure. It is helpful, too, to carry a piece of iron, a black cock, or one of the many herbs which are known to be charms against fairy spells.

Although the activities of fairies apparently continue unabated, the ordinary mortal must acquire second sight before he can see them. One of the ways to do this is to make a magic salve to rub on the eyes. A recipe for this can be found in an obscure book *Reliques of Ancient English Poetry:* "Take a pint of sallet oil and put it in a viall glass, first washing with rose water and marigold water, the flowers to be gathered towards the East. Add the buds of hollyhocks, flowers of marigold, flowers or tops of wild thyme gathered from the side of a fairy hill, and the buds of the young hazel. Add to the oil in the glass and allow to dissolve three days in the sun. Anoint the eyelids evening and morning."

Skye's magical prize is the magnificent Dunvegan Castle in the northwestern part of the island. It is beside its own private loch and was once approachable only by water until a "fairy bridge" was constructed across it, which, it is said, a horse would not cross without shying.

Inside the castle, for almost 600 years, has been preserved the famous "fairy flag," a tattered silken banner shot with gold thread and marked with crimson "elf spots," which came into the possession of the Mac-Leod family under mysterious circumstances. The fourth Lady MacLeod, hearing a strange noise from her infant son's room, disturbed a lady in a green petticoat who was apparently lulling her child to sleep.

The intruder immediately vanished leaving behind the flag which the MacLeods have preserved.

When Thomas Pennant visited the castle during his tour of Scotland (his book, *Tour of Scotland,* was published in 1769), he was told by clan chieftain Norman MacLeod that the flag was a gift to the clan from the fairy queen Titania "with powers of the first importance which were to be exerted on only three occasions," after which an "invisible being" would carry it back to its original owner. Supposedly the clan waved the banner and called upon the supernatural powers for help at two of its victories—the battles of Glendale (1490) and Waternish (1580)—and it is valid for one more occasion before its powers are spent.

The trip across the island to Dunvegan is exceptionally rewarding, the views, as in most parts of Scotland, playing will-o-the-wisp with the mist and clouds whose wraithlike shapes keep one's imagination constantly recharged.

Scotland's mist is not to be looked upon lightly. With the possible exception of Ireland, Scotland's weather is the most conducive to magical inclinations. The sun shines rarely, and when it does it seems to be filtered through a gossamer tapestry. Nothing is ever clear here. A hazy, muted vision prevails, predominantly in shades of gray-blue, and the landscape takes on softened, indistinct contours; what might appear to be a horse and man in ordinary light, blurs to surreal images. In the evening, all of this is heightened as the mist rolls in from the sea and lochs, filling the valleys with vaporous splendor. Buildings (usually of gray stone) recede into the distance, reappearing only when one is a few feet in front of them. Edges become fuzzy, especially when one is driving a car: where does the road leave off and the bank begin? Large shapes are contorted by the mist, corners rounded off to transform the most obvious into the extraordinary. The imagination needs little prodding, therefore, to make one believe while crouched in a fairy glen, that "little people" did make their homes in these parts, or to believe that ancient worship to the elements took place by Pictish stones cocooned by mist.

The evil eye used to be much feared on Skye, and there are people still living who keep sprigs of juniper wood around the cow byres (barns) to protect the cattle, or who tie three knots in a piece of red thread to make a charm to keep the witches away. But even more prevalent is the age-old belief about the kelpie, a playful water spirit, prone to change shapes. Typically, it would assume the shape of a horse and then with its victim securely on its back, it would plunge suddenly into deep water from which there was no escape.

Loch na Dubhrachen on Skye is said to be the traditional gathering place for kelpies, and there's a folksong, "Cumha an Eachwisge" ("Lament of the Waterhorse"), about such a creature who married a local girl; she discovered her mistake just in time and threw him out of the house.

Lots of islanders, and Scottish people in general, take kelpies seriously. In her poem "The Kelpie," Violet Jacobs says:

> I'm feart o' the road ayont the glen
> I'm sweir* to pass the place
> Whaur the water's rinnin, for a' fouk ten
> There's a kelpie site at the fit o' the den
> And there's them that's seen his face.

Possession of a kelpie's bridle is supposed to grant the power of second sight. By looking through its holes you gain special sight into the magic world and obtain views of "lill foak, always dressed in green," as a certain William Butterfield described them back in 1815. Needless to say, there have always been reports in Scotland of certain seers who possessed such trophies and were willing to dispense some of their insights for a fee.

The road southward down Skye's west coast is beautiful enough at any time, but if you are lucky it will be raining. Then you'll get to see the vivid purple of the rocks, the colorful flowers blooming, the quartet of majestic mountains at the island's southern tip turned into misty infernos, and the crowning glory, a double rainbow.

Lewis

From the port of Uig in northern Skye one can catch a ferry to the island of Lewis. Our major interest here is not with fairies but with Druids. The magnificent stone circle known as Callanish is believed to have been their last active site before they faded into myth sometime before the Dark Ages. There are those who feel a connection exists between fairies and Druids. Celtic lore reveals a long-standing belief that fairies are a kind of spiritual being who retain the otherwise extinct teachings of the Druids. Folklore of the British Isles and Ireland associates elves and fairies with the megalithic sites of a forgotten age.

The choppy seas between Skye and Lewis are inhabited by the mischievous Blue Men of the Minch, well-educated spirits who frequently amuse themselves by quoting poetry to passing sailors and challenging them to finish off the verses. Seafolk sometimes known as "selkies" are a common feature of the Hebrides, the Shetlands and the Orkneys where tales abound of them marrying the young fishermen. They correspond to the mermaids of other regions and invariably convey magical powers to those who capture them yet agree to release them. In Ross-shire, for example, there is a legend of the mermaid who was set free

*Reluctant.

only after she'd sworn that nobody would ever drown from any boat constructed in a certain builder's yard. On the other hand, further south, in Wales, the town of Conway is said to have suffered a fish famine one year after a captured mermaid had cursed the town when she died in captivity.

Lewis, like Skye, is crisscrossed with roads so narrow that "pull-in" areas every few yards must be used by passing vehicles. There seems to be only barrenness, but it does have a certain brooding charm.

Between the two main towns, Tarbert at the southern end and Stornoway toward the north, there is little to see along the thirty-nine miles of lonely road, with the exception of rocky mountains, sheep, and an occasional peat-digger. Apart from tourists, it can have changed little since 1785, when a certain "James Anderson, Scot," submitted to the Lords of the Treasury a report entitled *An account of the Hebrides and Western coasts of Scotland in which an attempt is made to explain the circumstances that have hitherto repressed the industry of the natives and some hints are suggested for encouraging the fisheries and promoting other improvements in those countries.*

In the elaborately printed tome, Mr. Anderson does make some sensible suggestions, for example, that the Western Highlands would be suitable for sheep and cattle.

An even earlier visitor to Lewis (from the Irish word *leog,* meaning "water lying on the surface of the ground") was "M. Martin, Gent," whose *Descriptions of the Western Islands of Scotland,* published in 1716, dwelt heavily on witchcraft and the survival of pagan customs.

Martin readily pinpointed the source of most of the pagan beliefs:

> Every great family in the isle had a chief Druid who foretold the future events and decided all causes civil and ecclesiastical. Caesar says they worshiped a deity under the name of Taramis or Taran, which in Welsh signifies Thunder, and in the ancient language of the Highlanders signifies Thunder also.
>
> Another God of the Britons was Belus or Belinus who seems to have been the Assyrian god Bel or Belus and probably from this pagan deity comes the Scottish term Beltin, the May Day having its first rise from the custom practiced by the Druids in the Isles of extinguishing all fires in the Parish until the Tythes were paid and upon payment of them the fires were kindled in each family and never till then. In those days malefactors were burnt between two fires, hence when they would express a man to be in a great strait they say he is between two fires of Bel. Some object that the Druids could not be in the Isles because there are no oaks growing in some of them.

His reference to the oak, of course, was based on the well-documented fact that the Druids regarded the tree as sacred and the mistletoe which grew upon it as all-healing. They believed that taken in drinks it imparted fertility to barren animals and was an antidote for all poisons. In Ireland, the word for mistletoe *(uilioc)* means "all-healing" and the

Greek word for oak tree, *drus,* may have been the basis of the word *Druid* itself.

Among the many customs of the seventeenth century that Martin reports on, one concerns the wrapping of a man in a cow's hide and leaving him outdoors all night while posing some problem "until his invisible friends relieved him by giving him a proper answer to the question at hand." Martin tells of a man whose curiosity had led him to spend such a night in the hide, "during which time he felt and heard such terrible things that he could not express them and the impression made upon him was such as could never again be concerned in the like performance, for this had disordered him to a high degree." Disordering of the senses was integral in all ancient ceremonies of magical initiation.

But even in Martin's day the ancient customs were beginning to disappear. He heard about how it had been customary to pour a little cow's milk on a big stone where a spirit named Browny was believed to lodge; thereupon Browny materialized as (not surprisingly) a tall man with brown hair. Local women said that their ancestors had taught them such a custom but that it had fallen into disuse. Similarly, remnants of the pagan fire ceremony had persisted with the custom of making a fiery circle about the houses, grain, and cattle and other possessions of the family. It was called "dessil," from the right hand *(dess)* in which the flaming brand was carried. A fire destroyed the farm of one man, twenty-four hours after he had practiced these rites, and so "this super-stitious custom is quite abolished now, for there has not been above this one instance of it in forty years past."

Still persisting, however, was the practice of carrying fire around a woman after childbirth "to preserve both mother and infant from the power of Evil Spirits who are ready at such times to do mischief and sometimes carry away the infant, and when they get them into their possession return them poor meager skeletons, and these infants are said to have voracious appetites instantly craving for meat."

One of Martin's most important stops on Lewis was the impressive stone circle of Callanish, the isolated megalithic monument overlooking the North Sea some miles beyond Stornoway.

One's first impression of Callanish is one of genuine awe. Arising from a grim, barren landscape, the monument looms on the horizon, dominating the surroundings. In late afternoon, the shadows lengthen dramatically and the dark stones capture the last of the sun's rays, held close by the center circle, as if gleaning some secret knowledge from it. But the northern sun is a cold one, and the stones hold court even over this powerful source of energy, seeming to draw in and consume the sun's efforts. Callanish rests supreme on its hillside, two or three smaller circles in the nearby fields pay respectful homage.

The circle of stones is adjoined by approachways also lined with stones, so that the whole design resembles a huge Celtic cross. The reference by Herodotus to a "winged temple" could conceivably have meant Callanish. Martin was assured by the local people that the whole area had been a pagan place of worship with the chief Druid standing near the center to address the crowd.

Callanish was definitely used as a burial ground because a grave was excavated in its center, but it seems more likely that some important personage chose to be buried in an already sacred place. The astronomer Boyle Somerville made an accurate survey of the site and published his findings in 1912. Of the fifty-six megaliths he surveyed in Scotland and Ireland, all but six were astronomically oriented. The brilliant engineer and mathematician Alexander Thom believes Callanish was designed as a lunar observatory. Professor Thom's research and interpretation of British stone circles and alignments has convinced him of the high intellect of megalithic man.

In his *Islands of Western Scotland,* W. H. Murray advances the argument that Callanish is too elaborate to be just a seasonal calendar, but if its primary purpose had been sun worship or fertility rites, then precise dating of the seasons by alignments might logically follow. There were stone circles, he says, known in Gaelic as *Bel Beachd,* meaning "the circle of Bel," the Celtic sun god, and the celebration of Beltane was still being observed in remote areas of Scotland as late as the eighteenth century. Murray recalls such old customs as walking sunwise around cairns or monuments; poor people making three sunwise turns around their benefactors; and young folk cutting a circular ditch on the moors and sitting around a lighted fire and choosing a "sacrificial victim" who would symbolically leap through the flames to ask Bel's favor for a productive year. Callanish, he believes, was built about 200 years after Stonehenge.

Christian legends aver that the megaliths are the ancient elders, turned to stone by St. Kiaran at their annual council because they declined to change their faith. But there are also hints of Atlantis and suggestions that its survivors arrived here with building skills long before the Christian era.

Whatever its purpose, Callanish is undeniably impressive. The circle stands high on a hilltop with the jagged, gray stones etched against the bleak, windswept blue-gray sky. A few cottages dot the surrounding countryside, but even so the hill remains aloof, silent. The breeze rarely abates and an occasional gull circles overhead with keening cries. The gray loch below is cold and menacing, shallow as it obviously is, and the low rocky hills that stretch for miles all around seem to be waiting, as they have for centuries.

Oddly, there is little regard for or interest in this impressive monument among the local residents, many of whom favor the proposal to demolish the circle and clear the site for building. The North Sea oil boom has affected nearby Stornoway, and its cobbled streets are filled with people whose eyes are dazzled by the gleam of money. Scottish Department of the Environment officials have made sympathetic noises but there has not, as yet, been any sign of concerted action to prevent the stones from being torn down: few people seem to care, least of all the tourists, most of whom visit and leave the area without even learning of their existence.

Iona

Our third magical island, the venerable island of Iona, was a pagan stronghold for centuries before the Christians arrived and claimed it for their own.

The tiny speck of land (3½ miles long by 1½ miles wide) is as beautiful today as it must have been when St. Columba landed there on May 12, 563. The colors of sea and sky are pristine, the beaches are of white sand, and great patches of wild daffodils turn the island into a blaze of yellow each spring. At both ends of the island the lovely low hills with their score of secret glens and hollows must hide a thousand memories of age-old ceremonials or gatherings under the moon. At dusk, even today, they seem to be haunted by spirits of long ago. The turf is chopped short everywhere by the ranging sheep, but the ground has probably never been uncovered to reveal the ancient treasures that must lie beneath.

Iona *feels* old: the air, the ground, the contours of the land seem saturated with ancient memories. Possibly because of its remoteness (no cars are allowed on the island), the island seems to shun contemporary life. The air is fresh and energizing but has the sweet aroma of hidden secrets; the ground is often rutted as though hundreds of thousands of feet have traversed the same routes.

Almost half a century ago, a mysterious death on the island was attributed to occult experimentation. A young student, Miss N. Fornario, was found lying nude atop a huge cross she had apparently carved into the turf with a knife that was found nearby. Rumors about the case, mentioned in the *Occult Review* for January 1930, were that mysterious blue lights had been spotted in the area where the body was found. The distinguished occultist Dion Fortune speculates in *Psychic Self-Defence* that Miss Fornario might have been on an astral trip and was unable to return to her body before dying of exposure.

The Hebrides writer Fiona Macdonald has written in several novels about the Druidic ceremonies imagined atop the islands's highest hill, Dun-I (332 feet), but it takes little imagination to re-create in the mind's eye some of the history of such magical spots as the Well of the North Wind and the Pool of Healing.

When Columba first landed, the tiny island had long been a pagan center. Its very name, *Innis-nam Druidbneach,* translated from the Gaelic, means "Island of the Druids," but before the century was out it was preeminently the island of Columba: Iona.

Once on Iona proselyting for Christianity, traveling, building churches and monasteries, and easing out the existing bishops on the grounds that their credentials were faulty, Columba soon found himself matching miracles with the Druid priests, as was the custom of the times. As all the chronicles that have come down to us are basically Christian, we have to accept that he usually won these contests. He blessed wells that were already holy, for example, expelled demons from milk pails, and in a confrontation with Broichan, Arch Druid and chief magical adviser to his foster father, King Brude, was able to sail off into a calm sea after the wizard had threatened serious storms.

And Columba continued the practice that had become popular in many regions as the Roman Church took over from their heathen predecessors—that of holding services at sites already considered sacred.

"If those temples are well built, it is requisite that they be converted from the worship of devils to the service of the true God," wrote Gregory the Great in 601 (quoted in Bede's *Ecclesiastical History*), "that the nations, seeing their temples are not destroyed, may remove error from their hearts and knowing and adoring the true God may the more freely resort to places to which they have been accustomed."

In 1561, to satisfy the desire of the Reformed Church in Scotland, an act was passed for the demolition of all the abbeys and monasteries of idolatry remaining in the realm, and armed with this authority fanatical reformers ruthlessly destroyed the learning of the ages. Tragically, they wiped out priceless records of the Scots, archives of remote antiquity, and many lovely buildings. Of the 360 crosses, some dating to pre-Columban times said to have stood on Iona, only three survive. Many of the books were carried away; some are in the Vatican, a few in Ireland.

Calling Druidism "that mysterious, poetic religion which more than any other expresses the voice of nature," the Anglo-American mystic Col. James Churchward, in *The Lost Continent of Mu,* speculated that the original Druids were descended from Egyptian priests who landed in Ireland and the west of England, bringing with them all their ancient beliefs in sun worship.

28

Ireland

WHERE IT ALL BEGAN

CONSIDERING THE ANTIPATHY of the ancient Irish to writing, and more particularly the attitude of the Druidic priests who regarded script as "an innovation unfit for recording ancient learning," it is amazing how much Irish history has been recorded.

Anyone who begins to delve into the subject of pagan Ireland soon finds himself struggling to separate fact from fantasy in a confusing welter of tales about fairies and magicians, of kings with supernatural powers and invincible weapons, and islands that mysteriously appear and disappear.

And all around the visitor to Ireland are the artifacts that retain the legends—the thousands of *raths,* or "earthworks," that traditionally have been, and in many cases still are called "fairy forts." Until comparatively recent times remedies for protection against witchcraft were commonplace, such as the custom in parts of County Roscommon of dressing a fir tree (stripped of its branches) in cap and jacket and setting it against the wall and roof of a cottage.

As in Italy, Catholicism in Ireland didn't destroy heathen sites and customs—except in a few isolated cases—but took them over wholesale,

Illustration: Interlacing ornament from The Book of Lindisfarne. *Late seventh century.*

Christianizing many of the ancient rituals but leaving them essentially unchanged. In a very real sense Catholicism has preserved paganism, changing only the names.

In a predominantly rural society much stock is still placed in old-fashioned remedies to cure sick animals: a mystical herb known as "mothan," which may be mugwort, sandwort, or a species of bog violet, is given to cattle as a protective charm; sick cows are often doctored by giving them "three measure" water from a stream where three townships meet and in which has been boiled a type of flint known as an elf dart.

Fairies pop up everywhere, not merely the wispy creatures with gossamer wings that frequent the pages of children's picture books but creatures of greater substance and more specific design who are as likely to trick mortals and make them lose their way as to invite the local athlete to a football match to play for the elfin team, granting some unlikely reward in return.

Among the more persistent tales are those of secret islands or communities where everything is enchantment, where beauty and tranquillity reign and time has no power over the years. No one who goes to such a place ever becomes old, and those who have passed whole years there have fancied the period as but a fleeting moment.

An early Irish legend concerns the enchanted island of Hy-Brasail which was supposed to be visible from Ireland's west coast every seven years and if once touched by fire would remain a delightful and accessible paradise instead of disappearing once more below the waves.

In the ancient tales of Ireland inanimate objects are the possessors of strange secrets and lives hang on threads. One of the early Celtic kings, Lavra (c. 268 B.C.) was said to have had ears like a horse, a fact known only to his barber who was sworn to secrecy on pain of death. But the barber was unable to avoid whispering the news to a willow tree which, when later cut down and formed into a harp, murmured: "Lavra Loingseach has the ears of a horse."

Clearly there are connections between the reincarnation beliefs of the Druids and the persistence of a belief in fairies. Some maintain that Ireland's early settlers, the Túatha Dé Danann, disappeared into the mystic underworld when they were supplanted by later conquerors at least one thousand years before the Christian era. So many legends have come down to us about the magical abilities of this tribe of the goddess Danu that it would seem there must have been substance to the tales.

For although little was written down before the Christian era when monks wrote chronicles there has always been a strong bardic tradition in the land. Poets ranked next to kings in social status (and in the variety of colors they were allowed to wear) and until a century or so ago, a poet's malediction was believed in Ireland to bring misfortune to those to whom it was addressed.

Any bard worth his salt was expected to be able to recite all the traditional "primary tales" on demand, and it was these stories that were later assembled in such collections as *The Book of Leinster* from the twelfth century.

The importance of such men of wisdom might best be described by the role they played during the rule by the three princely brothers— about 400 b.c.—when a compact that each should rule alternately for seven years was guaranteed by "seven Druids to crush them by their incantations, seven poets to lacerate them by their satires and seven young champions to slay and burn them should the proper man of them not receive the sovereignty at the end of each seventh year."

As unorthodox as this approach to kingship might be, two of the brothers couldn't accept the daughter of the third as their queen when their own reigns were over. This would-be queen was the redoubtable Macha who lost no time in raising an army, defeating her uncles in battle, and forcing them to build for her the great fort of Emhain (now called Navan Fort), traces of which remain in the hill west of Armagh. According to legend, the outlines of the immense, eleven-acre fort were marked out by Macha with a golden brooch.

There is still respect for arts and letters in Ireland today and still a sense of timelessness, too. "The troubles," as the Irish euphemistically term the conflict in the North, scarcely seem to have touched the pastoral countryside but two or three hours' drive away. And it is still possible in this green and pleasant land to forget contemporary society and lose oneself in an aura of the past. The romantic "twilight of memory," as the Tourist Board poetically puts it, "is stirred by silhouettes of yesterday." Traveling in Ireland can at times be an unnerving experience. Dark figures standing under roadside hedges late at night provoke their own mysteries; dogs run out everywhere at the approach of a car. Both, perhaps, share a curiosity about the more transient world that appears to be passing them by.

Getting to Ireland is easy via the excellent car ferries that sail from the Welsh ports of Fishguard in the south (to Rosslare) and Holyhead in the north (to Dublin) with car rentals readily available on the Irish side. Driving is pleasant in Ireland with roads that are by and large uncrowded, and it has the kind of countryside that encourages a slow pace to savor it fully. Bed and breakfast places abound, and an official list of accommodations is available free from the Tourist Information Center, 51 Dawson Street, Dublin. The center has comprehensive literature about almost every aspect of a visit to Ireland, including information about renting a horse-drawn caravan in which you can't expect to cover more than about ten miles per day.

Tara

The most sacred place in Ireland, for many centuries, was Tara of the Kings, although it is impressive today mostly to those with the imagination to conjure up its storied past. The Celts are most associated with it and they did rule there for several centuries. But this splendidly panoramic hilltop was undoubtedly sacred long before their arrival in the fourth century B.C. An old admonition "You shall not go righthand-wise around Tara" is a clear reference to go clockwise, or against the route of the sun.

This site of the royal residence of ancient Irish kings, where five highroads once converged, sits silent on a hill in County Meath, about twenty-three miles northwest of Dublin. Only a few mounds, ditches, and earthworks distinguish the grassy hillside from a dozen similar ones in the nearby placid countryside. Cows graze beside the walls of the adjacent St. Patrick's Church, and a grim-faced statue of the saint is symbolic of the usurpation of this pagan site by the fifth-century Christians.

Tara was the scene of the ritual marriage feast called *Feis Temhrach* at which the king mated with a beautiful woman who by certain mystic means became the personification of a goddess, a spirit of the land itself. Their union symbolically bound sovereign to realm and thus sanctified his reign.

An oblong enclosure measuring 759 feet in length and 46 feet in width with a series of entrances on each side was once Tara's grand Banqueting Hall. Here the *Tarbfeis,* or "bull feast," of legend took place. When a king died the men of Ireland would kill and roast a bull. A chosen man would eat his fill of the meat, drink its broth, and when he fell asleep an incantation was chanted over him. During his sleep, a vision of the future ruler would appear. The rite, called *Imbas Forosnai,* or "knowledge that illuminates," was later forbidden by St. Patrick.

Many references to Tara appear in Irish literature, particularly in *The Book of Leinster* and *The Yellow Book of Lecan,* both of which illustrate seating plans for the Banqueting Hall and enumerate the grades of society and appropriate food served to each. According to one old manuscript:

> Harmonious and stately was the carouse of the fiery chieftains and noblemen. There were none neglected of the number; three hundred cupbearers dispensed the liquor. Thrice fifty steaming cooks, in attendance unceasingly, with victuals, an abundant supply, on the jolly kings and chieftains.

It was at a betrothal feast in the Banqueting Hall where Grania, one of King Cormac's ten daughters, first set eyes on the handsome Diarmaid O' Duibhne. She so much preferred him to the older Finn MacCumhaill, the king's general to whom she was affianced, that she persuaded him to elope with her. The tale of Diarmaid and Grania—of how they were pursued all over Ireland by the vengeful Finn, of how they sheltered in innumerable cromlechs ("the beds of Diarmaid and Grania"), of how Diarmaid was finally killed by a wild boar and Grania was eventually won by Finn, the leader of the Fianna (Irish militia), the man she had formerly rejected—was a popular subject with the Irish bards, especially the warrior-poet Ossian, Finn's son.

Although Cormac, Grania's father, came by the throne dishonorably after having had his predecessor MacCon stabbed, his reign (A.D. 227–266) was probably Tara's most glorious era. He was not able to assume office immediately because a relative of the murdered MacCon vengefully set fire to his long hair. Until it grew again Cormac was bound by a rule which ordained that "No one having a personal blemish could rule at Tara." Eventually Cormac assumed the throne and constantly sought to enhance Tara's splendor. "The world was full of all goodness in the time of Cormac . . . there were fruit and fatness of the land, and abundant produce of the sea with peace and ease and happiness in his time."

The legendary Celtic hero Cú Chulainn (a famous statue of him is in Dublin's General Post Office) is closely associated with Tara. Indeed, his head and right hand are said to be buried there. The heroic qualities he represents and the magical feats he is reputed to have accomplished with his seagoing chariot and a helmet that proffered invisibility, are inextricably linked.

The Cuchulainn Mountains in Skye are a reminder of the days when that great Celtic hero studied in Scotland under the Amazonian instructress Scatha.

Most of what we know about pagan days in Ireland comes from a few large manuscripts written in medieval times. These are summarized in *The Tain* (translated by Thomas Kinsella from the Irish epic *Tain Bo Cuailnge*) and consist of three groups of stories: (1) mythological tales about the Túatha Dé Danann; (2) the Ulster cycle, dealing with the exploits of King Conchobhar (Conor) and the champions of the Red Branch with their chieftain Cú Chulainn; (3) the Fenian cycle, stories of Finn MacCumaill, his son Ossian and other warriors of the Fianna.

One of *The Tain*'s stories tells how a Druid prophecy that Cú Chulainn would be a famous warrior shaped his life. And how he, and his knightly companions of the Red Branch, defended Ulster against many enemies.

Although fearless in combat and superior in intelligence, Cú Chulainn was susceptible to the charms of ladies both mortal and supernatural, and one legend concerns his solicitation by one of the evil Morrigans (unearthly spirits who assume many forms) as he defended the ford on the Ulster border.

One of the last Celtic kings to rule at Tara before the arrival of St.

Patrick in A.D. 433 was Dathi, whose military expedition into Alba (Britain) and later to the Continent was said to have been ordained by the Druids. The expedition, celebrated with a magnificent Beltane feast at Tara, foundered when Dathi was struck down by lightning while storming a tower in the Rhine Valley. The area enclosed by the headwaters of the Danube and the Rhine rivers is said to have been the original home of the wandering Celtic tribes. Dathi's body was brought back to Ireland by his followers and lovingly buried at Religh na Righ, the royal cemetery at Ráth Cruachan, where a seven-foot pillar stone still stands marking his grave among the numerous earthworks.

When St. Patrick arrived in Ireland, King Laoghaire was on the throne and it was not long before the saint felt obliged to make a direct challenge to his rule. It was the eve of May and while waiting for the royal fire to be lit at Tara, the assembled Druids were amazed to see smoke rising from the nearby hill of Slane. Summoned into the king's presence to explain this sacrilege, St. Patrick (for it was he who had lit the fire) somehow managed to get royal assent for a contest of magic during which two huts were set afire, one containing a boy wearing the cloak of the royal magician and the other containing the magician with the robe of the saint wrapped around him.

According to the official (Christian) record of the event, the magician was incinerated leaving the saint's robe untouched; the boy was saved, but the magician's cloak around him was burned to a cinder. From then onward Christianity made great headway in Ireland despite the fact the king remained faithful to the old ways.

Appropriately enough, when King Laoghaire died it was from a stroke of lightning. He was buried standing up, sword in his hand, facing in the direction of Leinster from whence had come his perpetual enemies.

Tara was more or less abandoned during the sixth century and the centuries since have played havoc with the physical features that once gave the hill its splendor. All traces of the original wooden buildings have long ago disappeared, and plundering raids by Norsemen have removed any artifacts, or even bones, that might have existed.

Tara was always, apparently, more a place for special events—such as the triennial *Feis,* or parliamentry assembly, which always took place at Samhain early in November—than for day-to-day living. One of the old sagas notes that "Sunrise and sunset should not find a ruler within Tara's seven walls."

Although the walls are long gone, the banks and ditches that once marked the royal buildings can still be clearly discerned, especially the immense (950 by 800 feet) royal enclosure. The so-called Mound of the Hostages is a typical burial tumulus with a passageway and inner chambers. It was the custom for the winning armies to hold some of their princely opponents captive as a hostage against good behavior and this has been (probably fancifully) identified by some as the burial place of some such victims in King Cormac's time.

The most notable landmark at Tara, however, is the *Lia Fáil,* or "Stone of Destiny," which stands as an upright pillar close by St. Patrick's statue. According to legend, the stone was brought to Ireland by those early settlers, the Túatha Dé Danann, and was said to "cry out" with approval when the right king was crowned, remaining silent when the wrong candidate attempted to usurp the royal destiny. Irish historians seem unaware of the other Stone of Destiny which was taken from Scone in Scotland to Westminster Abbey and for centuries has fulfilled a similar royal role in English and Scottish tradition. Perhaps there were many such stones.

Pillar stones (known as *gallain*), many of which can be inspected in Dublin's National Museum, played an essential part in the religious beliefs of pagan Ireland, and after the Christians arrived many such stones were "taken over." Christian carvings or names were incised on them.

Some of the stone pillars became known as oracles. A pair at Farrana-glogh, County Meath, were often consulted until a man asked the same question twice. Insulted by such insensitivity, the story goes, the stones have remained silent ever since.

The most famous of the speaking stones is Cloch Labrhrais in County Waterford. It prepared those consulting it for disappointment by always accompanying its answer with the words, "The truth is often bitter."

Apart from the *Lia Fáil* there are other stones of interest at Tara, preserved in the graveyard of the tiny church. One of these stones, a five-foot sandstone pillar known as Adamnan's Stone (after the famous saint), bears a representation of what is believed to be Cernnunos, the horned god of the Celts whose image was also found at such other places as Kells and Clonmacnois.

By the time the Celtic tribes invaded Ireland in the middle of the fourth century B.C. an advanced civilization already existed there. The Celt's superior iron weapons assured their victory, but this contact with the indigenous mystical culture deeply influenced the nomadic warriors. Several centuries later when Greek and Roman writers came to describe the barbaric practices of the Celts on the Continent—including such perverse habits as head-hunting and human sacrifice—they also noted the tempering influence of the Druidic priests. It was undoubtedly the fruits of the Celtic encounter with the Old Irish that produced the civilizing themes.

Only a misty glimpse of Ireland's ancient history can be had today through the twin sources of archeological evidence and that controversial body of literature the myths and sagas of the Old Irish. Scholars are still at odds over details of a three-thousand-year interval preceding the time of written records. In spite of the disputes, we are indebted to monks who, in an unusual burst of intellectual activity, began in the sixth century A.D. to compile the Irish storytellers' wealth of legends. The strange beauty of the tales, kept alive by oral tradition, along with the extraordinary skill and taste of the Irish Bronze Age monuments and ornaments testify to the presence there of a culture so old that even Homer seems recent by comparison.

Ireland's first settlers are believed to have come from Spain across the Bay of Biscay. The many dolmens to be found in Ireland have their counterparts on the Iberian Peninsula. Some historians have surmised that the dolmen portals were once covered with turf and may have served as dwellings. If so, their distribution defines Ireland's earliest population centers. The ability to manipulate such heavy stones indicates an unusually high degree of social organization.

Stone Age tools, weapons, and artifacts reveal the presence of another wave of visitors. The evidence confirms that these people were akin to the Pict-like tribes who roamed through the northern perimeter of Europe. Legends tell of warriors called the Firbolgs and Fomorians, savage and uncouth, who swept down from the north in raiding parties.

The identity of another group of colonists is more in doubt, for no firm archeological evidence supports the tales of the "sons of Mil." The Milesians, like their kin the Phoenicians, were seafarers and traders. Cornwall was known to be a port of call because it was a major source of tin in ancient times. Because Ireland had no tin mines but still achieved such Bronze Age distinction (tin being necessary to the production of bronze), it is possible that the Irish not only worked but controlled Cornwall's mines. Gold in Wicklow's mountains would undoubtedly have attracted the traders from Asia Minor, and establishing outposts was a Milesian characteristic. The distinctive stone carving of Ireland's Bronze Age monuments suggests to many the influence of an eastern Mediterranean culture.

The mysterious people called the Túatha Dé Danann, children of the goddess Danu, are far and away the most intriguing folk to make Ireland their home. So strong was their influence that after a thousand or more years of blending, the opulent rulers the Celts met when they finally landed on Ireland's shores were still known by the ancient tribal name, the Túatha Dé Danann.

The Túatha Dé Danann were mystics said to have acquired their magic on faraway islands. Small in stature, dark-haired, elusive, the Celtic invaders frankly held them in awe. They would become legendary even during Celtic times and today the "little people" live only in folklore. Leprechauns guard their crocks of gold. (The gold mines of County Wicklow have never been found, yet golden ornaments of ancient Irish design dating from at least 1500 B.C. have been discovered throughout Europe.) The familiar folktale motif of the elfin wife who when offended by the rude manners of her tall, fair-haired mate would disappear into the side of a hill never to be seen again, echoes the merging of the Celtic warriors with refined daughters of the Túatha Dé Danann. The Celts are described in Classical texts as being unusually tall and blond. An old Celtic name for the Túatha Dé Danann was *aes sidh,* or "hill folk." As the two races became one, it seemed in folk memory that the "little people," when confronted by the Iron Age, preferred to retire into their fairy mounds.

While the Celts imposed iron, their language, and deities upon Ireland, they absorbed many cultural distinctions which would later form the Celtic image as observed by the Greeks and Romans at the beginning of the Christian era. Among these was the societal structure of Druid (sorcerer), vate (seer), and bard (storyteller). The Druids of old were more philosophers than priests. Many years of study and discipline were required to attain their special knowledge of the deities, the form and measurement of the earth, the movements of the heavenly bodies, the history of men, future life, and the otherworld. All knowledge was transmitted through a strictly oral tradition. A preference for subtle allusion, symbolism rather than direct statement, and an evident fondness for units of three are all part of an ancient Irish heritage, gifts to the Celts from the Túatha Dé Danann.

Specific dates are next to impossible to pin down, but most historians seem to agree that countless centuries before the Christian era, the Túatha Dé Danann were themselves the latest of a series of wandering tribes from the Mediterranean area to reach Irish shores. Preceding them had been the Partholians—wiped out en masse by a plague—and then the Nemedians. Down from the north came the Fomorians and the Firbolgs, who are credited with dividing the country into five provinces.

But from the earliest time it was the Túatha Dé Danann who seemed to invite the mystical imagination. They are credited with introducing magic and metallurgy to the country, having been taught their mystical wisdom by four wizards: Morfesa in Falia of the *l ia Fáil;* Esias in Gorias, from whence came Lugh's spear, invincible in battle; Uscias in Findias, which provided the sword of Nuada; and Simias in Murias, who was responsible for the bottomless cauldron of Dagda. The spear and the cauldron were to play an essential part in later legends about the Holy Grail.

A curious passage from the ancient *Leabhar Gabhála Éireann* ("The Book of Invasions" compiled by monastic scholars sometime before the twelfth century A.D.) refers to the arrival of the Túatha Dé Danann in Ireland. They were met by the Firbolgs, whose king describes his prophetic dream: "I saw a great flock of black birds coming to us from the depths of the ocean. They settled over all of us and fought with the people of Ireland. They brought confusion on us, and destroyed us. One of us, I thought, struck the noblest of the birds a blow and cut off one of its wings."

Then another narrator adds that the invaders came in dark clouds which "cast a darkness upon the sun for three days and three nights."

They are said by some historians to have burned their boats behind them, giving rise to a cloud that obscured their landing, but the popular legend avers that by means of sorcery and incantations the Túatha Dé Danann enveloped themselves in a mist and pursued the Firbolgs into what is today Connemara. Here at Moytura (on the Mayo-Galway border near the present-day village of Cong), in a four-day battle, the Firbolg king Eochaidh was killed (a cairn marks his grave on the strand at Ballysodare) and the invaders' king Nuada had his hand cut off. Because of the tradition that no king with a blemish could rule, this forced him into retirement, during which he constructed a lifelike, flexible silver hand.

King Nuada of the Silver Hand was succeeded by Bres, an unpopular leader who in his ignorance made the mistake of insulting a poet, a man of some distinction in those halcyon days. Instead of the customary formal banquet, King Bres served the poet, named Coirpre, a few small, dry cakes. Coirpre was so insulted that he wrote a satire about it. Whereupon a highly literate mob gathered, tossed out Bres and reinstated King Nuada, silver hand and all.

Bres, piqued, went off to the Hebrides where the remnants of Ireland's earlier settlers, the Fomorians, still lived. His father Elatha, a Fomorian chief helped him raise an army and a second battle of Moytura was fought which also ended in victory for the Túatha Dé Danann.

The notable event of this battle, which took place on the Sligo plain, was the slaying of the infamous Fomorian giant Balar of the Evil Eye by his grandson, Lugh. With this piece of giant-killing, Lugh, who had begun his career at King Eochaidh's court, became king of the Túatha Dé Danann. He was an accomplished man—smith, carpenter, champion, harpist, poet, physician, goldsmith, magician—and when he had first asked the Firbolg king Eochaidh for a job and had mentioned each of these talents singly, in turn, he was told by the doorkeeper that each post was filled. What clinched it for Lugh was his casual suggestion that maybe it might be useful to have them all in one man. He was appointed *ord-ollam,* chief professor of arts and sciences.

This whole pre-Celtic period, of course, swarmed with ambiguous figures who could have been gods or men, depending on whose accounts you read of their exploits. Lugh, who is often referred to as a sun god and who had prophetic ravens at his beck and call, gave his name to Lughnasa, the annual fair at Tailteann (now Teltown between Kells and Cavan) held every August 1. The grassy hollow where the fair was held, and where marriages were celebrated every Lughnasa right up to the thirteenth century, can still be seen to the left of the road between Kells and Donaghpatrick.

Lugh ruled Ireland for forty years, was killed at the battle of Uisneach, and was succeeded by the mysterious Dagda (sometimes known as "The Great Good Fire"), whose legendary cauldron was inexhaustible and whose wand had the capacity to kill with one end and restore life with the other. On one celebrated occasion Dagda is said to have mated, while standing astride a river, with Morrigan, one of the three "creatures of ill omen and of horrible appearance who foretold death and disaster, brooded over battlefields, and stimulated strife and slaughter." This trio of fierce goddesses—Morrigan, Macha, and Badhb—was said to live in a cave in Connacht. And from this cave occasionally emerged a flock of white birds that withered everything with their breath, as well as hordes of pigs which devastated the surrounding countryside.

Dagda's daughter, Brigit, was goddess of poetry, and his brother, Ogma, the god of learning, is presumed to have given his name to ogham, an alphabet system.

Newgrange and Northeast

Dagda ("The Great Good Fire," who is said to have ruled for seventy years) and his son Angus lived in Brugh na Bóinne, an area formed by a twist in the Boyne River between the present-day towns of Slane and Oldbridge. Bardic tradition attributes to him the mound of Newgrange, also known as the Túatha Dé Danann tumulus. This mound is, after Tara, the most important Bronze Age monument. And it is impressive, although the excavators (who only began work there in 1962) have now been superseded by builders, who are busily erecting a streamlined wall to slick up the exterior for the tourist trade.

Newgrange—Brugh na Bóinne—is an earth mound, 36 feet high and shaped like an inverted saucer. An entrance hall, lined with slabs of stone, stretches 60 feet deep into the mound, opening into a spacious circular chamber about 20 feet high The roof is of the corbel type, which means the stone slabs are piled up overlapping in a pyramid effect and are closed at the top with one final circular stone. In this case it is so close-fitting that the interior was bone-dry when it was discovered by a certain Edward Lhwyd in 1699. Later visitors—Thomas Molyneux (1726), Thomas Pownall (1773), George Wilkinson (1845), and William Wilde (1849)—also describe the mound and speculate that it was built by the Danes. The most astute observations of the site and its significance are contained in George Coffey's *New Grange and Other Incised Tumuli in Ireland,* published in 1912.

Excavations at Newgrange have revealed an unusual roof-box above the entranceway allowing the morning sun at winter solstice to shine into the central chamber and illuminate three linked spirals incised on the wall. What makes this even more remarkable is the fact that the passageway is slightly curved, yet at this one time of year the sun is able to slice through at a precise angle and light up the design.

Such sophisticated prehistoric engineering, coupled with the elegantly decorated stones both inside and outside the cairn, denotes a culture of much refinement. The stone carvings feature mostly spirals and circles, but there are occasional serpents, V's, and zigzags.

The so-called Entrance Stone is probably the most remarkable example of Megalithic art in Western Europe. It is incised with a complex pattern of spirals, concentric arcs, and diamond shapes. The entire surface of the slab is textured with fine dots giving it a rich green color. The spirals, similar to those of the Tarxien Temples on Malta and the decorated stones of Brittany, are infinitely more sophisticated—beautifully designed and skillfully executed. The spiral form calls to mind Archimedes' Screw (a machine for raising water) invented by the third-century B.C. mathematician to remove water from the hold of a king's ship. It is conceivable that the design on the stone signifies a principle of force known to the ancients and still a mystery to modern science.

Sir John Lubbock, in his *Prehistoric Times,* refers to the fern-leaf pattern on the stones at Newgrange and remarks their likeness to those on Malta and in Brittany. He adds, "The very frequent presence of the bones of quadrupeds in tumuli appears to show that sepulchral feasts were generally held in honor of the dead and the numerous cases in which interments were accompanied by burnt human bones tend to prove the prevalence of still more dreadful customs." Sir John may not have realized that cremation was common in ancient days, a custom still practiced by the Druids of Gaul, Britain, and Ireland at the turn of the Christian era. Cremation was forbidden in Christian countries for centuries and only within the last decade was the ban lifted by the Roman Catholic Church.

The mound, or cairn, at Newgrange was originally covered with glistening white quartz. Professor M. J. O'Kelly of University College, Cork, whose excavations are still in progress, has collected scores of the white pebbles with the view to their eventual restoration. Professor O'Kelly's wife, Claire, has written the definitive *Guide to Newgrange,* a detailed account of the history and new discoveries about the prehistoric monument. She recalls phrases in the old Irish literature describing the Brugh ("house" or "mansion") as "white-topped," "with the many lights," and "brilliant to approach." Although the eighteenth-century rediscoverers of Newgrange could conceive no greater antiquity than that it was built by the Danes, Claire O'Kelly surmises that "The Irish storytellers knew better."

The date of all this is in question. Radiocarbon dating places Newgrange at around 2500 B.C., but this method of establishing time is under reexamination at present, and archeologists are looking hopefully at such techniques as dating from tree rings. Some especially long-lived trees—the California bristle cone pine is one—survive 5,000 years, with all that history "coded" into their trunks. By calibrating radiocarbon datings with this living log, the former can be seen to be too conservative in its estimates. It is possible that as much as 500 years can be added to all radiocarbon datings of 2,500 years or more. If this is so, Newgrange's construction could have taken place at or prior to 3000 B.C. and conceivably be contemporary with the Egyptian pyramids.

Seeing Newgrange in relation to the stone monuments of the French coast and British Isles allows one to anticipate a time in the future when Ireland will be recognized as the center of a lost civilization: a supreme culture as yet unnamed whose elite class, the Druids, held sway for several thousand years.

What was in the Newgrange mound originally will never be known because it was plundered by the Norsemen in the ninth century A.D. But legend has always associated it with satellite mounds in the area, possibly tombs belonging to other chiefs and kings. An old tale persists that the great Celtic king Cormac, who established colleges for war, history, and jurisprudence and who died in 266 A.D., requested that he not be buried at Brugh because it was "a cemetery of idolators." After he died —with a salmon bone caught in his throat—his followers were crossing the river with his body to bury it at Brugh anyway when a torrent sprang up and swept the coffin downriver, depositing it at Ross-na-ree, where he was finally buried.

Newgrange, open 10 A.M. to 7 P.M. in summer and till 6 P.M. the rest of the year, is closed Mondays. There are similar but smaller mounds less than a mile away to the east and west. Knowth is closed for further excavations; Dowth is less impressive but still fascinating. Here you obtain a key and flashlight from Mrs. White's house, 300 yards down the road, and then return to descend some steps into a very narrow corridor, lined with stone slabs, which opens into a room just barely big enough to stand in. There is nothing much to see, but the mound is an impressive size.

While still in this area it's worth paying a visit to the ruins of Mellifont Abbey, four miles west of Drogheda, which was founded in 1142, and to Monasterboice, with the ruins of a monastery first founded in the sixth century A.D. There are some impressive High Crosses, one more than twenty feet tall, and a ninth-century Round Tower of the type in which people would take shelter with all their valuables when the Vikings raided. The entrance is fifteen feet off the ground and the last one in pulled up the ladder.

There is a certain irony to the fact that after centuries of pagan rule, an era of constantly marching armies, treachery, and pitched battles, Ireland turned Christian only to become the pawn of the still-pagan Norsemen. From the eighth century onward the invading Vikings poured in to ravage the land, caring nothing for ancient traditions or religious beliefs.

According to Lady Ferguson in *The Irish Before the Conquest:*

These invaders spared neither age, nor sex nor station. The monasteries were ever their first objects of attack. Here were deposited articles of chiefest value in the land; precious manuscripts which were only prized for rich decoration in gold and gems that graced the cases in which they were enclosed; shrines of exquisite workmanship, on which all that was costly and precious had been lavished, fit them for receptacles of the relics of some venerated saint; illuminated manuscripts, produce which had been the lifelong labor of pious and saintly men—all these were scattered to the winds by the ignorant and ruthless hands of these sea robbers. . . . Danes, during this period of their domination, were almost universally pagan and delighted in exhibiting their contempt for the sacred things of the Christian religion.

But back to the days of the Túatha Dé Danann whose magical rule came to an end shortly after Dagda's death. Continuance of the line by Dagda's three grandsons—MacColl (because he worshiped the hazel tree, *coll*), MacKeact (who worshiped the plow, *keact*), and MacGrene (sun, *grian*) and their wives Banba, Fola, and Eri (from whence came "Erin") —was aborted by the invasion of the Milesians.

The Milesians, one legend tells us, sailed from Corunna in Spain, apparently to avenge in Ireland the death of one of their chiefs who had been slain on an earlier peaceful visit there, and also to fulfill a prophesy that they would inhabit a country in which no venomous reptile would live and where they would seek and find the track of the setting sun. They came in a fleet of thirty ships, bearing a flag depicting a dead serpent and the rod of Moses. This commemorated an earlier miracle when their ancestor Gadelius had been bitten by a snake and was cured by the prophet at the nearby camp of the Israelites.

"Innisfail ["the isle of destiny"] is found!" the Milesians shouted as Innis Ealga ("the noble isle") came into view, but once again the defending Túatha Dé Danann were up to their magical tricks and the island disappeared from sight. Managing to effect a landing the following morning, the Milesians were confronted with the astonishing suggestion by the inhabitants that it had not been a fair contest so far and the only way to make amends would be for the invaders to withdraw "nine waves from shore" and try again. The Milesians, understandably feeling they'd had enough trouble already, nevertheless submitted the matter to the arbitration of their sorcerer Amergin, who somewhat surprisingly agreed with the defenders. And so the Milesians withdrew—only to be confronted by a tremendous hurricane which burst over the fleet scattering it in all directions.

The place where the Milesians attempted to land, Inver Sceine (today's Kenmare Bay), still retains historical traces of the event in a range of rocks named *Teach-Dhoinn,* or "Donn's House." Donn, one of the sons of Milesius, was wrecked there with his crew.

Nevertheless, the invasion eventually was effected and the Túatha Dé

Danann were chased and resoundingly beaten, first in Glen Scohene just south of Tralee (where their warrior queen Scota was killed and buried), and finally at Teltown in County Meath where the three Túatha Dé Danann princes were slain.

In those days, kings led their armies in person, but history assures us that their reigns were as long as those of recent eras. As well as being brave the kings were usually learned men, patrons of the arts, and appreciative of the sage advice, magical and otherwise, that helped them keep their countries and people together. It was an early Irish king who —over a thousand years before Christ—classified his people by alloting to them colors that may be worn on their garments. The dress of a slave was limited to one color; a peasant, two; a soldier or noble, three, and so on up to six colors for a man of learning. He ranked next to the king or queen whose multicolored robes (foreshadowing the Scottish tartan) might include seven hues.

The hurricane story is only one version of the arrival of the invading Milesians. Eoin Neeson in *Irish Myths and Legends* suggests that no actual battle took place but rather a contest of skills. Lugh, son of a Firbolg mother and a Dé Danann father, was said to have instituted a series of games at Tailteann similar to those held at Olympus. In these the Milesians may have participated and won.

The Milesians were not vindictive to their vanquished foe whose magical skills they had had every opportunity to appreciate, and they seem to have left the Túatha Dé Danann pretty much to their own devices. In time the vanquished would absorb the victors even though the legends say the Túatha Dé Danann disappeared, retreating into caves and underground haunts. Their identification with fairies and "little people" began countless centuries ago.

King Crimthan, who reigned for a solitary year much later (c. A.D. 74), is said to have been actually married to a fairy named Nair, whom he met while on a military campaign. Among the gifts she gave him, and which he brought back along with her to his fort of Dun Criffan on the Hill of Howth (just east of Dublin), were a gilt chariot, a golden chessboard inlaid with transparent gems, a multicolored cloak embroidered with gold, a sword ornamented with serpents, and a silver shield. Neither these objects nor his fairy queen's magic were enough to prolong his life when he fell from a horse shortly after his return.

Emphasizing the extent of belief in fairies, P. W. Joyce points to the prevalence of places in Ireland today whose names still contain *sidh,* or the modernized version, *shee.* "It must be borne in mind that every one of these places was once firmly believed to be a fairy mansion, inhabited by those mysterious beings," he writes in *Irish Names of Places,* "and that in the case of many of them, the same superstition lurks at this day in the minds of the peasantry." *Sidh,* originally applied to a fairy palace, was gradually transferred to the hill and ultimately to the fairies themselves. *Sidh-dhruim* ("fairy ridge," the old name of the Rock of Cashel) is still the name of six townlands in Armagh under the modern form, Sheetrim.

The eleventh-century *Annals of Clonmacnois,* and the later *Book of the Dun Cow,* both say the Túatha Dé Danann ruled Ireland for 197 years and were "most notable magicians who would work wonderful things by magick and other diabolical arts, wherein they were exceedingly well skilled in these days accounted the chiefest in the world in that profession." But as the myths tell us, 197 years might turn out to be ten times that long.

Clonmacnois, a great ecclesiastical center of learning, was associated with many curious legends. A ship seen sailing through the air was once said to have caught its anchor in the church steeple on the site; a bishop who resided there was said to know the date of everyone's death. Between 834 and 1204 it was plundered or burned a score of times, mostly by Vikings, one of whom set his wife on the high altar from which she gave forth oracles.

Today, stark and desolate, it is one of the most impressive spots in Ireland, particularly if seen for the first time by moonlight, its ruined buildings and ancient towers starkly outlined against the sky, with the silent Shannon barely moving a couple of hundred yards away. Apart from a barren car park, filled with coach parties by day, there's nowhere to stay nearer than Athlone, twelve miles to the north.

Despite its Christian significance it is worth noting that Clonmacnois is closely associated with the dun cows which are traditionally presumed to follow the geodetic currents of the earth, picking sites by natural geomancy. The Shannon River which flows so placidly by beside Clonmacnois owes its source, it is said, to an undersea spring—the well of Connla, overshadowed by a wonderful hazel tree whose nine nuts imparted supernatural wisdom to those (including the sacred salmon) who ate them.

Not far from here, on the Ballmore to Mullingar road in deserted countryside half a mile east of the pink-painted Ushnagh Inn, is what's said to be the exact center of Ireland: a cottage-sized rock locally called Cat-Ushnagh ("the cat stone") but originally the Stone of Divisions. This marked the meeting point of the five original provinces: Ulster, Meath, Munster, Leinster, and Connacht. Dagda's predecessor, Lugh, was slain here you may remember, but the spot owes its reputation to the eleventh-century king Tuathal who instituted the annual Feast of Beltane here every May 1, when cattle were driven between two fires with incantations designed to protect them from evil spirits. Games and pagan rites were celebrated and the various chiefs presented the king of Connacht with a horse as an annual tribute.

This is lakeland, a region that seems almost as much water as land; a region of beautiful lonely lakes, such as Lough Derg on the Shannon or the immense Lough Ree north of Athlone. Near Oldcastle is the choppy, brownish Lough Sheelin, originating, according to legend, from a well whose flood waters, released at the forbidden touch of a maiden, went on to submerge an ancient city. Like many lakes it has a tiny parking place adjoining it where one can sit and gaze over its tranquil setting.

Outside Mullingar, on the Longford Road, is little Lough Owel where the Danish chieftain Turgesius (who had earlier profaned Clonmacnois by setting his oracular wife on the altar) was drowned by the Irish king Malachy I. Turgesius had demanded Malachy's young daughter be sent to him, but the Irish king sent instead fifteen "beardless youths" in feminine garb. Those took Turgesius by surprise and captured his castle overlooking the lake.

But perhaps most famous of all the lakes is Lough Derravarragh, for so long the home of the Children of Lir, immortalized in one of Ireland's oldest and saddest tales, dating back to the dispute over which of the Túatha Dé Danann chieftains would succeed to the kingship when the great Dagda died. All the chiefs met in conclave and agreed that Bodbh Dearg should be the king—except for one, Lir of Sidhe Fionna, who was so affronted at not being himself chosen that he withdrew to his own territory in a fit of pique. He was already an unhappy man, but when his beautiful young wife died, life got even sadder for him. It was at this time that King Bodbh Dearg sent for him and offered one of his own lovely daughters. Lir gratefully accepted the offer of this new wife, and all would have been well but for the fact that she, too, died after giving birth to her second set of twins. Again the king offered his solicitations, and also his second daughter, Aoife, whom Lir also duly married.

But Aoife, having no children of her own, grew increasingly jealous of those born to her late sister, and her obsession led her first to trying to have them killed and then, while on an outing beside Lough Derravarragh, turning them magically into white swans with the aid of a golden druidical wand. Their fate, she vowed, would be to spend 300 years on the lake, a further 300 years plying the Sea of Moyle between Ireland and Scotland, and then, after a further 300 years in the sea off Ireland's Atlantic coast, they would be restored to human form when a new religion was destined to change the old pagan beliefs.

The ancient ballad goes on to relate how the child/swans lived out their nine centuries, singing sweetly and talking wisely to all who came to hear them, finally becoming humans briefly when the Christians arrived, then dying and being buried at Achill Island off the coast of County Mayo. As for the evil Aiofe, her magic availed her naught, for the Túatha Dé Danann's king was stronger: with his golden druidical wand he turned her into an ugly Morrigan, in the shape of a raven, which she remains to this day.

Heading up the Longford road from Mullingar just before the turnoff to Multyfernham near the lake, stop in at the pleasant pub called The Covert and have an Irish Mist, a basket of sandwiches, and a Gaelic coffee to fortify you for the drive through Multyfernham and the subsequent trip through a leafy tunnel leading through the woods to the lake. Beside the track a stray donkey from one of the farms scrounges cookies or candies from the rare passerby, otherwise there is no sign of life. The lake, wide at its northern end, thins out to a sliver in the south, and apart from an occasional discreet trailer, is in lovely scenic surroundings that are totally undeveloped.

Not far from here, just east of Castlepollard, is the tiny village of Fore, one of whose few buildings is a pub called the Seven Wonders. Here the resident tipplers are willing to talk to all comers of the "seven wonders" with which the village has long been associated. These are the monastery on a screw (meaning on swampy ground), the mill without a race (no water to drive its wheel), the cyclopean stone (it's about two tons) above the doorway of St. Fechin's ruined church, the well water which will not boil, the ash tree which will not burn, and the stream that flows uphill.

The remains of the seventh-century monastery just outside the village contain the mill, the dead tree (which not only won't burn but never blossoms either), and the well whose water supposedly won't boil (and, according to local residents, prevents sickness). St. Fechin's is across the road, and the river that allegedly runs uphill is near Lough Lene to the south.

The sharp-eyed reader will have noticed that these "wonders" add up to only six, a point not realized by your authors while on the spot and still in a position to make further inquiries.

The history of Ireland is found in many ancient books, most of them elaborately decorated by the monk-scholars at various abbeys. Most of these date back to the twelfth or thirteenth centuries, although a few are older: *The Book of Leinster, The Book of Ballymote, The Yellow Book of Lecan. The Annals of Loch Ce,* a chronicle of Irish affairs from the eleventh through sixteenth centuries, is comparatively recent.

Probably the most quoted of the histories is one of comparatively recent vintage: *The Annals of the Four Masters.* Four friars (Michael, Conary and Cucogny O'Clery, and Ferfeasa O'Mulconry) compiled their comprehensive work by collating all the ancient manuscripts they could lay their hands upon. They worked at the task in a Donegal monastery from January 22, 1632 to August 10, 1636, compiling an exhaustive history of Ireland that has no equal. And apart from prefacing every paragraph in the book with "The age of the world (2520)"—which, for example, is the year they gave for Parthalon's arrival in Ireland and is described by them as "278 years after The Deluge"—their history is as complete as could be imagined.

In 1851 the *Annals* were translated with a commentary by John

O'Donovan from the original manuscripts in the libraries of the Royal Irish Academy and Dublin's Trinity College, and it is this edition, in seven thick volumes, that is most often consulted today.

Apart from their value as history (and many manuscripts, despite their Christian parentage, had numerous unabashed references to magical pagan accomplishments), the books are also incredible works of art. One of them, *The Book of Kells,* which may date back to the early ninth century, is made from calfskin cut into 11-inch by 15-inch pages of which 340 still exist, all but two containing color illumination. Red, purple, green, blue, and yellow dyes were handmade by the monks to color their work, and for the last 300 years *The Book of Kells* has been in a locked case in Dublin's Trinity College where each day a guard solemnly turns one page of what bibliophiles have described as "the most beautiful book in the world."

Writing about these ancient books, the twelfth-century historian Giraldus Cambrensis comments: "If you look closely with all acuteness of sight you can command, and examine the inmost secrets of that wondrous art you discover such subtle, such fine and closely-wrought lines, twisted and interwoven in such intricate knots and adorned with such fresh and brilliant colors that you will readily acknowledge the whole to be the result of angelic rather than human skill."

The town of Kells, also known as Ceanannus Mór, is known for the Round Tower and several High Crosses in the old monastery churchyard. Leaning against the south wall of the church is a very old but undated stone sundial, and another High Cross, with a broken top, stands in the center of town.

Just south of Kells on the Navan Road is Teltown. "Teltown marriages," celebrated by young couples pledging their troth through a hole in a wooden door there, were traditionally said to last one year and one day after which the couple could part if they chose to do so.

It's worth making a diversion a few miles northwest of Kells to the twin hills of Sliabh na Caillighe where the Loughcrew megalithic graves and Witches' Hill dominate the landscape of gently rolling hills. A lengthy, windswept climb leads to a series of large cairns which are believed to contain passage graves, although only one or two have been opened up. Archeologists are unsure of the exact date of the graves but have commented admiringly on the interesting patterns and concentric circles on some of the inner stones.

South, Southwest, and Central

Any tour of southern Ireland begins with the obligatory visit to kiss the Blarney Stone. It's set high into the wall of the beautiful fifteenth-century castle at Blarney, not far from Cork in delightful countryside, and kissing it involves lying flat on one's back and bending over to reach the underside of the stone two feet below. The official photographer is usually standing by to assist solitary visitors by holding their ankles as they undergo the necessary acrobatics.

The origins of the stone are uncertain—one account says the four-foot limestone block was brought to Ireland from the Holy Land, another that it was the gift of a witch—but kissing it is popularly supposed to endow one with the gift of oratory. The effects are not particularly important: the ritual is just one of those things that everybody does.

The approach to the castle through its extensive grounds is very pastoral and tranquil, cows speckling the nearby fields and an amiable white horse sidling up to visitors as they cross the bridge over the sparkling brook. In the fragrant woods behind the ruins, moss-covered stones protrude from a springy bed of pine needles, sheltered by the spreading branches of immense trees, some of which must be several hundreds of years old. This is known locally as the fairy glen, and at twilight it is easy to believe the tales of those who claim to have seen the magical sprites who populate it.

Writing about the elves of Ireland in 1833, the astrologer Raphael comments: "During the summer nights when the moon shines, and particularly at harvest time, the elves come out of their secret dwellings and assemble for their dance in certain favorite spots which are hidden and secluded places. . . . In the first rays of the morning sun they again vanish with a noise resembling that of a swarm of bees or flies."

The glen is littered with enormous, strangely-shaped boulders, some arranged in rough circles, and for this reason there has been speculation that Druids once worshiped here; from what we know of their preference for sacred groves of this kind it would seem likely. The official booklet for Blarney Castle talks of the mysterious figure who has occasionally been seen leading a herd of white cattle through the glade to the minuscule lake at one end. Druids had a particular preference for such beasts, it reminds us. It becomes increasingly clear that the Druids, fairies, and the Túatha Dé Danann are all one and the same.

The southwestern corner of Ireland, a region honeycombed with quiet bays, rocky inlets, and gentle peninsulas extending into the stormy Atlantic, has always been a land of legend. The "big" towns—Skibbereen, Killarney, and Tralee—aren't big at all, more like busy villages and quite likely to be filled with people or animals, there for the weekly market, as you pass through.

A good place to start is just before Skibbereen, a town that suffered dreadfully in the disastrous potato famine of the last century. Just to the east, coming from Clonakilty into Glandore, a sign denotes the narrow road to the Drombeg stone circle, a group of seventeen standing stones so remarkably well preserved that they look almost new. Actually the circle is believed to date to around 150 B.C. and the nearby round huts to a few hundred years earlier. Whatever its purpose, and it has been suggested that it was a seasonal hunting place, it is delightfully situated, on a low ridge overlooking the sea. In fall the bracken-filled glens which surround it turn a vivid russet color, contrasting with the gently undulating green hills.

Be careful to take the path to the left (when facing the only house in sight) after parking; the field to the right is frequently occupied by an angry bull.

Glandore itself, only a mile or two away, is a charmingly uncommercial village consisting of little more than a sleepy harbor with boat rental, an old church, and the Marine Hotel. For centuries the harbor has been renowned for "a deep, hollow and melancholy roar" which occasionally issues from one of the caverns near the cliffs. Local residents say it is sometimes heard before storms, but legend attributes it to a banshee lament, formerly believed to foretell the death of a king. Banshees, or at least a belief in banshees, was once commonplace in this part of Ireland, their most famous site being Carrig Cleena, a great rock near Mallow. Here, Cleena, queen of the fairies of South Munster, was said to have had her palace.

The banshee has always been regarded as a rather particular kind of fairy, usually the possession of a specific family to which she appears to warn of an impending death. Sir Walter Scott suggested that only the Milesians, that ancient pre-Celtic tribe, inherited banshees. Writing more than half a century ago, folklorist Lewis Spence quoted a Mr. McAnally to the effect that different motives might impel the banshee's appearance.

"When the banshee loves those she calls," McAnally said, "the song is a low, soft chant giving notice, indeed, of the proximity of death but with a tenderness of tone that reassures the one destined to die and comforts the survivors; rather a welcome than a warning."

More than most countries, Ireland still reveals its origins through its place names. As previously mentioned, the tradition of banshees lives on in names which incorporate the prefix or suffix *shee.* There are seventy such place names today. Similarly there are 400 place names beginning with *ra, rah, raw,* or *ray,* and 700 more beginning with *rath,* all from *rath,* meaning "a ringfort."

The word *doire* has proliferated, too, occurring in innumerable places where oakwoods once flourished. *Dair* is the Irish word for "oak" and in various forms pops up all over the country from Adare in Limerick (once known as Ath-dara—"the ford of the oak tree") to Londonderry in Northern Ireland.

The words *drui* or *dree* are perpetuated in the names of several localities, notably Loughnashandree ("the lake of the Druids"), which lies near the head of Ardgroom on the peninsula to the north of Bantry Bay. The Druids were in the habit of consecrating water as well as fire on Beltane, and in his archeological sketch, *Pagan Ireland,* W. G. Wood-

Martin wrote (at the turn of this century) that certain springs were still held in special reverence. It was sometimes customary, he said, not to draw water from a well until after midnight on May Day Eve, and the people of each village were in the habit of sitting up to obtain the first pure draft on May Day; this was regarded as a powerful charm against witchcraft.

This whole region of the peninsulas might well be the most beautiful part of Ireland, the road invariably traversing spectacular hills covered with golden bracken and offering breathtaking views of the plains and sea below. Mist dances in the glens, the omnipresent rain crashes onto the shiny, black rock, and water streams into the valley. On a remote rock, high above the road, a whitewashed sign is scrawled: "Your Sins Will Catch up with You" and, a few hundred yards further on: "Macdonald's Is My Kind of Place."

The tiny town of Glengarriff (population: 400) is a renowned beauty spot favored by such famous writers as William Thackeray and George Bernard Shaw. Across the peninsula to the north the town of Kenmare is center of a prosperous woolens industry.

Westward from Kenmare, toward the end of the peninsula across the rocky moor dotted with bright pink or pale blue cottages, is Sneem, and beyond that the village of Castlecove. Here a right-hand turn on a winding, single-track road leads after 2½ miles to Staigue Fort, an amazingly well-preserved circular cashel almost 90 feet in diameter and with stone walls up to 13 feet thick. In pre-Christian days such a fort was a place of refuge, the defenders leading their families and livestock through its solitary gateway and into the shelter of its 18-foot walls. Two thousand years later the walls still stand, interior steps still leading to the platforms from which the fort was defended. The surrounding countryside, brooding hills flanking a rushing stream, must look pretty much as it always did.

Few things change in this part of Ireland. For uncounted centuries the water has poured down the hillsides in rivulets and streams to form the rivers and lakes around which so many legends have clustered. From Kenmare the road descends from the mountains skirting Upper Lake and Muckross Lake where, at Torc Bridge, a narrow path leads up through the woods to Torc waterfall. Plunging down the cliff the wild torrent tosses up a fine spray which obscures the smooth black rock of the cliffs behind. But, legend avers, the rock's smoothness is broken by the door to a cave in which endless treasures await the intrepid explorer bold enough to break through.

Centuries ago, the story goes, a wild black boar with red eyes and razor-sharp tusks explained to a local farmer that he'd been turned into his present shape by a bad-tempered Druid he'd unwittingly offended. In that state, he explained, he'd been obliged to ravage the farmer's sheep and cattle, but he wanted to make amends by presenting the latter with all the gold and silver he could carry from a cave in the side of Torc hill. The waterfall didn't yet exist in those days.

As in so many stories of this nature the lucky recipient couldn't keep the good news to himself, despite a warning that he must do so. And when the farmer's wife followed him to the cave one day and he told her the story the gold was transformed into useless granite and the red-eyed boar was whipped up in a pillar of flame to a lake at the top of Mangerton Mountain. Immediately the boiling water burst a hole in the mountain, causing the waterfall which exists to this day.

It must have been sometime after this that another popular legend gained currency. This one concerns the occasion when the devil invited a famous local chieftain named O'Donoghue for a drink at the Devil's Punchbowl high up on Mangerton Mountain. The devil got drunk and chased his guest over Torc waterfall. A piece of the mountain chewed off by the devil to spit at O'Donoghue landed short and formed one of the islands in the lake—or so the story goes.

This O'Donoghue features in many of the local legends, the most famous of which concerns his departure from this earth after practicing magic for seven weeks to attain the secret of eternal youth. One day, in the middle of giving one of his splendid feasts at which he had uttered many prophecies of things to come, he walked slowly into Lough Leane (now called Lower Lake), waved to his friends, and disappeared from view.

"The memory of the good O'Donoghue," wrote the Victorian folklorist T. Crofton Croker in *Traditions of the South of Ireland*, "has been cherished by successive generations with affectionate reverence and it is believed that at sunrise every May Day morning, the anniversary of his departure, he revisits his ancient domain. A favorite few only are permitted to see him and this distinction is always an omen of good fortune to the beholders."

Croker himself, born in Cork in the closing years of the eighteenth century, collected many of the folktales of southern Ireland during a lifetime in which he also served thirty years as an Admiralty clerk in London. His "successor" in the field was the multilingual Jeremiah Curtin who was born of Irish parents in Detroit and who visited Ireland several times after Croker was dead. Like his predecessor, Curtin took it upon himself to collect as many of the old tales as he could, but his specialty was in documenting the stories of ghosts or fairies, and in these the renowned O'Donoghue features as a kind of fairy king sometimes called the Knight of the Glen.

When he first published his book *Tales of the Fairies and of the Ghost World* in 1895, Curtin quoted one of his friends as bemoaning the fact that when he was a boy nine men out of ten believed in fairies but now the figure was a mere one in ten. To this Curtin adds: "It is interesting indeed to find a society with even ten per cent of the population professed believers in fairies."

The latter part of the last century seems to have been a golden period for documenting the fanciful tales of the Kerry and Munster regions. The last of the traditional storytellers were still to be found at that time; the oral tradition has almost disappeared today. Many of the stories covered the same ground and, wherever their origins, had similar explanations for purely local phenomena. The origin of the Killarney lakes, for example, was said to be one fulfillment of an old tradition that fearful tragedy would ensue if anybody left the cover off a well. Of course, this happened one day, and supposedly the well is still overflowing to keep Killarney (and dozens of other lakes around the country) brimful.

"Wells were the haunts of spirits that proved to be propitious if remembered, vindictive if neglected," Wood-Martin tells us. "These holy localities are approached from the north side, then moving from east to west, in imitation of the diurnal motion of the sun."

Even so ancient an authority as Giraldus Cambrensis documents the legend of the lake formed by the well overflowing—in this case referring to what is undoubtedly the largest lake in Ireland: Lough Neagh, west of Belfast. Oddly enough, there does appear to be early evidence for the sudden appearance of this lake, either through a minor earth tremor or a sudden inundation of some sort.

The Book of Lecan relates the origin of another well during the third-century rule of King Cormac who was fighting a war with the king of Munster. Cormac's Druids had by their magic caused all the lakes, rivers, and streams to be dried up, and in desperation the Munster king besought the most celebrated Druid of his time, Mogh-Ruith, to leave his home in Kerry and help relieve the army's thirst.

"Mogh-Ruith called for his disciple Canvore," the chronicle continues, "and said to him, 'Bring me my magical spear.' And his magical spear was brought and he cast it high in the air and told Canvore to dig up the ground where it fell. 'What shall be my reward?' said Canvore. 'Your name shall be for ever on the stream' said Mogh-Ruith. Then Canvore dug the ground and the living water burst asunder the spells that bound it and gushed forth from the earth in a great stream; and the multitudes of men and horses and cattle threw themselves upon it and drank till they were satisfied."

And at least until a few years ago the well still existed, beside the road three miles south of Knocklong in County Limerick. What's more, it was still known as Tober Canvore or Canvore's well.

"The face of the country," writes P. W. Joyce, "is a book which if it be deciphered correctly and read attentively will unfold more than ever did the cuneiform inscriptions of Persia or the hieroglyphics of Egypt. Not only are historical events and the names of innumerable remarkable persons recorded, but the whole social life of our ancestors—their customs, their superstitions, their battles, their amusements, their religious fervor and their crimes—are depicted in vivid and everlasting colors."

And in his book, *Irish Names of Places,* Joyce proceeds to prove his thesis with a thousand and one examples: the glen called Gleann-Samhaisce ("the valley of the heifer"), near Kenmare, which commemorates the time celebrated in *The Annals of Clonmacnois* when but one bull and one heifer remained in the country after a plague; the deep ravine on Connacht's Croagh Patrick called Lugnademon ("the hollow of the demons") into which St. Patrick is reputed to have driven all the evil spirits en route to banishment from Ireland; and all the place names bearing some derivation of Beltane, from that Druidic celebration on May 1 when the *bil-tene,* or "goodly fire," was lit to placate the pagan spirits.

Discussing this as well as the August Eve celebration known as Lughnasa and the end-of-summer celebration known as Samhain (November Eve), Joyce adds: "These primitive celebrations have descended through eighteen centuries; and even at the present time on the eve of the first of November, the people of this country practice many observances which are undoubted relics of ancient pagan ceremonials."

Leaving the pleasant town of Killarney where horse-drawn carts for tourists still vie with automobiles for space in the narrow streets we come to another town, Killorglin to the northwest, where a strange name has caused endless speculation. The name is Puck, as in the annual three-day Puck Fair which is held in the town every August. The official explanation for the fair's origins is that back in Oliver Cromwell's day a big male goat named Puck routed a group of English soldiers who were assembling secretly to attack the town, and the fair has honored this incident ever since. But the official brochure for the annual festival casts doubt on this story, as well as on others, and establishes only that it has been the tradition for the past 150 years to raise a he-goat to an elevated platform to overlook the celebrations.

Oddly enough, nowhere is mentioned the much likelier theory that the origin of *Puck* might be *Pooka,* a once-commonplace fairy spirit said to be "extremely obscure and indefinite in representation." *Raphael's Familiar Astrologer,* published in London in 1833, explains that "it appears as a black horse, an eagle or bat and compels the man of whom it has got possession, incapable of making any resistance, to go through various curious adventures in a short time. He hurries with him over precipices, carries him up to the moon and down into the bottom of the sea."

But that in itself is mere conjecture. What adds weight to the supposition about the Puck Fair is that there are actually places in Ireland once called Pollaphuca, and now called Puckstown. Joyce mentions two: Puckstown in the parish of Mosstown in County Louth and Puckstown near Artaine in Dublin.

The bridge of Ahaphuca which crosses the Ounageeragh River between Kilfinane in Limerick and Mitchelstown in Cork marks what was once a dangerous ford of evil repute. Strong currents and stormy winter nights combined to sweep many an unwary traveler to his death while he was attempting to cross the river, and the name Pooka's Ford is a reminder that these fatalities were once attributed to the evil spirit that haunted the place.

At any rate, Killorglin where the Puck Fair takes place is not especially attractive, resembling somewhat a northern England mining town, and scarcely needs to detain the visitor who is now within range of what is undoubtedly the star attraction of this region: the lovely Dingle Peninsula.

Beginning with the town of Tralee in the east and extending to Slea Head, the most westerly point in Europe, the Dingle Peninsula is about thirty-five miles long, mostly mountainous and extraordinarily lovely. The lofty Slieve Mish mountains (2,700 feet), mist-shrouded but gentle in aspect, descend almost to the road which skirts the sea past farms and pink-painted cottages. Dogs chase cars and cows interrupt their grazing to gaze mournfully at passing visitors. The legendary Irish hero Cú Chulainn, though not often heard of in these parts, is associated with one of the dark, forbidding tarns on the slopes of Slieve Mish. Regarded as unfathomable, it was believed to have once sheltered an enormous *peiste,* or "water monster," which frequently came out to gorge himself on the local inhabitants and their cattle. Everything fled before it and yes, even the great Cú Chulainn once passed up an opportunity to meet it face to face, preferring instead to take shelter in a nearby cashel. Slieve Mish was the scene of the fateful battle between the resident Túatha Dé Danann tribe and the invading Milesians, at least one thousand years before the Christian era. At this battle Scota, the widow of the late Milesian chief, was killed and her body buried in the glen, Glanaskagheen. A marker stone, three miles south of Tralee, sits atop the 800-foot Knockmichael.

Long life and ancient traditions dominate the Dingle Peninsula. The famous witch of Dingle is reputed to have lived to be more than 300 years old, telling inquirers that she always covered the top of her head, had never touched the earth with her feet, and never slept until sleepy.

The western end, near the fairly nondescript town of Dingle itself (population: 1,500) is Gaelic-speaking, and all the store signs are in that language.

Up Goat Street in Dingle is an immense neolithic stone with cup and ring markings and is traditionally sat upon by visitors.

There are many ogham stones in the area. One such stone sits in a field to the left of the road just west of Castlemaine, but a much finer example is farther up the peninsula in the graveyard of the twelfth-century church at Kilmalkedar. This fascinating ruined, roofless church where a fresh, crisp breeze from the sea blows constantly over the ancient graves, is rich in antiquities. In addition to the decorations of the church itself is the six-foot ogham pillar (its inscription memorializes a certain Mael Inbir, son of Brocan); an enormous cross carved from one stone; an early sundial; and the so-called "alphabet stone" with its clearly carved Latin letters, done probably at a time when there were few examples of this new-fangled language to study!

A mile or two to the west (take the road marked Ballyferriter) is one of Ireland's most famous monuments: the eighth-century Gallarus Oratory, a small chapel with a perfect, and still watertight, corbel roof. In appearance it looks like an overturned boat, being about 16 feet high and 22 feet long. There are more carved stones nearby.

Leaving Dingle, heading northeast, the road leads over the Connor Pass, follows the Brandon range for four or five miles, and drops down to the little town of Cloghane. Here a road runs left around the bay toward Brandon and following the sign marked Mount Brandon leads to a track off to the right which terminates beside an abandoned farm. Three immense standing stones overlook Brandon Bay here, their purpose totally unknown. Their 6- to 8-foot height is impressive as is their location on the brow of the foothills.

The town of Tralee (population: 11,000) is the biggest town hereabouts and is possibly best known for the song "The Rose of Tralee," composed by William Mulchinock for his childhood sweetheart. When, after a sojourn in America, he returned to the town in search of her in 1855 he found she was dead. He stayed on in Tralee where he himself died nine years later.

The triple-banked rath at Rathmore, between Tralee and Killarney, was the scene of a curious incident in this century when a local farmer sent his two sons to demolish the banks to make mowing easier. During the few moments when the men turned away to light their pipes, the horse and cart they had brought with them were separated and deposited in a nearby field. Local residents attributed the interference to fairies who resented intrusions on their terrain.

Our route now takes us northeast to Limerick (population: 50,000), whose original name, *Liminegh,* referred to a portion of land surrounded by a branch of the River Shannon. From the early ford that existed here the town grew up from the tenth century onward. There are some fascinating fifteenth-century carvings of mythical beasts on the oak choir stalls of St. Mary's Cathedral that are well worth looking at, and pagans are advised to head out of town to the lonely lake called Lough Gur about twelve miles south. Here around the horseshoe-shaped lake can be found numerous prehistoric remains including stone circles, megalithic tombs, and gallery graves. (The best map and listing is in Peter Harbison's excellent *Guide to the National Monuments of Ireland.*)

The lake is also the site of a story about Gerald, Earl of Desmond, whose castle and everybody in it was said to have sunk beneath the waters in 1583 after some experimental sorcery by the earl. He was said to have responded to his wife's entreaties to demonstrate his magical skill by changing successively into a vulture, a dwarf, a fish hag, and a huge serpent. Although he had warned his lady not to utter a sound during these demonstrations, she eventually screamed and the castle and its occupants immediately sank to the bottom of the lake.

In Maurice Lenihan's *History of Limerick* (1640), the story is told of a farmer who, on his way past the lake, was offered £4.10 for his horse and on accepting the offer was taken to a castle and showed a black horse who, his guide said, was the earl of Desmond. The horse had three shoes and when a fourth could be obtained the earl would be restored to normal life. The farmer, too confused to ask the obvious question, left hurriedly for home where he found the gold pieces in his pocket had turned to ivy leaves. Naturally he never saw the castle, his horse, or the mysterious stranger again.

North of Limerick is County Clare, its northern shores washed by Galway Bay. This is another region where fairy beliefs lingered and St. John D. Seymour tells the tale, in his *Irish Witchcraft and Demonology,* of a strolling vagabond named John Stewart who was struck on the head with a white rod by the king of the fairies. Blinded in one eye and rendered speechless for three years, he was restored to fitness three years later at Halloween. In the meantime, Seymour reports, the spot on his head on which he was struck was impervious to pain. He was also made privy to many fairy secrets (none of which the author reveals). Eventually Stewart was jailed for passing on spells and committed suicide by hanging himself in prison. Not a very cheerful story, but then fairy tales rarely seem to have the kind of happy ending that people often attribute to them.

In Galway, as elsewhere, things were not always what they seemed. One popular superstition, for example, insisted that the presence of a fox, or even mention of its name, would bring bad luck to a fisherman who, if such an encounter occurred, would spend that day on shore.

"The Irish appear to have believed not merely in the transmigration of one human soul to the body of another human being," writes Wood-Martin, "but the transformation of one body into another. Thus the soul of a man might pass into a deer, wolf, fox or bird—a state which may be described as a continual metamorphosical existence."

But back to our route. The charming little town of Tipperary (population: 4,800), despite its universal renown, seems scarcely to have entered the twentieth century. Its main street, lined with dozens of small shops, must hardly have changed in recent years and there's an old-world courtesy that treats the visitor like a native. (Carelessly forgetting the change from a five-pound note in one of the numerous souvenir shops, the authors returned half an hour later to find it sitting beside the cash desk waiting to be reclaimed.)

Near Tipperary used to be a pillar stone that was believed to be a remnant of the magic wheel, *Roth Fáil,* created by the Druid Mog-Ruith to carry him through the skies. This "wheel of light" was symbolic of the sun and over the centuries came to be confused with a mythical flying machine.

A few miles to the northeast is Cashel.

The famous Rock of Cashel, dramatically rising above the surrounding plains, dwarfs everything in sight. Since the fifth century when King Corc of Munster changed its name from Sidhruim ("fairy ridge") to Caiseal, there has been a building atop the massive rock. At first it was a pagan cashel, or stone fort, but with the coming of the Christians a church, and later a cathedral, was erected. St. Patrick converted King Aengus about A.D. 448 and there is a legend that the careless saint accidentally pierced the king's foot with his crozier during the ceremony. The saint was too wrapped up in his work to notice what had happened and the king, it is said, thought it was all part of the ceremony. So he kept his mouth shut (and his teeth clenched).

A somewhat battered seven-foot cross, known as St. Patrick's cross, stands on a massive block of granite which tradition says is a druidical altar. It is said that anyone suffering from a toothache can be cured by placing his head under the stone's southeast corner. There have been suggestions that this block might have been Ireland's original *Lia Fáil,* or "stone of destiny," but most historians seem agreed that the standing stone at Tara has the stronger claim to this honor. Certainly the stone at Cashel was used for the coronation of early Munster kings, from the fourth to eleventh centuries.

Adjoining the nearby parish church of St. John is Cashel's celebrated library which contains one of the finest collections of sixteenth- and seventeenth-century books in the country. Unfortunately it does not possess any trace of the famous *Psalter of Cashel,* a book first prepared in the fifth century and revised and expanded in the tenth and eleventh centuries. This was one of the earliest books to record the rights and privileges of various feudal lords and disappeared shortly after an imperfect copy of it was made in the fifteenth century. This copy now rests in Oxford's Bodleian Library.

Early in the thirteenth century the archbishopric of Cashel became vacant and the Pope offered the post to Michael Scot, the Scottish intellectual who was probably in Rome at the time. Unfortunately the renowned magician turned down the job; had he taken it the history of the Church might have taken a very different turn. Scot's potency as a wizard was such that it was written about him that "when in Salamanca's cave, he lifted his magic wand to wave . . . the bells would ring in Notre Dame."

In the year 1324 Alice Kyteler, hitherto known as a local banker and money lender, became the most notorious citizen of the little town of

Kilkenny. That was the year that Dame Alice was charged with witch-craft, accused of offering sacrifices (nine red cocks and nine peacocks' eyes) to demons, and obtaining her wealth from a certain incubus who appeared to her as a black dog with whom she had carnal relations. Shocking as these charges were, it was only the beginning: she was soon to be accused of disposing of at least the last two of her four husbands, making use of certain horrible unguents composed of "the entrails of cocks . . . certain horrible worms, various unspecified herbs, dead men's nails, the hair, brains and shreds of cerements [shrouds] of boys who were buried unbaptised and various other abominations, all of which were cooked with various incantations over a fire of oak logs in a vessel made out of the skull of a decapitated thief."

Apparently after hearing these outrageous charges the jury did not take long to convict the wealthy Dame Alice and she was imprisoned in the dungeon of Kilkenny Castle, only to escape on the eve of her execution. She fled to England, but the members of the coven she had gathered around her were not so lucky. Several of them were arrested and one, a certain Petronilla, was burned alive in Kilkenny on November 3, 1324.

Dame Alice's memory is preserved today in the form of a plaque on the wall of her original home, now the Kyteler Inn. It's a charming place, its bar and basement restaurant popular with young people, and the atmosphere a marked contrast to the shabby narrow street outside, which can't have changed very much since Dame Alice was in residence. Apart from having a good menu, the inn also serves some rather distinc-tive drinks: Burning Stake (Irish Mist and Irish whisky in flames), Witches' Brew, and Dame Alice's Revenge. There are now regular medieval banquets held at the inn, at which a local housewife dresses up as a witch and retells the Dame Alice story.

Although Giraldus Cambrensis referred to Irish witchcraft as far back as the twelfth century, maintaining that the native sorceresses could turn wisps of hay and straw into red-colored pigs which could be sold in the market but which resumed their original form as soon as they crossed running water, there was not as much persecution of witchcraft in Ireland as in neighboring countries. The Kyteler case was the major exception.

In *Irish Witchcraft and Demonology,* St. John D. Seymour explains: "Medieval witchcraft was a by-product of the civilization of the Roman empire. Ireland's civilization developed along other and more barbaric lines and so had no opportunity to assimilate the particular phases of that belief which obtained elsewhere in Europe." Although a minority firmly believed in witchcraft, he says, it had not sufficient strength to make the belief general and meanwhile the factional fights between Catholics "trampled it into the earth."

He does, however, refer to incomplete records of witchcraft trials at

Youghal in 1661; at Carrikfergus in 1808; and at Dungannon in 1890, among others.

Sligo

The prosperous town of Sligo was the birthplace, in 1865, of William Butler Yeats, the poet who devoted so much of his life to studying the occult. The area in which he was born in is rich in antiquities, the raths, dolmens, cairns, and tumuli with which fairies are so often associated and which local legend often credit with having been constructed in one night.

One such, the Heapstown cairn (turn right at the village of Castle Baldwin on the road to Lough Arrow), is twenty feet high and consists of literally hundreds of thousands of small stones piled atop one another. It probably contains a passage grave, but like so many others of this type has never been excavated.

There are traditions in these parts that such tumuli shelter not ancient bones but rather living, breathing elves or fairies whose subterranean palaces are lavishly decorated and are the scene of constant revelry which only the luckiest of mortals can share. The small, antique tobacco pipes that have been found in the vicinity of such places are supposed to belong to that species of elf known as the *cluricaine,* whose major pleasures are smoking and drinking and who is believed to have learned the secret the Danes brought into Ireland of making beer from heather.

Cluricaines have sometimes been seen in the daytime, if we are to believe the tales, and they usually make their appearance as aged little men with antiquated, pea-green coats, large metal buckles on their shoes, and cocked hats in the old French style.

Yeats, who spent several years in London associating with Aleister Crowley and other occultists of the Society of the Golden Dawn, was enticed back to his native land by Ireland's growing renaissance movement. From an early age he had been fascinated by fairy legends and although he must have been one of the most incongruous figures ever to enter politics (he served in the Senate from 1922 to 1928), he remained an artist, like his father and brothers. Much of his poetry reveals his deep interest in occult matters. In his book *Irish Fairy and Folk Tales* he referred to the fairies as "gentle people."

Dermot MacManus, author of a more recent work on Irish fairies called *The Middle Kingdom,* says they are gentle only when not crossed and that some Irish housewives are still cautious enough to leave a saucer of milk or bit of soda bread outside their cottage door for their diminutive visitors. Fairies were frequently familiars of witches, the author explains, and assisted their mentor "in her hurtful activities against her neighbors."

MacManus includes testimonials from various people of intelligence and education living in Ireland today who have sworn to seeing fairies, usually friendly, around four feet tall and wearing a turned-up hat and sometimes a bright red coat. Others have seen black-clothed figures of human size, standing motionless in a circle, only to have them reappear some distance away almost immediately.

"The thorn bush is locally reputed to be under fairy protection," MacManus avers, "but there are many popular misconceptions about the tree and inaccurate generalities have too often crept into those versions of local folklore which are held by people not close enough to the earth to distinguish between fact and fiction." The bourtree, the blackthorn, birch, and broom are localities for fairies and any tree growing inside or near a fairy ring, or a lone thorn tree in an otherwise rocky and isolated field, can be assumed to be "protected."

MacManus says his grandfather met with much local opposition when he tried to move a thorn tree from a fairy fort in Killeaden and suffered great misfortune in the years after he did move it to his garden. It is now in the grounds of the author's house, and wrens and robins, both "fairy birds," nest in it. The fairy fort from whence it came, Lis Ard, has long been known for another fairy phenomenon: the bewitched sod or piece of earth that causes whoever steps on it to lose his or her way.

Although Sligo itself is closely associated with Yeats—there is a collection of his manuscripts in the local museum (closed Mondays), and a full-blown Yeats Society quartered in a magnificent house near the riverside Silver Swan Hotel—he is probably better known for his immortalization of a tiny spot a few miles to the south. This is the famous "Lake Isle of Innisfree," a tiny island about 200 yards from the southwest shore of Lough Gill along a dead-end road. Lines from his famous poem,

> I will arise and go now, and go to Innisfree,
> And a small cabin build there, of clay and wattles made:
> Nine bean-rows will I have there, a hive for the honeybee,
> And live alone in the bee-loud glade.

which epitomize the dream of so many, are on a board at the edge of the lake. A beautiful spot.

"A latter-day pagan" is how Yeats is described by Stephen Brown in *Ireland in Fiction*. "His prose is that of a poet, full of changing color and strange rhythm and vague suggestion."

What we might term "the Brigadoon syndrome" lives on in Ireland, and tales of places that appear and disappear without warning are commonplace. One friend who lived in Sligo as a child told us of the occasion when she and her family came across an immensely beautiful valley while out exploring the countryside. It was distinctive enough for her mother to make some sketches of it. But, our friend added, try as they might they were never able to find the valley again even though they knew where it was—or had been.

Ancient stones play a major part in the legends of Sligo. At Kilross are some stones that reputedly were once a cow and the thieves who tried to steal it. A magician pursued them with his magical wand and accidentally petrified both the robbers and the cow. At Killery, in the graveyard of the old church, seven egg-shaped stones are surrounded with a string known as the "straining string," supposed to be an infallible cure for aches, pains, and strains if the sufferer replaces the string and turns each stone in succession.

Other oval or circular stones are known as "cursing stones" and can be used not only for curing ailments but also to wish harm on others. There are examples in the Sligo towns of Ballsummaghan and Barroe and also on the island of Inishmurray off the coast. For their curse to be effective the postulant is expected to undergo a ritual while barefooted and bare-headed; a way of averting the curse was for the person against whom the stones were turned to lie in a freshly-dug grave and have three shovelsfull of earth thrown over him while the gravedigger recited rhymes.

These oval or circular stones can often be found around the margins of holy wells whose traditions still maintain the remnants of the druidical cult once so strong in Ireland. The Druids were believed to have the power to dry up rivers, create springs, and make or withhold rain. One of their methods for inspiring rain was to empty the well with a wooden dish, throwing the water in batches in the direction from which a needed wind should blow. The ceremony was accompanied by various incantations and always ended with replacing the lid of the well lest a hurricane begin.

As in other parts of Ireland druidical traces remain in place names. Red Hill, near Skreen, used to be called Knocknadrooa, "the hill of the Druids."

Two miles southwest of Sligo itself, on the road from Ballysodare, are what remains of a rich collection of megalithic stone circles and tombs, most unfortunately destroyed by twentieth-century gravel quarrying. But the outstanding stone site, clearly visible from here, is the immense mound atop the 1,100-foot hill of Knocknarea, said to be the grave of the fiery first-century queen Maeve whose legend has been kept alive by Spenser's *Faerie Queene.*

Following the road from Ballysodare around the foot of the hill to a farm leads to a narrow pathway up the steepest side of Knocknarea hill. The path is often marshy, so boots are advisable. It takes about forty-five minutes to walk up the heather-covered slopes, past sheep and cows, to the enormous cairn (200 feet in diameter, 35 feet high) constructed of millions of stones which probably cover a passage grave. This, too, has never been excavated.

All around the cairn visitors have spelled out their names in white pebbles and the wind whistles eerily around the hill. The view is magnificent.

It has been astonishing to find that Ireland is still alive with magic: secrets buried deep in the earth and cleverly concealed within a tapestry of myth and legend.

And what is magic if not lost wisdom? It is as if the Western world has willfully denied a rich heritage of magic, scorning its precepts and ridiculing its truths. But the light from the past beckons and the riches are there waiting to be reclaimed.

Eunapius, the Greek historian and a hierophant of the Eleusinian mysteries writing in the fourth century A.D., sadly looked at the direction the West had chosen and saw "a fabulous and formless darkness mastering the loveliness of the world." Can the Dark Ages have lasted much longer than we supposed?

Bibliography

Adams, W. H. Davenport. *Dwellers on the Threshold.* London: John Maxwell, 1864.

Anderson, Patrick. *The Smile of Apollo.* London: Chatto & Windus, 1964.

Anon. *Thaumaturgia, or Elucidations of the Marvellous.* London: Edward Churton, 1835.

Ashe, Geoffrey. *King Arthur's Avalon.* New York: Dutton, 1958.

Barrett, Francis. *The Magus.* London: University Books, 1967.

Blackburn, Henry. *Travelling in Spain in the Present Day.* London: Sampson Low, Marston & Co., 1866.

Blight, J. T. *Ancient Stone Crosses in Cornwall.* London: Simpkin, Marshall & Co., 1872.

Blouet, Brian. *The Story of Malta.* London: Faber & Faber, 1967.

Briggs, Katharine M. *A Dictionary of British Folk-Tales.* London: Routledge & Kegan Paul, 1971.

Brouen, Stephen. *Ireland in Fiction.* London.

Burland, Cottie A. *Secrets of the Occult.* London: Ebury Press, [circa] 1968.

Butler, E. M. *Ritual Magic.* Cambridge: University Press, 1949.

Cavendish, Richard. *The Black Arts.* London: Routledge & Kegan Paul, 1967.

Charpentier, Louis. *The Mysteries of Chartres Cathedral.* Paris: Robert Laffont, 1966.

Churchward, James. *The Lost Continent of Mu.* New York: I. Washburn, 1932.

Colville, W. J. *Ancient Mysteries and Revelations.* New York: R. F. Fenno, 1910.

Cornish, F. Warre. *The Dictionary of Greek and Roman Antiquities.* London: John Murray, 1898.

Coxhead, J. R. W. *The Devil in Devon.* Bracknell: West Country Handbooks, [circa] 1959.

Croker, T. Crofton. *Fairy Legends and Traditions of the South of Ireland.* London: John Murray, 1825–28.

Crossing, William. *Crossing's Guide to Dartmoor.* 1912.

Cumont, Franz. *Mysteries of Mithra.* Translated by Thomas J. McCormick. Chicago: Open Court Publishing, 1910.

Daniel, Glyn. *The First Civilizations.* New York: Crowell, 1968.

de Camp, L. Sprague. *Lost Continents: The Atlantis Theme in History, Science and Literature.* New York: Dover Publications, 1970.

Dennie, John. *Rome of Today and Yesterday.* New York: G. P. Putnam's, 1904.

Dicks, D. R. *Early Greek Astronomy.* Ithica, N.Y.: Cornell University Press, 1970.

Dillon, Myles, ed. *Irish Sagas.* Dublin: Stationery Office, [published for Radio éireann] 1959.

Dinsdale, Tim. *The Story of the Loch Ness Monster.* London: Routledge & Kegan Paul, 1961.

Durant, Will. "Life of Greece." *The Story of Civilization,* Vol. IV. New York: Simon & Schuster, 1939.

Eliade, Mircea. *The Myth of the Eternal Return.* Translated by Willard Trask. New York: Pantheon, 1954.

Ennemoser, Joseph. *History of Magic.* London: Henry G. Bohn, 1854.

Evans, John D. *Malta.* London: Thames & Hudson, 1959.

Evans-Wentz, J. D. *The Fairy Faith in Celtic Countries.* London: Oxford University Press, 1911.

Faulkener, Edward. *Ephesus and the Temple of Diana.* London: Day & Sons, 1862.

Farrington, Benjamin. *Science and Politics in the Ancient World.* London: Allen & Unwin Ltd., 1939.

————. *Greek Science.* London, Baltimore: Pelican Books, 1953.

Ferguson. *The Irish Before the Conquest.* London: George Bell, 1903.

Flaceliere, Robert. *Greek Oracles.* London: Elek Books, 1965.

Fortune, Dion. *Avalon of the Heart.* London: Aquarian, 1971.

————. *Psychic Self-Defence.* London: Aquarian, 1971.

Gayley, Charles. *The Classic Myths.* New York: Ginn & Co., 1939.

Geoffrey of Monmouth. *The History of the Kings of Britain.* New York: Penguin, 1966.

Giles, J. A. *History of the Ancient Britons.* Oxford: W. Baxter, 1854.

Godwin, William. *Lives of the Necromancers.* New York: Harper & Bros., 1835.

Gould, F. J. *Concise History of Religion.* London: Watts & Co., 1907.

Graves, Robert. *The White Goddess.* New York: Creative Age Press, 1948.

Guinea, Miguel. *Altamira: The Beginning of Art.* Madrid, 1969.

Hall, Manly P. *The Secret Teachings of All Ages,* 18th edition. Los Angeles: Philosophical Research Society, 1972.

Harbison, Peter. *Guide to the National Monuments of Ireland.* Dublin: Gill & Macmillan, 1970.

Hawkes, Jacquetta. *Prehistoric Britain.* Cambridge, Mass.: Harvard University Press, 1953.

Hawkins, Gerald S. *Stonehenge Decoded.* Garden City: Doubleday, 1965.

Henderson, William. *Notes on the Folklore of the Northern Countries of England.* London: W. Satchell, Peyton, 1879.

Hill, Cecilia. *Moorish Towns in Spain.* London: Methuen, 1931.

Idries Shah [Ghulam Mustafa]. *The Secret Lore of Magic.* London: Fred Miller, 1965.

James, Montague R. *In Abbeys.* Garden City: Doubleday, 1926.

Jonas, Hans. *The Gnostic Religion.* Boston. Revised, 1963.

Jones, Francis. *The Holy Wells of Wales.* Cardiff: Univ. of Wales Press, 1954.

Joyce, P. W. *Irish Names of Places.* London; N.Y.: Longmans, Green, 1901.

Jung, C. G. and Kerenyi, C. *Introduction to a Science of Mythology.* Translation by R. F. C. Hull. London: Routledge & Kegan Paul, 1951.

Jung, C. G. *Man and His Symbols.* Garden City: Doubleday, 1964.

Lane-Poole, Stanley. *The Moors in Spain.* London: T. Fisher Unwin, 1887.

Lea, H. C. *A History of the Inquisition of the Middle Ages.* New York: Macmillan, 1922.

Lees, J. Cameron. *A History of the County of Inverness.* Edinburgh: Wm. Blackwood and Sons, 1897.

Leland, Charles Godfrey *Gypsies, Sorcery & Fortune-Telling.* Secaucus, N. J.: University Books, 1963.

Leland, John. *Itinerary.* Edited by Lucy Toulmin Smith. Carbondale: Southern Illinois University Press, 1964.

Lenihan, Maurice. *History of Limerick.* Dublin: J. Duffy, 1884.

Le Rouzic, Zacharie. *Carnac, Legends, Traditions, Coutumes et Contes du Pays.* Rennes: Imprimés Bretonne, 1954.

Lethbridge, T. C. *Gogmagog, the Buried Gods.* London: Routledge & Kegan Paul, 1957.

_____. *Legends of the Sons of God.* London: Routledge & Kegan Paul, [circa] 1957.

Levi, Eliphas. *Transcendental Magic.* London: Rider, 1962.

Linton, Ralph. *The Tree of Culture.* New York: Knopf, 1955.

Liversidge, Joan. *Britain in the Roman Empire.* London: Longmans, Green, 1958.

Lloyd, G. E. R. *Ancient Culture and Society.* London: Chatto & Windus.

Lomas, John. *Travelling in Spain.* London: A. & C. Black, 1908.

Long, Henry L. *Survey of the Early Geography of Western Europe.* London, 1859.

Long, William. *Stonehenge and Its Barrows.* Wiltshire: Devizes, 1876.

Lubbock, John. *Prehistoric Times.* New York: D. Appleton, 1887.

Luce, J. V. *Lost Atlantis.* New York: McGraw-Hill, 1969.

MacCana, Proinsias. *Celtic Mythology.* London: Hamlyn, 1970.

Macchioro, Vittorio. *Villa of the Mysteries.* Naples: Richter & Co.

MacManus, Diarmuid. *The Middle Kingdom.* London: M. Parrish, 1959.

McNeil, F. Marian. *The Silver Bough.* Glasgow: William MacLellan, 1957.

Maltwood, Katherine. *A Guide to Glastonbury's Temple of the Stars.* London: James Clarke, 1964.

Martin, M. *Descriptions of the Western Isles of Scotland,* 1716.

Michell, John. *The View Over Atlantis.* London: Distributed by Garnstone Press for Sago Press, 1969.

Mommsem, Theodor. *History of Rome.* Translated by Rev. William P. Dickson. New York: Scribner's, 1869.

Morwood, Vernon S. *Our Gypsies in City, Tent and Van.* London: Sampson Low, 1885.

Murphy, Gerard. *Saga and Myth in Ancient Ireland.* Dublin: C. O. Lochlainn, 1955.

Murray, Margaret. *Excavations in Malta.* London: Bernard Quaritch, 1923.

————. *The God of the Witches.* London: Oxford University Press, 1952.

Murray, W. H. *Islands of Western Scotland.* London: Eyre Methuen, 1973.

Neeson, Eoin. *Irish Myths and Legends,* I & II. Cork: Mercier, 1973.

Niebuhr, Alto Dodds. *Herbs of Greece.* Boston: New England Unit of the Herb Society of America.

O'Kelly, Claire. *Newgrange.* Wexford, Ireland: John English, 1971.

Oliphant, Margaret O. *Jeanne d'Arc.* New York: Putnam's, 1896.

Otto, Walter F. *Dionysus, Myth and Cult.* Bloomington: Indiana University Press, 1965.

————. *The Meaning of the Eleusinian Mysteries.* London, 1939.

Paulsen, Frederick. *Delphi.* London: Glydenhal, 1920.

Pennick, Nigel. *Geomancy.* Cokaygne, 1973.

Pepin, Eugene. *Chinon.* Paris: H. Laurenx, 1930.

Pepper, John Henry. *Play Book of Metals.* London: Routledge, Warne and Routledge, 1869.

Raftery, Joseph, ed. *The Celts.* London: Mercier, 1964.

Redgrove, H. Stanley. *Bygone Beliefs.* London: William Ryder, 1920.

Rhys, John. *Celtic Folklore.* Oxford: Clarendon, 1901.

Ribadeau, François Dumas. *Cagliostro, Scoundrel or Saint.* Translated by Elizabeth Abbott. London: Allen & Unwin, 1967.

Ricciotti, Guiseppe. *Julian the Apostate.* Milwaukee: Bruce Publishing, 1960.

Ritson, Joseph. *Folklore & Legends.* London: W. W. Gibbings, 1891.

Roberts, Anthony. *Atlantean Traditions in Ancient Britain.* Llanfynydd, Wales: Unicorn, 1974.

Ross, Anne. *Everyday Life of the Pagan Celts.* London: Carousel Books, [circa] 1967.

————. *Pagan Celtic Britain.* New York: Columbia University Press, 1967.

Seltman, Charles. *Wine and the Ancient World.* London: Routledge & Kegan Paul, 1957.

Seymour, St. John D. *Irish Witchcraft and Demonology.* Dublin: Hodges, Figgis & Co., 1913.

Sherrard, Philip. *The Pursuit of Greece.* London: John Murray, 1964.

Simpson, W. Douglas. *Julian the Apostate.* Aberdeen: Milne & Hutchinson, 1930.

Smith, Sir William. *A Smaller History of Rome.* London: J. Murray, 1898.

Spence, Lewis. *An Encyclopedia of Occultism.* New York: Dodd, Mead, 1920.

Summers, Montague. *Geography of Witchcraft.* Evanston, Illinois: University Books, 1958.

Taylor, Thomas, translator. *The Arguments of the Emperor Julian against the Christians.* London, 1818.

Thom, Alexander. *Megalithic Lunar Observatories.* Oxford: Clarendon Press, 1971.

————. *Megalithic Sites in Britain.* Oxford: Clarendon Press, 1967.

Thorndike, Lynn. *History of Magic.* New York: Macmillan, 1934.

Trump, David. *Malta: An Archaeological Guide.* London: Faber & Faber, 1972.

Underhill, Evelyn. *Mysticism.* New York: Dutton, 1912.

Underwood, Gary. *The Patterns of the Past.* London: Pitman.

Usherwood, Stephen. *Britain, Century by Century.* Devon: David & Charles.

Walker, D. P. *Spiritual and Demonic Magic from Ficino to Campanella.* London: University of London, 1958.

Waylen, James. *History of Marlborough.* London: J. R. Smith, 1854.

Whelpton, Eric. *Greece and the Islands.* London: Robert Hale, 1961.

Wigram, W. A. *Hellenic Travel.* London: Faber & Faber, [20th Century].

Wilson, Colin. *The Occult.* London: Hodder & Stoughton, 1971.

Wood, Edward J. *Giants and Dwarfs.* London: Richard Bentley, 1868.

Wood, J. T. *Discoveries at Ephesus.* London: Longmans, Green & Co., 1877.

Wright, Thomas. *Narratives of Sorcery and Magic.* London: Richard Bentley, 1851.

Zammitt, Themistocles. *Prehistoric Malta.* London: Oxford University Press, 1930.

Index